ISBN 978-1-330-34639-6
PIBN 10035483

English
Français
Deutsche
Italiano
Español
Português

www.forgottenbooks.com

Mythology Photography **Fiction**
Fishing Christianity **Art** Cooking
Essays Buddhism Freemasonry
Medicine **Biology** Music **Ancient
Egypt** Evolution Carpentry Physics
Dance Geology **Mathematics** Fitness
Shakespeare **Folklore** Yoga Marketing
Confidence Immortality Biographies
Poetry **Psychology** Witchcraft
Electronics Chemistry History **Law**
Accounting **Philosophy** Anthropology
Alchemy Drama Quantum Mechanics
Atheism Sexual Health **Ancient History**
Entrepreneurship Languages Sport
Paleontology Needlework Islam
Metaphysics Investment Archaeology
Parenting Statistics Criminology
Motivational

ESSAYS

IN

ENGLISH LITERATURE

VOLUME I

THE
COLLECTED ESSAYS
AND PAPERS OF
GEORGE
SAINTSBURY
1875–1920

VOLUME I

1923

LONDON & TORONTO

J. M. DENT & SONS LTD

NEW YORK : E. P. DUTTON & CO

PRINTED IN GREAT BRITAIN

PREFACE

WHEN MR DENT (who had originally published a certain part of this collection) asked me to collect still further from other volumes published some thirty years ago but long out of print, and to refresh the whole with yet other essays, papers, lectures (not *class*-lectures) and the like, I had to make up several minds—my own and other people's—on, as far as my own was concerned, several points. The "other people" gave me no trouble: my requests for permission to reprint were in every case granted in the kindest manner, details of which will be found annexed to this Preface. It was not quite so easy to make up my own mind as to the constituents of the collection. As far as quantity went there was not the slightest difficulty. I never thought of reproducing or asking permission to reproduce here the numerous and sometimes bulky "Introductions," which I have at different times contributed to editions of Thackeray, Balzac, Dryden, Fielding, Smollett, Sterne, Richardson, Donne, Herrick, Miss Austen, Marmontel, Molière and others, though I should rather like to see them together. And if I had begun to sort the chaos of old reviews and miscellaneous articles dating from my twenty years' general service to the Press there would have been no end to it. The present collection—itself somewhat laboriously sifted—consists, in addition to the reprints, of papers separately written or in a few cases delivered, some if not all of these latter having never been printed before. It seemed unnecessary to go through these and alter things like "*You* know" or "*You* will see" into "It is generally known" or "It will be seen." For they are all really spoken Essays and not in the least the sort of thing that I used to utter to my class in Edinburgh.

The collection, as I finally settled it, divided itself under several heads. The first and largest division consisted of Essays on English Literature, most of them concerning the period 1780–1860 and already published as such, but supplemented here by a few on other periods. Then there was the little group of *Corrected Impressions* which went, I think, through at least two editions when it was first published: and which, speaking as a fool, I think may have some interest as a sort of *point de repère.* Its subjects are the greatest authors, in prose and verse, of the Victorian period, and it was written and published just at the time when, though Queen Victoria herself occupied the throne for the best part of a decade longer, the revolt of the 'nineties had already begun and "Victorianism" itself was already beginning to seem fogeyish.

Then came a certain number of Essays on *French* Literature which are postponed for the present but have been very carefully prepared for publication. So much of them had already passed into more general books of mine on the subject that I did not care to rehash further: and some, written at the time as reviews of books new at that time, were not quite solid enough. Only one entire Essay is included from my *Essays on French Novelists* which, though not in most cases verbally reproduced, were largely re-worked in the second volume of my *History* of the subject. It was complained by reviewers, otherwise complimentary, that I had there treated Flaubert too slightly: and I had myself specially referred readers to this Essay. Unless I am wrongly informed it—or more probably somebody's account of it—pleased Flaubert himself when it originally appeared in the *Fortnightly Review* for 1878: and this may give it something of a life-buoy.

The last or "Miscellaneous" division actually appearing here needs little comment. I have selected its constituents with a view especially to variety. But they differ in one general respect from the others in that several of them have not merely not been collected but have never been printed before. One, which I should especially like to have included, *non est inventus -ta* or *-tum*—for there are substantives which would require all three genders. It was a lecture which I delivered at Leeds not very long before the war at the invitation of the late Professor Vaughan on "The Beginnings of Romanticism in Germany, England and France respectively." I liked it (to speak as a fool) as well as anything I have ever done: and Vaughan, who was not a gusher, seemed to think even better of it than I did. Some years before it would probably—and even now might possibly—have found an immediate home in some monthly or quarterly Review: but I was at the time rather out of touch with such periodicals. It was of course not fully reported anywhere: and my copy, which was the only one, disappeared somehow when I left Edinburgh. I have been told that students of the modern universities sometimes amuse themselves by taking shorthand notes of such things for their own private use, as their compeers in Scotland have long been in the habit of doing. If anybody at Leeds did this, and holds the transcript, he might hear of something modestly to his advantage by communicating with me.

I dare say, however, that there is already too much of my tediousness here as it is. So I will say no more about it except to give as exact indication as possible (in some of the newly printed pieces I have not myself got it to give) of the original dates of appearance; to thank those persons by whose kindness I am enabled to reprint for the first time, and to renew thanks to those whose releases years ago put in my hands the control of those which now appear for the second.

1 ROYAL CRESCENT,   GEORGE SAINTSBURY
   BATH.
     August 10, 1923

[Contents of original *Essays in English Literature*, 1780–1860:
Lockhart, *National Review*, Aug. 1884. Borrow, *Macmillan's Magazine*, Jan. 1886. Peacock, *do.*, April 1886. Wilson (under the title of "Christopher North"), *do.*, July 1886. Hazlitt, *do.*, March 1887. Jeffrey, *do.*, August 1887. Moore, *do.*, March 1888. Sydney Smith, *do.*, May 1888. Praed, *do.*, Sept. 1888. Leigh Hunt, *do.*, April 1889. Crabbe, *do.*, June 1889. Hogg, *do.*, Sept. 1889. De Quincey, *do.*, June 1890.

Except the Essay on Lockhart, which was written at the request of my friend the late Mr Courthope and originally reprinted by permission of the publishers of the *National Review*, all the above were kindly released originally by Messrs Macmillan. They had all been accepted, and were I think most of them suggested, by the late Mr Mowbray Morris, then editor of the *Magazine*, an intimate friend of mine (since, nearly sixty years ago, he came up to Merton College, Oxford, in my second year there) and a man of rare and various merits and abilities. They are now reprinted in this collection by similarly kind consent of Messrs Rivington, who first re-published them (under the firm-style of Percival) in 1890. My indebtedness to them extends (with a similar "throw-back" to the original editors and publishers) to the Essay on *Flaubert* (see above) originally appearing in the *Fortnightly Review* for 1878, under the editorship of the present Lord Morley of Blackburn and reprinted in *Essays on French Novelists* (1891), as well as to *Miscellaneous Essays* (Percival, 1892). This latter, and the corresponding throw-backs of acknowledgment, may be perhaps best discharged by reprinting part of the original *Preface*, it being understood that the French Essays are for the present held back.

'In the case of the first essay, which appeared originally as preface to a volume of *Specimens of English Prose Style*: London, 1885, I owe my best thanks for permission to reprint to Messrs Kegan Paul, Trench and Co. Similar thanks are due to Messrs Chapman and Hall, and the successive editors of the *Fortnightly Review*, in respect of the essays on "Ernest Renan" (May 1880), "Modern English Prose" (February 1876), "Saint-Evremond" (July 1879), "Charles Baudelaire" (October 1875), and a small part of "The Present State of the English Novel" (February 1888); in respect of "Thoughts on Republics," to the editor and proprietors of the *New Review* (February 1890); of "The Young England Movement," to the editor and proprietors of *Merry England* (May 1883); of "A Paradox on Quinet," to the editor and proprietors of the *National Review* (June 1883); of "The Contrasts of English and French Literature," to the editor of *Macmillan's Magazine* (March 1891), and Messrs Macmillan; and of the papers included in "A Frame of Miniatures," which appeared at various dates in the autumn and winter of 1879, to the editor and proprietors of the *Saturday Review.*'

The last named piece is the only representative of a general permission which I received from the editor and proprietors of the *Saturday* before it left their hands in the autumn of 1894.

For *Corrected Impressions* I owe my best thanks to Messrs Heinemann, who published it first.

The contents of the original second volume of *Essays in English Literature* issue once more from Messrs Dent's own hands. The original dates and places of appearance of these essays, except that on Madame D'Arblay, which was written for the book itself, are as follows: Miss Ferrier, *Fortnightly Review*, February 1882; Twenty Years of Political Satire, *Macmillan's Magazine*, March 1890; Hood, *do.*, September 1890; English War-Songs, *do.*, May 1891; Cobbett, *do.*, December 1891; Some Great Biographies, *do.*, June 1892; Landor, *do.*, February 1893; Three Humourists, *do.*, December 1893; The Historical Novel, *do.*, August-October 1894; Southey, *do.*, February 1895.

As for the matter not yet volumed or never printed at all, "Trollope Revisited" appeared in the Papers of the English Association for 1921 and the two Grand Style articles on Shakespeare and Dante in those for 1910 and 1912; the third of these articles on Milton in the tercentenary volume of the Royal Society of Literature, 190 ; the papers on H. Kingsley and Godwin in *The New World* for Nov. 1919 and Nov. 1920; those on "The End of a Chapter" and "Twenty Years of Reviewing" in *Blackwood's Magazine*, Jan. 1895 and Feb. 1897; the papers on the "Cookery of the Grouse and Partridge" in Messrs Longmans' Fur and Feather Series (1894–5). For these in their various aspects I owe thanks to the authorities of the two Societies and the publishers generally and to Mr George Blackwood and Mr C. J. Longman (both old acquaintances of mine) personally. The *New World* papers were written at the request and are now reissued with the sanction of Mr Lewis Melville. Some details as to the first origins of "Spelling Reform" and "The Permanent and the Temporary in Literature" are given in connection with the two pieces. "A French Man of Letters of All Work" was delivered at the Taylor Institution, Oxford, in the October Term of 1904.

The reason for giving these details is that I myself have often been very grateful to those authors who have furnished them in similar collections, and have sometimes been as much the reverse of grateful to those who have not.]

G. S.

CONTENTS

ESSAYS IN ENGLISH LITERATURE

I

CRABBE

THERE is a certain small class of persons in the history of literature the members of which possess, at least for literary students, an interest peculiar to themselves. They are the writers who having attained, not merely popular vogue, but fame as solid as fame can ever be, in their own day, having been praised by the praised, and having as far as can be seen owed this praise to none of the merely external and irrelevant causes—politics, religion, fashion or what not—from which it sometimes arises, experience in a more or less short time after their death the fate of being, not exactly cast down from their high place, but left respectfully alone in it, unvisited, unincensed, unread. Among these writers, over the gate of whose division of the literary Elysium the famous "Who now reads Bolingbroke?" might serve as motto, the author of *The Village* and *Tales of the Hall* is one of the most remarkable. As for Crabbe's popularity in his own day there is no mistake about that. It was extraordinarily long, it was extremely wide, it included the select few as well as the vulgar, it was felt and more or less fully acquiesced in by persons of the most diverse tastes, habits, and literary standards. His was not the case, which occurs now and then, of a man who makes a great reputation in early life and long afterwards preserves it because, either by accident or prudence, he does not enter the lists with his younger rivals, and therefore these rivals can afford to show him a reverence which is at once graceful and cheap. Crabbe won his spurs in full eighteenth century, and might have boasted, altering Landor's words, that he had dined early and in the best of company, or have parodied Goldsmith, and said, "I have Johnson and Burke: all the wits have been here." But when his studious though barren manhood was passed, and he again began, as almost an old man, to write poetry, he entered into full competition with the giants of the new school, whose ideals and whose education were utterly different from his. While *The Library* and *The Village* came to a public which still had Johnson, which had but just lost Goldsmith, and which had no other poetical novelty before it than Cowper, *The Borough* and the later Tales entered the lists with *Marmion* and *Childe Harold*, with *Christabel* and *The Excursion*, even with *Endymion* and *The Revolt of Islam*. Yet these later works of Crabbe met with the fullest recognition both from readers and from critics of the most opposite tendencies. Scott, the most generous, and Wordsworth[1], the most grudging, of all the poets of the day towards their fellows, united in praising Crabbe; and unromantic as the poet of *The Village* seems to us he was perhaps Sir Walter's favourite English bard. Scott read him constantly, he quotes him incessantly; and no one who has read it can ever forget how Crabbe figures in the most pathetic biographical pages ever written—Lockhart's account of the death at Abbotsford. Byron's criticism was as weak as his verse was powerful, but still Byron had no doubt

---

[1] In 1834, after Crabbe's death, Wordsworth wrote to his son: "Your father's works...will last, from their combined merit as poetry and truth, full as long as anything that has been expressed in verse since the date of their first appearance." A very different estimate by Wordsworth of Crabbe has been published in Mr Clayden's *Rogers and his Contemporaries*. Here he argues at great length that "Crabbe's verses can in no sense be called poetry," and that "nineteen out of twenty of his pictures are mere matter of fact." It is fair to say that this was in 1808, before the appearance of *The Borough* and of almost all Crabbe's best work.

about Crabbe. The utmost flight of memory or even of imagination can hardly get together three contemporary critics whose standards, tempers, and verdicts, were more different than those of Gifford, Jeffrey, and Wilson. Yet it is scarcely too much to say that they are all in a tale about Crabbe. In this unexampled chorus of eulogy there rose (for some others who can hardly have admired him much were simply silent) one single note, so far as I know, or rather one single rattling peal of thunder on the other side. It is true that this was significant enough, for it came from William Hazlitt.

Yet against this chorus, which was not, as has sometimes happened, the mere utterance of a loud-voiced few, but was echoed by a great multitude who eagerly bought and read Crabbe, must be set the almost total forgetfulness of his work which has followed. It is true that of living or lately living persons in the first rank of literature some great names can be cited on his side; and what is more, that these great names show the same curious diversity in agreement which has been already noticed as one of Crabbe's triumphs. The translator of Omar Khayyám, his friend the present Laureate[1], and the author of *The Dream of Gerontius*, are men whose literary ideals are known to be different enough; yet they add a third trinity as remarkable as those others of Gifford, Jeffrey, and Wilson, of Wordsworth, Byron, and Scott. Much more recently Mr Courthope has used Crabbe as a weapon in that battle of his with literary Liberalism which he has waged not always quite to the comprehension of his fellow-critics; Mr[2] Leslie Stephen has discussed him as one who knows and loves his eighteenth century. But who reads him? Who quotes him? Who likes him? I think I can venture

---

[1] Tennyson then (1923).   [2] Afterwards "Sir" (1923).

to say, with all proper humility, that I know Crabbe pretty well; I think I may say with neither humility nor pride, but simply as a person whose business it has been for some years to read books, and articles, and debates, that I know what has been written and said in England lately. You will find hardly a note of Crabbe in these writings and sayings. He does not even survive, as "Matthew Green, who wrote *The Spleen*," and others survive, by quotations which formerly made their mark, and are retained without a knowledge of their original. If anything is known about Crabbe to the general reader, it is the parody in *Rejected Addresses*, an extraordinarily happy parody no doubt, in fact rather better Crabbe in Crabbe's weakest moments than Crabbe himself. But naturally there is nothing of his best there; and it is by his best things, let it be repeated over and over in face of all opposition, that a poet must be judged.

Although Crabbe's life, save for one dramatic revolution, was one of the least eventful in our literary history, it is by no means one of the least interesting. Mr Kebbel's book[1] gives a very fair summary of it; but the *Life* by Crabbe's son which is prefixed to the collected editions of the poems, and on which Mr Kebbel's own is avowedly based, is perhaps the more interesting of the two. It is written with a curious mixture of the old literary state and formality, and of a feeling on the writer's part that he is not a literary man himself, and that not only his father, but Mr Lockhart, Mr Moore, Mr Bowles and the other high literary persons who assisted him were august beings of another sphere. This is all the more agreeable, in that Crabbe's sons had advantages of education and otherwise which were denied to their father, and might in the ordinary course

[1] *Great Writers; Crabbe:* by T. E. Kebbel. London, 1888.

of things have been expected to show towards him a lofty patronage rather than any filial reverence. The poet himself was born at Aldborough or Aldeburgh, a now well-known watering-place (the fortune of which was made by Mr Wilkie Collins in *No Name*), on Christmas Eve, 1754. That not uncommon infirmity of noble minds which seeks to prove distinguished ancestry seems to have had no hold on the plain common sense of the Crabbe family, who maintained themselves to be at the best Norfolk yeomen, and though they possessed a coat-of-arms, avowed with much frankness that they did not know how they got it. A hundred and forty years ago they had apparently lost even the dignity of yeomanhood, and occupied stations quite in the lower rank of the middle class as tradesmen, non-commissioned officers in the navy or the merchant service, and so forth. George Crabbe, the grandfather, was collector of customs at Aldborough, but his son, also a George, was a parish schoolmaster and a parish clerk before he returned to the Suffolk port as deputy collector and then as salt-master, or collector of the salt duties. He seems to have had no kind of polish, and late in life was a mere rough drinking exciseman; but his education, especially in mathematics, appears to have been considerable, and his ability in business not small. The third George, his eldest son, was also fairly though very irregularly educated for a time, and his father, perceiving that he was "a fool about a boat," had the rather unusual commonsense to destine him to a learned profession. Unluckily his will was better than his means, and while the profession which Crabbe chose or which was chosen for him—that of medicine—was not the best suited to his tastes or talents, the resources of the family were not equal to giving him a full education, even in that. He was still at intervals employed in the Customs warehouses at "piling up butter and cheese" even after he was apprenticed at fourteen to a country surgeon. The twelve years which he spent in this apprenticeship, in an abhorred return for a short time to the cheese and butter, in a brief visit to London, where he had no means to walk the hospitals, and in an attempt to practise with little or no qualification at Aldborough itself, present a rather dismal history of apprenticeship which taught nothing. But Love was, for once, most truly and literally Crabbe's solace and his salvation, his master and his patron. When he was barely eighteen, still an apprentice, and possessed, as far as can be made out, of neither manners nor prospects, he met a certain Miss Sarah Elmy. She was three or four years older than himself and much better connected, being the niece and eventual co-heiress of a wealthy yeoman squire. She was, it is said, pretty; she was evidently accomplished, and she seems to have had access to the country society of those days. But Mira, as Crabbe called her, perhaps merely in the fashion of the eighteenth century, perhaps in remembrance of Fulke Greville's heroine (for he knew his Elizabethans rather well for a man of those days), and no doubt also with a secret joy to think that the last syllables of her Christian name and surname in a way spelt the appellation, fell in love with the boy and made his fortune. But for her Crabbe would probably have subsided, not contentedly but stolidly, into the lot of a Doctor Slop of the time, consoling himself with snuff (which he always loved) and schnaps (to which we have hints that in his youth he was not averse). Mira was at once unalterably faithful to him and unalterably determined not to marry unless he could give her something like a position. Their long engagement (they were not married till he was twenty-nine and she was thirty-three) may, as we shall see, have carried with it some of the penalties of long engagements. But it is as certain as any such thing can be that but for it English literature would have lacked the name of Crabbe.

There is no space here to go through the sufferings of the novitiate. At last, at the extreme end of 1779, Crabbe made up his mind once more to seek his fortune, this time by aid of literature only, in London. His son has printed too rare scraps of a very interesting *Journal* to Mira which he kept during at least a part of the terrible year of struggle which he passed there. He saw the riots of '80; he canvassed, always more or less in vain, the booksellers and the peers; he spent three-and-sixpence of his last ten shillings on a copy of Dryden; he was much less disturbed about imminent starvation than by the delay of a letter from Mira ("my dearest Sally" she becomes with a pathetic lapse from convention, when the pinch is sorest) or by the doubt whether he had enough left to pay the postage of one. He writes prayers (but not for the public eye), abstracts of sermons for Mira, addresses (rather adulatory) to Lord Shelburne, which received no answer. All this has the most genuine note that ever man of letters put into his work, for whatever Crabbe was or was not, now or at any time, he was utterly sincere; and his sincerity makes his not very abundant letters and journals unusually interesting. At last, after a year, during which his means of subsistence are for the most part absolutely unknown, he, as he says himself, fixed "by some propitious influence, in some happy moment" on Edmund Burke as the subject of a last appeal.

Nothing in all literary history is, in a modest way and without pearls and gold, quite so like a fairy tale

as the difference in Crabbe's fortunes which this propitious influence brought about. On the day when he
wrote to Burke he was, as he said in the letter, "an
outcast, without friends, without employment, without
bread." In some twenty-four hours (the night-term
of which he passed in ceaselessly pacing Westminster
Bridge to cheat the agony of expectation) he was a
made man. It was not merely that, directly or indirectly, Burke procured him a solid and an increasing
income. He did much more than that. Crabbe, like
most self-educated men, was quite uncritical of his own
work: Burke took him into his own house for months,
encouraged him to submit his poems, criticised them
at once without mercy and with judgment, found him
publishers, found him a public, turned him from a raw
country boy into a man who at least had met society
of the best kind. It is a platitude to say that for a
hundred persons who will give money or patronage
there is scarcely one who will take trouble of this kind;
and if any devil's advocate objects the delight of producing a "lion," it may be answered that for Burke at
least this delight would not have been delightful at all.

The immediate form which the patronage of Burke
and that, soon added, of Thurlow took, is one which
rather shocks the present day. They made Crabbe turn
to the Church, and got a complaisant bishop to ordain
him. They sent him (a rather dangerous experiment)
to be curate in his own native place, and finally Burke
procured him the chaplaincy at Belvoir. The young
Duke of Rutland, who had been made a strong Tory
by Pitt, was fond of letters, and his Duchess Isabel,
who was,—like her elder kinswoman, Dryden's Duchess
of Ormond—

A daughter of the rose, whose cheeks unite
The varying beauties of the red and white,

in other words, a Somerset, was one of the most beautiful and gracious women in England. Crabbe, whose strictly literary fortunes I postpone for the present, was apparently treated with the greatest possible kindness by both; but he was not quite happy[1], and his ever-prudent Mira still would not marry him. At last Thurlow's patronage took the practical form (it had already taken that, equally practical, of a hundred pounds) of two small Chancellor's livings in Dorsetshire, residence at which was dispensed with by the easy fashions of the day. The Duke of Rutland, when he was appointed Lord Lieutenant of Ireland, did not take Crabbe with him, a circumstance which has excited some unnecessary discussion; but he gave him free quarters at Belvoir, where he and his wife lived for a time before they migrated to a neighbouring curacy—his wife, for even Mira's prudence had yielded at last to the Dorsetshire livings, and they were married in December 1783. They lived together for nearly thirty years, in, as it would seem, unbroken mutual devotion, but Mrs Crabbe's health seems very early to have broken down, and a remarkable endorsement of Crabbe's on a letter of hers has been preserved. I do not think Mr Kebbel quotes it; it ends, "And yet happiness was denied"—a sentence fully encouraging to Mr Browning and other good men who have denounced long engagements[2]. The story of Crabbe's life

[1] Although constantly patronised by the Rutland family in successive generations, and honoured by the attentions of "Old Q." and others, his poems are full of growls at patrons. These cannot be mere echoes of Oldham and Johnson, but their exact reason is unknown. His son's reference to it is so extremely cautious that it has been read as a confession that Crabbe was prone to his cups, and quarrelsome in them—a signal instance of the unwisdom of not speaking out.

[2] Rogers told Ticknor in 1838 that "Crabbe was nearly ruined by grief and vexation at the conduct of his wife for above seven years, at the end of which time she proved to be insane." But this was long after her death and Crabbe's, and it is not clear that while she was alive Rogers knew Crabbe at all. Nor is there the slightest reason for attaching to

after his marriage may be told very shortly. His first patron died in Ireland, but the duchess with some difficulty prevailed on Thurlow to exchange his former gifts for more convenient and rather better livings in the neighbourhood of Belvoir, at the chief of which, Muston, Crabbe long resided. The death of his wife's uncle made him leave his living and take up his abode for many years at Glemham, in Suffolk, only to find, when he returned, that (not unnaturally, though to his own great indignation) dissent had taken bodily possession of the parish. His wife died in 1813, and the continued kindness, after nearly a generation, of the house of Rutland, gave him the living of Trowbridge, in Wiltshire, with a small Leicestershire incumbency near Belvoir added, instead of Muston. At Trowbridge he lived nearly twenty years, revisiting London society, making the acquaintance personally (he had already known him by letter) of Sir Walter, paying a memorable visit to Edinburgh, flirting in an elderly and simple fashion with many ladies, writing much and being even more of a lion in the society of George the Fourth's reign than he had been in the days of George the Third. He died on 3rd February 1832.

Crabbe's character is not at all enigmatical, and emerges as clearly in those letters and diaries of his which have been published, as in anecdotes of him by others. Perhaps the famous story of his politely endeavouring to talk French to divers Highlanders, during George the Fourth's visit to Edinburgh, is slightly embroidered—Lockhart, who tells it, was a

the phrase "vexation at the conduct" the sense which it would usually have. A quatrain found after Crabbe's death wrapped round his wife's wedding-ring is touching, and graceful in its old-fashioned way.

> The ring so worn, as you behold,
> So thin, so pale, is yet of gold:
> The passion such it was to prove;
> Worn with life's cares, love yet was love.

mystifier without peer. If he did gently but firmly extinguish a candle-snuff while Wordsworth and Sir George Beaumont were indulging in poetic ecstasies over the beautiful undulations of the smoke, there may have been something to say for him as Anne Scott, to whom Wordsworth told the story, is said to have hinted, from the side of one of the senses. His life, no less than his work, speaks him a man of amiable though by no means wholly sweet temper, of more common-sense than romance, and of more simplicity than commonsense. His nature and his early trials made him not exactly sour, but shy, till age and prosperity mellowed him; but simplicity was his chief characteristic in age and youth alike.

The mere facts of his strictly literary career are chiefly remarkable for the enormous gap between his two periods of productiveness. In early youth he published some verses in the magazines and a poem called *Inebriety*, which appeared at Ipswich in 1775. His year of struggle in London saw the publication of another short piece, *The Candidate*, but with the ill-luck which then pursued him, the bookseller who brought it out became bankrupt. His despairing resort to Burke ushered in *The Library*, 1781, followed by *The Village*, 1783, which Johnson revised and improved not a little. Two years later again came *The Newspaper*, and then twenty-two years passed without anything appearing from Crabbe's pen. It was not that he was otherwise occupied, for he had little or nothing to do, and for the greater part of the time lived away from his parish. It was not that he was idle, for we have his son's testimony that he was perpetually writing, and that holocausts of manuscripts in prose and verse used from time to time to be offered up in the open air, for fear of setting the house on fire by their mass. At last,

in 1807, *The Parish Register* appeared, and three years
later *The Borough*—perhaps the strongest division of
his work. The miscellaneous Tales came in 1812, the
Tales of the Hall in 1819. Meanwhile and afterwards,
various collected editions appeared, the last and most
complete being in 1829—a very comely little book in
eight volumes. His death led to the issue of some
Posthumous Tales and to the inclusion by his son of
divers fragments both in the *Life* and in the *Works*.
It is understood, however, that there are still considerable remains in manuscript; perhaps they might be
published with less harm to the author's fame and with
less fear of incurring a famous curse than in the case
of almost any other poet[1].

For Crabbe, though by no means always at his best,
is one of the most curiously equal of verse-writers.
Inebriety and such other very youthful things are not
to be counted; but between *The Village* of 1783 and
the *Posthumous Tales* of more than fifty years later, the
difference is surprisingly small. Such as it is, it rather
reverses ordinary experience, for the later poems exhibit the greater play of fancy, the earlier the exacter
graces of form and expression. Yet there is nothing
really wonderful in this, for Crabbe's earliest poems
were published under severe surveillance of himself and
others, and at a time which still thought nothing of
such value in literature as correctness, while his later
were written under no particular censorship, and when
the Romantic revival had already, for better or worse,
emancipated the world. The change was in Crabbe's
case not wholly for the better. He does not in his later
verse become more prosaic, but he becomes consider-

---

[1] Much if not all of this has been given in Sir Adolphus Ward's
Cambridge Press edition: and it has done *no* "harm," if it has not put
the poet any higher (1923).

ably less intelligible. There is a passage in *The Old Bachelor*, too long to quote but worth referring to, which, though it may be easy enough to understand it with a little goodwill, I defy anybody to understand in its literal and grammatical meaning. Such welters of words are very common in Crabbe, and Johnson saved him from one of them in the very first lines of *The Village*. Yet Johnson could never have written the passages which earned Crabbe his fame. The great lexicographer knew man in general much better than Crabbe did; but he nowhere shows anything like Crabbe's power of seizing and reproducing man in particular. Crabbe is one of the first and certainly one of the greatest of the "realists" who, exactly reversing the old philosophical signification of the word, devote themselves to the particular only. Yet of the three small volumes by which he, after his introduction to Burke, made his reputation, and on which he lived for a quarter of a century, the first and the last display comparatively little of this peculiar quality. *The Library* and *The Newspaper* are characteristic pieces of the school of Pope, but not characteristic of their author. The first catalogues books as folio, quarto, octavo, and so forth, and then cross-catalogues them as law, physic, divinity, and the rest, but is otherwise written very much in the air. *The Newspaper* suited Crabbe a little better, because he pretty obviously took a particular newspaper and went through its contents —scandal, news, reviews, advertisements—in his own special fashion: but still the subject did not appeal to him. In *The Village*, on the other hand, contemporaries and successors alike have agreed to recognise Crabbe in his true vein. The two famous passages which attracted the suffrages of judges so different as Scott and Wordsworth, are still, after more than a hundred years, fresh, distinct, and striking. Here they are once more:—

Theirs is yon House that holds the parish poor,
Whose walls of mud scarce bear the broken door;
There, where the putrid vapours, flagging, play,
And the dull wheel hums doleful through the day;—
There children dwell who know no parents' care;
Parents who know no children's love dwell there!
Heart-broken matrons on their joyless bed,
Forsaken wives, and mothers never wed;
Dejected widows, with unheeded tears,
And crippled age with more than childhood fears;
The lame, the blind, and, far the happiest they!
The moping idiot and the madman gay.

———

Anon, a figure enters, quaintly neat,
All pride and business, bustle and conceit;
With looks unaltered by these scenes of woe,
With speed that, entering, speaks his haste to go,
He bids the gazing throng around him fly,
And carries fate and physic in his eye:
A potent quack, long versed in human ills,
Who first insults the victim whom he kills;
Whose murderous hand a drowsy Bench protect,
And whose most tender mercy is neglect.
Paid by the parish for attendance here,
He wears contempt upon his sapient sneer;
In haste he seeks the bed where Misery lies,
Impatience marked in his averted eyes;
And some habitual queries hurried o'er,
Without reply he rushes on the door:
His drooping patient, long inured to pain,
And long unheeded, knows remonstrance vain,
He ceases now the feeble help to crave
Of man; and silent, sinks into the grave.

The poet executed endless variations on this class of theme, but he never quite succeeded in discovering a new one, though in process of time he brought his narrow study of the Aldborough fishermen and towns-folk down still more narrowly to individuals. His landscape is always marvellously exact, the strokes selected with extraordinary skill *ad hoc* so as to show autumn rather than spring, failure rather than hope, the riddle of the painful earth rather than any joy of living. Attempts have been made to vindicate Crabbe from the charge of being a gloomy poet, but I cannot think them successful; I can hardly think that they have been quite serious. Crabbe, our chief realist poet, has an altogether astonishing likeness to the chief prose realist of France, Gustave Flaubert, so far as his manner of view goes, for in point of style the two have small resemblance. One of the most striking things in Crabbe's biography is his remembrance of the gradual disillusion of a day of pleasure which, as a child, he enjoyed in a new boat of his father's. We all of us, except those who are gifted or cursed with the proverbial duck's back, have these experiences and these remembrances of them. But most men either simply grin and bear it, or carrying the grin a little farther, console themselves by regarding their own disappointments from the ironic and humorous point of view. Crabbe, though not destitute of humour, does not seem to have been able or disposed to employ it in this way. Perhaps he never quite got over the terrible and, for the most part unrecorded, year in London: perhaps the difference between the Mira of promise and the Mira of possession —the "happiness denied"—had something to do with it: perhaps it was a question of natural disposition with him. But when, years afterwards, as a prosperous middle-aged man, he began his series of published poems once more with *The Parish Register*, the same manner of seeing is evident, though the minute elaboration of the views themselves is almost infinitely greater. Nor did he ever succeed in altering this manner, if he ever tried to do so.

With the exception of his few Lyrics, the most important of which, *Sir Eustace Grey* (one of his very best things), is itself a tale in different metre, and a few other occasional pieces of little importance, the entire work of Crabbe, voluminous as it is, is framed upon a single pattern, the vignettes of *The Village* being merely enlarged in size and altered in frame in the later books. The three parts of *The Parish Register*, the twenty-four Letters of *The Borough*, some of which have single and others grouped subjects, and the sixty or seventy pieces which make up the three divisions of Tales, consist almost exclusively of heroic couplets, shorter measures very rarely intervening. They are also almost wholly devoted to narratives, partly satirical, partly pathetic, of the lives of individuals of the lower and middle class chiefly. Jeffrey, who was a great champion of Crabbe and allotted several essays to him, takes delight in analysing the plots or stories of these tales; but it is a little amusing to notice that he does it for the most part exactly as if he were criticising a novelist or a dramatist. "The object," says he, in one place, "is to show that a man's fluency of speech depends very much upon his confidence in the approbation of his auditors": "In Squire Thomas we have the history of a mean, domineering spirit," and so forth. Gifford in one place actually discusses Crabbe as a novelist. I shall make some further reference to this curious attitude of Crabbe's admiring critics. For the moment I shall only remark that the singularly mean character of so much of Crabbe's style, the "style of drab stucco," as it has been unkindly called, which is familiar from the wicked wit that told how the youth at the theatre

Regained the felt and felt what he regained,

is by no means universal. The most powerful of all his pieces, the history of Peter Grimes, the tyrant of apprentices, is almost entirely free from it, and so are a few others. But it is common enough to be a very serious stumbling-block. In nine tales out of ten this is the staple:—

> Of a fair town where Dr Rack was guide,
> His only daughter was the boast and pride.

Now that is unexceptionable verse enough, but what is the good of putting it in verse at all? Here again:—

> For he who makes me thus on business wait,
> Is not for business in a proper state.

It is obvious that you cannot trust a man who, unless he is intending a burlesque, can bring himself to write like that. Crabbe not only brings himself to it, but rejoices and luxuriates in the style. The tale from which that last luckless distich is taken, *The Elder Brother*, is full of pathos and about equally full of false notes. If we turn to a far different subject, the very vigorously conceived *Natural Death of Love*, we find a piece of strong and true satire, the best thing of its kind in the author, which is kept up throughout. Although, like all satire, it belongs at best but to the outer courts of poetry, it is so good that none can complain. Then the page is turned and one reads:—

> "I met," said Richard, when returned to dine,
> "In my excursion with a friend of mine."

It may be childish, it may be uncritical, but I own that such verse as that excites in me an irritation which destroys all power of enjoyment, except the enjoyment of ridicule. Nor let any one say that pedestrian passages of the kind are inseparable from ordinary narrative in verse and from the adaptation of verse to miscellaneous themes. If it were so the argument would be fatal to such adaptation, but it is not. Pope seldom indulges in such passages, though he does sometimes: Dryden never does. He can praise, abuse, argue, tell stories, make questionable jests, do anything in verse that is still poetry, that has a throb and a quiver and a swell in it, and is not merely limp, rhythmed prose. In Crabbe, save in a few passages of feeling and a great many of mere description—the last an excellent setting for poetry but not necessarily poetical—this rhythmed prose is everywhere. The matter which it serves to convey is, with the limitations above given, varied, and it is excellent. No one except the greatest prose novelists has such a gallery of distinct, sharply etched characters, such another gallery of equally distinct scenes and manner-pieces, to set before the reader. Exasperating as Crabbe's style sometimes is, he seldom bores—never indeed except in his rare passages of digressive reflection. It has, I think, been observed, and if not the observation is obvious, that he has done with the pen for the neighbourhood of Aldborough and Glemham what Crome and Cotman have done for the neighbourhood of Norwich with the pencil. His observation of human nature, so far as it goes, is not less careful, true, and vivid. His pictures of manners, to those who read them at all, are perfectly fresh and in no respect grotesque or faded, dead as the manners themselves are. His pictures of motives and of facts, of vice and virtue, never can fade, because the subjects are perennial and are truly caught. Even his plays on words, which horrified Jeffrey—

Alas! your reverence, wanton thoughts I grant
Were once my motive, now the thoughts of want,

and the like—are not worse than Milton's jokes on the guns. He has immense talent, and he has the originality which sets talent to work in a way not tried by others, and may thus be very fairly said to turn it into genius. He is all this and more. But despite the warnings of a certain precedent, I cannot help stating the case which we have discussed in the old form, and asking, was Crabbe a poet?

And thus putting the question, we may try to sum up. It is the gracious habit of a summing-up to introduce, if possible, a dictum of the famous men our fathers that were before us. I have already referred to Hazlitt's criticism on Crabbe in *The Spirit of the Age*, and I need not here urge at very great length the cautions which are always necessary in considering any judgment of Hazlitt's[1]. Much that he says even in the brief space of six or eight pages which he allots to Crabbe is unjust; much is explicably, and not too creditably, unjust. Crabbe was a successful man, and Hazlitt did not like successful men: he was a clergyman of the Church of England, and Hazlitt did not love clergymen of the Church of England: he had been a duke's chaplain, and Hazlitt loathed dukes: he had been a Radical, and was still (though Hazlitt does not seem to have thought him so) a Liberal, but his Liberalism had been Torified into a tame variety. Again, Crabbe, though by no means squeamish, is the most unvoluptuous and dispassionate of all describers of inconvenient things; and Hazlitt was the author of *Liber Amoris*. Accordingly there is much that is untrue in the tissue of denunciation which the critic devotes to the poet. But there are two passages in this tirade which alone might show how great a critic Hazlitt himself was. Here in a couple of lines ("they turn, one and all, on the same sort of teasing, helpless, unimaginative distress") is the germ of one of the most famous and certainly of the best passages of the late Mr Arnold; and here again is one of those critical taps of the finger which shivers by a touch of the weakest part a whole Rupert's drop of misapprehension. Crabbe justified himself by Pope's example. "Nothing," says Hazlitt, "can be more dissimilar. Pope describes what

___
[1] See below, Essay on Hazlitt.

is striking: Crabbe would have described merely what was
there.... In Pope there was an appeal to the imagination,
you see what was passing *in a poetical point of view.*"

Even here (and I have not been able to quote the
whole passage) there is one of the flaws, which Hazlitt
rarely avoided, in the use of the word "striking"; for,
Heaven knows, Crabbe is often striking enough. But
the description of Pope as showing things "in a poetical
point of view" hits the white at once, wounds Crabbe
mortally, and demolishes realism, as we have been
pleased to understand it for the last generation or two.
Hazlitt, it is true, has not followed up the attack, as
I shall hope to show in an instant; but he has indicated
the right line of it. As far as mere treatment goes,
the fault of Crabbe is that he is pictorial rather than
poetic, and photographic rather than pictorial. He sees
his subject steadily, and even in a way he sees it whole;
but he does not see it in the poetical way. You are
bound in the shallows and the miseries of the individual;
never do you reach the large freedom of the poet who
looks at the universal. The absence of selection, of
the discarding of details that are not wanted, has no
doubt a great deal to do with this—Hazlitt seems to
have thought that it had everything to do. I do not
quite agree with him there. Dante, I think, was sometimes quite as minute as Crabbe; and I do not know
that any one less hardy than Hazlitt himself would
single out, as Hazlitt expressly does, the death-bed
scene of Buckingham as a conquering instance in Pope
to compare with Crabbe. We know that the bard of
Twickenham grossly exaggerated this. But suppose he
had not? Would it have been worse verse? I think not.
Although the faculty of selecting instead of giving all,
as Hazlitt himself justly contends, is one of the things
which make *poesis non ut pictura*, it is not all, and

I think myself that a poet, if he is a poet, could be almost absolutely literal. Shakespeare is so in the picture of Gloucester's corpse. Is that not poetry?

The defect of Crabbe, as it seems to me, is best indicated by reference to one of the truest of all dicta on poetry, the famous maxim of Joubert—that the lyre is a winged instrument and must transport. There is no wing in Crabbe, there is no transport, because, as I hold (and this is where I go beyond Hazlitt), there is no music. In all poetry, the very highest as well as the very lowest that is still poetry, there is something which transports, and that something in my view is always the music of the verse, of the words, of the cadence, of the rhythm, of the sounds superadded to the meaning. When you get the best music married to the best meaning, then you get, say, Shakespeare: when you get some music married to even moderate meaning, you get, say, Moore. Wordsworth can, as everybody not a Wordsworthian holds, and as some even of Wordsworthians admit, write the most detestable doggerel and platitude. But when any one who knows what poetry is reads—

> Our noisy years seem moments in the being
> Of the eternal silence,

he sees that, quite independently of the meaning, which disturbs the soul of no less a person than Mr John Morley[1], there is one note added to the articulate music of the world—a note that never will leave off resounding till the eternal silence itself gulfs it. He leaves Wordsworth, he goes straight into the middle of the eighteenth century, and he sees Thomson with his hands in his dressing-gown pockets biting at the peaches, and hears him between the mouthfuls murmuring—

> So when the Shepherd of the Hebrid Isles,
> Placed far amid the melancholy main,

[1] Lord Morley of Blackburn.

and there is another note, as different as possible in kind yet still alike, struck for ever. Yet again, to take example still from the less romantic poets, and in this case from a poet, whom Mr Kebbel specially and disadvantageously contrasts with Crabbe, when we read the old schoolboy's favourite—

> When the British warrior queen,
> Bleeding from the Roman rods,

we hear the same quality of music informing words, though again in a kind somewhat lower, commoner, and less. In this matter, as in all matters that are worth handling at all, we come of course *ad mysterium.* Why certain combinations of letters, sounds, cadences, should almost without the aid of meaning, though no doubt immensely assisted by meaning, produce this effect of poetry on men no man can say. But they do; and the chief merit of criticism is that it enables us by much study of different times and different languages to recognise some part of the laws, though not the ultimate and complete causes, of the production.

Now I can only say that Crabbe does not produce, or only in the rarest instances produces, this effect on me, and what is more, that on ceasing to be a patient in search of poetical stimulant and becoming merely a gelid critic, I do not discover even in Crabbe's warmest admirers any evidence that he produced this effect on them. Both in the eulogies which Mr Kebbel quotes, and in those that he does not quote, I observe that the eulogists either discreetly avoid saying what they mean by poetry, or specify for praise something in Crabbe that is not distinctly poetical. Cardinal Newman said that Crabbe "pleased and touched him at thirty years' interval," and pleaded that this answers to the "accidental definition of a classic." Most certainly; but not necessarily to that of a poetical classic.

Jeffrey thought him "original and powerful." Granted; but there are plenty of original and powerful writers who are not poets. Wilson gave him the superlative for "original and vivid painting." Perhaps; but is Hogarth a poet? Jane Austen "thought she could have married him." She had not read his biography; but even if she had would that prove him to be a poet? Lord Tennyson is said to single out the following passage, which is certainly one of Crabbe's best, if not his very best:—

> Early he rose, and looked with many a sigh
> On the red light that filled the eastern sky;
> Oft had he stood before, alert and gay,
> To hail the glories of the new-born day;
> But now dejected, languid, listless, low,
> He saw the wind upon the water blow,
> And the cold stream curled onward as the gale
> From the pine-hill blew harshly down the vale;
> On the right side the youth a wood surveyed,
> With all its dark intensity of shade;
> Where the rough wind alone was heard to move
> In this, the pause of nature and of love
> When now the young are reared, and when the old,
> Lost to the tie, grow negligent and cold:
> Far to the left he saw the huts of men,
> Half hid in mist that hung upon the fen:
> Before him swallows gathering for the sea,
> Took their short flights and twittered o'er the lea;
> And near the bean-sheaf stood, the harvest done,
> And slowly blackened in the sickly sun;
> All these were sad in nature, or they took
> Sadness from him, the likeness of his look
> And of his mind—he pondered for a while,
> Then met his Fanny with a borrowed smile.

It is good: it is extraordinarily good: it could not be better of its kind. It is as nearly poetry as anything that Crabbe ever did—but is it quite? If it is (and I am not careful to deny it) the reason, as it seems to me, is that the verbal and rhythmical music here, with its special effect of "transporting" of "making the common as if it were uncommon," is infinitely better than is usual with Crabbe, that in fact there is music as well as meaning. Hardly anywhere else, not even in the best passages of the story of Peter Grimes, shall we find such music; and in its absence it may be said of Crabbe much more truly than of Dryden (who carries the true if not the finest poetical undertone with him even into the rant of Almanzor and Maximin, into the interminable arguments of *Religio Laici* and *The Hind and the Panther*) that he is a classic of our prose.

Yet the qualities which are so noteworthy in him are all qualities which are valuable to the poet, and which for the most part are present in good poets. And I cannot help thinking that this was what actually deceived some of his contemporaries and made others content for the most part to acquiesce in an exaggerated estimate of his poetical merits. It must be remembered that even the latest generation which, as a whole and unhesitatingly, admired Crabbe, had been brought up on the poets of the eighteenth century, in the very best of whom the qualities which Crabbe lacks had been but sparingly and not eminently present. It must be remembered too, that from the great vice of the poetry of the eighteenth century, its artificiality and convention, Crabbe is conspicuously free. The return to nature was not the only secret of the return to poetry; but it was part of it, and that Crabbe returned to nature no one could doubt. Moreover he came just between the school of prose fiction which practically ended with *Evelina* and the school of prose fiction which opened its different branches with *Waverley* and *Sense and Sensibility*. His contemporaries found nowhere else the narrative power, the faculty of character-drawing, the genius for description of places and manners, which they found in Crabbe; and they knew that in almost all, if not in all the great poets there is narrative power, faculty of character-drawing, genius for description. Yet again, Crabbe put these gifts into verse which at its best was excellent in its own way, and at its worst was a blessed contrast to Darwin or to Hayley. Some readers may have had an uncomfortable though only half-conscious feeling that if they had not a poet in Crabbe they had not a poet at all. At all events they made up their minds that they had a poet in him.

But are we bound to follow their example? I think not. You could play on Crabbe that odd trick which used, it is said, to be actually played on some mediæval verse chroniclers and unrhyme him—that is to say, put him into prose with the least possible changes— and his merits would, save in rare instances, remain very much as they are now. You could put other words in the place of his words, keeping the verse, and it would not as a rule be much the worse. You cannot do either of these things with poets who are poets. Therefore I shall conclude that save at the rarest moments, moments of some sudden gust of emotion, some happy accident, some special grace of the Muses to reward long and blameless toil in their service, Crabbe was not a poet. But I have not the least intention of denying that he was great, and all but of the greatest among English writers.

II

HOGG

"WHAT on earth," it was once asked, "will you make of Hogg?" I think that there is something to be made of Hogg, and that it is something worth the making. In the first place, it is hardly possible, without studying "the Shepherd" pretty close, fully to appreciate three other persons, all greater, and one infinitely greater, than himself; namely, Wilson, Lockhart, and Scott. To the two first he was a client in the Roman sense, a plaything, something of a butt, and an invaluable source of inspiration or at least suggestion. Towards the last he occupied a very curious position, never I think quite paralleled elsewhere—the position of a Boswell who would fain be a Boswell and is not allowed to be, who has wild notions that he is really a greater man than Johnson and occasionally blasphemes against his idol, but who in the intervals is truly Boswellian. In the second place, he has usually hitherto been not criticised at all, but either somewhat sneered at or else absurdly over-praised. In the third place, as both Scott and Byron recognised, he is probably the most remarkable example we have of absolute self-education, or of no education: for Burns was an academically instructed student in comparison with Hogg. In the fourth, he produced, amid a mass of rubbish, some charming verse and one prose-story which, though it is almost overlooked by the general, some good judges are, I believe, agreed with me in regarding as one of the very best things of its kind, while it is also a very curious literary puzzle.

The anecdotic history, more or less authentic, of

the Ettrick Shepherd would fill volumes, and I must try to give some of the cream of it presently. The non-anecdotic part may be despatched in a few sentences. The exact date of his birth is not known, but he was baptised on 9th December 1770. His father was a good shepherd and a bad farmer—a combination of characteristics which Hogg himself inherited unimpaired and unimproved. If he had any early education at all, he forgot it so completely that he had, as a grown-up man, to teach himself writing if not reading a second time. He pursued his proper vocation for about thirty years, during the latter part of which time he became known as a composer of very good songs, "Donald Macdonald" being ranked as the best. He printed a few as a pamphlet in the first year of the century, but met with little success. Then he fell in with Scott, to whom he had been introduced as a purveyor of ballads, not a few of which his mother, Margaret Laidlaw, knew by heart. This old lady it was who gave Scott the true enough warning that the ballads were "made for singing and no for reading." Scott in his turn set Hogg on the track of making some money by his literary work, and Constable published *The Mountain Bard* together with a treatise called *Hogg on Sheep*, which I have not read, and of which I am not sure that I should be a good critic if I had. The two books brought Hogg three hundred pounds. This sum he poured into the usual Danaids' vessel of the Scotch peasant—the taking and stocking of a farm, which he had neither judgment to select, capital to work, nor skill to manage; and he went on doing very much the same thing for the rest of his life. The exact dates of that life are very sparely given in his own *Autobiography*, in his daughter's *Memorials*, and in the other notices of him that I have seen. He would appear to have spent four or five years in the promising attempt to run, not one but two large stock-farms. Then he tried shepherding again, without much success; and finally in 1810, being forty years old and able to write, he went to Edinburgh and "commenced," as the good old academic phrase has it, literary man. He brought out a new book of songs called *The Forest Minstrel*, and then he started a periodical, *The Spy*. On this, as he tells us, Scott very wisely remonstrated with him, asking him whether he thought he could be more elegant than Addison or Mackenzie. Hogg replied with his usual modesty that at any rate he would be "mair original." The originality appears to have consisted in personality; for Hogg acknowledges one exceedingly insolent attack on Scott himself, which Scott seems, after at first resenting it (and yet Hogg tells us elsewhere that he never resented any such thing), to have forgiven. He had also some not clearly known employments of the factorship or surveyorship kind; he was much patronised by two worthy hatters, Messrs Grieve and Scott, and in 1813 the book which contains all his best verse, *The Queen's Wake*, was published. It was deservedly successful; but, by a species of bad luck which pursued Hogg with extraordinary assiduity, the two first editions yielded nothing, as his publisher was not solvent. The third, which Blackwood issued, brought him in good profit. Two years later he became in a way a made man. He had very diligently sought the patronage of Harriet, Duchess of Buccleuch, and, his claims being warmly supported by Scott and specially recommended by the Duchess on her deathbed to her husband, Hogg received rent free, or at a peppercorn, the farm of Mossend, Eltrive or Altrive. It is agreed even by Hogg's least judicious admirers that if he had been satisfied with this endowment and had then devoted himself, as he actually did, to writing, he might have lived and died in comfort, even though his singular luck in not being paid continued to haunt him. But he must needs repeat his old mistake and take the adjacent farm of Mount Benger, which, with a certain reckless hospitable way of living for which he is not so blamable, kept him in difficulties all the rest of his life and made him die in them. He lived twenty years longer; married a good-looking girl much his superior in rank and twenty years his junior, who seems to have made him an excellent wife; engaged in infinite magazine- and book-writing, of which more presently; became the inspirer, model and butt of *Blackwood's Magazine*; constantly threatened to quarrel with it for traducing him, and once did so; loved Edinburgh convivialities more well than wisely; had the very ill-luck to survive Scott and to commit the folly of writing a pamphlet (more silly than anything else) on the "domestic manners" of that great man, which estranged Lockhart, hitherto his fast friend; paid a visit to London in 1832, whereby hang tales; and died himself on 21st November 1835.

Such, briefly but not I think insufficiently given, is the Hogg of history. The Hogg of anecdote is a much more considerable and difficult person. He mixes himself up with or becomes by turns (whichever phrase may be preferred) the Shepherd of the *Noctes* and the Hogg who is revealed to us, say his panegyrists, with "uncalled-for malignity" in Lockhart's *Life of Scott*. But these panegyrists seem to forget that there are two documents which happen not to be signed either "John Gibson Lockhart" or "Christopher North," and that these documents are Hogg's *Autobiography*, published by himself, and the *Domestic Manners of Sir Walter Scott*, likewise authenticated. In these two we have the Hogg of the *ana* put forward pretty vividly. For instance, Hogg tells us how, late in Sir Walter's life, he and his wife called upon Scott. "In we went and were received with all the affection of old friends. But his whole discourse was addressed to my wife, while I was left to shift for myself.... In order to attract his attention from my wife to one who I thought as well deserved it, I went close up to him with a scrutinising look and said, 'Gudeness guide us, Sir Walter, but ye hae gotten a braw gown.'" The rest of the story is not bad, but less characteristic. Immediately afterwards Hogg tells his own speech about being "not sae yelegant but mair original" than Addison. Then there is the other capital legend, also self-told, how he said to Scott, "Dear Sir Walter, ye can never suppose that I belang to your school of chivalry! Ye are the king of that school, but I'm the king of the mountain and fairy school, which is a far higher ane than yours!" "This," says Professor Veitch, a philosopher, a scholar, and a man of letters, "though put with an almost sublime egotism, is in the main true." Almost equally characteristic is the fact that, after beginning his pamphlet by calling Lockhart "the only man thoroughly qualified for the task" of writing Scott's life, Hogg elsewhere, in one of the extraordinary flings that distinguish him, writes: "Of Lockhart's genius and capabilities Sir Walter always spoke with the greatest enthusiasm: more than I thought he deserved. For I knew him a great deal better than Sir Walter did, and, whatever Lockhart may pretend, I knew Sir Walter a thousand times better than he did."

Now be it remembered that these passages are descriptive of Hogg's Hogg, to use the always useful classification of Dr Holmes. To complete them (the actual texts are too long to give here) it is only necessary to compare the accounts of a certain dinner at Bowhill given respectively by Hogg in the *Domestic Manners* and by Lockhart in his biography, and also those given in the same places of the one-sided quarrel between Scott and Hogg, because the former, according to his almost invariable habit, refused to collaborate in Hogg's *Poetic Mirror*. In all this we have the man's own testimony about himself. It is not in the least incompatible with his having been, as his panegyrists contend, an affectionate friend, husband, and father; a very good fellow when his vanity or his whims were not touched; and inexhaustibly fertile in the kind of rough profusion of flower and weed that uncultivated soil frequently produces. But it most certainly is also not inconsistent, but on the contrary highly consistent, with the picture drawn by Lockhart in his great book; and it shows how, to say the least and mildest, the faults and foibles of the curious personage known as "the Shepherd of the *Noctes*" were not the parts of the character on which Wilson need have spent, or did spend, most of his invention. Even if the "boozing buffoon" had been a boozing buffoon and nothing more, Hogg, who confesses with a little affected remorse, but with evident pride, that he once got regularly drunk every night for some six weeks running, till "an inflammatory fever" kindly pulled him up, could not have greatly objected to this part of the matter. The wildest excesses of the *Eidolon*-Shepherd's vanity do not exceed that speech to Scott which Professor Veitch thinks so true; and the quaintest pranks played by the same shadow do not exceed in quaintness the immortal story of Hogg being introduced to Mrs Scott for the first time, extending himself on a sofa at full length (on the excuse that he "thought he could never do wrong to copy the lady of the house," who happened at the time to be in a delicate state of health), and ending by addressing her as "Charlotte." This is the story that Mrs Garden, Hogg's daughter, without attempting to contest its truth, describes as told by Lockhart with "uncalled-for malignity." Now when anybody who knows something of Lockhart comes across "malignant," "scorpion," or any term of the kind, he, if he is wise, merely shrugs his shoulders. All the literary copy-books have got it that Lockhart was malignant, and there is of course no more to be said[1]. But something may be done by a little industrious clearing away of fiction in particulars. It may be most assuredly and confidently asserted that no one reading the *Life of Scott* without knowing what Hogg's friends have said of it would dream of seeing malignity in the notices which it contains of the Shepherd. Before writing this paper I gave myself the trouble, or indulged myself in the pleasure (for perhaps that is the more appropriate phrase in reference to the most delightful of biographies, if not of books), of marking with slips of paper all the passages in Lockhart referring to Hogg, and reading them consecutively. I am quite sure that any one who does this, even knowing little or nothing of the circumstances, will wonder where on earth the "ungenerous assaults," the "virulent detraction," the "bitter words," the "false friendship," and so forth, with which Lockhart has been charged, are to be found. But any one who knows that Hogg had, just before his own death, and while the sorrow of Sir Walter's end was fresh, published the possibly not ill-intentioned but certainly ill-mannered pamphlet referred to—a pamphlet which contains among other things, besides the grossest impertinences about Lady Scott's origin, at least one insinuation that

---

[1] For something more, however, see the Essay on Lockhart below.

Scott wrote Lockhart's books for him—if any one further knows (I think the late Mr Scott Douglas was the first to point out the fact) that Hogg had calmly looted Lockhart's biography of Burns, then he will think that the "scorpion," instead of using his sting, showed most uncommon forbearance. This false friend, virulent detractor and ungenerous assailant describes Hogg as "a true son of nature and genius with a naturally kind and simple character." He does indeed remark that Hogg's "notions of literary honesty were exceedingly loose." But (not to mention the Burns affair, which gave me some years ago a clue to this sentence) the remark is subjoined to a letter in which Hogg placidly suggests that he shall write an autobiographic sketch, and that Scott, transcribing it and substituting the third person for the first, shall father it as his own. The other offence I suppose was the remark that "the Shepherd's nerves were not heroically strung." This perhaps might have been left out, but if it was the fact (and Hogg's defenders never seem to have traversed it) it suggested itself naturally enough in the context, which deals with Hogg's extraordinary desire, when nearly forty, to enter the militia as an ensign. Moreover the same passage contains plenty of kindly description of the Shepherd. Perhaps there is "false friendship" in quoting a letter from Scott to Byron which describes Hogg as "a wonderful creature," or in describing the Shepherd's greeting to Wilkie, "Thank God for it! I did not know you were so young a man" as "graceful," or in the citation of Jeffrey's famous blunder in selecting for special praise a fabrication of Hogg's among the *Jacobite Ballads*, or in the genial description, without a touch of ridicule, of Hogg at the St Ronan's Games. The sentence on Hogg's death is indeed severe: "It had been better for his memory had his end been of earlier date; for he did not follow his benefactor until he had insulted his dust." It is even perhaps a little too severe, considering Hogg's irresponsible and childlike nature. But Lockhart might justly have retorted that men of sixty-four have no business to be irresponsible children; and it is certainly true that in this unlucky pamphlet Hogg distinctly accuses Scott of anonymously puffing himself at his, Hogg's, expense, of being over and over again jealous of him, of plagiarising his plots, of sneering at him, and, if the passage has any meaning, of joining a conspiracy of "the whole of the aristocracy and literature of the country" to keep Hogg down and "crush him to a nonentity." Neither could Lockhart have been exactly pleased at the passage where Scott is represented as afraid to clear the character of an innocent friend to the boy Duke of Buccleuch.

He told me that which I never knew nor suspected before; that a certain gamekeeper, on whom he bestowed his maledictions without reserve, had prejudiced my best friend, the young Duke of Buccleuch, against me by a story; and though he himself knew it to be a malicious and invidious lie, yet seeing his grace so much irritated, he durst not open his lips on the subject, further than by saying, "But, my lord duke, you must always remember that Hogg is no ordinary man, although he may have shot a stray moorcock." And then turning to me he said, "Before you had ventured to give any saucy language to a low scoundrel of an English gamekeeper, you should have thought of Fielding's tale of Black George."

"I never saw that tale," said I, "and dinna ken ought about it. But never trouble your head about that matter, Sir Walter, for it is awthegither out o' nature for our young chief to entertain ony animosity against me. The thing will never mair be heard of, an' the chap that tauld the lees on me will gang to hell, that's aye some comfort."

Part of my reason for quoting this last passage is to recall to those who are familiar with the *Noctes Ambrosianæ* the extraordinary felicity of the imitation. This, which Hogg with his own pen represents himself as speaking with his own mouth, might be found textually in any page of the *Noctes* without seeming in the least out of keeping with the ideal Hogg.

And this brings me to the second charge of Hogg's friends, that Wilson wickedly caricatured his humble friend, if indeed he did not manufacture a Shepherd out of his own brain. This is as uncritical as the other, and even more surprising. That any one acquainted with Hogg's works, especially his autobiographic productions, should fail to recognise the resemblance is astonishing enough; but what is more astonishing is that any one interested in Hogg's fame should not perceive that the Shepherd of the *Noctes* is Hogg magnified and embellished in every way. He is not a better poet, for the simple reason that the verses put in his mouth are usually Hogg's own and not always his best. But out of the *Confessions of a Sinner*, Hogg has never signed anything half so good as the best prose passages assigned to him in the *Noctes*. They are what he might have written if he had taken pains: they are in his key and vein; but they are much above him. Again, unless any reader is so extraordinarily devoid of humour as to be shocked by the mere horse-play, it must be clear to him that the Shepherd's manners are dressed up with extraordinary skill, so as to be just what he would have liked them to be. As for the drinking and so forth, it simply comes to this—that the habits which were fashionable when the century was not yet in its teens, or just in them, were getting to be looked on askance when it was entering or had entered on its thirties. But, instead of being annoyed at this Socrates-Falstaff, as somebody has called it, one might have thought that both Hogg himself and his admirers would have taken it as an immense compliment. The only really bad turn that Wilson seems to have done his friend was posthumous and pardonable. He undertook the task of writing the Shepherd's life and editing his *Remains* for the benefit of his family, who were left very badly off; and he not only did not do it but appears to have lost the documents with which he was entrusted. It is fair to say that after the deaths, which came close together, of his wife, of Blackwood, and of Hogg himself, Wilson was never fully the same man; and that his strongly sentimental nature, joined to his now inveterate habit of writing rapidly as the fancy took him, would have made the task of hammering out a biography and of selecting and editing *Remains* so distasteful from different points of view as to be practically impossible. But in that case of course he should not have undertaken it, or should have relinquished it as soon as he found out the difficulties. Allan Cunningham, it is said, would have gladly done the business; and there were few men better qualified.

And now, having done a by no means unnecessary task in this preliminary clearance of rubbish, let us see what sort of a person in literature and life this Ettrick Shepherd really was—the Shepherd whom Scott not only befriended with unwearied and lifelong kindness, but ranked very high as an original talent, whom Byron thought Scott's only second worth speaking of, whom Southey, a very different person from either, esteemed highly, whom Wilson selected as the mouthpiece and model for one of the most singular and (I venture to say despite a certain passing wave of unpopularity) one of the most enduring of literary character-parts, and to whom Lockhart was, as Hogg himself late in life sets down, "a warm and disinterested friend." We have seen what Professor Veitch thinks of him—that he is the king of a higher school than Scott's. On the other hand, I fear the general English impression of

him is rather that given by no Englishman, but by
Thomas Carlyle, at the time of Hogg's visit to
London in 1832. Carlyle describes him as talking and
behaving like a "gomeril," and amusing the town
by walking about in a huge gray plaid, which was
supposed to be an advertisement, suggested by his
publisher.

The king of a school higher than Scott's and the
veriest gomeril—these surely, though the judges be
not quite of equal competence, are judgments of a
singularly contradictory kind. Let us see what middle
term we can find between them.

The mighty volume (it has been Hogg's ill-fortune
that the most accessible edition of his work is in two
great double-columned royal octavos, heavy to the
hand and not too grateful to the eye) which contains
the Shepherd's collected poetical work is not for every
reader. "Poets? where are they?" Wordsworth is said,
on the authority of De Quincey, to have asked, with
a want of graciousness of manners uncommon even in
him and never forgiven by Hogg, when the latter used
the plural in his presence, and in that of Wilson and
Lloyd. It was unjust as well as rude, but endless
allowance certainly has to be made for Hogg as a poet.
I do not know to whom the epigram that "everything
that is written in Scotch dialect is not necessarily
poetry" is originally due, but there is certainly some
justice in it. Scotch, as a language, has grand accommodations; it has richer vowels and a more varied and
musical arrangement of consonants than English, while
it falls not much short of English in freedom from that
mere monotony which besets the richly-vowelled con-
tinental languages. It has an almost unrivalled provision
of poetical *clichés* (the sternest purist may admit a
French word which has no English equivalent), that

is to say, the stock phrases which Heaven knows who first minted and which will pass till they are worn out of all knowledge. It has two great poets—one in the vernacular, one in the literary language—who are rich enough to keep a bank for their inferiors almost to the end of time. The depreciation of it by "glaikit Englishers" (I am a glaikit Englisher who does not depreciate), simply because it is unfamiliar and rustic-looking, is silly enough. But its best practitioners are sometimes prone to forget that nothing ready-made will do as poetry, and that you can no more take a short cut to Parnassus by spelling good "guid" and liberally using "ava," than you can execute the same journey by calling a girl a nymph and a boy a swain. The reason why Burns is a great poet, and one of the greatest, is that he seldom or never does this in Scots. When he takes to the short cut, as he does sometimes, he usually "gets to his English." Of Hogg, who wrote some charming things and many good ones, the same cannot be said. No writer known to me, not even the eminent Dr Young, who has the root of the poetical matter in him at all, is so utterly uncritical as Hogg. He does not seem even to have known when he borrowed and when he was original. We have seen that he told Scott that he was not of his school. Now a great deal that he wrote, perhaps indeed actually the major part of his verse, is simply imitation and not often very good imitation of Scott. Here is a passage:—

> Light on her airy steed she sprung,
> Around with golden tassels hung.
> No chieftain there rode half so free,
> Or half so light and gracefully.
> How sweet to see her ringlets pale
> Wide-waving in the Southland gale,
> Which through the broom-wood odorous flew
> To fan her cheeks of rosy hue!
> Whene'er it heaved her bosom's screen
> What beauties in her form were seen!

> And when her courser's mane it swung,
> A thousand silver bells were rung.
> A sight so fair, on Scottish plain,
> A Scot shall never see again.

I think we know where this comes from. Indeed Hogg had a certain considerable faculty of conscious parody as well as of unconscious imitation, and his *Poetic Mirror*, which he wrote as a kind of humorous revenge on his brother bards for refusing to contribute, is a fair second to *Rejected Addresses*. The amusing thing is that he often parodied where he did not mean parody in the least, and nowadays we do not want Scott-and-water. Another vein of Hogg's, which he worked mercilessly, is a similar imitation, not of Scott, but of the weakest echoes of Percy's *Reliques*:—

> O sad, sad, was young Mary's plight:
> She took the cup, no word she spake,
> She had even wished that very night
> To sleep and never more to wake.

Sad, sad indeed is the plight of the poet who publishes verses like this, of which there are thousands of lines to be found in Hogg. And then one comes to "Kilmeny," and the note changes with a vengeance:—

> Bonny Kilmeny gaed up the glen;
> But it wasna to meet Duneira's men,
> Nor the rosy monk of the isle to see,
> For Kilmeny was pure as pure could be.
> It was only to hear the yorlin sing,
> And pu' the cress-flower round the spring,
> The scarlet hip and the hindberry,
> For Kilmeny was pure as pure could be.
>
> .   .   .   .   .
>
> Kilmeny looked up with a lovely grace,
> But nae smile was seen on Kilmeny's face;
> As still was her look and as still was her ee
> As the stillness that lay on the emeraut lea,
> Or the mist that sleeps on a waveless sea.
> For Kilmeny had been she kent not where,
> And Kilmeny had seen what she could not declare;
> Kilmeny had been where the cock never crew,
> Where the rain never fell and the wind never blew.

No matter that it is necessary even here to make a cento, that the untutored singer cannot keep up the song by natural force and has not skill enough to dissemble the lapses. "Kilmeny" at its best is poetry—such poetry as, to take Hogg's contemporaries only, there is none in Rogers or Crabbe, little I fear in Southey, and not very much in Moore. Then there is no doubt at all that he could write ballads. "The Witch of Fife" is long and is not improved by being written (at least in one version) in a kind of Scots that never was on land or sea, but it is quite admirable of its class. "The Good Grey Cat," his own imitation of himself in the *Poetic Mirror*, comes perhaps second to it, and "The Abbot McKinnon" (which is rather close to the imitations of Scott) third. But there are plenty of others. As for his poems of the more ambitious kind, *Mador of the Moor, Pilgrims of the Sun*, and even *Queen Hynde*, let blushing glory—the glory attached to the literary department—hide the days on which he produced those. She can very well afford it, for the hiding leaves untouched the division of Hogg's poetical work which furnishes his highest claims to fame except "Kilmeny," the division of the songs. These are numerous and unequal as a matter of course. Not a few of them are merely variations on older scraps and fragments of the kind which Burns had made popular; some of them are absolute rubbish; some of them are mere imitations of Burns himself. But this leaves abundance of precious remnants, as the Shepherd's covenanting friends would have said. The beforementioned "Donald Macdonald" is a famous song of its kind: "I'll no wake wi' Annie" comes very little short of Burns's "Green grow the rashes O!" The piece on the lifting of the banner of Buccleuch, though a curious contrast with Scott's "Up with the Banner"

does not suffer too much by the comparison: "Cam'
ye by Athole" and "When the kye comes hame"
everybody knows, and I do not know whether it is
a mere delusion, but there seems to me to be a rare
and agreeable humour in "The Village of Balmaquhapple."

> D'ye ken the big village of Balmaquhapple?
> The great muckle village of Balmaquhapple?
> 'Tis steeped in iniquity up to the thrapple,
> An' what's to become o' poor Balmaquhapple?

Whereafter follows an invocation to St Andrew, with
a characteristic suggestion that he may spare himself
the trouble of intervening for certain persons such as

> Geordie, our deacon for want of a better,
> And Bess, wha delights in the sins that beset her—

ending with the milder prayer:

> But as for the rest, for the women's sake save them,
> Their bodies at least, and their sauls if they have them.
>
> .   .   .   .
>
> And save, without word of confession auricular,
> The clerk's bonny daughters, and Bell in particular;
> For ye ken that their beauty's the pride and the stapple
> Of the great wicked village of Balmaquhapple!

"Donald McGillavry," which deceived Jeffrey, is
another of the half-inarticulate songs which have the
gift of setting the blood coursing;

> Donald's gane up the hill hard an' hungry;
> Donald's come down the hill wild an' angry:
> Donald will clear the gowk's nest cleverly;
> Here's to the King and Donald McGillavry!
>
> .   .   .   .   .   .
>
> Donald has foughten wi' reif and roguery,
> Donald has dinnered wi' banes and beggary;
> Better it war for Whigs an' Whiggery
> Meeting the deevil than Donald McGillavry.
> Come like a tailor, Donald McGillavry,
> Come like a tailor, Donald McGillavry,
> Push about, in an' out, thimble them cleverly.
> Here's to King James an' Donald McGillavry!

"Love is Like a Dizziness," and the "Boys' Song,"

> Where the pools are bright and deep,
> Where the grey trout lies asleep,
> Up the river and over the lea,
> That's the way for Billy and me—

and plenty more charming things will reward the explorer of the Shepherd's country. Only let that explorer be prepared for pages on pages of the most unreadable stuff, the kind of stuff which hardly any educated man, however great a "gomeril" he might be, would ever dream of putting to paper, much less of sending to press. It is fair to repeat that the educated man who thus refrained would probably be a very long time before he wrote "Kilmeny," or even "Donald McGillavry" and "The Village of Balmaquhapple."

Still (though to say it is enough to make him turn in his grave) if Hogg had been a verse-writer alone he would, except for "Kilmeny" and his songs, hardly be worth remembering, save by professed critics and literary free-selectors. A little better than Allan Cunningham, he is but for that single, sudden, and unsustained inspiration of "Kilmeny," and one or two of his songs, so far below Burns that Burns might enable us to pay no attention to him and not lose much. As for Scott, "Proud Maisie" (an unapproachable thing), the fragments that Elspeth Cheyne sings, even the single stanza in *Guy Mannering*, "Are these the Links of Forth? she said," any one of a thousand snatches that Sir Walter has scattered about his books with a godlike carelessness will "ding" Hogg and all his works on their own field. But then it is not saying anything very serious against a man to say that he is not so great as Scott. With those who know what poetry is, Hogg will keep his corner ("not a polished corner," as Sydney Smith would say) of the temple of Apollo.

Hogg wrote prose even more freely than he wrote verse, and after the same fashion—a fashion which he describes with equal frankness and truth by the phrases, "dashing on," "writing as if in desperation," "mingling pathos and absurdity," and so forth. Tales, novels, sketches, all were the same to him; and he had the same queer mixture of confidence in their merits and doubt about the manner in which they were written. *The Brownie of Bodsbeck*, *The Three Perils of Man* (which appears refashioned in the modern editions of his works as *The Siege of Roxburgh*), *The Three Perils of Woman*, *The Shepherd's Calendar* and numerous other uncollected tales exhibit for the most part very much the same characteristics. Hogg knew the Scottish peasantry well, he had abundant stores of unpublished folklore, he could invent more when wanted, he was not destitute of the true poetic knowledge of human nature, and at his best he could write strikingly and picturesquely. But he simply did not know what self-criticism was, he had no notion of the conduct or carpentry of a story, and though he was rather fond of choosing antique subjects, and prided himself on his knowledge of old Scots, he was quite as likely to put the baldest modern touches in the mouth of a heroine of the fourteenth or fifteenth century as not. If anybody takes pleasure in seeing how a good story can be spoilt, let him look at the sixth chapter of the *Shepherd's Calendar*, "The Souters of Selkirk"; and if any one wants to read a novel of antiquity which is not like Scott, let him read *The Bridal of Polmood*.

In the midst, however, of all this chaotic work, there is still to be found, though misnamed, one of the most remarkable stories of its kind ever written—a story which, as I have said before, is not only extraordinarily good of itself, but insists peremptorily that the reader shall wonder how the devil it got where it is. This is the book now called *The Private Memoirs and Confessions of a Fanatic*, but by its proper and original title, *The Confessions of a Justified Sinner*. Hogg's reference to it in his *Autobiography* is sufficiently odd. "The next year (1824)," he says, "I published *The Confessions of a Fanatic* [*Sinner*], but, it being a story replete with horrors, after I had written it I durst not venture to put my name to it, so it was published anonymously, and of course did not sell very well—so at least I believe, for I do not remember ever receiving anything for it, and I am sure if there had been a reversion [he means return] I should have had a moiety. However I never asked anything, so on that point there was no misunderstanding." And he says nothing more about it, except to inform us that his publishers, Messrs Longman, who had given him for his two previous books a hundred and fifty pounds each "as soon as the volumes were put to press," and who had published the *Confessions* on half profits, observed, when his next book was offered to them, that "his last publication (the *Confessions*) had been found fault with in some very material points, and they begged leave to decline the present one until they consulted some other persons." That is all. But the Reverend Thomas Thomson, Hogg's editor, an industrious and not incompetent man of letters, while admitting that it is "in excellence of plot, concentration of language and vigorous language, one of the best and most interesting [he might have said the best without a second] of Hogg's tales," observes that it "alarmed the religious portion of the community who hastily thought that the author was assailing Christianity." "Nothing could be more unfounded," says the Reverend Thomas Thomson with much justice. He might have added

that it would have been much more reasonable to suspect the author of practice with the Evil One in order
to obtain the power of writing anything so much better
than his usual work.

For, in truth, *The Confessions of a Justified Sinner*,
while it has all Hogg's merits and more, is quite
astoundingly free from his defects. His tales are generally innocent of the most rudimentary notions of
construction: this goes closely ordered, with a few
pardonable enough digressions, from beginning to end.
He has usually little concentrated grasp of character:
the few personages of the *Confessions* are consistent
throughout. His dialogue is, as a rule, extraordinarily
slipshod and unequal: here there is no fault to find with
it. His greatest lack, in short, is the lack of form: and
here, though the story might perhaps have been cur-
tailed, or rather "cut" in the middle, with advantage,
the form is excellent. As its original edition, though
an agreeable volume, is rare, and its later ones are
buried amidst discordant rubbish, it may not be improper to give some account of it. The time is pitched
just about the Revolution and the years following, and,
according to a common if not altogether praiseworthy
custom, the story consists of an editor's narrative and
of the *Confessions* proper imbedded therein. The narrative tells how a drinking Royalist laird married an
exceedingly precise young woman, how the dissension
which was probable broke out between them, how a
certain divine, the Reverend Robert Wringhim, endeavoured to convert the sinner at the instances of
the saint, and perhaps succeeded in consoling the saint
at the expense of the sinner; how the laird sought more
congenial society with a certain cousin of his named
Arabella Logan, and how, rather out of jealousy than
forgiveness, such a union or quasi-union took place

between husband and wife that they had two sons, George and Robert, the elder of whom was his father's favourite and like, while the younger was pretty much left to the care of Mr Wringhim. The tale then tells how, after hardly seeing one another in boyhood, the brothers met as young men at Edinburgh, where on extreme provocation the elder was within an ace of killing the younger. The end of it was that, after Robert had brought against George a charge of assaulting him on Arthur's Seat, George himself was found mysteriously murdered in an Edinburgh close. His mother cared naught for it; his father soon died of grief; the obnoxious Robert succeeded to the estates, and only Arabella Logan was left to do what she could to clear up the mystery, which, after certain strange passages, she did. But when warrants were made out against Robert he had disappeared, and the whole thing remained wrapped in more mystery than ever.

To this narrative succeed the confessions of Robert himself. He takes of course the extreme side both of his mother and of her doctrines, but for some time, though an accomplished Pharisee, he is not assured of salvation, till at last his adopted (if not real) father Wringhim announces that he has wrestled sufficiently in prayer and has received assurance.

Thereupon the young man sallies out in much exaltation of feeling and full of contempt for the unconverted. As he goes he meets another young man of mysterious appearance, who seems to be an exact double of himself. This wraith, however, presents himself as only a humble admirer of Robert's spiritual glory, and holds much converse with him. He meets this person repeatedly, but is never able to ascertain who he is. The stranger says that he may be called Gil Martin if Robert likes, but hints that he is some great one—perhaps the Czar Peter, who was then known to be travelling incognito about Europe. For a time Robert's Illustrious Friend (as he generally calls him) exaggerates the extremest doctrines of Calvinism, and slips easily from this into suggestions of positive crime. A minister named Blanchard, who has overheard his conversation, warns Robert against him, and Gil Martin in return points out Blanchard as an enemy to religion whom it is Robert's duty to take off. They lay wait for the minister and pistol him, the Illustrious Friend managing not only to avert all suspicion from themselves, but to throw it with capital consequences on a perfectly innocent person. After this initiation in blood Robert is fully reconciled to the "great work" and, going to Edinburgh, is led by his Illustrious Friend without difficulty into the series of plots against his brother which had to outsiders so strange an appearance, and which ended in a fresh murder. When Robert in the course of events above described becomes master of Dalchastel, the family estate, his Illustrious Friend accompanies him and the same process goes on. But now things turn, less happily for Robert. He finds himself, without any consciousness of the acts charged, accused on apparently indubitable evidence, first of peccadillos, then of serious crimes. Seduction, forgery, murder, even matricide are hinted against him, and at last, under the impression that indisputable proofs of the last two crimes have been discovered, he flies from his house. After a short period of wandering, in which his Illustrious Friend alternately stirs up all men against him and tempts him to suicide, he finally in. despair succumbs to the temptation and puts an end to his life. This of course ends the *Memoir*, or rather the *Memoir* ends just before the catastrophe. There is then a short postscript in which the editor tells a tale of a suicide found with some such legend attaching to him on a Border hillside, of an account given in *Blackwood* of the searching for the grave, and of a visit to it made by himself (the editor), his friend Mr L——t of C——d [Lockhart of Chiefswood], Mr L——w [Scott's Laidlaw] and others. The whole thing ends with a very well written bit of rationalisation of the now familiar kind, discussing the authenticity of the *Memoirs*, and concluding that they are probably the work of some one suffering from religious mania, or perhaps a sort of parable or allegory worked out with insufficient skill.

Although some such account as this was necessary, no such account, unless illustrated with the most copious citation, could do justice to the book. The first part or Narrative is not of extraordinary, though it is of considerable merit, and has some of Hogg's usual faults. The *Memoirs* proper are almost wholly free from these faults. In no book known to me is the grave treatment of the topsy-turvy and improbable better managed; although, by an old trick, it pleases the "editor" to depreciate his work in the passage just mentioned. The writer, whoever he was, was fully qualified for the task. The possibility of a young man of narrow intellect—his passion against his brother already excited, and his whole mind given to the theology of predestination—gliding into such ideas as are here described is undoubted; and it is made thoroughly credible to the reader. The story of the pretended Gil Martin, preposterous as it is, is told by the unlucky maniac exactly in the manner in which a man deluded, but with occasional suspicions of his delusion, would tell it. The gradual change from intended and successful rascality and crime into the incurring or the supposed incurring of the most hideous guilt without any actual consciousness of guilty action may seem an almost hopeless thing to treat probably. Yet it is so treated here. And the final gathering and blackening of the clouds of despair (though here again there is a very slight touch of Hogg's undue prolongation of things) exhibits literary power of the ghastly kind infinitely different from and far above the usual raw-head-and-bloody-bones story of the supernatural.

Now, who wrote it?

No doubt, so far as I know, has been generally entertained of Hogg's authorship, though, since I myself entertained doubts on the subject, I have found some good judges not unwilling to agree with me. Although admitting that it appeared anonymously, Hogg claims it, as we have seen, not only without hesitation but apparently without any suspicion that it was a particularly valuable or meritorious thing to claim, and without any attempt to shift, divide, or in any way disclaim the responsibility, though the book had been a failure. His publishers do not seem to have doubted then that it was his; nor, I have been told, have their representatives any reason to doubt it now. His daughter, I think, does not so much as mention it in her *Memorials*, but his various biographers have never, so far as I know, hinted the least hesitation. At the same time I am absolutely unable to believe that it is Hogg's unadulterated and unassisted work. It is not one of those cases where a man once tries a particular style, and then from accident, disgust, or what not, relinquishes it. Hogg was always trying the supernatural, and he failed in it, except in this instance, as often as he tried it. Why should he on this particular occasion have been saved from himself? and who saved him?—for that great part of the book at least is his there can be no doubt.

By way of answer to these questions I can at least point out certain coincidences and probabilities. It has been seen that Lockhart's name actually figures in the postscript to the book. Now at this time and for long afterwards Lockhart was one of the closest of Hogg's literary allies; and Hogg, while admitting that the author of *Peter's Letters* hoaxed him as he hoaxed everybody, is warm in his praise. He describes him in his *Autobiography* as "a warm and disinterested friend." He tells us in the book on Scott how he had a plan, even later than this, that Lockhart should edit all his (the Shepherd's) works, for discouraging which plan he was very cross with Sir Walter. Further, the vein of the *Confessions* is very closely akin to, if not wholly identical with, a vein which Lockhart not only worked on his own account but worked at this very same time. It was in these very years of his residence at Chiefswood that Lockhart produced the little masterpiece of *Adam Blair* (where the terrors and temptations of a convinced Presbyterian minister are dwelt upon), and *Matthew Wald*, which is itself the history of a lunatic as full of horrors, and those of no very different kind, as the *Confessions* themselves. That editing, and perhaps something more than editing, on Lockhart's part would have been exactly the thing necessary to prune and train and direct the Shepherd's disorderly luxuriance into the methodical madness of the Justified Sinner—to give Hogg's loose though by no means vulgar style the dress of his own polished manner—to weed and shape and correct and straighten the faults of the Boar of the Forest—nobody who knows the undoubted writing of the two men will deny. And Lockhart, who was so careless of his work that to this day it is difficult, if not impossible, to ascertain what he did or did not write unassisted, would certainly not have been the man to claim a share in the book, even had it made more noise; though he may have thought of this as well as of other things when, in his wrath over the foolish blethering about Scott, he wrote that the Shepherd's views of literary morality were peculiar. As for Hogg himself, he would never have thought of acknowledging any such editing or collaboration if it did take place; and that not nearly so much from vanity or dishonesty as from simple carelessness, dashed perhaps with something of the habit of literary *supercherie* which the society in which he lived affected, and which he carried as far at least as any one of its members.

It may seem rather hard after praising a man's ewe lamb so highly to question his right in her. But I do not think there is any real hardship. I should think that the actual imagination of the story is chiefly Hogg's, for Lockhart's forte was not that quality, and his own novels suffer rather for want of it. If this be the one specimen of what the Shepherd's genius could turn out when it submitted to correction and training, it gives us a useful and interesting explanation why the mass of his work, with such excellent flashes, is so flawed and formless as a whole. It explains why he wished Lockhart to edit the others. It explains at the same time why (for the Shepherd's vanity was never far off) he set apparently little store by the book. It is only a hypothesis of course, and a hypothesis which is very unlikely ever to be proved, while in the nature of things it is even less capable of disproof. But I think there is good critical reason for it.

At any rate, I confess for myself, that I should not take anything like the same interest in Hogg, if he were not the putative author of the *Confessions*. The book is in a style which wearies soon if it be overdone, and which is very difficult indeed to do well. But it is one of the very best things of its kind, and that is a claim which ought never to be overlooked. And if Hogg in some lucky moment did really "write it all by himself," as the children say, then we could make up for him a volume composed of it, of "Kilmeny," and of the best of the songs, which would be a very remarkable volume indeed. It would not represent a twentieth part of his collected work, and it would probably represent a still smaller fraction of what he wrote, while all the rest would be vastly inferior. But it would be a title to no inconsiderable place in literature, and we know that good judges did think Hogg, with all his personal weakness and all his literary shortcomings, entitled to such a place.

III

SYDNEY SMITH

THE hackneyed joke about biographers adding a new terror to death holds still as good as ever. But biography can sometimes make a good case against her persecutors; and one of the instances which she would certainly adduce would be the instance of Sydney Smith. I more than suspect that his actual works are less and less read as time goes on, and that the brilliant virulence of *Peter Plymley*, the even greater brilliance, not marred by virulence at all, of the *Letters to Archdeacon Singleton*, the inimitable quips of his articles in the *Edinburgh Review*, are familiar, if they are familiar at all, only to the professed readers of the literature of the past, and perhaps to some intelligent newspaper men who find Sydney[1] to be what Fuseli pronounced Blake, "d—d good to steal from." But the *Life* which Lady Holland, with her mother's and Mrs Austin's aid, produced more than thirty years ago has had a different fate; and a fresh lease of popularity seems to have been secured by another *Life*, published by Mr Stuart Reid in 1883. This was partly abridged from the first, and partly supplied with fresh matter by a new sifting of the documents which Lady Holland had used. Nor do the authors of these works, however great must be our gratitude to them, take to themselves any such share of the credit as is due to Boswell in the case of Johnson, to Lockhart in the case of Scott, to Carlyle in the case of Sterling. Neither can lay claim to the highest

---

[1] To speak of him in this way is not impertinence or familiarity. He was most generally addressed as "Mr Sydney," and his references to his wife are nearly always to "Mrs Sydney," seldom or never to "Mrs Smith."

literary merit of writing or arrangement; and the latter of the two contains digressions, not interesting to all readers, about the nobility of Sydney's cause. It is because both books let their subject reveal himself by familiar letters, scraps of journal, or conversation, and because the revelation of self is so full and so delightful, that Sydney Smith's immortality, now that the generation which actually heard him talk has all but disappeared, is still secured without the slightest fear of disturbance or decay. With a few exceptions (the Mrs Partington business, the apologue of the dinners at the synod of Dort, "Noodle's Oration," and one or two more), the things by which Sydney is known to the general, all come, not from his works, but from his *Life* or *Lives*. No one with any sense of fun can read the Works without being delighted; but in the Life and the letters the same qualities of wit appear, with other qualities which in the Works hardly appear at all. A person absolutely ignorant of anything but the Works might possibly dismiss Sydney Smith as a brilliant but bitter and not too consistent partisan who fought desperately against abuses when his party was out, and discovered that they were not abuses at all when his party was in. A reader of his Life and of his private utterances knows him better, likes him better, and certainly does not admire him less.

He was born in 1771, the son of an eccentric and apparently rather provoking person, who for no assigned reason left his wife at the church door in order to wander about the world, and who maintained his vagabond principles so well that, as his granddaughter ruefully records, he bought, spent money on, and sold at a loss, no less than nineteen different houses in England and Wales. Sydney was also the second of four clever brothers, the eldest and cleverest being the

somewhat famous "Bobus," who co-operated in the
Microcosm with Canning and Frere, survived his better
known brother but a fortnight, founded a family, and
has left one of those odd reputations of immense talent
not justified by any producible work, to which our
English life of public schools, universities, and Parliament gives peculiar facilities. Bobus and Cecil, the third
brother, were sent to Eton: Sydney and Courtenay, the
fourth, to Winchester, after a childhood spent in precocious reading and arguing among themselves. From
Winchester Sydney (of whose school-days some trifling
but only trifling anecdotes are recorded) proceeded in
regular course to New College, Oxford, and being
elected of right to a Fellowship, then worth about a
hundred pounds a year, was left by his father to "do
for himself" on that not extensive revenue. He did
for himself at Oxford during the space of nine years;
and it is supposed that his straitened circumstances
had something to do with his dislike for universities,
which however was a kind of point of conscience among
his Whig friends. It is at least singular that this
residence of nearly a decade has left hardly a single
story or recorded incident of any kind; and that though
three generations of undergraduates passed through
Oxford in his time, no one of them seems in later years
to have had anything to say of not the least famous
and one of the most sociable of Englishmen. At that
time, it is true, and for long afterwards, the men of
New College kept more to themselves than the men of
any other college in Oxford; but still it is odd. Another
little mystery is, Why did Sydney take orders? Although
there is not the slightest reason to question his being,
according to his own standard, a very sincere and
sufficient divine, it obviously was not quite the profession for him. He is said to have wished for the Bar,

but to have deferred to his father's wishes for the Church. That Sydney was an affectionate and dutiful son nobody need doubt: he was always affectionate, and in his own way dutiful. But he is about the last man one can think of as likely to undertake an uncongenial profession out of high-flown dutifulness to a father who had long left him to his own resources, and who had neither influence nor prospects in the Church to offer him. The Fellowship would have kept him, as it had kept him already, till briefs came. However, he did take orders; and the later *Life* gives more particulars than the first as to the incumbency which indirectly determined his career. It was the curacy of Netheravon on Salisbury Plain; and its almost complete seclusion was tempered by a kindly squire, Mr Hicks-Beach, great-grandfather of the present Sir Michael Hicks-Beach[1]. Mr Hicks-Beach offered Sydney the post of tutor to his eldest son; Sydney accepted it, started for Germany with his pupil, but (as he picturesquely though rather vaguely expresses it) "put into Edinburgh under stress of war" and stayed there for five years.

The sojourn at Edinburgh began in June 1798: it ended in August 1803. It will thus be seen that Sydney was by no means a very young man even when he began reviewing, the year before leaving the Scotch capital. Indeed the aimless prolongation of his stay at Oxford, which brought him neither friends, money, nor professional experience of any kind, threw him considerably behindhand all his life; and this delay, much more than Tory persecution or Whig indifference, was the cause of the comparative slowness with which he made his way. His time at Edinburgh was, however, usefully spent even before that invention of the *Review*,

[1] The late Lord St Aldwyn (1923).

over which there is an amicable and unimportant dispute between himself and Jeffrey. His tutorship was
so successful that Mr Hicks-Beach rewarded it with a
cheque for a thousand pounds: he did duty in the
Episcopal churches of Edinburgh: he made friends with
all the Whigs and many of the Tories of the place: he
laughed unceasingly at Scotchmen and liked them very
much. Also, about the middle of his stay, he got
married, but not to a Scotch girl. His wife was Miss
Catherine Pybus, of Cheam, and the marriage was as
harebrained a one, from the point of view of settlements,
as Jeffrey's own[1]. Sydney's settlement on his wife is
well known: it consisted of "six small silver teaspoons
much worn," with which worldly goods he did her
literally endow by throwing them into her lap. It
would appear that there never was a happier marriage;
but it certainly seemed for some years as if there might
have been many more prosperous in point of money.
When Sydney moved to London he had no very definite
prospect of any income whatever; and had not Mrs
Smith sold her mother's jewels (which came to her just
at the time), they would apparently have had some
difficulty in furnishing their house in Doughty Street.
But Horner, their friend (the "parish bull" of Scott's
irreverent comparison), had gone to London before
them, and impressed himself, apparently by sheer
gravity, on the political world as a good young man.
Introduced by him, Sydney Smith soon became one
of the circle at Holland House. It is indeed not easy
to live on invitations and your mother-in-law's pearls;
but Sydney reviewed vigorously, preached occasionally,
before very long received a regular appointment at the
Foundling Hospital, and made some money by lecturing
very agreeably at the Royal Institution on Moral

[1] See next Essay.

Philosophy—a subject of which he honestly admits that he knew, in the technical sense, nothing. But his hearers did not want technical ethics, and in Sydney Smith they had a moral philosopher of the practical kind who could hardly be excelled either in sense or in wit. One little incident of this time, however, throws some light on the complaints which have been made about the delay of his promotion. He applied to a London rector to license him to a vacant chapel, which had not hitherto been used for the services of the Church. The immediate answer has not been preserved; but from what followed it clearly was a civil and rather evasive but perfectly intelligible request to be excused. The man was of course quite within his right, and a dozen good reasons can be guessed for his conduct. He may really have objected, as he seems to have said he did, to take a step which his predecessors had refused to take, and which might inconvenience his successors. But Sydney would not take the refusal, and wrote another very logical, but extremely injudicious, letter pressing his request with much elaboration, and begging the worthy Doctor of Divinity to observe that he, the Doctor, was guilty of inconsistency and other faults. Naturally this put the Doctor's back up, and he now replied with a flat and very high and mighty refusal. We know from another instance that Sydney was indisposed to take "No" for an answer. However he obtained, besides his place at the Foundling, preacherships in two proprietary chapels, and seems to have had both business and pleasure enough on his hands during his London sojourn, which was about the same length as his Edinburgh one. It was, however, much more profitable, for in three years the ministry of "All the Talents" came in, the Holland House interest was exerted, and the Chancellor's living of Foston, near York, valued at five hundred pounds a year, was given to Sydney. He paid for it, after a fashion which in a less zealous and convinced Whig might seem a little dubious, by the famous lampoons of the *Plymley Letters*, advocating the claims of Catholic emancipation, and extolling Fox and Grenville at the expense of Perceval and Canning. Very edifying is it to find Sydney Smith objecting to this last that he is a "diner out," a "maker of jokes and parodies," a trifler on important subjects—in fact each and all of the things which the Rev. Sydney Smith himself was, in a perfection only equalled by the object of his righteous wrath. But of Peter more presently.

Even his admiring biographers have noticed, with something of a chuckle, the revenge which Perceval, who was the chief object of Plymley's sarcasm, took, without in the least knowing it, on his lampooner. Had it not been for the Clergy Residence Bill, which that very respectable, if not very brilliant, statesman passed in 1808, and which put an end to perhaps the most flagrant of all then existing abuses, Sydney, the enemy of abuses, would no doubt have continued with a perfectly clear conscience to draw the revenues of Foston, and while serving it by a curate, to preach, lecture, dine out, and rebuke Canning for making jokes, in London. As it was he had to make up his mind, though he obtained a respite from the Archbishop, to resign (which in the recurring frost of Whig hopes was not to be thought of), to exchange, which he found impossible, or to bury himself in Yorkshire. This was a real hardship upon him, because Foston, as it was, was uninhabitable, and had had no resident clergyman since the seventeenth century. But whatever bad things could be said of Sydney (and I really do not know what they are, except that the combination of a sharp wit, a ready pen, and strong political prejudices sometimes made him abuse his talents), no one could say that he ever shirked either a difficulty or a duty. When his first three years' leave expired, he went up in 1809 with his family to York, and established himself at Heslington, a village near the city and not far from his parish. And when a second term of dispensation from actual residence was over, he set to work and built the snuggest if the ugliest parsonage in England, with farm-buildings and all complete, at the cost of some four thousand pounds. Of the details of that building his own inimitable account exists, and is or ought to be well known. The brick-pit and kiln on the property, which were going to save fortunes and resulted in nothing but the production of exactly a hundred and fifty thousand unusable bricks: the four oxen, Tug, Lug, Haul and Crawl, who were to be the instruments of another economy and proved to be, at least in Sydneian language, equal to nothing but the consumption of "buckets of sal volatile": the entry of the distracted mother of the household on her new domains with a baby clutched in her arms and one shoe left in the circumambient mud: the great folks of the neighbourhood (Lord and Lady Carlisle) coming to call graciously on the strangers, and being whelmed, coach and four, outriders and all, in a ploughed field of despond: the "universal scratcher" in the meadows, inclined so as to let the brute creation of all heights enjoy that luxury: Bunch the butler, a female child of tender years but stout proportions: Annie Kay the factotum: the "Immortal," a chariot which was picked up at York in the last stage of decay, and carried the family for many years half over England—all these things and persons occur in divers delightful scraps of autobiography and in innumerable letters, after a fashion impossible to better and at a length too long to quote.

Sydney Smith was for more than twenty years rector of Foston, and for fully fifteen actually resided there. During this time he made the acquaintance of Lord and Lady Grey, next to Lord and Lady Holland his most constant friends, visited a little, entertained in his own unostentatious but hearty fashion a great deal, wrote many articles for the *Edinburgh Review*, found himself in a minority of one or two among the clergy of Yorkshire on the subject of Emancipation and similar matters, but was on the most friendly terms possible with his diocesan, Archbishop Vernon Harcourt. Nor was he even without further preferment, for he held for some years (on the then not discredited understanding of resignation when one of the Howards was ready for it) the neighbouring and valuable living of Londesborough. Then the death of an aunt put an end to his monetary anxieties, which for years had been considerable, by the legacy of a small but sufficient fortune. And at last, when he was approaching sixty, the good things of the Church, which he never affected to despise, came in earnest. The Tory Chancellor Lyndhurst gave him a stall at Bristol, which carried with it a small Devonshire living, and soon afterwards he was able to exchange Foston (which he had greatly improved) for Combe Florey near Taunton. When his friend Lord Grey became Prime Minister, the stall at Bristol was exchanged for a much more valuable one at St Paul's; Halberton, the Devonshire vicarage, and Combe Florey still remaining his. These made up an ecclesiastical revenue not far short of three thousand a year, which Sydney enjoyed for the last fifteen years of his life. He never got anything more, and it is certain that for a time he was very sore at not being made a bishop, or at least offered a bishopric. Lord Holland had rather rashly explained the whole difficulty years before, by reporting a conversation of his with Lord Grenville, in which they had hoped that when the Whigs came into power they would be more grateful to Sydney than the Tories had been to Swift. Sydney's acuteness must have made him wince at the omen. For my part I do not see why either Harley or Grey should have hesitated, as far as any scruples of their own went. But I think any fair-minded person must admit the possibility of a scruple, though he may not share it, about the effect of seeing either the *Tale of a Tub* or *Peter Plymley's Letters*, with "By the Right Rev. the Lord Bishop of——" on the title-page. The people who would have been shocked might in each case have been fools: there is nothing that I at least can see, in either book, inconsistent with sound religion and churchmanship. But they would have been honest fools, and of such a Prime Minister has to take heed. So Amen Corner (or rather, for he did not live there, certain streets near Grosvenor Square) in London, and Combe Florey in the country, were Sydney Smith's abodes till his death. In the former he gave his breakfasts and dinners in the season, being further enabled to do so by his share (some thirty thousand pounds) of his brother Courtenay's Indian fortune. The latter, after rebuilding it,—for he had either a fate or a passion for bricks and mortar,—he made on a small scale one of the most beautiful and hospitable houses in the West of England.

To Combe Florey, as to Foston, a sheaf of fantastic legends attaches itself; indeed, as Lady Holland was not very fond of dates, it is sometimes not clear to which of the two residences some of them apply. At both Sydney had a huge storeroom, or rather grocer's and chemist's shop, from which he supplied the wants, not merely of his household, but of half the neighbourhood. It appears to have been at Combe Florey (for though no longer poor he still had a frugal mind) that he hit upon the device of "putting the cheapest soaps in the dearest papers," confident of the result upon the female temper. It was certainly there that he fitted up two favourite donkeys with a kind of holiday-dress of antlers, to meet the objection of one of his lady-visitors that he had no deer; and converted certain large bay-trees in boxes into the semblance of an orangery, by fastening some dozens of fine fruit to the branches. I like to think of the mixed astonishment and disgust of a great Russian, and a not very small Frenchman, both not long deceased, M. Tourguénieff and M. Paul de Saint-Victor, if they had heard of these pleasing tom-fooleries. But tomfoolery, though, when properly and not inordinately indulged, one of the best things in life, must, like the other good things of life, come to an end. After an illness of some months Sydney Smith died at his house in Green Street, of heart disease, on 22nd February, 1845, in the seventy-fourth year of his age.

The memorials and evidences of his peculiar if not unique genius consist of three different kinds; reported or remembered conversations and jokes, letters, and formal literary work. He was once most famous as a talker; but conversation is necessarily the most perishable of all things, and its recorded fragments bear keeping less than any other relics. Some of the verbal jests assigned to him (notably the famous one about the tortoise, which, after being long known by the initiated not to be his, has at last been formally claimed by its rightful owner)[1] are certainly or probably borrowed or falsely attributed, as rich conversationalists always

[1] The late Sir Frederick Pollock (1923).

borrow or receive. And always the things have some-thing of the mangled air which sayings detached from their context can hardly escape. It is otherwise with the letters. The best letters are always most like the actual conversation of their writers, and probably no one ever wrote more as he talked than Sydney Smith. The specially literary qualities of his writing for print are here too in great measure; and on the whole, though of course the importance of subject is nearly always less, and the interest of sustained work is wholly absent, nowhere can the entire Sydney be better seen. Of the three satirists of modern times with whom he may not unfairly claim to rank—Pascal, Swift, and Voltaire—he is most like Voltaire in his faculty of presenting a good thing with a preface which does not in the least prepare you for it, and then leaving it without the slightest attempt to go back on it, and elaborate it, and make sure that his hearer has duly appreciated it and laughed at it. And of the two, though the palm of concentration must be given to Voltaire, the palm of absolute simplicity must be given to Sydney. Hardly any of his letters are without these unforced flashes of wit, from almost his first epistle to Jeffrey (where, after rallying that great little man on being the "only male despondent he has met," he adds the postscript, "I beg to except the Tuxford waiter, who desponds exactly as you do") to his very last to Miss Harcourt, in which he mildly dismisses one of his brethren as "anything but a *polished* corner of the Temple." There is the "usual establishment for an eldest landed baby": the proposition, advanced in the grave and chaste manner, that "the information of very plain women is so inconsiderable, that I agree with you in setting no store by it": the plaintive ex-postulation with Lady Holland (who had asked him to dinner on the ninth of the month, after previously asking him to stay from the fifth to the twelfth), "it is like giving a gentleman an assignation for Wednesday when you are going to marry him on the previous Sunday—an attempt to combine the stimulus of gallantry with the security of connubial relations": the simple and touching information that "Lord Tankerville has sent me a whole buck. This necessarily takes up a good deal of my time"; that "geranium-fed bacon is of a beautiful colour, but it takes so many plants to fatten one pig that such a system can never answer"; that "it is a mistake to think that Dr Bond could be influenced by partridges. He is a man of very independent mind, with whom pheasants at least, or perhaps even turkeys, are necessary"; and scores more with references to which I find the fly-leaves of my copy of the letters covered. If any one wants to see how much solid there is with all this froth, let him turn to the passages showing the unconquerable manliness, fairness, and good sense with which Sydney treated the unhappy subject of Queen Caroline, out of which his friends were so ready to make political capital; or to the admirable epistle in which he takes seriously, and blunts once for all, the points of certain foolish witticisms as to the readiness with which he, a man about town, had taken to catechisms and cabbages in an almost uninhabited part of the despised country. In conversation he would seem sometimes to have a little, a very little, "forced the note." The Quaker baby, and the lady "with whom you might give an assembly or populate a parish," are instances in point. But he never does this in his letters. I take particular pleasure in the following passage written to Miss Georgiana Harcourt within two years of his death: "What a charming existence! To live in the midst of holy people;

to know that nothing profane can approach you; to be certain that a Dissenter can no more be found in the Palace than a snake can exist in Ireland, or ripe fruit in Scotland! To have your society strong, and undiluted by the laity; to bid adieu to human learning; to feast on the Canons and revel in the Thirty-Nine Articles! Happy Georgiana!" Now if Sydney had been what some foolish people think him, merely a scoffer, there would be no fun in this; it would be as impertinent and in as bad taste as the stale jokes of the eighteenth century about Christianity. But he was much else.

Of course, however, no rational man will contend that in estimating Sydney Smith's place in the general memory, his deliberate literary work, or at least that portion of it which he chose to present on reflection, acknowledged and endorsed, can be overlooked. His *Life* contains (what is infinitely desirable in all such Lives and by no means always or often furnished) a complete list of his contributions to the *Edinburgh Review*, and his Works contain most of them. To these have to be added the pamphlets, of which the chief and incomparably the best are, at intervals of thirty years, *Peter Plymley* and the *Letters to Archdeacon Singleton*, together with sermons, speeches, and other miscellaneous matter. The whole, except the things which he did not himself care to reprint, can be obtained now in one volume; but the print is not to be recommended to aged or weakly sight.

Sydney Smith had no false modesty, and in not a few letters to Jeffrey he speaks of his own contributions to the *Edinburgh* with the greatest freedom, combating and quite refusing to accept his editor's suggestion as to their flippancy and fantasticality, professing with much frankness that this is the way he can write and no other, and more than once telling Jeffrey that whatever they may think in solemn Scotland, his, Sydney's, articles are a great deal more read in England and elsewhere than any others. Although there are maxims to the contrary effect, the judgment of a clever man, not very young and tolerably familiar with the world, on his own work, is very seldom far wrong. I should say myself that, putting aside the historic estimate, Sydney Smith's articles are by far the most interesting nowadays of those contributed by any one before the days of Macaulay, who began just as Sydney ceased to write anonymously in 1827, on his Bristol appointment. They are also by far the most distinct and original. Jeffrey, Brougham, and the rest wrote, for the most part, very much after the fashion of the ancients: if a very few changes were made for date, passages of Jeffrey's criticism might almost be passages of Dryden, certainly passages of the better critics of the eighteenth century, as far as manner goes. There is nobody at all like Sydney Smith before him in England, for Swift's style is wholly different. To begin with, Sydney had a strong prejudice in favour of writing very short articles, and a horror of reading long ones—the latter being perhaps less peculiar to himself than the former. Then he never made the slightest pretence at systematic or dogmatic criticism of anything whatever. In literature proper he seems indeed to have had no particular principles, and I cannot say that he had very good taste. He commits the almost unpardonable sin of not merely blaspheming Madame de Sévigné, but preferring to her that second-rate leader-writer in petticoats, Madame de Staël. On the other hand, if he had no literary principles, he had (except in rare cases where politics came in, and not often then) few literary prejudices, and his happily incorrigible good sense and good humour were proof against the frequent bias of his associates. Though he could not have been very sensible, from what he himself says, of their highest qualities, he championed Scott's novels incessantly against the Whigs and prigs of Holland House. He gives a most well-timed warning to Jeffrey that the constant running-down of Wordsworth had very much the look of persecution, though with his usual frankness he avows that he has not read the particular article in question, because the subject is "quite uninteresting to" him. I think he would, if driven hard, have admitted with equal frankness that poetry, merely as poetry, was generally uninteresting. Still he had so many interests of various kinds, that few books failed to appeal to one or the other, and he, in his turn, has seldom failed to give a lively if not a very exact or critical account of his subject. But it is in his way of giving this account that the peculiarity, glanced at above as making a parallel between him and Voltaire, appears. It is, I have said, almost original, and what is more, endless as has been the periodical writing of the last eighty years, and sedulously as later writers have imitated earlier, I do not know that it has ever been successfully copied. It consists in giving rapid and apparently business-like summaries, packed, with apparent negligence and real art, full of the flashes of wit so often noticed and to be noticed. Such are, in the article "The Island of Ceylon," the honey-bird "into whose body the soul of a common informer seems to have migrated," and "the chaplain of the garrison, all in black, the Rev. Mr Somebody or other whose name we have forgotten," the discovery of whose body in a serpent his ruthless clerical brother pronounces to be "the best history of the kind he remembers." Very likely there may be people who can read this, even the "all in black," without laughing, and among them I should suppose must be the somebody or other, whose name we too have forgotten, who is said to have imagined that he had more than parried Sydney's unforgiven jest about the joke and the surgical operation, by retorting, "Yes! an *English* joke." I have always wept to think that Sydney did not live to hear this retort. The classical places for this kind of summary work are the article just named on Ceylon, and that on Waterton. But the most inimitable single example, if it is not too shocking to this very proper age[1], is the argument of Mat Lewis's tragedy: "Ottilia becomes quite furious from the conviction that Cæsario has been sleeping with a second lady called Estella; whereas he has really been sleeping with a third lady called Amelrosa."

Among the most important of these essays are the two famous ones on Methodism and on Indian missions, which gave far more offence to the religious public of evangelical persuasion than all Sydney's jokes on bishops, or his arguments for Catholic emancipation, and which (owing to the strong influence which then, as now, Nonconformists possessed in the counsels of the Liberal party) probably had as much to do as anything else with the reluctance of the Whig leaders, when they came into power, to give their friend the highest ecclesiastical preferment. These subjects are rather difficult to treat in a general literary essay, and it may perhaps be admitted that here, as in dealing with poetry and other subjects of the more transcendental kind, Sydney showed a touch of Philistinism, and a distinct inability to comprehend exaltation of sentiment and thought. But the general sense is admirably sound and perfectly orthodox; and the way in which so

[1] "But this was forty years ago" or nearly so and before even the "naughty nineties" (1923).

apparently light and careless a writer has laboriously supported every one of his charges, and almost every one of his flings, with chapter and verse from the writings of the incriminated societies, is very remarkable. Nor can it, I think, be doubted that the publication, in so widely read a periodical, of the nauseous follies of speech in which well-meaning persons indulged, had something to do with the gradual disuse of a style than which nothing could be more prejudicial to religion, for the simple reason that nothing else could make religion ridiculous. The medicine did not of course operate at once, and silly people still write silly things. But I hardly think that the Wesleyan body or the Church Missionary Society would now officially publish such stuff as the passage about Brother Carey, who, while in the actual paroxysm of sea-sickness, was "wonderfully comforted by the contemplation of the goodness of God," or that about Brother Ward "in design clasping to his bosom" the magnanimous Captain Wickes, who subsequently "seemed very low," when a French privateer was in sight. Jeffrey was, it seems, a little afraid of these well-deserved exposures, which, from the necessity of abundant quotation, are an exception to the general shortness of Sydney's articles. Sydney's interest in certain subjects led him constantly to take up fresh books on them; and thus a series of series might be made out of his papers, with some advantage to the reader perhaps, if a new edition of his works were undertaken. The chief of such subjects is America, in dealing with which he pleased the Americans by descanting on their gradual emancipation from English prejudices and abuses, but infuriated them by constant denunciations of slavery, and by laughing at their lack of literature and cultivation. With India he also dealt often, his brothers' connection with it giving him an interest therein. Prisons were another favourite subject, though, in his zeal for making them uncomfortable, he committed himself to one really atrocious suggestion—that of dark cells for long periods of time. It is odd that the same person should make such a truly diabolical proposal, and yet be in a perpetual state of humanitarian rage about man-traps and spring-guns, which were certainly milder engines of torture. It is odd, too, that Sydney, who was never tired of arguing that prisons ought to be made uncomfortable, because nobody need go there unless he chose, should have been furiously wroth with poor Mr Justice Best for suggesting much the same thing of spring-guns. The greatest political triumph of his manner is to be found no doubt in the article "Bentham on Fallacies," in which the unreadable dia-tribes of the apostle of utilitarianism are somehow spirited and crisped up into a series of brilliant argu-ments, and the whole is crowned by the famous "Noodle's Oration," the summary and storehouse of all that ever has been or can be said on the Liberal side in the lighter manner. It has not lost its point even from the fact that Noodle has now for a long time changed his party, and has elaborated for himself, after his manner, a similar stock of platitudes and absurdities in favour of the very things for which Sydney was fighting.

The qualities of these articles appear equally in the miscellaneous essays, in the speeches, and even in the sermons, though Sydney Smith, unlike Sterne, never condescended to buffoonery or theatrical tricks in the pulpit. In *Peter Plymley's Letters* they appear concen-trated and acidulated: in the *Letters to Archdeacon Singleton*, in the *Repudiation Letters*, and the *Letters on Railways* which date from his very last days, con-

centrated and mellowed. More than one good judge
has been of the opinion that Sydney's powers increased
to the very end of his life, and it is not surprising that
this should have been the case. Although he did plenty
of work in his time, the literary part of it was never
of an exhausting nature. Though one of the most
original of commentators, he was a commentator pure
and simple, and found, but did not supply, his matter.
Thus there was no danger of running dry, and as his
happiest style was not indignation but good-natured
raillery, his increasing prosperity, not chequered, till
quite the close of his life, by any serious bodily ailment,
put him more and more in the right atmosphere and
temper for indulging his genius. *Plymley*, though very
amusing, and, except in the Canning matter above
referred to, not glaringly unfair for a political lampoon,
is distinctly acrimonious, and almost (as "almost" as
Sydney could be) ill-tempered. It is possible to read
between the lines that the writer is furious at his party
being out of office, and is much more angry with
Mr Perceval for having the ear of the country than for
being a respectable nonentity. The main argument,
moreover, is bad in itself, and was refuted by facts.
Sydney pretends to be, as his friend Jeffrey really was,
in mortal terror lest the French should invade England,
and, joined by rebellious Irishmen and wrathful Catholics
generally, produce an English revolution. The Tories
replied, "We will take good care that the French shall
not land, and that Irishmen shall *not* rise." And they
did take the said good care, and they beat the Frenchmen thorough and thorough while Sydney and his
friends were pointing their epigrams. Therefore, though
much of the contention is unanswerable enough, the
thing is doubtfully successful as a whole. In the *Letters
to Archdeacon Singleton* the tone is almost uniformly

good-humoured, and the argument, whether quite consistent or not in the particular speaker's mouth, is
absolutely sound, and has been practically admitted
since by almost all the best friends of the Church. Here
occurs that inimitable passage before referred to:

I met the other day, in an old Dutch chronicle, with a passage
so apposite to this subject, that, though it is somewhat too light
for the occasion, I cannot abstain from quoting it. There was a
great meeting of all the clergy at Dordrecht, and the chronicler
thus describes it, which I give in the language of the translation:
"And there was great store of Bishops in the town, in their robes
goodly to behold, and all the great men of the State were there,
and folks poured in in boats on the Meuse, the Merse, the Rhine,
and the Linge, coming from the Isle of Beverlandt and Isselmond,
and from all quarters in the Bailiwick of Dort; Arminians and
Gomarists, with the friends of John Barneveldt and of Hugh Grote.
And before my Lords the Bishops, Simon of Gloucester, who was
a Bishop in those parts, disputed with Vorstius and Leoline the
Monk, and many texts of Scripture were bandied to and fro; and
when this was done, and many propositions made, and it waxed
towards twelve of the clock, my Lords the Bishops prepared to set
them down to a fair repast, in which was great store of good things
—and among the rest a roasted peacock, having in lieu of a tail
the arms and banners of the Archbishop, which was a goodly sight
to all who favoured the Church—and then the Archbishop would
say a grace, as was seemly to do, he being a very holy man; but
ere he had finished, a great mob of townspeople and folks from the
country, who were gathered under the windows, cried out *Bread!
bread!* for there was a great famine, and wheat had risen to three
times the ordinary price of the *sleich*; and when they had done
crying *Bread! bread!* they called out *No Bishops!* and began to cast
up stones at the windows. Whereat my Lords the Bishops were in
a great fright, and cast their dinner out of the window to appease
the mob, and so the men of that town were well pleased, and did
devour the meats with a great appetite; and then you might have
seen my Lords standing with empty plates, and looking wistfully
at each other, till Simon of Gloucester, he who disputed with
Leoline the Monk, stood up among them and said, *Good my Lords,
is it your pleasure to stand here fasting, and that those who count
lower in the Church than you do should feast and fluster? Let us order
to us the dinner of the Deans and Canons which is making ready for
them in the chamber below.* And this speech of Simon of Gloucester
pleased the Bishops much; and so they sent for the host, one
William of Ypres, and told him it was for the public good, and he,
much fearing the Bishops, brought them the dinner of the Deans
and Canons; and so the Deans and Canons went away without
dinner, and were pelted by the men of the town. because they had

not put any meat out of the windows like the Bishops; and when the Count came to hear of it, he said it was a pleasant conceit, *and that the Bishops were right cunning men, and had ding'd the Canons well.*"

Even in the Singleton Letters, however, there are some little lapses of the same kind (worse, indeed, because these letters were signed) as the attack on Canning in the Plymley Letters. Sydney Smith exclaiming against "derision and persiflage, the great principle by which the world is now governed," is again edifying. But in truth Sydney never had the weakness (for I have known it called a weakness) of looking too carefully to see what the enemy's advocate is going to say. Take even the famous, the immortal apologue of Mrs Partington. It covered, we are usually told, the Upper House with ridicule, and did as much as anything else to carry the Reform Bill. And yet, though it is a watery apologue, it will not hold water for a moment. The implied conclusion is, that the Atlantic beat Mrs Partington. Did it? It made, no doubt, a great mess in her house, it put her to flight, it put her to shame. But when I was last at Sidmouth the line of high-water mark was, I believe, much what it was before the great storm of 1824, and though the particular Mrs Partington had no doubt been gathered to her fathers, the Mrs Partington of the day was, equally without doubt, living very comfortably in the house which the Atlantic had threatened to swallow up.

It was, however, perhaps part of Sydney's strength that he never cared to consider too curiously, or on too many sides. Besides his inimitable felicity of expression (the Singleton Letters are simply crammed with epigram), he had the sturdiest possible common sense and the liveliest possible humour. I have known his claim to the title of "humourist" called in question by precisians: nobody could deny him the title of good-humourist. Except that the sentimental side of Toryism would never have appealed to him, it was chiefly an accident of time that he was a polemical Liberal. He would always and naturally have been on the side opposite to that on which most of the fools were. When he came into the world, as the straitest Tory will admit, there were in that world a great many abuses as they are called, that is to say, a great many things which, once useful and excellent, had either decayed into positive nuisances, or dried up into neutral and harmless but obstructive rubbish. There were also many silly and some mischievous people, as well as some wise and useful ones, who defended the abuses. Sydney Smith was an ideal soldier of reform for his time, and in his way. He was not extraordinarily long-sighted—indeed (as his famous and constantly-repeated advice to "take short views of life" shows) he had a distinct distrust of taking too anxious thought for political or any other morrows. But he had a most keen and, in many cases, a most just scent and sight for the immediate inconveniences and injustices of the day, and for the shortest and most effective ways of mending them. He was perhaps more destitute of romance and of reverence (though he had too much good taste to be positively irreverent) than any man who ever lived. He never could have paralleled, he never could have even understood, Scott's feelings about the Regalia, or that ever-famous incident of Sir Walter's life, when returning with Jeffrey and other Whig friends from some public meeting, Scott protested against the innovations which, harmless or even beneficial individually and in themselves, would by degrees destroy every thing that made Scotland Scotland. I am afraid that his warmest admirers, even those of his own political complexion, must admit that he was, as has been said, more than a little of a Philistine; that he expressed, and expressed capitally in one way, that curious middle-class sentiment, or denial of sentiment, which won its first triumph in the first Reform Bill and its last in the Exhibition of twenty years later, which destroyed no doubt much that was absurd, and some things that were noxious, but which induced in England a reign of shoddy in politics, in philosophy, in art, in literature, and, when its own reign was over, left England weak and divided, instead of, as it had been under the reign of abuses, united and strong. The bombardment of Copenhagen may or may not have been a dreadful thing: it was at any rate better than the abandonment of Khartoum. Nor can Sydney any more than his friends be acquitted of having held the extraordinary notion that you can "rest and be thankful" in politics, that you can set Demos at bishops, but stave and tail him off when he comes to canons; that you can level beautifully down to a certain point, and then stop levelling for ever afterwards; that because you can laugh Brother Ringletub out of court, laughter will be equally effective with Cardinal Newman; and that though it is the height of "anility" (a favourite word of his) to believe in a country gentleman, it is the height of rational religion to believe in a ten-pound householder.

But however open to exception his principles may be, and that not merely from the point of view of high-flying Toryism, his carrying out of them in life and in literature had the two abiding justifications of being infinitely amusing, and of being amusing always in thoroughly good temper. It is, as I have said, impossible to read Sydney Smith's *Life*, and still more impossible to read his letters, without liking him warmly and personally, without seeing that he was not only a man who liked to be comfortable (that is not very rare),

that he was not only one who liked others to be comfortable (that is rarer), but one who in every situation
in which he was thrown, did his utmost to make others
as well as himself comfortable (which is rarest of all).
If the references in *Peter Plymley* to Canning were
unjustifiable from him, there is little or no reason to
think that they were prompted by personal jealousy;
and though, as has been said, he was undoubtedly sore,
and unreasonably sore, at not receiving the preferment
which he thought he had deserved, he does not seem
to have been personally jealous of any man who had
received it. The parson of Foston and Combe Florey
may not have been (his latest biographer, admiring
though he be, pathetically laments that he was not)
a spiritually minded man. But happy beyond almost
all other parishioners of the time were the parishioners
of Combe Florey and Foston, though one of them did
once throw a pair of scissors at his provoking pastor.
He was a fast and affectionate friend; and though he
was rather given to haunting rich men, he did it not
only without servility, but without that alternative of
bearishness and freaks which has sometimes been
adopted. As a prince of talkers he might have been
a bore to a generation which (I own I think in that
perhaps single point), wiser than its fathers, is not so
ambitious as they were to sit as a bucket and be
pumped into. But in that infinitely happier system
of conversation by books, which any one can enjoy as
he likes and interrupt as he likes at his own fireside,
Sydney is still a prince. There may be living somewhere
some one who does not think so very badly of slavery,
who is most emphatically of opinion that "the fools
were right," in the matters of Catholic emancipation
and Reform, who thinks well of public schools and
universities, who even, though he may not like spring-

guns much, thinks that John Jones had only himself to blame if, after ample warning and with no business except the business of supplying a London poulterer with his landlord's game, he trespassed and came to the worst. Yet even this monster, if he happened to be possessed of the sense of fun and literature (which is perhaps impossible), could not read even the most acrid of Sydney's political diatribes without shrieking with laughter, if, in his ogreish way, he were given to such violent demonstrations; could certainly not read the *Life* and the letters without admitting, in a moment of unwonted humanity, that here was a man who, for goodness as well as for cleverness, for sound practical wisdom as well as for fantastic verbal wit, has had hardly a superior and very few equals.

IV

JEFFREY

"JEFFREY and I," says Christopher North in one of his more malicious moments, "do nothing original; it's porter's work." A tolerably experienced student of human nature might almost, without knowing the facts, guess the amount of truth contained in this fling. North, as North, had done nothing that the world calls original: North, as Wilson, had done a by no means inconsiderable quantity of such work in verse and prose. But Jeffrey really did underlie the accusation contained in the words. A great name in literature, nothing stands to his credit in permanent literary record but a volume (a sufficiently big one, no doubt[1]) of criticisms on the work of other men; and though this volume is only a selection from his actual writings, no further gleaning could be made of any different material. Even his celebrated, or once celebrated, "Treatise on Beauty" is but a review article, worked up into an encyclopædia article, and dealing almost wholly with pure criticism. Against him, if against any one, the famous and constantly repeated gibe about the fellows who have failed in literature and art, falls short and harmless. In another of its forms, "the corruption of a poet is the generation of a critic," it might be more appropriate. For Jeffrey, as we know from his boyish letters, once thought, like almost every boy who is not an idiot, that he might be a poet, and scribbled verses in plenty. But the distinguishing

---

[1] To prevent mistakes it may be as well to say that Jeffrey's *Contributions to the Edinburgh Review* appeared first in four volumes, then in three, then in one.

feature in this case was, that he waited for no failure, for no public ridicule or neglect, not even for any private nipping of the merciful, but so seldom effective, sort, to check those sterile growths. The critic was sufficiently early developed in him to prevent the corruption of the poet from presenting itself, in its usual disastrous fashion, to the senses of the world. Thus he lives (for his political and legal renown, though not inconsiderable, is comparatively unimportant) as a critic pure and simple.

His biographer, Lord Cockburn, tells us that "Francis Jeffrey, the greatest of British critics, was born in Edinburgh on 23rd October, 1773." It must be at the end, not the beginning, of this paper that we decide whether Jeffrey deserves the superlative. He seems certainly to have begun his critical practice very early. He was the son of a depute-clerk of the Court of Session, and respectably, though not brilliantly, connected. His father was a great Tory, and, though it would be uncharitable to say that this was the reason why Jeffrey was a great Liberal, the two facts were probably not unconnected in the line of causation. Francis went to the High School when he was eight, and to the College at Glasgow when he was fourteen. He does not appear to have been a prodigy at either; but he has an almost unequalled record for early work of the self-undertaken kind. He seems from his boyhood to have been addicted to filling reams of paper, and shelves full of note-books, with extracts, abstracts, critical annotations, criticisms of these criticisms, and all manner of writing of the same kind. I believe it is the general experience that this kind of thing does harm in nineteen cases, for one in which it does good; but Jeffrey was certainly a striking exception to the rule, though perhaps he might not have been so if his producing, or at least publishing, time had not been unusually delayed. Indeed, his whole mental history appears to have been of a curiously piecemeal character; and his scrappy and self-guided education may have conduced to the priggishness which he showed early, and never entirely lost, till fame, prosperity, and the approach of old age mellowed it out of him. He was not sixteen when his sojourn at Glasgow came to an end; and, for more than two years, he seems to have been left to a kind of studious independence, attending only a couple of law classes at Edinburgh University. Then his father insisted on his going to Oxford: a curious step, the reasons for which are anything but clear. For the paternal idea seems to have been that Jeffrey was to study not arts, but law; a study for which Oxford may present facilities now, but which most certainly was quite out of its way in Jeffrey's time, and especially in the case of a Scotch boy of ordinary freshman's age.

It is painful to have to say that Jeffrey hated Oxford, because there are few instances on record in which such hatred does not show the hater to have been a very bad man indeed. There are, however, some special excuses for the little Scotchman. His college (Queen's) was not perhaps very happily selected; he had been sent there in the teeth of his own will, which was a pretty strong will; he was horrified, after the free selection of Scotch classes, to find a regular curriculum which he had to take or leave as a whole; the priggishness of Oxford was not his priggishness, its amusements (for he hated sport of every kind) were not his amusements; and, in short, there was a general incompatibility. He came up in September and went down in July, after doing nothing except having, according to a not ill-natured jest, "lost the broad Scotch, but gained only the narrow English,"—a peculiarity which sometimes brought a little mild ridicule on him both from Scotchmen and Englishmen.

Very soon after his return to Edinburgh, he seems to have settled down steadily to study for the Scotch bar, and during his studies distinguished himself as a member of the famous Speculative Society, both in essay-writing and in the debates. He was called on 16th December, 1794.

Although there have never been very quick returns at the bar, either of England or Scotland, the smaller numbers of the latter might be thought likely to bring young men of talent earlier to the front. This advantage, however, appears to have been counterbalanced partly by the strong family interests which made a kind of aristocracy among Scotch lawyers, and partly by the influence of politics and of Government patronage. Jeffrey was, comparatively speaking, a "kinless loon"; and, while he was steadily resolved not to put himself forward as a candidate for the Tory manna of which Dundas was the Moses, his filial reverence long prevented him from declaring himself a very violent Whig. Indeed, he gave an instance of this reverence which might serve as a pretty text for a casuistical discussion. Henry Erskine, Dean of the Faculty of Advocates, was in 1796 deprived by vote of that, the most honourable position of the Scotch bar, for having presided at a Whig meeting. Jeffrey, hke Gibbon, sighed as a Whig, but obeyed as a son, and stayed away from the poll. His days were certainly long in the land; but I am inclined to think that, in a parallel case, some Tories at least would have taken the chance of shorter life with less speckled honour. However, it is hard to quarrel with a man for obeying his parents; and perhaps, after all, the Whigs did not think the matter of so much importance as they affected to do. It is certain that Jeffrey was a little dashed by the slowness of his success at the bar. Towards the end of 1798, he set out for London with a budget of letters of introduction, and thoughts of settling down to literature. But the editors and publishers to whom he was introduced did not know what a treasure lay underneath the scanty surface of this Scotch advocate, and they were either inaccessible or repulsive. He returned to Edinburgh, and, for another two years, waited for fortune philosophically enough, though with lingering thoughts of England, and growing ones of India. It was just at the turn of the century, that his fortunes began, in various ways, also to take a turn. For some years, though a person by no means given to miscellaneous acquaintances, he had been slowly forming the remarkable circle of friends from whose combined brains was soon to start the *Edinburgh Review*. He fell in love, and married his second cousin, Catherine Wilson, on 1st November, 1801—a bold and by no means canny step, for his father was ill-off, the bride was tocherless, and he says that he had never earned a hundred pounds a year in fees. They did not, however, launch out greatly, and their house in Buccleuch Place (not the least famous locality in literature) was furnished on a scale which some modern colleges, conducted on the principles of enforced economy, would think Spartan for an undergraduate. Shortly afterwards, and very little before the appearance of the Blue and Yellow, Jeffrey made another innovation, which was perhaps not less profitable to him, by establishing a practice in ecclesiastical causes; though he met with a professional check in his rejection, on party principles, for the so-called collectorship, a kind of reporter's post of some emolument and not inconsiderable distinction.

The story of the *Edinburgh Review* and its foundation

has been very often told on the humorous, if not exactly historical, authority of Sydney Smith. It is unnecessary to repeat it. It is undoubted that the idea was Sydney's. It is equally undoubted that, but for Jeffrey, the said idea might never have taken form at all, and would never have retained any form for more than a few months. It was only Jeffrey's long-established habit of critical writing, the untiring energy with which he whipped up his no doubt gifted but quite untrained contributors, and the skill which he almost at once developed in editing proper—that is to say in selecting, arranging, adapting, and, even to some extent, re-writing contributions—which secured success. Very different opinions have been expressed at different times on the intrinsic merits of this celebrated pro-duction; and perhaps, on the whole, the principal feeling of explorers into the long and dusty ranges of its early volumes, has been one of disappointment. I believe myself that, in similar cases, a similar result is very common indeed, and that it is due to the operation of two familiar fallacies. The one is the delusion as to the products of former times being necessarily better than those of the present; a delusion which is not the less deluding because of its counterpart, the delusion about progress. The other is a more peculiar and subtle one. I shall not go so far as a very experienced journalist who once said to me commiseratingly, "My good sir, I won't exactly say that literary merit hurts a newspaper." But there is no doubt that all the great successes of journalism, for the last hundred years, have been much more due to the fact of the new venture being new, of its supplying something that the public wanted and had not got, than to the fact of the supply being extraordinarily good in kind. In nearly every case, the intrinsic merit has improved as the thing went on, but it has ceased to be a novel merit. Nothing would be easier than to show that the early *Edinburgh* articles were very far from perfect. Of Jeffrey we shall speak presently, and there is no doubt that Sydney at his best was, and is always, delightful. But the blundering bluster of Brougham, the solemn ineffectiveness of Horner (of whom I can never think without also thinking of Scott's delightful Shandean jest on him), the respectable erudition of the Scotch professors, cannot for one single moment be compared with the work which, in Jeffrey's own later days, in those of Macvey Napier, and in the earlier ones of Empson, was contributed by Hazlitt, by Carlyle, by Stephen, and, above all, by Macaulay. The *Review* never had any one who could emulate the ornateness of De Quincey or Wilson, the pure and perfect English of Southey, or the inimitable insolence, so polished and so intangible, of Lockhart. But it may at least claim that it led the way, and that the very men who attacked its principles and surpassed its practice had, in some cases, been actually trained in its school, and were in all, imitating and following its model. To analyse, with chemical exactness, the constituents of a literary novelty is never easy, if it is ever possible. But some of the contrasts between the style of criticism most prevalent at the time, and the style of the new venture are obvious and important. The older rivals of the *Edinburgh* maintained for the most part a decent and amiable impartiality; the *Edinburgh*, whatever it pretended to be, was violently partisan, unhesitatingly personal, and more inclined to find fault, the more distinguished the subject was. The reviews of the time had got into the hands either of gentlemen and ladies who were happy to be thought literary, and only too glad to write for nothing, or else into those of the lowest booksellers' hacks, who praised or blamed according to orders, wrote without interest and without vigour, and were quite content to earn the smallest pittance. The *Edinburgh* started from the first on the principle that its contributors should be paid, and paid well, whether they liked it or not, thus establishing at once an inducement to do well and a check on personal eccentricity and irresponsibility; while whatever partisanship there might be in its pages, there was at any rate no mere literary puffery.

From being, but for his private studies, rather an idle person, Jeffrey became an extremely busy one. The *Review* gave him not a little occupation, and his practice increased rapidly. In 1803 the institution, at Scott's suggestion, of the famous Friday Club, in which, for the greater part of the first half of this century, the best men in Edinburgh, Johnstone and Maxwell, Whig and Tory alike, met in peaceable conviviality, did a good deal to console Jeffrey, who was now as much given to company as he had been in his early youth to solitude, for the partial breaking up of the circle of friends— Allen, Horner, Smith, Brougham, Lord Webb Seymour —in which he had previously mixed. In the same year he became a volunteer, an act of patriotism the more creditable, that he seems to have been sincerely convinced of the probability of an invasion, and of the certainty of its success if it occurred. But I have no room here for anything but a rapid review of the not very numerous or striking events of his life. Soon, however, after the date last mentioned, he met with two afflictions peculiarly trying to a man whose domestic affections were unusually strong. These were the deaths of his favourite sister in May 1804, and of his wife in October 1807. The last blow drove him nearly to despair; and the extreme and open-mouthed "sensibility" of his private letters, on this and similar occasions, is very valuable as an index of character, oddly as it contrasts, in the vulgar estimate, with the supposed cynicism and savagery of the critic. In yet another year occurred the somewhat ludicrous duel, or beginning of a duel, with Moore, in which several police constables did perform the friendly office which Mr Winkle vainly deprecated, and in which Jeffrey's, not Moore's, pistol was discovered to be leadless. There is a sentence in a letter of Jeffrey's concerning the thing which is characteristic and amusing: "I am glad to have gone through this scene, both because it satisfies me that my nerves are good enough to enable me to act in conformity to my notions of propriety without any suffering, and because it also assures me that I am really as little in love with life as I have been for some time in the habit of professing." It is needless to say that this was an example of the excellence of beginning with a little aversion, for Jeffrey and Moore fraternised immediately afterwards and remained friends for life. The quarrel, or half quarrel, with Scott as to the review of *Marmion*, the planning and producing of the *Quarterly Review*, *English Bards and Scotch Reviewers*, not a few other events of the same kind, must be passed over rapidly. About six years after the death of his first wife, Jeffrey met, and fell in love with, a certain Miss Charlotte Wilkes, great-niece of the patriot, and niece of a New York banker, and of a Monsieur and Madame Simond, who were travelling in Europe. He married her two years later, having gone through the very respectable probation of crossing and re-crossing the Atlantic (he was a very bad sailor) in a sailing ship, in winter, and in time of war, to fetch his bride. Nor had he long been married before he took the celebrated country house of Craigcrook, where, for more than thirty years, he spent all the spare time of an exceedingly happy life. Then we may jump some fifteen years to the great Reform contest which gave Jeffrey the reward, such as it was, of his long constancy in opposition, in the shape of the Lord Advocateship. He was not always successful as a debater; but he had the opportunity of adding a third reputation to those which he had already gained in literature and in law. He had the historical duty of piloting the Scotch Reform Bill through Parliament, and he had the, in his case, pleasurable and honourable pain of taking the official steps in Parliament necessitated by the mental incapacity of Sir Walter Scott. Early in 1834 he was provided for by promotion to the Scotch Bench. He had five years before, on being appointed Dean of Faculty, given up the editorship of the *Review*, which he had held for seven-and-twenty years. For some time previous to his resignation, his own contributions, which in early days had run up to half a dozen in a single number, and had averaged two or three for more than twenty years, had become more and more intermittent. After that resignation he contributed two or three articles at very long intervals. He was perhaps more lavish of advice than he need have been to Macvey Napier, and after Napier's death it passed into the control of his own son-in-law, Empson. Long, however, before the reins passed from his own hands, a rival more galling if less formidable than the *Quarterly* had arisen in the shape of *Blackwood's Magazine*. The more ponderous and stately publication always affected, to some extent, to ignore its audacious junior; and Lord Cockburn (perhaps instigated not more by prudence than by regard for Lockhart and Wilson, both of whom were living) passes over in complete silence the establishment of the magazine, the publication of the Chaldee manuscript, and the still greater hubbub which arose around the supposed attacks of Lockhart on Playfair, and the *Edinburgh* reviewers generally, with regard to their religious opinions. How deep the feelings really excited were, may be seen from a letter of Jeffrey's, published, not by Cockburn, but by Wilson's daughter in the life of her father. In this Jeffrey practically drums out a new and certainly most promising recruit for his supposed share in the business, and inveighs in the most passionate terms against the imputation. It is undesirable to enter at length into any such matters here. It need only be said that Allen, one of the founders of the *Edinburgh*, and always a kind of standing counsel to it, is now acknowledged to have been something uncommonly like an atheist, that Sydney Smith (as I believe most unjustly) was often and is sometimes still, regarded as standing towards his profession very much in the attitude of a French *abbé* of the eighteenth century, that almost the whole staff of the *Review*, including Jeffrey, had, as every Edinburgh man of position knew, belonged to the so-called Academy of Physics, the first principle of which was that only three facts (the words are Lord Cockburn's) were to be admitted without proof: (1) Mind exists; (2) matter exists; (3) every change indicates a cause. Nowadays the most orthodox of metaphysicians would admit that this limitation of position by no means implied atheism. But seventy years ago it would have been the exception to find an orthodox metaphysician who did admit it; and Lockhart, or rather Baron von Lauerwinkel, was perfectly justified in taking the view which ordinary opinion took.

These jars, however, were long over when Jeffrey became Lord Jeffrey, and subsided upon the placid

bench. He lived sixteen years longer, alternating between Edinburgh, Craigcrook, and divers houses which
he hired from time to time, on Loch Lomond, on the
Clyde, and latterly at some English watering-places in
the west. His health was not particularly good, though
hardly worse than any man who lives to nearly eighty,
with constant sedentary and few out-of-door occupations, and with a cheerful devotion to the good things
of this life, must expect. And he was on the whole
singularly happy, being passionately devoted to his
wife, his daughter, and his grandchildren; possessing
ample means, and making a cheerful and sensible use
of them; seeing the increasing triumph of the political
principles to which he had attached himself; knowing
that he was regarded by friends and foes alike, as the
chief living English representative of an important
branch of literature; and retaining to the last an almost
unparalleled juvenility of tastes and interests. His
letters to Dickens are well known, and, though I should
be very sorry to stake his critical reputation upon them,
there could not be better documents for his vivid
enjoyment of life. He died on 26th January 1850, in
his seventy-seventh year, having been in harness almost
to the very last. He had written a letter the day before
to Empson, describing one of those curious waking
visions known to all sick folk, in which there had
appeared part of a proof-sheet of a new edition of the
Apocrypha, and a new political paper filled with discussions on Free Trade.

In reading Jeffrey's work[1] nowadays, the critical
reader finds it considerably more difficult to gain and

[1] In the following remarks, reference is confined to the *Contributions
to the Edinburgh Review*, 1 vol. London, 1853. This is not merely a matter
of convenience; the selection having been made with very great care by
Jeffrey himself at a time when his faculties were in perfect order, and
including full specimens of every kind of his work.

keep the author's own point of view than in the case of any other great English critic. With Hazlitt, with Coleridge, with Wilson, with Carlyle, with Macaulay, we very soon fall into step, so to speak, with our author. If we cannot exactly prophesy what he will say on any given subject, we can make a pretty shrewd guess at it; and when, as it seems to us, he stumbles and shies, we have a sort of feeling beforehand that he is going to do it, and a decided inkling of the reason. But my own experience is, that a modern reader of Jeffrey, who takes him systematically, and endeavours to trace cause and effect in him, is liable to be constantly thrown out before he finds the secret. For Jeffrey, in the most puzzling way, lies between the ancients and the moderns in matter of criticism, and we never quite know where to have him. It is ten to one, for instance, that the novice approaches him with the idea that he is a "classic" of the old rock. Imagine the said novice's confusion, when he finds Jeffrey not merely exalting Shakespeare to the skies, but warmly praising Elizabethan poetry in general, anticipating Mr Matthew Arnold almost literally, in the estimate of Dryden and Pope as classics of our prose, and hailing with tears of joy the herald of the emancipation in Cowper. Surely our novice may be excused if, despite certain misgiving memories of such reviews as that of *The Lay of the Last Minstrel*, he concludes that Jeffrey has been maligned, and that he was really a Romantic before Romanticism. Unhappy novice! he will find his new conclusion not less rapidly and more completely staggered than his old. Indeed, until the clue is once gained, Jeffrey must appear to be one of the most incomprehensibly inconsistent of writers and of critics. On one page he declares that Campbell's extracts from Chamberlayne's *Pharonnida* have made him "quite impatient for an opportunity of perusing the whole poem,"—Romantic surely, quite Romantic. "The tameness and poorness of the serious style of Addison and Swift,"—Romantic again, quite Romantic. Yet when we come to Jeffrey's own contemporaries, he constantly appears as much bewigged and befogged with pseudo-classicism as M. de Jouy himself. He commits himself, in the year of grace 1829, to the statement that "the rich melodies of Keats and Shelley, and the fantastical emphasis of Wordsworth are melting fast from the field of our vision," while he contrasts with this "rapid withering of the laurel" the "comparative absence of marks of decay" on Rogers and Campbell. The poets of his own time whom he praises most heartily, and with least reserve, are Campbell and Crabbe; and he is quite as enthusiastic over *Theodric* and *Gertrude* as over the two great war-pieces of the same author, which are worth a hundred *Gertrudes* and about ten thousand *Theodrics*. Reviewing Scott, not merely when they were personal friends (they were always that), but when Scott was a contributor to the *Edinburgh*, and giving general praise to *The Lay*, he glances with an unmistakable meaning at the "dignity of the subject," regrets the "imitation and antiquarian researches," and criticises the versification in a way which shows that he had not in the least grasped its scheme. It is hardly necessary to quote his well-known attacks on Wordsworth; but, though I am myself anything but a Wordsworthian, and would willingly give up to chaos and old night nineteen-twentieths of the "extremely valooable chains of thought" which the good man used to forge, it is in the first place quite clear that the twentieth ought to have saved him from Jeffrey's claws; in the second, that the critic constantly selects the wrong things as well as the right for con-

demnation and ridicule; and in the third, that he would
have praised, or at any rate not blamed, in another,
the very things which he blames in Wordsworth. Even
his praise of Crabbe, excessive as it may now appear,
is diversified by curious patches of blame which seem
to me at any rate, singularly uncritical. There are, for
instance, a very great many worse jests in poetry than,

Oh, had he learnt to make the wig he wears!

—which Jeffrey pronounces a misplaced piece of
buffoonery. I cannot help thinking that if Campbell
instead of Southey had written the hnes,

To see brute nature scorn him and renounce
Its homage to the human form divine,

Jeffrey would, to say the least, not have hinted that
they were "little better than drivelling." But I do not
think that when Jeffrey wrote these things, or when he
actually perpetrated such almost unforgivable phrases
as "stuff about dancing daffodils," he was speaking
away from his sincere conviction. On the contrary,
though partisanship may frequently have determined
the suppression or the utterance, the emphasising or
the softening, of his opinions, I do not think that he
ever said anything but what he sincerely thought. The
problem, therefore, is to discover and define, if possible,
the critical standpoint of a man whose judgment was
at once so acute and so purblind; who could write the
admirable surveys of English poetry contained in the
essays on Mme de Staël and Campbell, and yet be
guilty of the stuff (we thank him for the word) about
the dancing daffodils; who could talk of "the splendid
strains of Moore" (though I have myself a relatively
high opinion of Moore) and pronounce *The White,
Doe of Rylstone* (though I am not very fond of that
animal as a whole) "the very worst poem he ever saw
printed in a quarto volume"; who could really ap-

preciate parts even of Wordsworth himself, and yet sneer at the very finest passages of the poems he partly admired. It is unnecessary to multiply inconsistencies, because the reader who does not want the trouble of reading Jeffrey must be content to take them for granted, and the reader who does read Jeffrey will discover them in plenty for himself. But they are not limited, it should be said, to purely literary criticism; and they appear, if not quite so strongly, in his estimates of personal character, and even in his purely political arguments.

The explanation, as far as there is any (and perhaps such explanations, as Hume says of another matter, only push ignorance a stage farther back), seems to me to lie in what I can only call the Gallicanism of Jeffrey's mind and character. As Horace Walpole has been pronounced the most French of Englishmen, so may Francis Jeffrey be pronounced the most French of Scotchmen. The reader of his letters, no less than the reader of his essays, constantly comes across the most curious and multiform instances of this Frenchness. The early priggishness is French; the effusive domestic affection is French; the antipathy to dogmatic theology, combined with general recognition of the Supreme Being, is French; the talk (I had almost said the chatter) about virtue and sympathy, and so forth, is French; the Whig recognition of the rights of man, joined to a kind of bureaucratical distrust and terror of the common people (a combination almost unknown in England), is French. Everybody remembers the ingenious argument in *Peter Simple* that the French were quite as brave as the English, indeed more so, but that they were extraordinarily ticklish. Jeffrey, we have seen, was very far from being a coward, but he was very ticklish indeed. His private letters throw the most curious light possible on the secret, as far as he was concerned, of the earlier Whig opposition to the war, and of the later Whig advocacy of reform. Jeffrey by no means thought the cause of the Revolution divine, like the Friends of Liberty, or admired Napoleon like Hazlitt, or believed in the inherent right of Manchester and Birmingham to representation like the zealots of 1830. But he was always dreadfully afraid of invasion in the first place, and of popular insurrection in the second; and he wanted peace and reform to calm his fears. As a young man he was, with a lack of confidence in his countrymen probably unparalleled in a Scotchman, sure that a French corporal's guard might march from end to end of Scotland, and a French privateer's boat's crew carry off "the fattest cattle and the fairest women" (these are his very words) "of any Scotch seaboard county." The famous, or infamous, Cevallos article—an ungenerous and pusillanimous attack on the Spanish patriots, which practically founded the *Quarterly Review*, by finally disgusting all Tories and many Whigs with the *Edinburgh*—was, it seems, prompted merely by the conviction that the Spanish cause was hopeless, and that maintaining it, or assisting it, must lead to mere useless bloodshed. He felt profoundly the crime of Napoleon's rule; but he thought Napoleon unconquerable, and so did his best to prevent him from being conquered. He was sure that the multitude would revolt if reform was not granted; and he was, therefore, eager for reform. Later, he got into his head the oddest crotchet of all his life, which was that a Conservative government, with a sort of approval from the people generally, and especially from the English peasantry, would scheme for a *coup d'état*, and (his own words again) "make mincemeat of their opponents in a single year." He may be said almost to have left the world in a state of despair over the probable results of the Revolutions of 1848–49; and it is impossible to guess what would have happened to him if he had survived to witness the Second of December. Never was there such a case, at least among Englishmen, of timorous pugnacity and plucky pessimism. But it would be by no means difficult to parallel the temperament in France; and, indeed, the comparative frequency of it there, may be thought to be no small cause of the political and military disasters of the country.

In literature, and especially in criticism, Jeffrey's characteristics were still more decidedly and un-questionably French. He came into the world almost too soon to feel the German impulse, even if he had been disposed to feel it. But, as a matter of fact, he was not at all disposed. The faults of taste of the German Romantic School, its alternate homeliness and extravagance, its abuse of the supernatural, its un-doubted offences against order and proportion, scanda-lised him only a little less than they would have scandalised Voltaire and did scandalise the later Voltairians. Jeffrey was perfectly prepared to be Romantic up to a certain point,—the point which he had himself reached in his early course of independent reading and criticism. He was even a little inclined to sympathise with the Reverend Mr Bowles on the great question whether Pope was a poet; and, as I have said, he uses, about the older English literature, phrases which might almost satisfy a fanatic of the school of Hazlitt or of Lamb. He is, if anything, rather too severe on French as compared with English drama. Yet, when he comes to his own contemporaries, and sometimes even in reference to earlier writers, we find him slipping into those purely arbitrary severities of condemnation, those capricious stigmatisings of this as improper, and that as vulgar, and the other as unbecoming, which are the characteristics of the pseudo-correct and pseudo-classical school of criticism. He was a great admirer of Cowper, and yet he is shocked by Cowper's use, in his translation of Homer, of the phrases, "to entreat Achilles to a calm" (evidently he had forgotten Shakespeare's "pursue him and entreat him to a peace"), "this wrangler here," "hke a fellow of no worth." He was certainly not likely to be unjust to Charles James Fox. So he is unhappy, rather than contemptuous, over such excellent phrases as "swearing away the lives," "crying injustice," "fond of ill-treating." These appear to Mr Aristarchus Jeffrey too "homely and familiar," too "low and vapid"; while a harmless and rather agreeable Shakespearian parallel of Fox's seems to him downright impropriety. The fun of the thing is that the passage turns on the well-known misuse of "flat burglary"; and if Jeffrey had had a little more sense of humour (his deficiency in which, for all his keen wit, is another Gallic note in him), he must have seen that the words were ludicrously applicable to his own condemnation and his own frame of mind. These settings-up of a wholly arbitrary canon of mere taste, these excommunicatings of such and such a thing as "low" and "improper," without assigned or assignable reason, are eminently Gallic. They may be found not merely in the older school before 1830, but in almost all French critics up to the present day: there is perhaps not one, with the single exception of Sainte-Beuve, who is habitually free from them. The critic may be quite unable to say why *tarte à la crème* is such a shocking expression, or even to produce any important authority for the shockingness of it. But he is quite certain that it is shocking. Jeffrey is but too much given to protesting against *tarte à la crème*; and the reasons for his error are almost exactly the same as in the case of the usual Frenchman; that is to say, a very just and wholesome preference for order, proportion, literary orthodoxy, freedom from will-worship and eccentric divagations, unfortunately distorted by a certain absence of catholicity, by a tendency to regard novelty as bad, merely because it is novelty, and by a curious reluctance, as Lamb has it of another great man of the same generation, to go shares with any newcomer in literary commerce.

But when these reservations have been made, when his standpoint has been clearly discovered and marked out, and when some little tricks, such as the affectation of delivering judgments without appeal, which is still kept up by a few, though very few, reviewers, have been further allowed for, Jeffrey is a most admirable essayist and critic. As an essayist, a writer of *causeries*, I do not think he has been surpassed among Englishmen in the art of interweaving quotation, abstract, and comment. The best proof of his felicity in this respect is that in almost all the books which he has reviewed (and he has reviewed many of the most interesting books in literature) the passages and traits, the anecdotes and phrases, which have made most mark in the general memory, and which are often remembered with very indistinct consciousness of their origin, are to be found in his reviews. Sometimes the very perfection of his skill in this respect makes it rather difficult to know where he is abstracting or paraphrasing, and where he is speaking outright and for himself; but that is a very small fault. Yet his merits as an essayist, though considerable, are not to be compared, even to the extent to which Hazlitt's are to be compared, with his merits as a critic, and especially as a literary critic. It would be interesting to criticise his political criticism; but it is always best to keep politics out where it can be managed. Besides, Jeffrey as a political critic is a subject of almost exclusively historical interest, while as a literary critic he is important at this very day, and perhaps more important than he was in his own. For the spirit of merely æsthetic criticism, which was in his day only in its infancy, has long been full grown and rampant; so that, good work as it has done in its time, it decidedly needs chastening by an admixture of the dogmatic criticism, which at least tries to keep its impressions together and in order, and to connect them into some coherent doctrine and creed.

Of this dogmatic criticism Jeffrey, with all his shortcomings, is perhaps the very best example that we have in English. He had addressed himself more directly and theoretically to literary criticism than Lockhart. Prejudiced as he often was, he was not affected by the wild gusts of personal and political passion which frequently blew Hazlitt a thousand miles off the course of true criticism. He keeps his eye on the object, which De Quincey seldom does. He is not affected by that desire to preach on certain pet subjects which affects the admirable critical faculty of Carlyle. He never blusters and splashes at random hke Wilson. And he never indulges in the mannered and rather superfluous graces which marred, to some tastes, the work of his successor in critical authority, if there has been any such, the author of *Essays in Criticism*.

Let us, as we just now looked through Jeffrey's work to pick out the less favourable characteristics which distinguish his position, look through it again to see those qualities which he shares, but in greater measure than most, with all good critics. The literary essay which stands first in his collected works is on Madame de Staël. Now that good lady, of whom some judges in these days do not think very much, was a kind of goddess on earth in literature, however much she might bore them in life, to the English Whig party in general; while Jeffrey's French tastes must have made her, or at least her books, specially attractive to him. Accordingly he has written a great deal about her, no less than three essays appearing in the collected works. Writing at least partly in her lifetime and under the influences just glanced at, he is of course profuse in compliments. But it is very amusing and highly instructive to observe how, in the intervals of these compliments, he contrives to take the good Corinne to pieces, to smash up her ingenious Perfectibilism, and to put in order her rather rash literary judgments. It is in connection also with her, that he gives one of the best of not a few general sketches of the history of literature which his work contains. Of course there are here, as always, isolated expressions as to which, however much we admit that Jeffrey was a clever man, we cannot agree with Jeffrey. He thinks Aristophanes "coarse" and "vulgar" while (though nobody of course can deny the coarseness) Aristophanes and vulgarity are certainly many miles asunder. We may protest against the chronological, even more than against the critical, blunder which couples Cowley and Donne, putting Donne, moreover, who wrote long before Cowley was born, and differs from him in genius almost as the author of the *Iliad* does from the author of the *Henriade*, second. But hardly anything in English criticism is better than Jeffrey's discussion of the general French imputation of "want of taste and politeness" to English and German writers, especially English. It is a very general, and a very mistaken, notion that the Romantic movement in France has done away with this imputation to a great extent. On the contrary, though it has long been a kind of fashion in France to admire Shakespeare, and though since the labours of MM. Taine and Montégut, the study of English literature generally has grown and flourished, it is, I believe, the very rarest thing to find a Frenchman who, in his heart of hearts, does not cling to the old "pearls in the dung-heap" idea, not merely in reference to Shakespeare, but to English writers, and especially English humorists, generally[1]. Nothing can be more admirable than Jeffrey's comments on this matter. They are especially admirable because they are not made from the point of view of a *Romantique à tous crins*; because, as has been already pointed out, he himself is largely penetrated by the very preference for order and proportion which is at the bottom of the French mistake; and because he is, therefore, arguing in a tongue understanded of those whom he censures. Another essay which may be read with especial advantage is that on Scott's edition of Swift. Here, again, there was a kind of test subject, and perhaps Jeffrey does not come quite scatheless out of the trial: to me, at any rate, his account of Swift's political and moral conduct and character seems both uncritical and unfair. But here, too, the value of his literary criticism shows itself. He might very easily have been tempted to extend his injustice from the writer to the writings, especially since, as has been elsewhere shown, he was by no means a fanatical admirer of the Augustan age, and thought the serious style of Addison and Swift tame and poor. It is possible of course, here also, to find things that seem to be errors, both in the general sketch which Jeffrey, according to his custom, prefixes, and in the particular remarks on Swift himself. For

[1] Things have continuously improved in this respect but the above remarks still have a good deal of truth (1923).

instance, to deny fancy to the author of the *Tale of a Tub*, of *Gulliver*, and of the *Polite Conversation*, is very odd indeed. But there are few instances of a greater triumph of sound literary judgment over political and personal prejudice than Jeffrey's description, not merely of the great works just mentioned (it is curious, and illustrates his defective appreciation of humour, that he likes the greatest least, and is positively unjust to the *Tale of a Tub*), but also of those wonderful pamphlets, articles, lampoons, skits (libels if any one likes), which proved too strong for the generalship of Marlborough and the administrative talents of Godolphin; and which are perhaps the only literary works that ever really changed, for a not inconsiderable period, the government of England. "Considered," he says, "with a view to the purposes for which they were intended, they have probably never been equalled in any period of the world." They certainly have not; but to find a Whig, and a Whig writing in the very moment of Tory triumph after Waterloo, ready to admit the fact, is not a trivial thing. Another excellent example of Jeffrey's strength, by no means unmixed with examples of his weakness, is to be found in his essays on Cowper. I have already given some of the weakness: the strength is to be found in his general description of Cowper's revolt, thought so daring at the time, now so apparently moderate, against poetic diction. These instances are to be found under miscellaneous sections, biographical, historical, and so forth; but the reader will naturally turn to the considerable divisions headed Poetry and Fiction. Here are the chief rocks of offence already indicated, and here also are many excellent things which deserve reading. Here is the remarkable essay, quoted above, on Campbell's *Specimens*. Here is the criticism of

Weber's edition of Ford, and another of those critical surveys of the course of English literature which Jeffrey was so fond of doing, and which he did so well, together with some remarks on the magnificently spendthrift style of our Elizabethan dramatists which would deserve almost the first place in an anthology of his critical beauties. The paper on Hazlitt's *Characters of Shakespeare* (Hazlitt was an *Edinburgh* reviewer, and his biographer, not Jeffrey's, has chronicled a remarkable piece of generosity on Jeffrey's part towards his wayward contributor) is a little defaced by a patronising spirit, not, indeed, of that memorably mistaken kind which induced the famous and unlucky sentence to Macvey Napier about Carlyle, but something in the spirit of the schoolmaster who observes, "See this clever boy of mine, and only think how much better I could do it myself." Yet it contains some admirable passages on Shakespeare, if not on Hazlitt; and it would be impossible to deny that its hinted condemnation of Hazlitt's "desultory and capricious acuteness" is just enough. On the other hand, how significant is it of Jeffrey's own limitations that he should protest against Hazlitt's sympathy with such "conceits and puerilities" as the immortal and unmatchable

Take him and cut him out in little stars,

with the rest of the passage. But there you have the French spirit. I do not believe that there ever was a Frenchman since the seventeenth century (unless perchance it was Gérard de Nerval, and he was not quite sane), who could put his hand on his heart and deny that the little stars seemed to him puerile and conceited.

Jeffrey's dealings with Byron (I do not now speak of the article on *Hours of Idleness*, which was simply a just rebuke of really puerile and conceited rubbish) are not, to me, very satisfactory. The critic seems, in the rather numerous articles which he has devoted to the "noble Poet," as they used to call him, to have felt his genius unduly rebuked by that of his subject. He spends a great deal, and surely an unnecessarily great deal, of time in solemnly, and no doubt quite sincerely, rebuking Byron's morality; and in doing so he is sometimes almost absurd. He calls him "not more obscene perhaps than Dryden or Prior," which is simply ludicrous, because it is very rare that this particular word can be applied to Byron at all, while even the staunchest champion must admit that it applies to glorious John and to dear Mat Prior. He helps, unconsciously no doubt, to spread the very contagion which he denounces, by talking about Byron's demoniacal power, going so far as actually to contrast *Manfred* with Marlowe to the advantage of the former. And he is so completely overcome by what he calls the "dreadful tone of sincerity" of this "puissant spirit," that he never seems to have had leisure or courage to apply the critical tests and solvents of which few men have had a greater command. Had he done so, it is impossible not to believe that, whether he did or did not pronounce Byron's sentiment to be as theatrical, as vulgar, and as false as it seems to some later critics, he would at any rate have substituted for his edifying but rather irrelevant moral denunciations some exposure of those gross faults in style and metre, in phrase and form, which now disgust us.

There are many essays remaining on which I should like to comment if there were room enough. But I have only space for a few more general remarks on his general characteristics, and especially those which, as Sainte-Beuve said to the altered Jeffrey of our altered days, are "important to us." Let me repeat then that the peculiar value of Jeffrey is not, as is that of Coleridge, of Hazlitt, or of Lamb, in very subtle, very profound, or very original views of his subjects. He is neither a critical Columbus nor a critical Socrates; he neither opens up undiscovered countries, nor provokes and stimulates to the discovery of them. His strength lies in the combination of a fairly wide range of sympathy with an extraordinary shrewdness and good sense in applying that sympathy. Tested for range alone, or for subtlety alone, he will frequently be found wanting; but he almost invariably catches up those who have thus outstripped him, when the subject of the trial is shifted to soundness of estimate, intelligent connection of view, and absence of eccentricity. And it must be again and again repeated that Jeffrey is by no means justly chargeable with the Dryasdust failings so often attributed to academic criticism. They said that on the actual Bench he worried counsel a little too much, but that his decisions were almost invariably sound. Not quite so much perhaps can be said for his other exercise of the judicial function. But however much he may sometimes seem to carp and complain, however much we may sometimes wish for a little more equity and a little less law, it is astonishing how weighty Jeffrey's critical judgments are after three-quarters of a century which has seen so many seeming heavy things grow light. There may be much that he does not see; there may be some things which he is physically unable to see; but what he does see, he sees with a clearness, and co-ordinates in its bearings on other things seen with a precision, which are hardly to be matched among the fluctuating and diverse race of critics.

V
HAZLITT

THE following paper was in great part composed, when I came across some sentences on Hazlitt, written indeed before I was born, but practically unpublished until the other day. In a review of the late Mr Horne's *New Spirit of the Age*, contributed to the *Morning Chronicle* in 1845 and but recently[1] included in his collected works, Thackeray writes thus of the author of the book whose title Horne had rather rashly borrowed:

The author of the *Spirit of the Age* was one of the keenest and brightest critics that ever lived. With partialities and prejudices innumerable, he had a wit so keen, a sensibility so exquisite, an appreciation of humour, or pathos, or even of the greatest art, so lively, quick, and cultivated, that it was always good to know what were the impressions made by books or men or pictures on such a mind; and that, as there were not probably a dozen men in England with powers so varied, all the rest of the world might be rejoiced to listen to the opinions of this accomplished critic. He was of so different a caste to the people who gave authority in his day—the pompous big-wigs and schoolmen, who never could pardon him his familiarity of manner so unlike their own—his popular—too popular habits—and sympathies so much beneath their dignity; his loose, disorderly education gathered round those bookstalls or picture galleries where he laboured a penniless student, in lonely journeys over Europe tramped on foot (and not made, after the fashion of the regular critics of the day, by the side of a young nobleman in a postchaise), in every school of knowledge from St Peter's at Rome to St Giles's in London. In all his modes of life and thought, he was so different from the established authorities, with their degrees and white neck-cloths, that they hooted the man down with all the power of their lungs, and disdained to hear truth that came from such a ragged philosopher.

Some exceptions, no doubt, must be taken to this enthusiastic, and in the main just, verdict. Hazlitt himself denied himself wit, yet if this was mock humility, I am inclined to think that he spoke truth

[1] 1886.

unwittingly. His appreciation of humour was fitful
and anything but impartial, while, biographically
speaking, the hardships of his apprenticeship are very
considerably exaggerated. It was not, for instance, in
a penniless or pedestrian manner that he visited
St Peter's at Rome; but journeying with comforts of
wine, *vetturini*, and partridges, which his second wife's
income paid for. But this does not matter much, and,
on the whole, the estimate is as just as it is generous.
Perhaps something of its inspiration may be set down
to fellow-feeling, both in politics and in the unsuccessful cultivation of the arts of design. But as high
an estimate of Hazlitt is quite compatible with the
strongest political dissent from his opinions, and with a
total freedom from the charge of wearing the willow for
painting.

There is indeed no doubt that Hazlitt is one of the
most absolutely unequal writers in English, if not in
any, literature, Wilson being perhaps his only compeer.
The term absolute is used with intention and precision.
There may be others who, in different parts of their
work, are more unequal than he is; but with him the
inequality is pervading, and shows itself in his finest
passages, in those where he is most at home, as much
as in his hastiest and most uncongenial taskwork. It
could not, indeed, be otherwise, because the inequality
itself is due less to an intellectual than to a moral
defect. The clear sunshine of Hazlitt's admirably acute
intellect is always there; but it is constantly obscured
by driving clouds of furious prejudice. Even as the
clouds pass, the light may still be seen on distant and
scattered parts of the landscape; but wherever their
influence extends, there is nothing but thick darkness,
gusty wind and drenching rain. And the two phenomena, the abiding intellectual light, and the fits and

squalls of moral darkness, appear to be totally independent of each other, or of any single will or cause of any kind. It would be perfectly easy, and may perhaps be in place later, to give a brief collection of some of the most absurd and outrageous sayings that any writer, not a mere fool, can be charged with: of sentences not representing quips and cranks of humour, or judgments temporary and one-sided, though having a certain relative validity, but containing blunders and calumnies so gross and palpable, that the man who set them down might seem to have forfeited all claim to the reputation either of an intelligent or a responsible being. And yet, side by side with these, are other passages (and fortunately a much greater number) which justify, and more than justify, Hazlitt's claims to be as Thackeray says, "one of the keenest and brightest critics that ever lived"; as Lamb had said earlier, "one of the wisest and finest spirits breathing."

The only exception to be taken to the well-known panegyric of Elia is, that it bestows this eulogy on Hazlitt "in his natural and healthy state." Unluckily, it would seem, by a concurrence of all testimony, even the most partial, that the unhealthy state was quite as natural as the healthy one. Lamb himself plaintively wishes that "he would not quarrel with the world at the rate he does"; and De Quincey, in his short, but very interesting, biographical notice of Hazlitt (a notice entirely free from the malignity with which De Quincey has been sometimes charged), declares with quite as much truth as point, that Hazlitt's guiding principle was, "Whatever is, is wrong." He was the very ideal of a literary Ishmael; and after the fullest admission of the almost incredible virulence and unfairness of his foes, it has to be admitted, likewise, that he was quite as ready to quarrel with his friends. He succeeded, at least once, in forcing a quarrel even upon Lamb. His relations with Leigh Hunt (who, whatever his faults were, was not unamiable) were constantly strained, and at least once actually broken by his infernal temper. Nor were his relations with women more fortunate or more creditable than those with men. That the fault was entirely on his side in the rupture with his first wife is, no doubt, not the case; for Mrs Hazlitt's, or Miss Stoddart's, own friends admit that she was of a peculiar and rather trying disposition. It is indeed evident that she was the sort of person (most teasing of all others to a man of Hazlitt's temperament) who would put her head back as he was kissing her, to ask if he would like another cup of tea, or interrupt a declaration to suggest shutting the window. As for the famous and almost legendary episode of Sarah Walker, the lodging-house keeper's daughter, and the *Liber Amoris*, the obvious and irresistible attack of something hke erotic madness which it implies absolves Hazlitt partly—but only partly, for there is a kind of shabbiness about the affair which shuts it out from all reasonable claim to be regarded as a new act of the endless drama of *All for Love, or The World Well Lost!* Of his second marriage, the only persons who might be expected to give us some information either can or will say next to nothing. But when a man with such antecedents marries a woman of whom no one has anything bad to say, lives with her for a year, chiefly on her money, and is then quitted by her with the information that she will have nothing more to do with him, it is not, I think, uncharitable to conjecture that most of the fault is his.

It is not, however, only of Hazlitt's rather imperfectly known life, or of his pretty generally acknowledged character, that I wish to speak here. His strange

mixture of manly common-sense and childish prejudice, the dislike of foreigners which accompanied his
Liberalism and his Bonapartism, and other traits, are
very much more English than Irish. But Irish, at least
on the father's side, his family was, and had been for
generations. He was himself the son of a Unitarian
minister, was born at Maidstone in 1778, accompanied
his parents as a very little boy to America, but passed
the greater part of his youth at Wem in Shropshire,
where the interview with Coleridge, which decided his
fate, took place. Yet for some time after that, he was
mainly occupied with studies, not of literature, but of
art. He had been intended for his father's profession,
but had early taken a disgust to it. At such schools as
he had been able to frequent, he had gained the
character of a boy rather insusceptible of ordinary
teaching; and his letters (they are rare throughout his
life) show him to us as something very like a juvenile
prig. According to his own account, he "thought for
at least eight years" without being able to pen a line,
or at least a page; and the worst accusation that can
truly be brought against him is that, by his own confession, he left off reading when he began to write.
Those who (for their sins or for their good) are condemned to a life of writing for the press know that such
an abstinence as this is almost fatal. Perhaps no man
ever did good work in periodical writing, unless he had
previously had a more or less prolonged period of
reading, with no view to writing. Certainly no one ever
did other than very faulty work if, not having such a
store to draw on, when he began writing he left off
reading.

The first really important event in Hazlitt's life,
except the visit from Coleridge in 1798, was his own
visit to Paris after the Peace of Amiens in 1802—a

visit authorised and defrayed by certain commissions to copy pictures at the Louvre, which was then, in consequence of French conquests, the picture-gallery of Europe. The chief of these commissioners was a Mr Railton, a person of some fortune at Liverpool, and the father of a daughter who, if she was anything like her portrait, had one of the most beautiful faces of modern times. Miss Railton was one of Hazlitt's many loves: it was, perhaps, fortunate for her that the course of the love did not run smooth. Almost immediately on his return, he made acquaintance with the Lambs, and, as Mr W. C. Hazlitt, his grandson and biographer, thinks, with Miss Stoddart, his future wife. Miss Stoddart, there is no doubt, was an elderly coquette, though perfectly "proper." Besides the "William" of her early correspondence with Mary Lamb, we hear of three or four other lovers of hers between 1803 and 1808, when she married Hazlitt. It so happens that one, and only one, letter of his to her has been preserved. His biographer seems to think it in another sense unique; but it is, in effect, a very typical letter from a literary lover of a rather passionate temperament. The two were married, in defiance of superstition, on Sunday, the first of May; and certainly the superstition had not the worst of it.

At first, however, no evil results seemed likely. Miss Stoddart had a certain property settled on her at Winterslow, on the south-eastern border of Salisbury Plain, and for nearly four years the couple seem to have dwelt there (once, at least, entertaining the Lambs), and producing children, of whom only one lived. It was not till 1812 that they removed to London, and that Hazlitt engaged in writing for the newspapers. From this time till the end of his life, some eighteen years, he was never at a loss for employment—a succession of daily and weekly papers, with occasional employment on the *Edinburgh Review*, providing him, it would seem, with sufficiently abundant opportunities for copy. The *London*, the *New Monthly* (where Campbell's dislike did him no harm), and other magazines also employed him. For a time, he seems to have joined "the gallery," and written ordinary press-work. During this time, which was very short, and this time only, his friends admit a certain indulgence in drinking, which he gave up completely, but which was used against him with as much pitilessness as indecency in *Blackwood*; though heaven only knows how the most Tory soul alive could see fitness of things in the accusation of gin-drinking brought against Hazlitt by the whiskey-drinkers of the *Noctes*. For the greater part of his literary life he seems to have been almost a total abstainer, indulging only in the very strongest of tea. He soon gave up miscellaneous press-work, as far as politics went; but his passion for the theatre retained him as a theatrical critic almost to the end of his life. He gradually drifted into the business really best suited to him, that of essay-writing, and occasionally lecturing on literary and miscellaneous subjects. During the greatest part of his early London life, he was resident in a famous house, now destroyed, in York Street, Westminster, next door to Bentham and reputed to have once been tenanted by Milton; and he was a constant attendant on Lamb's Wednesday evenings. The details of his life, it has been said, are not much known. The chief of them, besides the breaking out of his lifelong war with *Blackwood* and the *Quarterly*, was, perhaps, his unlucky participation in the duel which proved fatal to Scott, the editor of the *London*. It is impossible to imagine a more deplorable muddle than this affair. Scott, after refusing the challenge of Lockhart[1], with whom he had, according to the customs of those days, a sufficient ground of quarrel, accepted that of Christie, Lockhart's second, with whom he had no quarrel at all. Moreover, when his adversary had deliberately spared him in the first fire, he insisted (it is said owing to the stupid conduct of his own second) on another, and was mortally wounded. Hazlitt, who was more than indirectly concerned in the affair, had a professed objection to duelling, which would have been more creditable to him if he had not been avowedly of a timid temper. But, most unfortunately, he was said, and believed, to have spurred Scott on to the acceptance of the challenge, nor do his own champions deny it. The scandal is long bygone, but is, unluckily, a fair sample of the ugly stories which cluster round Hazlitt's name, and which have hitherto prevented that justice being done to him which his abilities deserve and demand.

This wretched affair occurred in February 1821, and, shortly afterwards, the crowning complications of Hazlitt's own life, the business of the *Liber Amoris* and the divorce with his first wife, took place. The first could only be properly described by an abundance of extracts, for which there is here no room. Of the second, which, it must be remembered, went on simultaneously with the first, it is sufficient to say that the circumstances are nearly incredible. It was conducted under the Scotch law with a blessed indifference to collusion: the direct means taken to effect it were, if report may be trusted, scandalous; and the parties met during the whole time, and placidly wrangled over money matters, with a callousness which is ineffably disgusting. I have hinted, in reference to Sarah Walker,

---

[1] For some further remarks on this duel as it concerns Lockhart see essay on him and Appendix thereto.

that the tyranny of "Love unconquered in battle" may be taken by a very charitable person to be a sufficient excuse. In this other affair there is no such palliation; unless the very charitable person should hold that a wife, who could so forget her own dignity, justified any forgetfulness on the part of her husband; and that a husband, who could haggle and chaffer about the terms on which he should be disgracefully separated from his wife, justified any forgetfulness of dignity on the wife's part.

Little has to be said about the rest of Hazlitt's life. Miss Sarah Walker would have nothing to say to him; and it has been already mentioned that the lady whom he afterwards married, a Mrs Bridgewater, had enough of him after a year's experience. He did not outlive this last shock more than five years; and unfortunately his death was preceded by a complete financial break-down, though he was more industrious during these later years than at any other time, and though he had abundance of well-paid work. The failure of the publishers, who were to have paid him five hundred pounds for his *magnum opus*, the partisan and almost valueless *Life of Napoleon*, had something to do with this, and the dishonesty of an agent is said to have had more, but details are not forthcoming. He died on the eighteenth of September 1830, saying, "Well, I have had a happy life"; and despite his son's assertion that, like Goldsmith, he had something on his mind, I believe this to have been not ironical but quite sincere. He was only fifty-two, so that the infirmities of age had not begun to press on him. Although, except during the brief duration of his second marriage, he had always lived by his wits, it does not appear that he was ever in any want, or that he had at any time to deny himself his favourite pleasures of wandering

about and being idle when he chose. If he had not
been completely happy in his life, he had lived it; if
he had not seen the triumph of his opinions, he had
been able always to hold to them. He was one of those
men, such as an extreme devotion to literature now
and then breeds, who, by the intensity of their enjoyment of quite commonplace delights—a face passed in
the street, a sunset, a quiet hour of reflection, even a
well-cooked meal—make up for the suffering of not
wholly commonplace woes. I do not know whether
even the joy of literary battle did not overweigh the
pain of the dishonest wounds which he received from
illiberal adversaries. I think that he had a happy life,
and I am glad that he had. For he was in literature
a great man. I am myself disposed to hold that, for
all his accesses of hopelessly uncritical prejudice, he
was the greatest critic that England has yet produced;
and there are some who hold (though I do not agree
with them) that he was even greater as a miscellaneous
essayist than as a critic. It is certainly upon his essays,
critical and other, that his fame must rest; not on the
frenzied outpourings of the *Liber Amoris* (full as these
are of flashes of genius), or upon the one-sided and ill-
planned *Life of Napoleon*; still less on his clever-boy
essay on the *Principles of Human Action*, or on his
attempts in grammar, in literary compilation and
abridgment, and the like. Seven volumes of Bohn's
Standard Library, with another published elsewhere
containing his writings on Art, contain nearly all the
documents of Hazlitt's fame: a few do not seem to have
been yet collected from his *Remains* and from the
publications in which they originally appeared.

These books—the *Spirit of the Age*, *Table-Talk*, *The
Plain Speaker*, *The Round Table* (including the *Conversations with Northcote* and *Characteristics*), *Lectures*

on the English Poets and Comic Writers, Elizabethan Literature and *Characters of Shakespeare, Sketches and Essays* (including *Winterslow*)—represent the work, roughly speaking, of the last twenty years of Hazlitt's life; for in the earlier and longer period he wrote very little, and, indeed, declares that for a long time he had a difficulty in writing at all. They are all singularly homogeneous in general character, the lectures written as lectures differing very little from the essays written as essays, and even the frantic diatribes of the "Letter to Gifford" bearing a strong family likeness to the good-humoured *reportage* of "On going to a Fight," or the singularly picturesque and pathetic egotism of the "Farewell to Essay-writing." This family resemblance is the more curious because, independently of the diversity of subject, Hazlitt can hardly be said to possess a style or, at least, a manner—indeed, he somewhere or other distinctly disclaims the possession. Yet, irregular as he is in his fashion of writing, no less than in the merit of it, the germs of some of the most famous styles of this century may be discovered in his casual and haphazard work. Everybody knows Jeffrey's question to Macaulay, "Where the devil did you get that style?" If any one will read Hazlitt (who, be it remembered, was a contributor to the *Edinburgh*) carefully, he will see where Macaulay got that style, or at least the beginning of it, much as he improved on it afterwards. Nor is there any doubt that, in a very different way, Hazlitt served as a model to Thackeray, to Dickens, and to many not merely of the most popular, but of the greatest, writers of the middle of the century. Indeed, in the *Spirit of the Age* there are distinct anticipations of Carlyle. He had the not uncommon fate of producing work which, little noted by the public, struck very strongly those of his juniors who had any literary faculty. If he had been, just by a little, a greater man than he was, he would, no doubt, have elaborated an individual manner, and not have contented himself with the hints and germs of manners. As it was, he had more of seed than of fruit. And the secret of this is, undoubtedly, to be found in the obstinate individuality of thought which characterised him all through. Hazlitt may sometimes have adopted an opinion partly because other people did not hold it, but he never adopted an opinion because other people did hold it. And all his opinions, even those which seem to have been adopted simply to quarrel with the world, were genuine opinions. He has himself drawn a striking contrast in this point, between himself and Lamb, in one of the very best of all his essays, the beautiful "Farewell to Essay-writing" reprinted in *Winterslow*. The contrast is a remarkable one, and most men, probably, who take great interest in literature or politics, or indeed in any subject admitting of principles, will be able to furnish similar contrasts from their own experience.

In matters of taste and feeling, one proof that my conclusions have not been quite shallow and hasty, is the circumstance of their having been lasting. I have the same favourite books, pictures, passages that I ever had; I may therefore presume that they will last me my life—nay, I may indulge a hope that my thoughts will survive me. This continuity of impression is the only thing on which I pride myself. Even Lamb, whose relish of certain things is as keen and earnest as possible, takes a surfeit of admiration, and I should be afraid to ask about his select authors or particular friends after a lapse of ten years. As for myself, any one knows where to have me. What I have once made up my mind to, I abide by to the end of the chapter.

This is quite true if we add a proviso to it—a proviso, to be sure, of no small importance. Hazlitt is always the same when he is not different, when his political or personal ails and angers do not obscure his critical judgment. His uniformity of principle extends only to the two subjects of literature and of art; unless a third may be added, to wit, the various good things of this life, as they are commonly called. He was not so great a metaphysician as he thought himself. He "shows to the utmost of his knowledge, and that not deep"; a want of depth not surprising when we find him confessing that he had to go to Taylor, the Platonist, to tell him something of Platonic ideas. It may be more than suspected that he had read little but the French and English philosophers of the eighteenth century; a very interesting class of persons, but, except Condillac, Hume, and Berkeley, scarcely metaphysicians. As for his politics, Hazlitt seems to me to have had no clear political creed at all. He hated something called "the hag legitimacy," but for the hag despotism, in the person of Bonaparte, he had nothing but love. How any one possessed of brains could combine Liberty and the first Napoleon in one common worship is, I confess, a mystery too great for me; and I fear that any one who could call "Jupiter Scapin" "the greatest man who ever lived," must be entirely blind to such constituents of greatness as justice, mercy, chivalry, and all that makes a gentleman. Indeed, I am afraid that "gentleman" is exactly what cannot be predicated of Hazlitt. No gentleman could have published the *Liber Amoris*, not at all because of its so-called voluptuousness, but because of its shameless kissing and telling. But the most curious example of Hazlitt's weaknesses is the language he uses in regard to those men with whom he had both political and literary differences. That he had provocation in some cases (he had absolutely none from Sir Walter Scott) is perfectly true. But what provocation will excuse such things as the following, all taken from one book, the *Spirit of the Age*? He speaks of Scott's "zeal to restore the spirit of loyalty, of passive obedience, and of non-resistance," as an acknowledgment for his having been "created a baronet by a prince of the House of Brunswick." Alas for dates and circumstances, for times and seasons, when they stand in the way of a fling of Hazlitt's! In the character of Scott himself an entire page and a half is devoted to an elaborate peroration in one huge sentence, denouncing him in such terms as "pettifogging," "littleness," "pique," "secret and envenomed blows," "slime of rankling malice and mercenary scorn," "trammels of servility," "lies," "garbage," etc. etc. The Duke of Wellington he always speaks of as a brainless noodle, forgetting apparently that the description does not make his idol's defeat more creditable to the vanquished. As for the character of Gifford, and the earlier "Letter to Gifford," I should have to print them entire to show the state of Hazlitt's mind in regard to this notorious, and certainly not very amiable person. His own words, "the dotage of age and the fury of a woman," form the best short description of both. He screams, he foams at the mouth, he gnashes and tears and kicks, rather than fights. Nor is it only on living authors and living persons (as some of his unfavourable critics have said) that he exercises his spleen. His remarks on Burke (*Round Table*, p. 150) suggest temporary insanity. Sir Philip Sidney (as Lamb, a perfectly impartial person who had no politics at all, pointed out) was a kind of representative of the courtly monarchist school in literature. So down must Sir Philip go; and not only the *Arcadia*, that "vain and amatorious poem" which Milton condemned, but the sonnets which one would have thought such a lover of poetry as Hazlitt must have spared, go down also before his remorseless bludgeon.

But there is no need to say any more of these faults

of his, and there is no need to say much of another and more purely literary fault with which he has been charged—the fault of excessive quotation. In him the error lies rather in the constant repetition of the same, than in a too great multitude of different borrowings. Almost priding himself on limited study, and (as he tells us) very rarely reading his own work after it was printed, he has certainly abused his right of press most damnably in some cases. "Dry as a remainder biscuit," and "of no mark or likelihood," occur to me as the most constantly recurrent tags; but there are many others.

These various drawbacks, however, only set off the merits which almost every lover of literature must perceive in him. In most writers, in all save the very greatest, we look for one or two, or for a few special faculties and capacities, and we know perfectly well that other (generally many other) capacities and faculties will not be found in them at all. We do not dream of finding rollicking mirth in Milton, or gorgeous embroidery of style in Swift, or unadorned simplicity in Browne. But in Hazlitt you may find something of almost everything, except the finer kinds of wit and humour; to which last, however, he makes a certain side-approach by dint of his appreciation of the irony of Nature and Fate. Almost every other grace of matter and form that can be found in prose may be found at times in his. He is generally thought of as, and for the most part is, a rather plain and straightforward writer, with few tricks and frounces of phrase and style. Yet most of the fine writing of these latter days is but as crumpled tarlatan to brocaded satin beside the passage on Coleridge in the *English Poets*, or the description of Winterslow and its neighbourhood in the "Farewell to Essay-writing," or "On a Land-

scape of Nicolas Poussin" in the *Table-Talk*. Read
these pieces and nothing else, and an excusable impression might be given that the writer was nothing
if not florid. But turn over a dozen pages, and the
most admirable examples of the grave and simple
manner occur. He is an inveterate quoter, yet few men
are more original. No man is his superior in lively,
gossiping description, yet he could, within his limits,
reason closely and expound admirably. It is, indeed,
almost always necessary, when he condemns anything,
to inquire very carefully as to the reasons of the condemnation. But nothing that he likes (except Napoleon)
is ever bad: everything that he praises will repay the
right man who, at the right time, examines it to see for
what Hazlitt likes it. I have, for my part, no doubt
that Miss Sarah Walker was a very engaging young
woman; but (though the witness is the same) I have
the gravest doubts as to Hazlitt's charges against her.

We shall find this same curious difference everywhere in Hazlitt. He has been talking, for instance,
with keen relish of the "Conversation of Authors" (it
is he, be it remembered, who has handed down to us
the immortal debate at one of Lamb's Wednesdays on
"People one would Like to have Seen"), and saying
excellent things about it. Then he changes the key,
and tells us that the conversation of "Gentlemen and
Men of Fashion" will not do. Perhaps not; but the
wicked critic stops and asks himself whether Hazlitt
had known much of the conversation of "Gentlemen
and Men of Fashion"? We can find no record of any
such experiences of his. In his youth he had no opportunity: in his middle age he was notoriously recalcitrant
to all the usages of society, would not dress, and
scarcely ever dined out except with a few cronies. This
does not seem to be the best qualification for a pro-

nouncement on the question. Yet this same essay is full of admirable things, the most admirable being, perhaps, the description of the man who "had you at an advantage by never understanding you." I find, indeed, in looking through my copies of his books, re-read for the purpose of this paper, an innumerable and bewildering multitude of essays, of passages, and of short phrases, marked for reference. In the seven volumes above referred to (to which, as has been said, not a little has to be added) there must be hundreds of separate articles and conversations; not counting as separate the short maxims and thoughts of the *Characteristics*, and one or two other similar collections, in which, indeed, several passages are duplicated from the essays. At least two out of every three are characteristic of Hazlitt: not one in any twenty is not well worth reading and, if occasion served, commenting on. They are, indeed, as far from being consecutive as (according to the Yankee) was the conversation of Edgar Poe; and the multitude and diversity of their subjects fit them better for occasional than for continuous reading[1]. Perhaps, if any single volume deserves to be recommended to a beginner in Hazlitt it had better be *The Plain Speaker*, where there is the greatest range of subject, and where the author is seen in an almost complete repertory of his numerous parts. But there is not much to choose between it and *The Round Table* (where, however, the papers are shorter as a rule), *Table-Talk*, and the volume called, though not by the author, *Sketches and Essays*. I myself care considerably less for the *Conversations with Northcote*, the personal element in which has often attracted readers; and the attempts referred to above as *Charac-*

---

[1] Since this paper was first published Mr Alexander Ireland has edited a most excellent selection from Hazlitt.

teristics, avowedly in the manner of La Rochefoucauld, are sometimes merely extracts from the essays, and rarely have the self-containedness, the exact and chiselled proportion, which distinguishes the true *pensée* as La Rochefoucauld and some other Frenchmen, and as Hobbes perhaps alone of Englishmen, wrote it. But to criticise these numerous papers is like sifting a cluster of motes, and the mere enumeration of their titles would fill up more than half the room which I have to spare. They must be criticised or characterised in two groups only, the strictly critical and the miscellaneous, the latter excluding politics. As for art, I do not pretend to be more than a connoisseur according to Blake's definition, that is to say, one who refuses to let himself be connoisseured out of his senses. I shall only, in reference to this last subject, observe that the singularly germinal character of Hazlitt's work is noticeable here also; for no one who reads the essay on Nicolas Poussin will fail to add Mr Ruskin to Hazlitt's fair herd of literary children.

His criticism is scattered through all the volumes of general essays; but is found by itself in the series of lectures, or essays (they are rather the latter than the former), on the characters of Shakespeare, on Elizabethan Literature, on the English Poets, and on the English Comic Writers. I cannot myself help thinking that in these four Hazlitt is at his best; though there may be nothing so attractive to the general, and few such brilliant passages as may be found in the "Farewell to Essay-writing," in the paper on Poussin, in "Going to a Fight," in "Going a Journey," and others of the same class. The reason of the preference is by no means a greater interest in the subject of one class, than in the subject of another. It is that, from the very nature of the case, Hazlitt's unlucky prejudices interfere much more seldom with his literary work. They interfere sometimes, as in the case of Sidney, as in some remarks about Coleridge and Wordsworth, and elsewhere; but these instances are rare indeed compared with those that occur in the other division. On the other hand, there are always present Hazlitt's enthusiastic appreciation of what is good in letters, his combination of gusto with sound theory as to what is excellent in prose and verse, his felicitous method of expression, and the acuteness that kept him from that excessive and paradoxical admiration which both Lamb and Coleridge affected, and which has gained many more pupils than his own moderation. Nothing better has ever been written as a general view of the subject than his introduction to his Lectures on Elizabethan Literature; and almost all the faults to be found in it are due merely to occasional deficiency of information, not to error of judgment. He is a little paradoxical on Jonson; but not many critics could furnish a happier contrast than his enthusiastic praise of certain passages of Beaumont and Fletcher, and his cool toning down of Lamb's extravagant eulogy on Ford. He is a little unfair to the Caroline poets; but here the great disturbing influence comes in. If his comparison of ancient and modern literature is rather weak, that is because Hazlitt was anything but widely acquainted with either; and, indeed, it may be said in general that wherever he goes wrong, it is not because he judges wrongly on known facts, but because he either does not know the facts, or is prevented from seeing them by distractions of prejudice. To go through his Characters of Shakespeare would be impossible, and besides, it is a point of honour for one student of Shakespeare to differ with all others. I can only say that I know no critic with whom on this point I differ so seldom as with Hazlitt. Even better, perhaps, are the two sets of lectures on the Poets and Comic Writers. The generalisations are not always sound, for, as must be constantly repeated, Hazlitt was not widely read in literatures other than his own, and his standpoint for comparison is therefore rather insufficient. But take him where his information is sufficient, and how good he is! Of the famous four treatments of the dramatists of the Restoration—Lamb's, Hazlitt's, Leigh Hunt's, and Macaulay's—his seems to me by far the best. In regard to Butler, his critical sense has for once triumphed over his political prejudice; unless some very unkind devil's advocate should suggest that the supposed ingratitude of the King to Butler reconciled Hazlitt to him. He is admirable on Burns; and nothing can be more unjust or sillier than to pretend, as has been pretended, that Burns's loose morality engaged Hazlitt on his side. De Quincey was often a very acute critic, but anything more uncritical than his attack on Hazlitt's comparison of Burns and Wordsworth in relation to passion, it would be difficult to find. Hazlitt "could forgive Swift for being a Tory," he tells us—which is at any rate more than some other people, who have a better reputation for impartiality than his, seem to have been able to do. No one has written better than he on Pope, who still seems to have the faculty of distorting some critical judgments. His chapter on the English novelists (that is to say, those of the eighteenth century) is perhaps the best thing ever written on the subject; and is particularly valuable nowadays when there is a certain tendency to under-value Smollett in order to exalt Fielding, who certainly needs no such illegitimate and uncritical leverage. I do not think that he is, on the whole, unjust to Campbell; though his Gallican, or rather Napoleonic, mania made him commit the literary crime of slighting "The Battle of the Baltic." But in all his criticism of English literature (and he has attempted little else, except by way of digression) he is, for the critic, a study never to be wearied of, always to be profited by. His very aberrations are often more instructive than other men's right-goings; and if he sometimes fails to detect or acknowledge a beauty, he never praises a defect.

It is less easy to sum up the merits of the miscellaneous pieces, for the very obvious reason that they can hardly be brought under any general form or illustrated by any small number of typical instances. Perhaps the best way of "sampling" this undisciplined multitude is to select a few papers by name, so as to show the variety of Hazlitt's interests. The one already mentioned, "On Going to a Fight," which shocked some proprieties even in its own day, ranks almost first; but the reader should take care to accompany it with the official record of that celebrated contest between Neate and the Gasman. All fights are good reading; but this particular effort of Hazlitt's makes one sigh for a *Boxiana* or *Pugilistica* edited by him. Next, I think, must be ranked "On Going a Journey," with its fine appreciation of solitary travelling which does not exclude reminiscences of pleasant journeys in company. But these two, with the article on Poussin and the "Farewell to Essay-writing," have been so often mentioned that it may seem as if Hazlitt's store were otherwise poor. Nothing could be farther from the truth. The "Character of Cobbett" is the best thing the writer ever did of the kind, and the best thing known to me on Cobbett[1]. "Of the Past and the Future" is perhaps the height of the popular metaphysical style—the style from which, as was noted,

[1] *V. inf.* on him (vol. i. p. 269) (1923).

Hazlitt may never have got free as far as philosophising is concerned, but of which he is a master. "On the Indian Jugglers" is a capital example of what may be called improving a text; and it contains some of the most interesting and genial examples of Hazlitt's honest delight in games such as rackets and fives, a delight which (heaven help his critics) was frequently regarded at the time as "low." "On Paradox and Commonplace" is less remarkable for its contribution to the discussion of the subject, than as exhibiting one of Hazlitt's most curious critical megrims—his dislike of Shelley. I wish I could think that he had any better reason for this than the fact that Shelley was a gentleman by birth and his own contemporary. Most disappointing of all, perhaps, is "On Criticism," which the reader (as his prophetic soul, if he is a sensible reader, has probably warned him beforehand) soon finds to be little but an open or covert diatribe against the contemporary critics whom Hazlitt did not like, or who did not hke Hazlitt. The apparently promising "On the Knowledge of Character" chiefly yields the remark that Hazlitt could not have admired Cæsar if he had resembled (in face) the Duke of Wellington. But "My first Acquaintance with Poets" is again a masterpiece; and to me, at least, "Merry England" is perfect. Hazlitt is almost the only person up to his own day who dared to vindicate the claims of nonsense, though he seems to have talked and written as little of it as most men. The chapter "On Editors" is very amusing, though perhaps not entirely in the way in which Hazlitt meant it; but I cannot think him happy "On Footmen," or on "The Conversation of Lords," for reasons already sufficiently stated. A sun-dial is a much more promising subject than a broomstick, yet many essays might be written on sun-dials without there being any fear of Hazlitt's being surpassed. Better still is "On Taste," which, if the twenty or thirty best papers in Hazlitt were collected (and a most charming volume they would make), would rank among the very best. "On Reading New Books" contains excellent sense, but perhaps is, as Hazlitt not seldom is, a little deficient in humour; while the absence of any necessity for humour makes the discussion "Whether Belief is Voluntary" a capital one. Hazlitt is not wholly of the opinion of that Ebrew Jew who said to M. Renan, "*On fait ce qu'on veut mais on croit ce qu'on peut.*"

The shorter papers of the *Round Table* yield perhaps a little less freely in the way of specially notable examples. They come closer to a certain kind of Addisonian essay, a short lay-sermon, without the charming divagation of the longer articles. To see how nearly Hazlitt can reach the level of a rather older and cleverer George Osborne, turn to the paper here on Classical Education. He is quite orthodox for a wonder: perhaps because opinion was beginning to veer a little to the side of Useful Knowledge; but he is as dry as his own favourite biscuit, and as guiltless of freshness. He is best in this volume where he notes particular points such as Kean's Iago, Milton's versification (here, however, he does not get quite to the heart of the matter), "John Buncle," and "The Excursion." In this last he far outsteps the scanty confines of the earlier papers of the *Round Table*, and allows himself that score of pages which seems to be with so many men the normal limit of a good essay. Of his shortest style one sample from "Trifles light as Air" is so characteristic, in more ways than one, that it must be quoted whole.

I am by education and conviction inclined to Republicanism and Puritanism. In America they have both. But I confess I feel a little staggered as to the practical efficacy and saving grace of first principles, when I ask myself, Can they throughout the United States from Boston to Baltimore, produce a single head like one of Titian's Venetian Nobles, nurtured in all the pride of aristocracy and all the blindness of popery? Of all the branches of political economy the human face is perhaps the best criterion of value.

If I were editing Hazlitt's works I should put these sentences on the title-page of every volume; for, dogmatist as he thought himself, it is certain that he was in reality purely æsthetic, though, I need hardly say, not in the absurd sense, or no-sense, which modern misuse of language has chosen to fix on the word. Therefore he is very good (where few are good at all) on Dreams; and, being a great observer of himself, singularly instructive on Application to Study. "On Londoners and Country People" is one of his liveliest efforts; and the pique at his own inclusion in the Cockney School fortunately evaporates in some delightful reminiscences, including one of the few classic passages on the great game of marbles. His remarks on the company at the Southampton coffee-house, which have been often and much praised, please me less: they are too much like attempts in the manner of the Queen Anne men, and Hazlitt is always best when he imitates nobody. "Hot and Cold" (which might have been more intelligibly called "North and South") is distinctly curious, bringing out again what may be called Hazlitt's fanciful observation; and it may generally be said that, however alarming and however suggestive of commonplace the titles "On Respectable People," "On People of Sense," "On Novelty and Familiarity," may be, Hazlitt may almost invariably be trusted to produce something that is not commonplace, that is not laboured paradox, that is eminently literature.

I know that a haphazard catalogue of the titles of

essays (for it is little more) such as fills the last paragraph or two may not seem very succulent. But within moderate space there is really no other means of indicating the author's extraordinary range of subject, and at the same time the pervading excellence of his treatment. To exemplify a difference which has sometimes been thought to require explanation, his work as regards system, connection with anything else, immediate occasion (which with him was generally what his friend, Mr Skimpole, would have called "pounds") is always Journalism: in result, it is almost always Literature. Its staple subjects, as far as there can be said to be any staple where the thread is so various, are very much those which the average newspaper-writer since his time has had to deal with—politics, book-reviewing, criticism on plays and pictures, social etceteras, the minor morals, the miscellaneous incidents of daily life. It is true that Hazlitt was only for a short time in the straitest shafts, the most galling traces, of periodical hack-work. His practice was rather that of George Warrington, who worked till he had filled his purse, and then lay idle till he had emptied it. He used (an indulgence agreeable in the mouth, but bitter in the belly) very frequently to receive money beforehand for work which was not yet done. Although anything but careful, he was never an extravagant man, his tastes being for the most part simple; and he never, even during his first married life, seems to have been burdened by an expensive household. Moreover, he got rid of Mrs Hazlitt on very easy terms. Still he must constantly have had on him the sensation that he lived by his work, and by that only. It seems to be (as far as one can make it out) this sensation which more than anything else jades and tires what some very metaphorical men of letters are pleased to call their Pegasus. But Hazlitt, though he served in the shafts, shows little trace of the harness. He has frequent small carelessnesses of style, but he would probably have had as many or more if he had been the easiest and gentlest of easy-writing gentlemen. He never seems to have allowed himself to be cramped in his choice of his subjects, and wrote for the editors, of whom he speaks so amusingly, with almost as much freedom of speech as if he had had a private press of his own, and had issued dainty little tractates on Dutch paper to be fought for by bibliophiles. His prejudices, his desultoriness, his occasional lack of correctness of fact (he speaks of "Fontaine's Translation" of Æsop, and makes use of the extraordinary phrase, "The whole Council of Trent with Father Paul at their head," than which a more curious blunder is hardly conceivable), his wayward inconsistencies, his freaks of bad taste, would in all probability have been aggravated rather than alleviated by the greater freedom and less responsibility of an independent or an endowed student. The fact is that he was a born man of letters, and that he could not help turning whatsoever he touched into literature, whether it was criticism on books or on pictures, a fight or a supper, a game at marbles, a political diatribe, or the report of a literary conversation. He doubtless had favourite subjects; but I do not know that it can be said that he treated one class of subjects better than another, with the exception that I must hold him to have been first of all a literary critic. He certainly could not write a work of great length; for the faults of his *Life of Napoleon* are grave even when its view of the subject is taken as undisputed, and it holds among his productions about the same place (that of longest and worst) which the book it was designed to counterwork holds among Scott's. Nor was he, as it seems to me, quite at home in very short papers—in papers of the length of the average newspaper article. What he could do, as hardly any other man has ever done it in England, was a *causerie* of about the same length as Sainte-Beuve's or a little shorter, less limited in range, but also less artfully proportioned than the great Frenchman's literary and historical studies, giving scope for considerable digression, but coming to an end before the author was wearied of his subject, or had exhausted the fresh thoughts and the happy borrowings and analogies which he had ready for it. Of what is rather affectedly called "architectonic," Hazlitt has nothing. No essay of his is ever an exhaustive or even a symmetrical treatment of its nominal, or of any, theme. He somewhere speaks of himself as finding it easy to go on stringing pearls when he has once got the string; but, for my part, I should say that the string was much more doubtful than the pearls. Except in a very few set pieces, his whole charm consists in the succession of irregular, half-connected, but unending and infinitely variegated thoughts, fancies, phrases, quotations, which he pours forth not merely at a particular "Open Sesame," but at "Open barley," "Open rye," or any other grain in the corn-chandler's list. No doubt the charm of these is increased by the fact that they are never quite haphazard, never absolutely promiscuous, despite their desultory arrangement; no doubt also a certain additional interest arises from the constant revelation which they make of Hazlitt's curious personality, his enthusiastic appreciation flecked with spots of grudging spite, his clear intellect clouded with prejudice, his admiration of greatness and nobility of character coexisting with the faculty of doing very mean and even disgraceful things, his abundant relish of life contrasted with almost constant repining. He must have been one of the most uncomfortable of all English men of letters, who can be called great, to know as a friend. He is certainly, to those who know him only as readers, one of the most fruitful both in instruction and in delight[1].

---

[1] Since this essay was written, Hazlitt has been re-edited in greater fulness, and in selection, more than once; and far greater attention has been paid to him by fellows of his own craft. This is all to the good. But I do not find it necessary to alter anything. Indeed, my friend Professor Elton, whose competence is unsurpassed, while thinking me rather hard on the man admits my full justice to the writer (1923).

VI

MOORE

It would be interesting, though perhaps a little impertinent, to put to any given number of well-informed persons under the age of forty or fifty the sudden query, who was Thomas Brown the Younger? And it is very possible that a majority of them would answer that he had something to do with Rugby. It is certain that with respect to that part of his work in which he was pleased so to call himself, Moore is but little known. The considerable mass of his hack-work has gone whither all hack-work goes, fortunately enough for those of us who have to do it. The vast monument erected to him by his pupil, friend, and literary executor, Lord Russell, or rather Lord John Russell, is a monument of such a Cyclopean order of architecture, both in respect of bulk and in respect of style, that most honest biographers and critics acknowledge themselves to have explored its recesses but cursorily. Less of him, even as a poet proper, is now read than of any of the brilliant group of poets of which he was one, with the possible exceptions of Crabbe and Rogers; while, more unfortunate than Crabbe, he has had no Mr Courthope to come to his rescue. But he has recently had what is an unusual thing for an English poet, a French biographer[1]. I shall not have very much to say of the details of M. Vallat's very creditable and useful monograph. It would be possible, if I were merely reviewing it, to pick out some of the curious

[1] *Etude sur la Vie et les Œuvres de Thomas Moore*; by Gustave Vallat. Paris: Rousseau. London: Asher and Co. Dublin: Hodges, Figgis, and Co. 1887. Such biographies and criticisms have become much more frequent in the interval (1923).

errors of hasty deduction which are rarely wanting in a book of its nationality. If (and no shame to him) Moore's father sold cheese and whisky, *le whisky d'Irlande* was no doubt his staple commodity in the one branch, but scarcely *le 'fromage de Stilton* in the other. An English lawyer's studies are not even now, except at the universities and for purposes of perfunctory examination, very much in "Justinian," and in Moore's time they were still less so. And if Bromham Church is near Sloperton, then it will follow as the night the day that it is not *dans le Bedfordshire*. But these things matter very little. They are found, in their different kinds, in all books; and if we English bookmakers (at least some of us) are not likely to make a Bordeaux wine merchant sell Burgundy as his chief commodity, or say that a village near Amiens is *dans le Béarn*, we no doubt do other things quite as bad. On the whole, M. Vallat's sketch, though of moderate length, is quite the soberest and most trustworthy sketch of Moore's life and of his books, as books merely, that I know. In matters of pure criticism M. Vallat is less blameless. He quotes authorities with that apparent indifference to, or even ignorance of, their relative value which is so yawning a pit for the feet of the foreigner in all cases; and perhaps a wider knowledge of English poetry in general would have been a better preparation for the study of Moore's in particular. "Never," says M. Renan very wisely, "never does a foreigner satisfy the nation whose history he writes"; and this is as true of literary history as of history proper. But M. Vallat satisfies us in a very considerable degree; and even putting aside the question whether he is satisfactory altogether, he has given us quite sufficient text in the mere fact that he has bestowed upon Moore an amount of attention and competence which no compatriot of the author of *Lalla Rookh* has cared to bestow for many years.

I shall also here take the liberty of neglecting a very great—as far as bulk goes, by far the greatest—part of Moore's own performance. He has inserted so many interesting autobiographical particulars in the prefaces to his complete works, that visits to the great mausoleum of the Russell memoirs are rarely necessary, and still more rarely profitable. His work for the booksellers was done at a time when the best class of such work was much better done than the best class of it is now; but it was after all work for the booksellers. His *History of Ireland*, his *Life of Lord Edward Fitzgerald*, etc., may be pretty exactly gauged by saying that they are a good deal better than Scott's work of a merely similar kind (in which it is hardly necessary to say that I do not include the *Tales of a Grandfather* or the introductions to the Dryden, the Swift, and the Ballantyne novels), not nearly so good as Southey's, and not quite so good as Campbell's. The *Life of Byron* holds a different place. With the poems, or some of them, it forms the only part of Moore's literary work which is still read; and though it is read much more for its substance than for its execution, it is still a masterly performance of a very difficult task. The circumstances which brought it about are well known, and no discussion of them would be possible without plunging into the Byron controversy generally, which the present writer most distinctly declines to do. But these circumstances, with other things among which Moore's own comparative faculty for the business may be not unjustly mentioned, prevent it from taking rank at all approaching that of Boswell's or Lockhart's inimitable biographies. The chief thing to note in it as regards Moore himself, is the help it gives in a matter to which we shall have to refer again, his attitude towards those whom his time still called "the great."

And so we are left with the poems—not an inconsiderable companion seeing that its stature is some seven hundred small quarto pages closely packed with verses in double columns. Part of this volume is, however, devoted to the *Epicurean*, a not unremarkable example of ornate prose in many respects resembling the author's verse. Indeed, as close readers of Moore know, there exists an unfinished verse form of it which, in style and general character, is not unlike a more serious *Lalla Rookh*. As far as poetry goes, almost everything that will be said of *Lalla Rookh* might be said of *Alciphron*: this latter, however, is a little more Byronic than its more famous sister, and in that respect not quite so successful.

Moore's life, which is not uninteresting as a key to his personal character, is very fairly treated by M. Vallat, chiefly from the poet's own authority; but it need not detain us very long. He was born at Dublin on 28th May 1779. There is no mystery about his origin. His father, John Moore, was a small grocer and liquor-shop keeper who received later the place of barrack-master from a patron of his son. The mother, Anastasia Codd, was a Wexford girl, and seems to have been well educated and somewhat above her husband in station. Thomas was sent to several private schools, where he appears to have attained to some scholarship and to have early practised composition in the tongue of the hated Saxon. When he was fourteen, the first measure of Catholic Emancipation opened Trinity College to him, and that establishment, "the intellectual eye of Ireland" as Sir William Harcourt has justly called it, received him a year later. The "silent sister" has fostered an always genial, if sometimes inexact, fashion of scholarship, in which Moore's talents were well suited to shine, and a pleasant social atmosphere wherein he was also not misplaced. But the time drew near to '98, and Moore, although he had always too much good sense to dip deeply into sedition, was, from his sentimental habits, likely to run some risk of being thought to have dipped in it. Although it is certain that he would have regarded what is called Nationalism in our days with disgust and horror[1], he cannot be acquitted of using, to the end of his life, the loosest of language on subjects where precision is particularly to be desired. Robert Emmet was his contemporary, and the action which the authorities took was but too well justified by the outbreak of the insurrection later. A Commission was named for purifying the college. Its head was Lord Clare, one of the greatest of Irishmen, the base or ignorant vilifying of whom by some persons in these days has been one of the worst results of the Home Rule movement. It had a rather comic assessor in Dr Duigenan, the same, I believe, of whom it has been recorded that, at an earlier stage of his academic career and when a junior Fellow, he threatened to "bulge the Provost's eye." The oath was tendered to each examinate, and on the day before Moore's appearance Emmet and others had gone by default, while it was at least whispered that there had been treachery in the camp. Moore's own performance was, by his own account, heroic and successful: by another, which he very fairly gives, a little less heroic but still successful. Both show clearly that Clare was nothing like the stage-tyrant which the imagination of the seditious has chosen to represent him as being. That M. Vallat should talk rather foolishly about Emmet was to be expected; for Emmet's rhetorical rubbish was sure to impose, and

[1] And what has followed! (1923).

has always imposed, on Frenchmen. The truth of course is that this young person—though one of those whom every humane man would like to keep mewed up till they arrived, if they ever did arrive, which is improbable, at years of discretion—was one of the most mischievous of agitators. He was one of those who light a bonfire and then are shocked at its burning, who throw a kingdom into anarchy and misery and think that they are cleared by a reference to Harmodius and Aristogeiton. It is one of the most fearful delights of the educated Tory to remember what the grievance of Harmodius and Aristogeiton really was. Moore (who had something of the folly of Emmet, but none of his reckless conceit) escaped, and his family must have been exceedingly glad to send him over to the Isle of Britain. He entered at the Middle Temple in 1799, but hardly made even a pretence of reading law. His actual experience is one of those puzzles which continually meet the student of literary history in the days when society was much smaller, the makers of literature fewer, and the resources of patronage greater. Moore toiled not, neither did he spin. He slipped, apparently on the mere strength of an ordinary introduction, into the good graces of Lord Moira, who introduced him to the exiled Royal Family of France, and to the richest members of the Whig aristocracy—the Duke of Bedford, the Marquis of Lansdowne and others, not to mention the Prince of Wales himself. The young Irishman had indeed, as usual, his "proposals" in his pocket —proposals for a translation of Anacreon which appeared in May 1800. The thing which thus founded one of the easiest, if not the most wholly triumphant, of literary careers is not a bad thing. The original, now abandoned as a clever though late imitation, was known even in Moore's time to be in parts of very doubtful authenticity, but it still remains, as an original, a very pretty thing. Moore's version is not quite so pretty, and is bolstered out with paraphrase and amplification to a rather intolerable extent. But there was considerable fellow-feeling between the author, whoever he was, and the translator, and the result is not despicable. Still there is no doubt that work as good or better might appear now, and the author would be lucky if he cleared a hundred pounds and a favourable review or two by the transaction. Moore was made for life. These things happen at one time and do not happen at another. We are inclined to accept them as ultimate facts into which it is useless to inquire. There does not appear to be among the numerous fixed laws of the universe any one which regulates the proportion of literary desert to immediate reward, and it is on the whole well that it should be so. At any rate the publication increased Moore's claims as a "lion," and encouraged him to publish next year the *Poems of the late Thomas Little* (he always stuck to the Christian name), which put up his fame and rather put down his character.

In later editions Thomas Little has been so much subjected to the fig-leaf and knife that we have known readers who wondered why on earth any one should ever have objected to him. He was a good deal more uncastrated originally, but there never was much harm in him. It is true that the excuse made by Sterne for *Tristram Shandy*, and often repeated for Moore, does not quite apply. There is not much guilt in Little, but there is certainly very little innocence. He knows that a certain amount of not too gross indecency will raise a snigger, and, like Voltaire and Sterne himself, he sets himself to raise it. But he does not do it very wickedly. The propriety of the nineteenth century, moreover, had not then made the surprisingly rapid strides of a few years later, and some time had to pass before Moore was to go out with Jeffrey, and nearly challenge Byron, for questioning his morality. The rewards of his harmless iniquity were at hand; and in the autumn of 1803 he was made Secretary of the Admiralty in Bermuda. Bermuda, it is said, is an exceedingly pleasant place; but either there is no Secretary of the Admiralty there now, or they do not give the post to young men four-and-twenty years old who have written two very thin volumes of light verses. The Bermoothes are not still vexed with that kind of Civil Servant. The appointment was not altogether fortunate for Moore, inasmuch as his deputy (for they not only gave nice berths to men of letters then, but let them have deputies) embezzled public and private moneys, with disastrous results to his easy-going principal. But for the time it was all, as most things were with Moore, plain sailing. He went out in a frigate, and was the delight of the gun-room. As soon as he got tired of the Bermudas, he appointed his deputy and went to travel in America, composing large numbers of easy poems. In October 1804 he was back in England, still voyaging at His Majesty's expense, and having achieved his fifteen months' trip wholly on those terms. Little is heard of him for the next two years, and then the publication of his American and other poems, with some free reflections on the American character, brought down on him the wrath of *The Edinburgh*, and provoked the famous leadless or half-leadless duel at Chalk Farm. It was rather hard on Moore, if the real cause of his castigation was that he had offended democratic principles, while the ostensible cause was that, as Thomas Little, he had five years before written loose and humorous verses. So thinks M. Vallat, with whom we are not wholly disposed to agree, for Jeffrey, though a

Whig, was no Democrat, and he was a rather strict moralist. However, no harm came of the meeting in any sense, though its somewhat burlesque termination made the irreverent laugh. It was indeed not fated that Moore should smell serious powder, though his courage seems to have been fully equal to any such occasion. The same year brought him two unquestioned and unalloyed advantages, the friendship of Rogers and the beginning of the Irish Melodies, from which he reaped not a little solid benefit, and which contain by far his highest and most lasting poetry. It is curious, but by no means unexampled, that, at the very time at which he was thus showing that he had found his right way, he also diverged into one wholly wrong— that of the serious and very ineffective Satires, *Corruption*, *Intolerance*, and others. The year 1809 brought *English Bard's and Scotch Reviewers* with a gibe from Byron and a challenge from Moore. But Moore's challenges were fated to have no other result than making the challenged his friends for life. All this time he had been more or less "about town." In 1811 he married Elizabeth Dyke ("Bessy"), an actress of virtue and beauty, and wrote the very inferior comic opera of "The Blue Stocking." Lord Moira gave the pair a home first in his own house, then at Kegworth near Donington, whence they moved to Ashbourne. Moore was busy now. The politics of *The Two-penny Postbag* are of course sometimes dead enough to us; but sometimes also they are not, and then the easy grace of the satire, which is always pungent and never venomed, is not much below Canning. Its author also did a good deal of other work of the same kind, besides beginning to review for *The Edinburgh*. Considering that he was in a way making his bread and butter by lampooning, however good-humouredly, the ruler of his country, he seems to have been a little unreasonable in feeling shocked that Lord Moira, on going as viceroy to India, did not provide for him. In the first place he was provided for already; and in the second place you cannot reasonably expect to enjoy the pleasures of independence and those of dependence at the same time. At the end of 1817 he left Mayfield (his cottage near Ashbourne) and Lord Moira, for Lord Lansdowne and Sloperton, a cottage near Bowood, the end of the one sojourn and the beginning of the other being distinguished by the appearance of his two best works, next to the Irish Melodies—*Lalla Rookh* and *The Fudge Family at Paris*. His first and almost his only heavy stroke of ill-luck now came on him: his deputy at Bermuda levanted with some six thousand pounds, for which Moore was liable. Many friends came to his aid, and after some delay and negotiations, during which he had to go abroad, Lord Lansdowne paid what was necessary. But Moore afterwards paid Lord Lansdowne, which makes a decided distinction between his conduct and that of Theodore Hook in a similar case.

Although the days of Moore lasted for half an ordinary lifetime after this, they saw few important events save the imbroglio over the Byron memoirs. They saw also the composition of a great deal of literature and journalism, all very well paid, notwithstanding which Moore seems to have been always in a rather unintelligible state of pecuniary distress. That he made his parents an allowance, as some allege in explanation, will not in the least account for this; for, creditable as it was in him to make it, this allowance did not exceed one hundred pounds a year. He must have spent little in an ordinary way, for his Sloperton establishment was of the most modest character, while his wife was an excellent manager, and never went into society.

Probably he might have endorsed, if he had been asked, the great principle which somebody or other has formulated, that the most expensive way of living is staying in other people's houses. At any rate his condition was rather precarious till 1835, when Lord John Russell and Lord Lansdowne obtained for him a Civil List pension of three hundred pounds a year. In his very last days this was further increased by an additional hundred a year to his wife. His end was not happy. The softening of the brain, which set in about 1848, and which had been preceded for some time by premonitory symptoms, can hardly, as in the cases of Scott and Southey, be set down to overwork, for though Moore had not been idle, his literary life had been mere child's play to theirs. He died on 26th February 1852.

Of Moore's character not much need be said, nor need what is said be otherwise than favourable. Not only to modern tastes, but to the sturdier tastes of his own day, and even of the days immediately before his, there was a little too much of the parasite and the hanger-on about him. It is easy to say that a man of his talents, when he had once obtained a start, might surely have gone his own way and lived his own life, without taking up the position of a kind of superior gamekeeper or steward at rich men's gates. But race, fashion, and a good many other things have to be taken into account; and it is fair to Moore to remember that he was, as it were from the first, bound to the chariot-wheels of "the great," and could hardly liberate himself from them without churlishness and violence. Moreover, it cannot possibly be denied by any fair critic that if he accepted to some extent the awkward position of led-poet, he showed in it as much independence as was compatible with the function.

Both in money matters, in his language to his patrons, and in a certain general but indefinable tone of behaviour, he contrasts not less favourably than remarkably, both with the ultra-Tory Hook, to whom we have already compared him, and with the ultra-Radical Leigh Hunt. Moore had as little of Wagg as he had of Skimpole about him; though he allowed his way of life to compare in some respects perilously with theirs. It is only necessary to look at his letters to Byron—always ready enough to treat as spaniels those of his inferiors in station who appeared to be of the spaniel kind—to appreciate his general attitude, and his behaviour in this instance is by no means different from his behaviour in others. As a politician there is no doubt that he at least thought himself to be quite sincere. It may be that, if he had been, his political satires would have galled Tories more than they did then, and could hardly be read by persons of that persuasion with such complete enjoyment as they can now. But the insincerity was quite unconscious, and indeed can hardly be said to have been insincerity at all. Moore had not a political head, and in English as in Irish politics his beliefs were probably not founded on any clearly comprehended principles. But such as they were he held to them firmly. Against his domestic character nobody has ever said anything; and it is sufficient to observe that not a few of the best as well as of the greatest men of his time, Scott as well as Byron, Lord John Russell as well as Lord Moira, appear not only to have admired his abilities and liked his social qualities, but to have sincerely respected his character. And so we may at last find ourselves alone with the plump volume of poems in which we shall hardly discover with the amiable M. Vallat "the greatest lyric poet of England," but in which we shall find a poet certainly, and if not a very great poet, at any rate a poet who has done many things well, and one particular thing better than anybody else.

The volume opens with *Lalla Rookh*, a proceeding which, if not justified by chronology, is completely justified by the facts that Moore was to his contemporaries the author of that poem chiefly, and that it is by far the most considerable thing not only in mere bulk, but in arrangement, plan, and style, that he ever did. Perhaps I am not quite a fair judge of *Lalla Rookh*. I was brought up in what is called a strict household where, though the rule was not, as far as I can remember, enforced by any penalties, it was a point of honour that in the nursery and schoolroom none but "Sunday books" should be read on Sunday. But this severity was tempered by one of the easements often occurring in a world which, if not the best, is certainly not the worst of all possible worlds. For the convenience of servants, or for some other reason, the children were much more in the drawing-room on Sundays than on any other day, and it was an unwritten rule that any book that lived in the drawing-room was fit Sunday-reading. The consequence was that from the time I could read, till childish things were put away, I used to spend a considerable part of the first day of the week in reading and re-reading a collection of books, four of which were Scott's poems, *Lalla Rookh*, *The Essays of Elia* (First Edition,—I have got it now), and Southey's *Doctor*[1]. Therefore it may be that I rank *Lalla Rookh* rather too high. At the same time I confess that it still seems to me a very respectable poem indeed of the second rank. Of course it is artificial. The parade of second, or third, or twentieth-hand learning in the notes makes one smile, and the whole

---

[1] *Elia* and *The Doctor* are still with me (1923).

reminds one (as I daresay it has reminded many others before) of a harp of the period with the gilt a little tarnished, the ribbons more than a little faded, and the silk stool on which the young woman in ringlets used to sit much worn. All this is easy metaphorical criticism, if it is criticism at all. For I am not sure that, when the last age has got a little farther off from our descendants, they will see anything more ludicrous in such a harp than we see in the faded spinets of a generation earlier still. But much remains to Lalla if not to Feramorz. The prose interludes have lost none of their airy grace. Even Mr Burnand has not been able to make Mokanna ridiculous, nor have the recent accounts of the actual waste of desert and felt huts banished at least the poetical beauty of "Merou's bright palaces and groves." There are those who laugh at the bower of roses by Bendemeer's stream: I do not. *Paradise and the Peri* is perhaps the prettiest purely sentimental poem that English or any other language can show. *The Fire Worshippers* are rather long, but there is a famous fight—more than one indeed—in them to relieve the monotony. For *The Light of the Harem* alone I have never been able to get up much enthusiasm; but even *The Light of the Harem* is a great deal better than Moore's subsequent attempt in the style of *Lalla Rookh*, or something like it, *The Loves of the Angels*. There is only one good thing that I can find to say of that: it is not so bad as the poem which similarity of title makes one think of in connection with it—Lamartine's disastrous *Chute d'un Ange*.

As *Lalla Rookh* is far the most important of Moore's serious poems, so *The Fudge Family at Paris* is far the best of his humorous poems. I do not forget *The Two-penny Postbag*, nor many capital later verses of the same kind, the best of which perhaps is the Epistle from Henry of Exeter to John of Tchume. But *The Fudge Family* has all the merits of these, with a scheme and framework of dramatic character which they lack. Miss Biddy and her vanities, Master Bob and his guttling, the eminent turncoat Phil Fudge, Esq. himself and his politics, are all excellent. But I avow that Phelim Connor is to me the most delightful, though he has always been rather a puzzle. If he is intended to be a satire on the class now[1] represented by the O'Briens and the McCarthys he is exquisite, and it is small wonder that Young Ireland has never loved Moore much. But I do not think that Thomas Brown the Younger meant it, or at least wholly meant it, as satire, and this is perhaps the best proof of his unpractical way of looking at politics. For Phelim Connor is a much more damning sketch than any of the Fudges. Vanity, gluttony, the scheming intrigues of eld, may not be nice things, but they are common to the whole human race. The hollow rant which enjoys the advantages of liberty and declaims against the excesses of tyranny is in its perfection Irish alone. However this may be, these lighter poems of Moore are great fun, and it is no small misfortune that the younger generation of readers pays so little attention to them. For they are full of acute observation of manners, politics, and society by an accomplished man of the world, put into pointed and notable form by an accomplished man of letters. Our fathers knew them well, and many a quotation familiar enough at second hand is due originally to the Fudge Family in their second appearance (not so good, but still good) many years later, to *The Two-penny Postbag* and to the long list of miscellaneous satires and skits. The last sentence is,

---

[1] *I.e.* 1887. "But [this] though bad is followed by a worse" as Dryden has it (1923).

however, to be taken as most strictly excluding *Corruption, Intolerance*, and *The Sceptic*. *Rhymes on the Road*, travel-pieces out of Moore's line, may also be mercifully left aside: and *Evenings in Greece*; and *The Summer Fête* (any universal provider would have supplied as good a poem with the supper and the rout-seats) need not delay the critic and will not extraordinarily delight the reader. Not here is Moore's spur of Parnassus to be found.

For that domain of his we must go to the songs which, in extraordinary numbers, make up the whole of the divisions headed Irish Melodies, National Airs, Sacred Songs, Ballads and Songs, and some of the finest of which are found outside these divisions in the longer poems from *Lalla Rookh* downwards. The singular musical melody of these pieces has never been seriously denied by any one, but it seems to be thought, especially nowadays, that because they are musically melodious they are not poetical. It is probably useless to protest against a prejudice which, where it is not due to simple thoughtlessness or to blind following of fashion, argues a certain constitutional defect of the understanding powers. But it may be just necessary to repeat pretty firmly that any one who regards, even with a tincture of contempt, such work (to take various characteristic examples) as Dryden's lyrics, as Shenstone's, as Moore's, as Macaulay's Lays, because he thinks that, if he did not contemn them, his worship of Shakespeare, of Shelley, of Wordsworth would be suspect, is most emphatically not a critic of poetry and not even a catholic lover of it. Which said, let us betake ourselves to seeing what Moore's special virtue is. It is acknowledged that it consists partly in marrying music most happily to verse; but what is not so fully acknowledged as it ought to be is, that it also consists in marrying music not merely to verse, but to poetry. Among the more abstract questions of poetical criticism few are more interesting than this, the connection of what may be called musical music with poetical music; and it is one which has not been much discussed. Let us take the two greatest of Moore's own contemporaries in lyric, the two greatest lyrists as some think (I give no opinion on this) in English, and compare their work with his. Shelley has the poetical music in an unsurpassable and sometimes in an almost unapproached degree, but his verse is admittedly very difficult to set to music. I should myself go farther and say that it has in it some indefinable quality antagonistic to such setting. Except the famous Indian Serenade, I do not know any poem of Shelley's that has been set with anything approaching to success, and in the best setting that I know of this the honeymoon of the marriage turns into a "red moon" before long. That this is not merely due to the fact that Shelley likes intricate metres any one who examines Moore can see. That it is due merely to the fact that Shelley, as we know from Peacock, was almost destitute of any ear for music is the obvious and common explanation. But neither will this serve, for we happen also to know that Burns, whose lyric, of a higher quality than Moore's, assorts with music as naturally as Moore's own, was quite as deficient as Shelley in this respect. So was Scott, who could yet write admirable songs to be sung. It seems therefore almost impossible, on the comparison of these three instances, to deny the existence of some peculiar musical music in poetry, which is distinct from poetical music, though it may coexist with it or may be separated from it, and which is independent both of technical musical training and even of what is commonly called "ear" in the poet. That Moore possessed

it in probably the highest degree will, I think, hardly
be denied. It never seems to have mattered to him
whether he wrote the words for the air or altered the air
to suit the words. The two fit like a glove, and if, as is
sometimes the case, the same or a similar poetical
measure is heard set to another air than Moore's, this
other always seems intrusive and wrong. He draws
attention in one case to the extraordinary irregularity
of his own metre (an irregularity to which the average
pindaric is a mere jog-trot), yet the air fits it exactly[1].
Of course the two feet which most naturally go to
music, the anapæst and the trochee, are commonest
with him; but the point is that he seems to find no more
difficulty, if he does not take so much pleasure, in
setting combinations of a very different kind. Nor is
this peculiar gift by any means unimportant from the
purely poetical side, the side on which the verse is
looked at without any regard to air or accompaniment.
For the great drawback to "songs to be sung" in
general since Elizabethan days (when, as Mr Arber and
Mr Bullen have shown, it was very different) has been
the constant tendency of the verse-writer to sacrifice
to his musical necessities either meaning or poetic
sound or both. The climax of this is of course reached
in the ineffable balderdash which usually does duty
for the libretto of an opera, but it is quite as noticeable
in the ordinary songs of the drawing-room. Now Moore
is quite free from this blame. He may not have the
highest and rarest strokes of poetic expression; but at
any rate he seldom or never sins against either reason
or poetry for the sake of rhythm and rhyme. He is
always the master not the servant, the artist not the

---

[1] I do not wish to multiply references to other books of my own. But
the treatment of Moore in my *History of Prosody*, vol. III. completes
this Essay in a rather unusual degree.

clumsy craftsman. And this I say not by any means as
one likely to pardon poetical shortcomings in consideration of musical merit, for, shameful as the confession
may be, a little music goes a long way with me; and
what music I do like, is rather of the kind opposite to
Moore's facile styles. Yet it is easy, even from the
musical view, to exaggerate his facility. Berlioz is not
generally thought a barrel-organ composer, and he
bestowed early and particular pains on Moore.

To many persons, however, the results are more
interesting than the analysis of their qualities and
principles; so let us go to the songs themselves. To my
fancy the three best of Moore's songs, and three of the
finest songs in any language, are *Oft in the stilly Night,*
When in Death I shall calm recline, and *I saw from the
Beach.* They all exemplify what has been pointed out
above, the complete adaptation of words to music and
music to words, coupled with a decidedly high quality
of poetical merit in the verse, quite apart from the
mere music. It can hardly be necessary to quote them,
for they are or ought to be familiar to everybody; but
in selecting these three I have no intention of distinguishing them in point of general excellence from
scores, nay hundreds of others. *Go where Glory waits
thee* is the first of the Irish Melodies, and one of those
most hackneyed by the enthusiasm of bygone Pogsons.
But its merit ought in no way to suffer on that account
with persons who are not Pogsons. It ought to be
possible for the reader, it is certainly possible for the
critic, to dismiss Pogson altogether, to wave Pogson
off, and to read anything as if it had never been read
before. If this be done we shall hardly wonder at the
delight which our fathers, who will not compare
altogether badly with ourselves, took in Thomas Moore.
When he who adores thee is supposed on pretty good

evidence to have been inspired by the most hollow and senseless of all pseudo-patriotic delusions, a delusion of which the best thing that can be said is that "the pride of thus dying for" it has been about the last thing that it ever did inspire, and that most persons who have suffered from it have usually had the good sense to take lucrative places from the tyrant as soon as they could get them, and to live happily ever after. But the basest, the most brutal, and the bloodiest of Saxons may recognise in Moore's poem the expression of a possible, if not a real, feeling given with infinite grace and pathos. The same string reverberates even in the thrice and thousand times hackneyed Harp of Tara. *Rich and rare were the Gems she wore* is chiefly comic opera, but it is very pretty comic opera; and the two pieces, *There is not in the wide world* and *How dear to me* exemplify, for the first but by no means for the last time, Moore's extraordinary command of the last phase of that curious thing called by the century that gave him birth Sensibility. We have turned Sensibility out of doors; but he would be a rash man who should say that we have not let in seven worse devils of the gushing kind in her comparatively innocent room.

Then we may skip not a few pieces, only referring once more to *The Legacy* ("When in Death I shall calm recline"), an anacreontic quite unsurpassable in its own kind. We need dwell but briefly on such pieces as *Believe me if all those endearing young Charms*, which is typical of much that Moore wrote, but does not reach the true devil-may-care note of Suckling, or as *By the Hope within us springing*, for Moore's warlike pieces are seldom or never good. But with *Love's Young Dream* we come back to the style of which it is impossible to say less than that it is quite admirable in its kind. Then after a page or two we come to the chief *cruces* of Moore's pathetic and of his comic manner, *The Last Rose of Summer, The Young May Moon,* and *The Minstrel Boy.* I cannot say very much for the last, which is tainted with the unreality of all Moore's Tyrtean efforts; but *The Young May Moon* could not be better, and I am not going to abandon the Rose, for all her perfume be something musty—a *pot-pourri* rose rather than a fresh one. The song of O'Ruark with its altogether fatal climax—

> On our side is virtue and Erin,
> On theirs is the Saxon and guilt—

(which carries with it the delightful reflection that it was an Irishman running away with an Irish woman that occasioned this sweeping moral contrast) must be given up; but surely not so "Oh had we some bright little Isle of our own." For indeed if one only had some bright little isle of that kind, some *rive fidèle où l'on aime toujours,* and where things in general are adjusted to such a state, then would Thomas Moore be the Laureate of that bright and tight little island.

But it is alarming to find that we have not yet got through twenty-five pages out of some hundred or two, and that the Irish Melodies are not yet nearly exhausted. Not a few of the best known of Moore's songs, including *Oft in the stilly Night,* are to be found in the division of National Airs, which is as a whole a triumph of that extraordinary genius for setting which has been already noticed. Here is *Flow on thou shining River,* here the capital *When I touch the String,* on which Thackeray loved to make variations. But *Oft in the stilly Night* itself is far above the others. We do not say "stilly" now: we have been taught by Coleridge (who used to use it freely himself before he laughed at it) to laugh at "stilly" and "paly" and so forth. But the most acrimonious critic may be challenged to point out another weakness of the same kind, and on the whole the straightforward simplicity of the phrase equals the melody of the rhythm.

The Sacred Songs need not delay us long; for they are not better than sacred songs in general, which is saying remarkably little. Perhaps the most interesting thing in them is the well-known couplet,

This world is but a fleeting show
For man's illusion given—

which, as has justly been observed, contains one of the most singular estimates of the divine purpose anywhere to be found. But Moore might, like Mr Midshipman Easy, have excused himself by remarking, "Ah! well, I don't understand these things." The miscellaneous division of Ballads, Songs, etc., is much more fruitful. *The Leaf and the Fountain*, beginning "Tell me, kind seer, I pray thee," though rather long, is singularly good of its kind—the kind of half-narrative ballad. So in a lighter strain is *The Indian Bark*. Nor is Moore less at home after his own fashion in the songs from the Anthology. It is true that the same fault which has been found with his *Anacreon* may be found here, and that it is all the more sensible because at least in some cases the originals are much higher poetry than the pseudo-Teian. To the form and style of Meleager Moore could not pretend; but as these are rather songs on Greek motives than translations from the Greek, the slackness and dilution matter less. But the strictly miscellaneous division holds some of the best work. We could no doubt dispense with the well-known ditty (for once very nearly the "rubbish" with which Moore is so often and so unjustly charged) where Posada rhymes of necessity to Granada, and where, quite against the author's habit, the ridiculous term "Sultana" is fished out to do similar duty in reference to the Dulcinea, or rather to the Maritornes, of a muleteer. But this is quite an exception, and as a rule the facile verse is as felicitous as it is facile. Perhaps no one stands out very far above the rest; perhaps all have more or less the mark of easy variations on a few well-known themes. The old comparison that they are as numerous as motes, as bright, as fleeting, and as in-dividually insignificant, comes naturally enough to the mind. But then they are very numerous, they are very bright, and if they are fleeting, their number provides plenty more to take the place of that which passes away. Nor is it by any means true that they lack individual significance.

This enumeration of a few out of many ornaments of Moore's muse will of course irritate those who object to the "brick-of-the-house" mode of criticism; while it may not be minute enough, or sufficiently bolstered by actual quotation, to please those who hold that simple extract is the best, if not the only tolerable form of criticism. But the critic is not alone in finding that, whether he carry his ass or ride upon it, he cannot please all his public. What has been said is probably enough, in the case of a writer whose work, though as a whole rather unjustly forgotten, survives in parts more securely even than the work of greater men, to remind readers of at least the outlines and bases of his claim to esteem. And the more those outlines are followed up, and the structure founded on those bases is examined, the more certain, I think, is Moore of recovering, not the position which M. Vallat would assign to him of the greatest lyrist of England (a position which he never held and never could hold except with very prejudiced or very incompetent judges), not that of the equal of Scott or Byron or Shelley or Wordsworth, but still a position high enough and singularly isolated at its height. Viewed from the point of strictly poetical criticism, he no doubt ranks only with those poets who have expressed easily and acceptably the likings and passions and thoughts and fancies of the average man, and who have expressed these with no extraordinary cunning or witchery. To go further in limitation, the average man, of whom he is thus the bard, is a rather sophisticated average man, without very deep thoughts or feelings, without a very fertile or fresh imagination or fancy, with even a touch —a little touch—of cant and "gush" and other defects incident to average and sophisticated humanity. But this humanity is at any time and every time no small portion of humanity at large, and it is to Moore's credit that he sings its feelings and its thoughts so as always to get the human and durable element in them visible and audible through the "trappings of convention." Again, he has that all-saving touch of humour which enables him, sentimentalist as he is, to be an admirable comedian as well. Yet again, he has at least something of the two qualities which one must demand of a poet who is a poet, and not a mere maker of rhymes. His note of feeling, if not full or deep, is true and real. His faculty of expression is not only considerable, but it is also distinguished; it is a faculty which in the same measure and degree nobody else has possessed. On one side he had the gift of singing those admirable songs of which we have been talking. On the other, he had the gift of right satiric verse to a degree which only three others of the great dead men of the century in England —Canning, Praed, and Thackeray—have reached[1]. Besides all this, he was a "considerable man of letters." But your considerable men of letters, after flourishing, turn to dust in their season, and other considerable or inconsiderable men of letters spring out of it. The true poets and even the true satirists abide, and both as a poet and a satirist Thomas Moore abides and will abide with them.

[1] I should add my then living but now dead friend H. D. Traill (1923).

VII

LEIGH HUNT

To compare the peaceful and home-keeping art of criticism to the adventurous one of lighthouse-building may seem an excursion into the heroi-comic, if not into the tragic-burlesque. Neither is it in the least my intention to dwell on a tolerably obvious metaphorical resemblance between the two. It is certainly the business of the critic to warn others off from the mistakes which have been committed by his forerunners, and perhaps (for let us anticipate the crushing wit) from his own. But that is not my reason for the suggestion. There is a story of I forget what lighthouse which Smeaton, or Stevenson, or somebody else, had unusual difficulty in establishing. The rock was too near the surface for it to be safe or practicable to moor barges over it; and it was uncovered for too short a time to enable any sohd foundations to be laid or even begun during one tide. So the engineer, with other adventurous persons, got himself landed on it, succeeded after a vain attempt or two in working an iron rod into the middle, and then hung on bodily while the tide was up, that he and his men might begin again as soon as it receded. In a mild and unexciting fashion, that is what the critic has to do—to dig about till he makes a lodgment in his author, hang on to it, and then begin to build. It is not always very easy work, and it is never less easy than in the case of the author whom somebody has kindly called "the Ariel of criticism." Leigh Hunt is an extremely difficult person upon whom to make any critical lodgment, for the reason that (I do not intend any disrespect by the comparison) he has much less of the rock about him than of the shifting sand. I do not now speak of the great Skimpole problem—we shall come to that presently—but merely of the writer as shown in his works.

The works themselves are not particularly easy to get together in any complete form, some of them being almost inextricably entangled in defunct periodicals, and others reappearing in different guises in the author's many published volumes. Mr Kent's bibliography gives forty-six different entries; Mr Alexander Ireland's (to which he refers) gives, I think, over eighty. Some years ago I remember receiving the catalogue of a second-hand bookseller who offered what he very frankly confessed to be far from a complete collection of the first editions, at the price of a score or two of pounds; and here at least the first are in some cases the only issues. Probably this is one reason why selections from Leigh Hunt, of which Mr Kent's is the latest and best, have been frequent. I have seen two certainly, and I think three, within as many years. Luckily, however, quite enough for the reader's if not for the critic's purpose is easily obtainable. The poems can be bought in more forms than one; Messrs Smith and Elder have reprinted cheaply the *Autobiography*, *Men, Women and Books*, *Imagination and Fancy*, *The Town*, *Wit and Humour*, *Table Talk*, and *A Jar of Honey*. Other reprints of *One Hundred Romances of Real Life* (one of his merest pieces of book-making) and of his *Stories from the Italian Poets*, one of his worst pieces of criticism, but agreeably reproduced in every respect save the hideous American spelling, have recently appeared. The complete and uniform issue, the want of which to some lovers of books (I own myself among them) is never quite made up by a scratch company of volumes of all dates, sizes, and prints, is indeed wanting. But still you can get a working Leigh Hunt together.

It is when you have got him that your trouble begins; and before it is done the critic, if he be one of those who are not satisfied with a mere *compte rendu*, is likely to acknowledge that Leigh Hunt, if "Ariel" be in some respects too complimentary a name for him, is at any rate a most tricksy spirit. The finest taste in some ways, contrasting with what can only be called the most horrible vulgarity in others; a light hand tediously boring again and again at obviously miscomprehended questions of religion, philosophy, and politics; a keen appetite for humour condescending to thin and repeated jests; a reviler of kings going out of his way laboriously to beslaver royalty; a man of letters, of talent almost touching genius, who seldom writes a dozen consecutive good pages:—these are only some of the inconsistencies that meet us in Leigh Hunt.

He has related the history of his immediate and remoter forbears with considerable minuteness—with more minuteness indeed by far than he has bestowed upon all but a few passages of his own life. For the general reader, however, it is quite sufficient to know that his father, the Reverend Isaac Hunt, who belonged to a clerical family in Barbados, went for his education to the still British Provinces of North America, married a Philadelphia girl, Mary Shewell, practised as a lawyer till the Revolution broke out, and then being driven from his adopted country as a loyalist, settled in England, took orders, drifted into Unitarianism or anythingarianism, and ended his days, after not infrequent visits to the King's Bench, comfortably enough, but hanging rather loose on society, his friends, and a pension. Leigh Hunt (his godfathers and godmothers gave him also the names of James Henry, which he dropped) was the youngest son, and was born on 19th October 1784. His best youthful remembrance, and one of the most really humorous things he ever said, was that he used, after a childish indulgence in bad language, to think to himself with a shudder when he received any mark of favour, "Ah! they little suspect I'm the boy who said 'd——n.'" But at seven years old he went to Christ's Hospital, and continued there for another seven. His reminiscences of that seminary, put down pretty early, and afterwards embodied in the *Autobiography*, are even better known from the fact that they served as a text, and as the occasion of a little gentle raillery, to Elia's famous essay than in themselves. For some years after leaving school he did nothing definite but write verses, which his father (who seems to have been gifted with a plentiful lack of judgment in most incidents and relations of life) published when the boy was but sixteen. They are as nearly as possible valueless, but they went through three editions in a very short time. It ought to be remembered that except Cowper, who was just dead, and Crabbe, who had for years intermitted writing, the public had only Rogers and Southey for poets, for it would none of the *Lyrical Ballads*, and the *Lay of the Last Minstrel* had not yet been published. So that it did not make one of its worst mistakes in taking up Leigh Hunt, who certainly had poetry in him, if he did not put it forth quite so early as this. He was made a kind of lion, but, fortunately or unfortunately for him, only in middle-class circles where there were no patrons. He was quite an old man— nearly twenty—when he made regular entry into the periodical writing which kept him (with the aid of his friends) for nearly sixty years. "Mr Town, Junior" (altered from an old signature of Colman's) contributed theatrical criticisms, which do not seem to have been paid for, to an evening paper, the *Traveller*, now[1] surviving as a second title to the *Globe*. His bent in this direction was assisted by the fact that his elder brother John had been apprenticed to a printer, and had desires to be a publisher. In January 1808, the two brothers started the *Examiner*, and Leigh Hunt edited it with a great deal of courage for fourteen years. He threw away for this the only piece of solid pre-ferment that he ever had, a clerkship in the War Office which Addington gave him. The references to this act of recklessness or self-sacrifice in the *Autobiography* are rather enigmatical. His two functions were no doubt incompatible at best, especially considering the violent Opposition tone which the *Examiner* took. But Leigh Hunt, whatever faults he had, was not quite a hypo-crite; and he hints pretty broadly that if he had not resigned he might have been asked to do so, not from any political reasons, but simply because he did his work very badly. He was much more at home in the *Examiner* (with which for a short time was joined the quarterly *Reflector*), though his warmest admirers can-didly admit that he knew nothing about politics. In 1809 he married a Miss Marianne Kent, whose station was not very exalted, and whose son admits with un-usual frankness that she was "the reverse of handsome, and without accomplishments," adding rather whimsi-cally that this person, "the reverse of handsome," had "a pretty figure, beautiful black hair and magnificent eyes," and though "without accomplishments" had "a very strong natural turn for plastic art." At any rate she seems to have suited Leigh Hunt admirably.

---

[1] And till yesterday; but not to-day (1923).

The *Examiner* soon became ill-noted with Government, but it was not till the end of 1812 that a grip could be got out of it. Leigh Hunt's offence is in the ordinary books rather undervalued. That he (or his contributor) called the Prince Regent, as is commonly said, "a fat Adonis of fifty" (the exact words are, "this Adonis in loveliness is a corpulent man of fifty") may have been the chief sting, but was certainly not the chief legal offence. Leigh Hunt called the ruler of his country "a violator of his word, a libertine over head and ears in disgrace, a despiser of domestic ties, the companion of demireps, a man who had just closed half a century without one single claim on the gratitude of his country or the respect of posterity." It might be true or it might be false; but certainly there was then not a country in Europe where it would have been allowed to be said of the chief of the state. And I am not sure that it could be said now[1] anywhere but in Ireland, where considerably worse things were said with impunity of Lord Spencer and Sir George Trevelyan. At any rate the brothers were prosecuted and fined five hundred pounds each, with two years' imprisonment. The sentence was carried out; but Leigh Hunt's imprisonment in Horsemonger Lane Gaol was the merest farce of incarceration. He could not indeed go beyond the prison walls. But he had a comfortable suite of rooms which he was permitted to furnish and decorate just as he liked; he was allowed to have his wife and family with him; he had a tiny garden of his own, and free access to that of the prison; there was no restriction on visitors, who brought him presents just as they chose; and he became a kind of fashion with the Opposition. Jeremy Bentham came and played at battledore and shuttlecock with him—an almost

[1] 1887 (1923).

appalling idea, for it will not do to trust too implicitly to Leigh Hunt's declaration that Jeremy's object was to suggest "an improvement in the constitution of shuttlecocks." The *Examiner* itself continued undisturbed, and except for the "I can't get out" feeling, which even of itself cannot be compared for one moment to that of a modern prisoner condemned to his cell and the exercising-ground, it is rather difficult to see much reason for Leigh Hunt's complaints. The imprisonment may have affected his health, but it certainly brought him troops of friends, and gave him leisure to do not only his journalist's work, but things much more serious. Here he wrote and published his first poem since the *Juvenilia*, *A Feast of the Poets* (not much of a thing), and here he wrote, though he did not publish it till his liberation, the *Story of Rimini*, by far his most important poem, both for intrinsic character and for influence on others. He had known Lamb from boyhood, and Shelley some years; he now made the acquaintance of Keats, Hazlitt, and Byron.

In the next five years after his liberation he did a great deal of work, the best by far being the periodical called the *Indicator*, a weekly paper which ran for sixty-six numbers. The *Indicator* was the first thing that I ever read of Hunt's, and, by no means for that reason only, I think it the best. Its buttonholing papers, of a kind since widely imitated, were the most popular; but there are romantic things in it, such as *The Daughter of Hippocrates* (paraphrased and expanded from Sir John Mandeville with Hunt's peculiar skill), which seem to me better. It was at the end of these five years that Leigh Hunt resolved upon the second adventure (his imprisonment being the first and involuntary) of his otherwise easy-going life—an adventure the immediate consequences of which were unfortunate in many ways, but which supplied him with a good deal of literary material. This was his visit to Italy as a kind of literary *attaché* to Lord Byron, and editor of a quarterly magazine, the *Liberal*. The idea was Shelley's, and if Shelley had lived, it might not have resulted quite so disastrously, for Shelley was absolutely untiring as a helper of lame dogs over stiles. As it was, the excursion distinctly contradicted the saying (condemned by some as immoral) that a bad beginning makes a good ending. The Hunt family, which now included several children, embarked, in November of all months in the year, on a small ship bound for Italy. They were something like a month getting down the Channel in tremendous weather, and at last when their ship had to turn tail from near Scilly and run into Dartmouth, Hunt, whose wife was extremely ill of lung-disease, made up his mind to stay for the winter in Devonshire. He passed the time pleasantly enough at Plymouth, which they left once more in May, 1822, reaching Leghorn at the end of June. Shelley's death happened within ten days of their arrival, and Byron and Leigh Hunt were left to get on together. How badly they got on is pretty generally known, might have been foreseen from the beginning, and is not very profitable to dwell on. Leigh Hunt's mixture of familiarity and "airs" could not have been worse mixed to suit the taste of Byron. The "noble poet" too was not a person who liked to be spunged upon; and his coolest admirers may sympathise with his disgust when he found that he had upon his hands a man of letters with a large family whom he was literally expected to keep, whose society was disagreeable to him, who lampooned his friends, who differed with him on every point of taste, and who did not think it necessary to be grateful. For Leigh Hunt, somewhat on Lamb's system of compensation for coming late by going away early, combined his readiness to receive favours with a practice of not acknowledging the slightest obligation for them. Byron's departure for Greece was in its way lucky, but it left Hunt stranded. He remained in Italy for rather more than three years and then returned home across the Continent. The *Liberal*, which contains work of his, of Byron's, of Shelley's, and of Hazlitt's, is interesting enough and worth buying in its original form, but it did not pay. Of the unlucky book on his relations with Byron which followed—the worst act by far of his life —I shall not say much. No one has attempted to defend it, and he himself apologises for it frankly and fully in his *Autobiography*. It is impossible, however, not to remark that the offence was much aggravated by its deliberate character. For the book was not published in the heat of the moment, but three years after Hunt's return to England and four after Byron's death.

The remaining thirty years of Hunt's life were wholly literary. As for residences, he hovered about London, living successively at Highgate, Epsom, Brompton, Chelsea, Kensington, and divers other places. At Chelsea he was very intimate with the Carlyles, and, while he was perhaps of all living men of letters most leniently judged by those not particularly lenient judges, we have nowhere such vivid glimpses of Hunt's peculiar weaknesses as in the memoirs of Carlyle and his wife. Why Leigh Hunt was always in such difficulties is not at first obvious, for he was the reverse of an idle man; he seems, though thriftless, to have been by no means very sumptuous in his way of living; everybody helped him, and his writing was always popular. He appears to have felt not a little sore that nothing was done for him when his political friends came into power after the Reform Bill—and remained there for almost the whole of the rest of his life. He had certainly in some senses borne the burden and heat of the day for Liberalism. But he was one of those reckless people who, without meaning to offend anybody in particular, offend friends as well as foes; the days of sinecures were even then passing or passed; and it is very difficult to conceive any office, even with the lightest duties, in which Leigh Hunt would not have come to grief. As for his writing, his son's earnest plea as to his not being an idle man is no doubt true enough, but he never seems to have reconciled himself to the regular drudgery of miscellaneous article writing for newspapers which is almost the only kind of journalism that really pays, and his books did not sell very largely. In his latter days, however, things became easier for him. The unfailing kindness of the Shelley family gave him (in 1844 when Sir Percy Shelley came into his property) a regular annuity of £120; two royal gifts of £200 each and in 1847 a pension of the same amount were added; and two benefit nights of Dickens's famous amateur company brought him in something like a cool thousand, as Dickens himself would have said. Of his last years Mr Kent, who was intimate with him, gives much the pleasantest account known to me. He died on 28th August, 1859, surviving his wife only two years.

I can imagine some one, at the name of Dickens in the preceding paragraph, thinking or saying, that if the author of *Bleak House* raised a thousand pounds for his old friend, he took the value of it and infinitely more out of him. It is impossible to shirk the Skimpole affair in any really critical notice of Leigh Hunt. To put unpleasant things briefly, that famous character was at once recognised by every one as a caricature, perhaps ill-natured but certainly brilliant, of what an enemy might have said of the author of *Rimini*. Thornton Hunt, the eldest of Leigh Hunt's children, and a writer of no small power, took the matter up and forced from Dickens a contradiction, or disavowal, with which I am afraid the recording angel must have had some little difficulty. Strangely enough the last words of Macaulay's that we have concern this affair; and they may be quoted as Sir George Trevelyan gives them, written by his uncle in those days at Holly Lodge when the shadow of death was heavy on him.

December 23, 1859. An odd declaration by Dickens that he did not mean Leigh Hunt by Harold Skimpole. Yet he owns that he took the light externals of the character from Leigh Hunt, and surely it is by those light externals that the bulk of mankind will always recognise character. Besides, it is to be observed that the vices of H. S. are vices to which L. H. had, to say the least, some little leaning, and which the world generally attributed to him most unsparingly. That he had loose notions of *meum* and *tuum*; that he had no high feeling of independence; that he had no sense of obligation; that he took money wherever he could get it; that he felt no gratitude for it; that he was just as ready to defame a person who had relieved his distress as a person who had refused him relief—these were things which, as Dickens must have known, were said, truly or falsely, about L. H., and had made a deep impression on the public mind.

Now Macaulay has not always been leniently judged; but I do not think that, with the single exception of Croker's case, he can be accused of having borne hardly on the moral character of any one of his contemporaries. He had befriended Leigh Hunt in every way; he had got him into the *Edinburgh*; he had lent (that is to say given) him money freely, and I do not think that his fiercest enemy can seriously think that he bore Hunt a grudge for having told him, as he himself records, that the *Lays* were not so good as Spenser, whom Macaulay in one of the rare lapses of his memory had unjustly blasphemed, and whom Leigh Hunt adored. To my mind, if there were any doubt about Dickens's intention, or about the fitting in a certain sense of the cap, this testimony of Macaulay's would settle it. But I cannot conceive any doubt remaining in the mind of any person who has read Leigh Hunt's works, who has even read the *Autobiography*. Of the grossest faults in Skimpole's character, such as the selling of Jo's secret, Leigh Hunt was indeed incapable, and the insertion of these is at once a blot on Dickens's memory and a kind of excuse for his disclaimer; but as regards the lighter touches the likeness is unmistakable. Skimpole's most elaborate jests about "pounds" are hardly an exaggeration of the man who gravely and more than once tells us that his difficulties and irregularities with money came from a congenital incapacity to appreciate arithmetic, and who admits that Shelley (whose affairs he knew very well) once gave him no less than fourteen hundred pounds (that is to say, some sixteen months of Shelley's income at his wealthiest) to clear him, and that he was not cleared, though apparently he gave Shelley to understand that he was.

There are many excuses for him which Skimpole had not. His own pleas of tropical blood and so forth will not greatly avail. But the old patron-theory and its more subtle transformation (the influence of which is sometimes shown even by Thackeray in the act of denouncing it), to the effect that the State or the public, or somebody, is bound to look after your man of genius, had bitten deep into the being of the literary man of our grandfathers' time. Anybody who has read *Thomas Poole and his Friends* must have seen how not merely Coleridge, of whose known liability to the weakness the book furnished new proofs, but even, to some extent and vicariously, the austere Wordsworth, cherished the idea. But for the most part, men kept it to themselves. Leigh Hunt never could keep anything to himself, and

he has left record on record of the easy manner in which
he acted on his beliefs.

For this I own that I care little, especially since he
never borrowed money of me. There is a Statute of
Limitations for all such things in letters as well as in
law. What is much harder to forgive is the ill-bred
pertness, often if not always innocent enough in intention, but rather the worse than the better for that,
which mars so much of his actual literary work. When
almost an old man he wrote—when a very old man he
quotes, with childlike surprise that any one should see
anything objectionable in them—the following lines:

> Perhaps you have known what it is to feel longings,
> To pat buxom shoulders at routs and mad throngings—
> Well—think what it was at a vision like that!
> A Grace after dinner! a Venus grown fat!

It would be almost unbelievable of any man but
Leigh Hunt that he placidly remarks in reference to
this impertinence that "he had not the pleasure of
Lady Blessington's acquaintance," as if that did not
make things ten times worse. He had laid the foundation of not a few of the literary enmities he suffered
from, by writing, thirty years earlier, a *Feast of the
Poets*, on the pattern of Suckling, in which he took,
though much more excusably, the same kind of ill-bred
liberties; and similar things abound in his works. It is
scarcely surprising that the good Macvey Napier (rather
awkwardly, and giving Macaulay much trouble to patch
things up) should have said that he would like a
"gentleman-like" article from Mr Hunt for the
Edinburgh; and the taunt about the Cockney School
undoubtedly derived its venom from this weakness of
his. Lamb was not descended from the kings that long
the Tuscan sceptre swayed, and had some homely ways;
Keats had to do with livery-stables, Hazlitt with shady

lodging-houses and lodging-house keepers. But Keats might have been, whatever his weaknesses, his own and Spenser's Sir Calidore for gentle feeling and conduct; the man who called Lamb vulgar would only prove his own vulgarity; and Hazlitt, though he had some darker stains on his character than any that rest on Hunt, was far too potent a spirit for the fire within him not to burn out mere vulgarity. Leigh Hunt I fear must be allowed to be now and then merely vulgar—a Pogson of talent, of genius, of immense amiability, of rather hard luck, but still of the Pogsons, Pogsonic.

As I shall have plenty of good to say of him, I may as well despatch at once whatever else I have to say that is bad, which is little. The faults of taste which have just been noticed passed easily into occasional, though only occasional, faults of criticism. I do not recommend anybody who has not the faculty of critical adjustment, and who wants to like Leigh Hunt, to read his essay on Dante in the *Italian Poets*. For flashes of crass insensibility to great poetry it is difficult to match anywhere, and impossible to match in Leigh Hunt. His favourite theological doctrine, like that of Béranger's hero, was, *Ne damnons personne.* He did not like monarchy, and he did not understand metaphysics. So the great poet, who, more than any other great poet except Shakespeare, grows on those who read him, receives from Leigh Hunt not an honest confession, like Sir Walter's, that he does not like him, which is perhaps the first honest impression of the majority of Dante's readers, but tirade upon tirade of abuse and bad criticism. Further, Leigh Hunt's unfortunate necessity of preserving his own journalism has made him keep a thousand things that he ought to have left to the kindly shade of the newspaper files—a cemetery where, thank Heaven, the tombs are not open as in the other city of Dis. The book called *Table Talk*, for instance, contains, with a little better matter, chiefly mere rubbish like this section:

BEAUMARCHAIS

Beaumarchais, author of the celebrated comedy of "Figaro," an abridgment of which has been rendered more famous by the music of Mozart, made a large fortune by supplying the American republicans with arms and ammunition, and lost it by speculations in salt and printing. His comedy is one of those productions which are accounted dangerous, from developing the spirit of intrigue and gallantry with more gaiety than objection; and they would be more unanimously so, if the good humour and self-examination to which they excite did not suggest a spirit of charity and inquiry beyond themselves.

Leigh Hunt tried almost every conceivable kind of literature, including a historical novel, *Sir Ralph Esher*, several dramas (one or two of which, the *Legend of Florence* being the chief, got acted), and at nearly the beginning and nearly the end of his career two religious works, or works on religion, an attack on Methodism and *The Religion of the Heart*. All this we may not unkindly brush away, and consider him first as a poet, secondly as a critic, and thirdly as what can be best, though rather unphilosophically, called a miscellanist.

Few good judges nowadays, I think, would deny that Leigh Hunt had a certain faculty for poetry, and fewer still would rank it very high. To something like, but less than, the tunefulness of Moore, he joined a very much better taste in models and an infinitely wider and deeper study of them. There is no doubt that his versification in *Rimini* (which may be described as Chaucerian in basis with a strong admixture of Dryden, further crossed and dashed slightly with the peculiar music of the followers of Spenser, especially Browne and Wither) had a very strong influence both on Keats and on Shelley, and that it drew from them music much better than itself. This fluent, musical, many-coloured verse was a capital medium for tale-telling, and Leigh Hunt is always at his best when he employs it. The more varied measures and the more ambitious aim of *Captain Sword and Captain Pen* seem to me very much less successful. Not only was Leigh Hunt far from strong enough for a serious argument, but the cheery, sentimental optimism of which he was one of the most persevering exponents—the kind of thing which vehemently protests that in the good time coming nobody shall be damned, or starved, or put in prison, or subjected to the perils of villainous saltpetre, or prevented from doing just what he likes, and that all existence ought to be and shortly will be a vaguely refined beer and skittles—did not lend itself very well to verse. Nor are Hunt's lyrics particularly strong. His best thing by far is the charming trifle (the heroine[1] being, it has been said and also denied, Mrs Carlyle) which he called a "rondeau," though it is not one.

> Jenny kissed me when we met,
> Jumping from the chair she sat in:
> Time, you thief, who love to get
> Sweets into your list, put *that* in!
> Say I'm weary, say I'm sad,
> Say that health and wealth have missed me,
> Say I'm growing old—but add,
>   Jenny kissed me.

Even here it may be noticed that though the last four lines could hardly be bettered, the second couplet is rather weak. Some of Leigh Hunt's sonnets, especially that which he wrote on the Nile in rivalry with Shelley and Keats, are very good.

> It flows through old hushed Egypt and its sands,
> Like some grave mighty thought threading a dream;
> And times and things, as in that vision, seem
> Keeping along it their eternal stands;—

---

[1] She was originally "Nelly" not "Jenny"; but this can be worked both ways (1923)

Caves, pillars, pyramids, the shepherd-bands
That roamed through the young earth, the glory extreme
Of high Sesostris, and that southern beam,
The laughing queen that caught the world's great hands.
Then comes a mightier silence, stern and strong,
As of a world left empty of its throng,
And the void weighs on us; and then we wake,
And hear the fruitful stream lapsing along
'Twixt villages, and think how we shall take
Our own calm journey on for human sake.

This was written in 1818, and I think it will be admitted that the italicised line is a rediscovery of a cadence which had been lost for centuries, and which has been constantly borrowed and imitated since.

Every now and then he had touches of something much above his usual style, as in the concluding lines of the whimsical "flyting," as the Scotch poets of the fifteenth century would have called it, between the Man and the Fish:

Man's life is warm, glad, sad, 'twixt loves and graves,
    Boundless in hope, honoured with pangs austere,
Heaven-gazing; and his angel-wings he craves:
    The fish is swift, small-needing, vague yet clear,
A cold, sweet, silver life, wrapped in round waves,
    Quickened with touches of transporting fear.

As a rule, however, his poetry has little or nothing of this kind, and he will hold his place in the English *corpus poetarum*, first, because he was an associate of better poets than himself; secondly, because he invented a medium for the poetic tale which was as poetical as Crabbe's was prosaic; thirdly, because of all persons perhaps who have ever attempted English verse on their own account, he had the most genuine affection for, and the most intimate and extensive acquaintance with, the triumphs of his predecessors in poetry. Of prose he was a much less trustworthy judge, as may be instanced once for all by his pronouncing Gibbon's style to be bad; but of poetry he could tell with an extraordinary mixture of sympathy and discretion.

And this will introduce us to his second faculty, the faculty of literary criticism, in which he is, with all his drawbacks, on a level with Coleridge, with Lamb, and with Hazlitt, his defects as compared with them being in each case made up by compensatory, or more than compensatory, merits.

How considerable a critic Leigh Hunt was, may be judged from the fact that he himself confesses the great critical fault of his principal poem—the selection, for amplification and paraphrase, of a subject which has once for all been treated with imperial and immortal brevity by a great poet. With equal ingenuousness and equal truth he further confesses that, at the time, he not only did not see this fault, but was critically incapable of seeing it. For there is that one comfort about this discomfortable and discredited art of ours, that age at any rate does not impair it. The first sprightly runnings of criticism are never the best; and in the case of all really great critics, from Dryden to Sainte-Beuve, the critical faculty has gone on constantly increasing. The chief examples of Leigh Hunt's critical accomplishment are to be found in the two books called respectively, *Wit and Humour*, and *Imagination and Fancy*, both being selections from the English poets, with critical remarks interspersed as a sort of running commentary. But hardly any book of his is quite barren of such examples; for he neither would, nor indeed apparently could, restrain his desultory fancy from this as from other indulgences. His criticism is very distinct in kind. It is almost purely and in the strict and proper sense æsthetic—that is to say, it does hardly anything but reproduce the sensations produced upon Hunt himself by the reading of his favourite passages. As his sense of poetry was extraordinarily keen and accurate, there is perhaps no body of "beauties" of English poetry to be found anywhere in the language which is selected with such uniform and unerring judgment as this or these. Even Lamb, in his own favourite subjects and authors, misses treasure-trove which Leigh Hunt unfailingly discovers, as in the now pretty generally acknowledged case of the character of De Flores in Middleton's *Changeling*. And Lamb had a much less wide and a much more crotchety system of admissions and exclusions. Macaulay was perfectly right in fixing, at the beginning of his essay on the dramatists of the Restoration, upon this catholicity of Hunt's taste as the main merit in it; and it is really a great pity that the two volumes referred to were not, as they were intended to be, followed up by others respectively devoted to Action and Passion, Contemplation, and Song. But Leigh Hunt was sixty when he planned them, and age, infirmity, perhaps also the less pressing need which the comparative affluence of his later years brought, prevented the completion. It has also to be remarked that Hunt is much better as a taster than as a professor or expounder. He says, indeed, many happy things about his favourite passages, but they evidently represent rather afterthought than forethought. He is not good at generalities, and when he tries them is apt, instead of flying (as an Ariel of criticism should do), to sprawl. Yet it was impossible for a man who was so almost invariably right in particulars to go very wrong in general; and the worst that can be said of Leigh Hunt's general critical axioms and conclusions is that they are much better than the reasons that support them. For instance, he is probably right in calling the famous "intellectual" and "henpecked you all" in *Don Juan*, "the happiest triple rhyme ever written." But when he goes on to say that " the sweepingness of the assumption completes the flowing breadth of the effect," he goes very near to talking nonsense. For most people, however, a true opinion persuasively stated is of much more consequence than the most elaborate logical justification of it; and it is this that makes Leigh Hunt's criticism such excellent good reading. It is impossible not to feel that when a guide (which after all a critic should be) is recommended with cautions that, though an invaluable fellow for the most part, he is not unlikely in certain places to lead the traveller over a precipice, it is a very dubious kind of recommendation. Yet this is the way in which one has to speak of Jeffrey and Hazlitt, of Wilson and De Quincey. Of Leigh Hunt it need hardly ever be said; for in the unlucky diatribes on Dante above cited, the most unwary reader can see that his author has lost his temper and with it his head. As a rule he avoids the things that he is not qualified to judge, such as the rougher and sublimer parts of poetry. Of its sweetness and its music, of its grace and its wit, of its tenderness and its fancy, no better judge ever existed than Leigh Hunt. He jumped at such things, when he came near them, almost as involuntarily as a needle to a magnet.

He was, however, perhaps most popular in his own time, and certainly he gained most of the not excessive share of pecuniary profit which fell to his lot, as what I have called a miscellanist. One of the things which have not yet been sufficiently done in the criticism of English literary history, is a careful review of the successive steps by which the periodical essay of Addison and his followers during the eighteenth century passed into the magazine-paper of our own days. The later examples of the eighteenth century, the *Observers* and *Connoisseurs*, the *Loungers* and *Mirrors* and *Lookers-On*, are fairly well worth reading in themselves, especially as the little volumes of the *British Essayists* go capitally in a travelling-bag; but the gap between them and the productions of Leigh Hunt, of Lamb, and of the *Blackwood* men, with Praed's schoolboy attempts not left out, is a very considerable one. Leigh Hunt is himself entitled to a high place in the new school so far as mere priority goes, and to one not low in actual merit. He relates himself, more than once, with the childishness which is the good side of his Skimpolism, how not merely his literary friends but persons of quality had special favourites among the miscellaneous papers of the *Indicator*, like (he would certainly have used the parallel himself if he had known it or thought of it) the Court of France with Marot's Psalms. This miscellaneous work of his extends, as it ought to do, to all manner of subjects. The pleasantest example to my fancy is the book called *The Town*, a gossiping description of London from St Paul's to St James's, which he afterwards followed up with books on the West End and Kensington, and which, though of course second-hand as to its facts, is by no means uncritical, and by far the best reading of any book of its kind. Even the *Autobiography* might take rank in this class; and the same kind of stuff made up the staple of the numerous periodicals which Leigh Hunt edited or wrote, and of the still more numerous books which he compounded out of the dead periodicals. It may be that a severe criticism will declare that, here as well as elsewhere, he was more original than accomplished; and that his way of treating subjects was pursued with better success by his imitators than by himself. Such a paper, for instance, as *On Beds and Bedrooms* suggests (and is dwarfed by the suggestion) Lamb's *Convalescent* and other similar work. *Jack Abbott's Breakfast*, which is, or was, exceedingly popular with

Hunt's admirers, is an account of the misfortunes of a luckless young man who goes to breakfast with an absent-minded pedagogue, and, being turned away empty, orders successive refreshments at different coffee-houses, each of which proves a feast of Tantalus. The idea is not bad; but the carrying out suits the stage better than the study, and is certainly far below such things as Maginn's adventures of Jack Ginger and his friends, with the tale untold that Humphries told Harlow. *A Few Remarks on the Rare Vice called Lying* is a most promising title; he must be a very good-natured judge who finds appended to it a performing article. *The Old Lady* and *The Old Gentleman* were once great favourites; they seem to have been studied from Earle's *Microcosmography*, not the least excellent of the books that have proceeded from foster-children of Walter de Merton, but they are over-laboured in particulars. So too are *The Adventures of Carfington Blundell* and *Inside of an Omnibus*. Leigh Hunt's humour is so devoid of bitterness that it sometimes becomes insipid; his narrative so fluent and gossiping that it sometimes becomes insignificant. His enemies called him immoral, which appears to have been a gross calumny so far as his private life was concerned, and is certainly a gross exaggeration as regards his writing. But he was rather too much given to dally about voluptuous subjects with a sort of chuckling epicene triviality. He is so far from being passionate that he sometimes becomes almost offensive. He is terribly apt to labour a conceit or a prettiness till it becomes vapid; and his *Criticism on Female Beauty*, though it contains some extremely sensible remarks, also contains much which is suggestive of Mr Tupman. Yet his miscellaneous writing has one great merit (besides its gentle playfulness and its untiring variety) which might procure pardon for worse faults. With no one perhaps are those literary memories which transform and vivify life so constantly present as with Leigh Hunt. Although the world was a perfectly real thing to him, and not by any means seen only through the windows of a library, he took everywhere with him the remembrances of what he had read, and they helped him to clothe and colour what he saw and what he wrote. Between him, therefore, and readers who themselves have read a good deal, and loved what they have read not a little, there is always something in common; and yet probably no bookish writer has been less resented by his unbookish readers as a thruster of the abominable things— superior knowledge and superior scholarship—upon them. Some vices of the snob Leigh Hunt undoubtedly had, but he was never in the least a pretentious snob. He quotes his books not in the spirit of a man who is looking down on his fellows from a proper elevation, but in the spirit of a kindly host who is anxious that his guests should enjoy the good things on his table.

It is this sincere and unostentatious love of letters, and anxiety to spread the love of letters, that is the redeeming point of Leigh Hunt throughout: he is saved *quia multum amavit.* It was this which prompted that rather grandiose but still admirable palinode of Christopher North, in August, 1834,—"the Animosities are mortal: but the Humanities live for ever,"—an apology which naturally enough pleased Hunt very much. He is one of those persons with whom it is impossible to be angry, or at least to be angry long. "The bailiff who took him was fond of him," it is recorded of Captain Costigan; and in milder moments the same may be said of the critical bailiffs who are compelled to "take" Leigh Hunt. Even in his least happy books (such as the *Jar of Honey from Mount Hybla,* where all sorts of matter, some of it by no means well known to the writer, have been hastily cobbled together) this love, and for the most part intelligent and animated love, for literature appears. If in another of his least happy attempts, the critical parts of the already mentioned *Stories from the Italian Poets*, he is miles below the great argument of Dante, and if he is even guilty to some extent of vulgarising the lesser but still great poets with whom he deals, he never comes, even in Dante, to any passage he can understand without exhibiting such a warmth of enthusiasm and enjoyment that it softens the stoniest readers. He can gravely call Dante's Hell "geologically speaking a most fantastical formation" (which it certainly is), and joke clumsily about the poet's putting Cunizza and Rahab in Paradise. He can write, in the true spirit of vulgarising, that "the Florentine is thought to have been less strict in his conduct in regard to the sex than might be supposed from his platonical aspirations," heedless of the great confessions implied in the swoon at Francesca's story, and the passage through the fire at the end of the seventh circle of Purgatory. But when he comes to things like "Dolce color d' oriental zaffiro," and "Era già l'ora," it is hardly possible to do more justice to the subject. The whole description of his Italian sojourn in the *Autobiography* is an example of the best kind of such writing. Again, of all the people who have rejoiced in Samuel Pepys, Leigh Hunt "does it most natural," being indeed a kind of nineteenth-century Pepys himself, whom the gods had made less comfortable in worldly circumstances and no man of business, but to whom as a compensation they had given the feeling for poetry which Samuel lacked. At different times Dryden, Spenser, and Chaucer were respectively his favourite English poets; and as there was nothing faithless in his inconstancy, he took up his new loves without ceasing to love the old. It is perhaps rather more surprising that he should have liked Spenser than that he should have liked the other two; and we must suppose that the profusion of beautiful pictures in the *Faerie Queene* enabled him, not to appreciate (for he never could have done that), but to tolerate or pass over the deep melancholy and the occasional philosophisings of the poet. But the attraction of Dryden and Chaucer for him is very easily understood. Both are eminently cheerful poets, Dryden with the cheerfulness born of manly sense, Chaucer with that of youth and abounding animal spirits. Leigh Hunt seems to have found this cheerfulness as akin to his own, as the vigour of both was complementary and satisfactory to his own, I shall not say weakness, but fragility. Add yet again to this that Hunt seems—a thing very rarely to be said of critics—never to have disliked a thing simply because he could not understand it. If he sometimes abused Dante, it was not merely because he could not understand him, though he certainly could not, but because Dante trod (and when Dante treads he treads heavily) on his most cherished prejudices. Now he had not very many prejudices, and so he had an advantage here also.

Lastly, as he may be read with pleasure, so he may be skipped without shame. There are some writers whom to skip may seem to a conscientious devotee of letters both wicked and unwise—wicked because it is disrespectful to them, unwise because it is quite likely to inflict loss on the reader. Now nobody can ever think of respecting Leigh Hunt; he is not unfrequently amiable, but never in the least venerable. Even at his best he seldom or never affects the reader with admiration, only with a mild pleasure. It is at once a penalty for his sins and a compliment to his good qualities, that to make any kind of fuss over him would be absurd. Nor is there any selfish risk run by treating him, in the literary sense, in an unceremonious manner. His writing of all kinds carries desultoriness to the height; and may be begun at the beginning, or at the end, or in the middle, and left off at any place, without the least risk of serious loss. He is excellent good company for half an hour, sometimes for much longer; but the reader rarely thinks very much of what he has said when the interview is over, and never experiences any violent hunger or thirst for its renewal, though such renewal is agreeable enough in its way. Such an author is a convenient possession on the shelves: a possession so convenient that occasionally a blush of shame may suggest itself at the thought that he should be treated so cavalierly. But this is quixotic. The very best things that he has done hardly deserve more respectful treatment, for they are little more than a faithful and fairly lively description of his own enjoyments; the worst things deserve treatment much less respectful. Yet let us not leave him with a harsh mouth; for, as has been said, he loved the good literature of others very much, and he wrote not a little that was good literature of his own[1].

---

[1] I might almost repeat here *mutatis mutandis* the note above on Hazlitt (p. 133). But one important addition occurs. Mr Milford's edition of the *Poems* (Oxford, 1922) reinforces Hunt's claims as a poet very notably—for instance, in giving the extremely pretty piece of *The Nymphs* (1923).

VIII

WILSON

AMONG those judgments of his contemporaries which make a sort of Inferno of the posthumous writings of Thomas Carlyle, that passed upon "Christopher North" has always seemed to me the most interesting, and perhaps on the whole the fairest. There is enough and to spare of onesidedness in it, and of the harshness which comes from onesidedness. But it is hardly at all sour, and, when allowance is made for the point of view, by no means unjust. The whole is interesting from the literary side, but as it fills two large pages it is much too long to quote. The personal description, "the broad-shouldered stately bulk of the man struck me: his flashing eye, copious dishevelled head of hair, and rapid unconcerned progress like that of a plough through stubble," is characteristically graphic, and far the best of the numerous pen sketches of "the Professor." As for the criticism, the following is the kernel passage of it:—

Wilson had much nobleness of heart and many traits of noble genius, but the central tie-beam seemed wanting always; very long ago I perceived in him the most irreconcilable contradictions: Toryism with sansculottism; Methodism of a sort with total incredulity; a noble loyal and religious nature not strong enough to vanquish the perverse element it is born into. Hence a being all split into precipitous chasms and the wildest volcanic tumults; rocks overgrown indeed with tropical luxuriance of leaf and flower but knit together at the bottom—that was my old figure of speech —only by an ocean of whisky punch. On these terms nothing can be done. Wilson seems to me always by far the most *gifted* of our literary men either then or still. And yet intrinsically he has written nothing that can endure. The central gift was wanting.

Something in the unfavourable part of this must no doubt be set down to the critic's usual forgetfulness of his own admirable dictum, "he is not thou, but himself; other than thou." John was quite other than Thomas, and Thomas judged him somewhat summarily as if he were a failure of a Thomas. Yet the criticism, if partly harsh and as a whole somewhat incomplete, is true enough. Wilson has written "intrinsically nothing that can endure," if it be judged by any severe test. An English Diderot, he must bear a harder version of the judgment on Diderot, that he had written good pages but no good book. Only very rarely has he even written good pages, in the sense of pages good throughout. The almost inconceivable haste with which he wrote (he is credited with having on one occasion actually written fifty-six pages of print for *Blackwood* in two days, and in the years of its double numbers he often contributed from a hundred to a hundred and fifty pages in a single month)—this prodigious haste would not of itself account for the puerilities, the touches of bad taste, the false pathos, the tedious burlesque, the more tedious jactation which disfigure his work. A man writing against time may be driven to dulness, or commonplace, or inelegance of style; but he need never commit any of the faults just noticed. They were due beyond doubt, in Wilson's case, to a natural idiosyncrasy, the great characteristic of which Carlyle has happily hit off in the phrase, "want of a tie-beam," whether he has or has not been charitable in suggesting that the missing link was supplied by whisky punch. The least attractive point about Wilson's work is undoubtedly what his censor elsewhere describes as his habit of "giving a kick" to many men and things. There is no more unpleasant feature of the *Noctes* than the apparent inability of the writer to refrain from sly "kicks" even at the objects of his greatest veneration. A kind of mania of detraction seizes him at times, a mania which some of his admirers have more kindly than wisely endeavoured to shuffle off as a humorous dramatic touch intentionally administered to him by his Eidolon North. The most disgraceful, perhaps the only really disgraceful, instance of this is the carping and offensive criticism of Scott's *Demonology*, written and published at a time when Sir Walter's known state of health and fortunes might have protected him even from an enemy, much more from a friend, and a deeply obliged friend such as Wilson. Nor is this the only fling at Scott. Wordsworth, much more vulnerable, is also much more frequently assailed; and even Shakespeare does not come off scot-free when Wilson is in his ugly moods.

It need hardly be said that I have no intention of saying that Scott or Wordsworth or Shakespeare may not be criticised. It is the way in which the criticism is done which is the crime; and for these acts of literary high treason, or at least leasing-making, as well as for all Wilson's other faults, nothing seems to me so much responsible as the want of bottom which Carlyle notes. I do not think that Wilson had any solid fund of principles, putting morals and religion aside, either in politics or in literature. He liked and he hated much and strongly, and being a healthy creature he on the whole liked the right things and hated the wrong ones; but it was for the most part a merely instinctive liking and hatred, quite un-coördinated, and by no means unlikely to pass the next moment into hatred or liking as the case might be.

These are grave faults. But for the purpose of providing that pleasure which is to be got from literature (and this, like one or two other chapters here, is partly an effort in literary hedonism) Wilson stands very high, indeed so high that he can be ranked only below the highest. He who will enjoy him must be an intelligent voluptuary, and especially well versed in the art of skipping. When Wilson begins to talk fine, when he begins to wax pathetic, and when he gets into many others of his numerous altitudes, it will behove the reader, according to his own tastes, to skip with discretion and vigour. If he cannot do this, if his eye is not wary enough, or if his conscience forbids him to obey his eyes' warnings, Wilson is not for him. It is true that Mr Skelton has tried to make a "Comedy of the *Noctes Ambrosianæ*," in which the skipping is done ready to hand. But, with all the respect due to the author of *Thalatta*, the process is not, at least speaking according to my judgment, successful. No one can really taste that eccentric book unless he reads it as a whole; its humours arbitrarily separated and cut-and-dried are nearly unintelligible. Indeed Professor Ferrier's original attempt to give Wilson's work only, and not all of that work when it happened to be mixed with others, seems to me to have been a mistake. But of that further, when we come to speak of the *Noctes* themselves.

Wilson's life, for more than two-thirds of it a very happy one and not devoid of a certain eventfulness, can be summarised pretty briefly, especially as a full account of it is available in the very delightful work of his daughter Mrs Gordon. Born in 1785, the son of a rich manufacturer of Paisley and a mother who boasted gentle blood, he was brought up first in the house of a country minister (whose parish he has made famous in several sketches), then at the University of Glasgow, and then at Magdalen College, Oxford. He was early left possessor of a considerable fortune, and his first love, a certain "Margaret," having proved unkind, he established himself at Elleray on Windermere and entered into all the Lake society. Before very long (he was twenty-six at the time) he married Miss Jane Penny, daughter of a Liverpool merchant, and kept open house at Elleray for some years. Then his fortune disappeared in the keeping of a dishonest relation, and he had, in a way, his livelihood to make. I say "in a way," because the wind appears to have been considerably tempered to this shorn but robust lamb. He had not even to give up Elleray, though he could not live there in his old style. He had a mother who was able and willing to entertain him at Edinburgh, on the sole understanding that he did not "turn Whig," of which there was very little danger. He was enabled to keep not too exhausting or anxious terms as an advocate at the Scottish bar; and before long he was endowed, against the infinitely superior claims of Sir William Hamilton, and by sheer force of personal and political influence, with the lucrative Professorship of Moral Philosophy in the University of Edinburgh. But even before this he had been exempted from the necessity of cultivating literature on a little oatmeal by his connection with *Blackwood's Magazine.* The story of that magazine has often been told; never perhaps quite fully, but sufficiently. Wilson was not at any time, strictly speaking, editor; and a statement under his own hand avers that he never received any editorial pay, and was sometimes subject to that criticism which the publisher, as all men know from a famous letter of Scott's, was sometimes in the habit of exercising rather indiscreetly. But for a very great number of years, there is no doubt that he held a kind of quasi-editorial position, which included the censorship of other men's work and an almost, if not quite, unlimited right of printing his own. For some time the even more masterful spirit of Lockhart (against whom by the way Mrs Gordon seems to have had a rather unreasonable prejudice) qualified his control over *Maga*. But Lockhart's promotion to the *Quarterly* removed this influence, and from 1825 (speaking roughly) to 1835 Wilson was supreme. The death of William Blackwood and of the Ettrick Shepherd in the last-named year, and of his own wife in 1837 (the latter a blow from which he never recovered), strongly affected not his control over the publication but his desire to control it; and after 1839 his contributions (save in the years 1845 and 1848) were very few. Ill-health and broken spirits disabled him, and in 1852 he had to resign his professorship, dying two years later after some months of almost total prostration. Of the rest of the deeds of Christopher, and of his pugilism, and of his learning, and of his pedestrian exploits, and of his fishing, and of his cock-fighting, and of his hearty enjoyment of life generally, the books of the chronicles of Mrs Gordon, and still more the twelve volumes of his works and the unreprinted contributions to *Blackwood*, shall tell.

It is with those works that our principal business is, and some of them I shall take the liberty of at once dismissing. His poems are now matters of interest to very few mortals. It is not that they are bad, for they are not; but that they are almost wholly without distinction. He came just late enough to have got the seed of the great romantic revival; and his verse work is rarely more than the work of a clever man who has partly learnt and partly divined the manner of Burns, Scott, Campbell, Coleridge, Wordsworth, Byron, and the rest. Nor, to my fancy, are his prose tales of much more value. I read them many years ago and cared little for them. I re-read, or attempted to re-read, them the other day and cared less. There seems, from the original prospectus of the edition of his works, to have been an intention of editing the course of moral philosophy which, with more or fewer variations, obtained him the agreeable income of a thousand a year or so for thirty years. But whether (as Mrs Gordon seems to hint) the notes were in too dilapidated and chaotic a condition for use, or whether Professor Ferrier, his son-in-law and editor (himself, with Dean Mansel, the last of the exact philosophers of Britain), revolted at the idea of printing anything so merely literary, or what it was, I know not—at any rate they do not now figure in the list. This leaves us ten volumes of collected works, to wit, four of the *Noctes Ambrosianæ*, four of *Essays Critical and Imaginative*, and two of *The Recreations of Christopher North*, all with a very few exceptions reprinted from *Blackwood*. Mrs Gordon filially groans because the reprint was not more extensive, and without endorsing her own very high opinion of her father's work, it is possible to agree with her. It is especially noteworthy that from the essays are excluded three out of the four chief critical series which Wilson wrote— that on Spenser, praised by a writer so little given to reckless praise as Hallam, the *Specimens of British Critics*, and the *Dies Boreales*,—leaving only the series on Homer with its quasi-Appendix on the Greek dramatists, and the *Noctes* themselves.

It must be confessed that the *Noctes Ambrosianæ* are not easy things to commend to the modern reader, if I may use the word "commend" in its proper sense and with no air of patronage. Even Scotchmen (perhaps, indeed, Scotchmen most of all) are wont nowadays to praise them rather apologetically, as may be seen in the case of their editor and abridger Mr Skelton. Like most other very original things they drew after them a flock of imbecile imitations; and up to the present day[1] those who have lived in the remoter parts of Scotland must know, or recently remember, dreary compositions in corrupt following of the *Noctes*, with exaggerated attempts at Christopher's worst mannerisms, and invariably including a ghastly caricature of the Shepherd. Even in themselves they abound in stumbling-blocks, which are perhaps multiplied, at least at the threshold, by the arbitrary separation in Ferrier's edition of Wilson's part, and not all his part, from the whole series; eighteen numbers being excluded bodily to begin with, while many more and parts of more are omitted subsequently. The critical mistake of this is evident, for much of the machinery and all the characters of the *Noctes* were given to, not by, Wilson, and in all probability he accepted them not too willingly. The origin of the fantastic personages, the creation of which was a perfect mania with the early contributors to *Blackwood*, and who are, it is to be feared, too often a nuisance to modern readers, is rather dubious. Maginn's friends have claimed the origination of the *Noctes* proper, and of its well-known motto paraphrased from Phocylides, for "The Doctor," or, if his chief *Blackwood* designation be preferred, for the Ensign—Ensign O'Doherty. Professor Ferrier, on the other hand, has shown a not unnatural but by no means critical or exact desire to hint that Wilson invented the whole. There is no doubt that the real original is to be found in the actual suppers at "Ambrose's." These Lockhart had described, in *Peter's Letters*, before the appearance of the first *Noctes* (the reader must not be shocked, the false concord is invariable in the book itself) and not long after the establishment of *Maga*. As was the case with the magazine generally, the early numbers were extremely

---

[1] 1886. Things have changed somewhat (1923).

local and extremely personal. Wilson's glory is that he to a great extent, though not wholly, lifted them out of this rut, when he became the chief if not the sole writer after Lockhart's removal to London, and, with rare exceptions, reduced the personages to three strongly marked and very dramatic characters, Christopher North himself, the Ettrick Shepherd, and "Tickler." All these three were in a manner portraits, but no one is a mere photograph from a single person. On the whole, however, I suspect that Christopher North is a much closer likeness, if not of what Wilson himself was, yet at any rate of what he would have liked to be, than some of his apologists maintain. These charitable souls excuse the egotism, the personality, the violence, the inconsistency, the absurd assumption of omniscience and Admirable-Crichtonism, on the plea that "Christopher" is only the ideal Editor and not the actual Professor. It is quite true that Wilson, who, like all men of humour, must have known his own foibles, not unfrequently satirises them; but it is clear from his other work and from his private letters that they *were* his foibles. The figure of the Shepherd, who is the chief speaker and on the whole the most interesting, is a more debatable one. It is certain that many of Hogg's friends, and, in his touchy moments he himself, considered that great liberty was taken with him, if not that (as the *Quarterly* put it in a phrase which evidently made Wilson very angry) he was represented as a mere "boozing buffoon." On the other hand it is equally certain that the Shepherd never did anything that exhibited half the power over thought and language which is shown in the best passages of his *Noctes* eidolon. Some of the adventures described as having happened to him are historically known as having happened to Wilson himself, and his sentiments are much more the writer's than the speaker's. At the same time the admirably imitated patois and the subtle rendering of Hogg's very well known foibles—his inordinate and stupendous vanity, his proneness to take liberties with his betters, his irritable temper, and the rest—give a false air of identity which is very noteworthy. The third portrait is said to have been the farthest from life, except in some physical peculiarities, of the three. "Tickler," whose original was Wilson's maternal uncle Robert Sym, an Edinburgh "writer," and something of a humorist in the flesh, is very skilfully made to hold the position of common-sense intermediary between the two originals, North and the Shepherd. He has his own peculiarities, but he has also a habit of bringing his friends down from their altitudes in a Voltairian fashion which is of great benefit to the dialogues, and may be compared to Peacock's similar use of some of his characters. The few occasional interlocutors are of little moment, with one exception; and the only female characters, Mrs and Miss Gentle, would have been very much better away. They are not in the least life-like, and usually exhibit the namby-pambiness into which Wilson too often fell when he wished to be refined and pathetic. The "English" or half-English characters, who come in sometimes as foils, are also rather of the stick, sticky. On the other hand, the interruptions of Ambrose, the host, and his household, though a little farcical, are well judged. And of the one exception above mentioned, the live Thomas De Quincey, who is brought in without disguise or excuse in some of the very best of the series, it can only be said that the imitation of his written style is extraordinary, and that men who knew his conversation say that the rendering of that is more extraordinary still.

The same designed exaggeration which some uncritical persons have called Rabelaisian (not noticing that the very fault of the *Noctes* is that, unlike Rabelais, their author mixes up probabilities and improbabilities so that there is a perpetual jarring) is maintained throughout the scenery and etceteras. The comfortable but modest accommodations of Ambrose's hotels in Gabriel's Road and Picardy Place are turned into abodes of not particularly tasteful luxury which put Lord Beaconsfield's famous upholstery to shame, and remind one of what they probably suggested, Edgar Poe's equally famous and much more terrible sketch of a model drawing-room. All the plate is carefully described as "silver"; if it had been gold there might have been some humour in it. The "wax" candles and "silken" curtains (if they had been *Arabian Nights* lamps and oriental drapery the same might be said) are always insisted on. If there is any joke here it seems to lie in the contrast with Wilson's actual habits, which were very simple. For instance, he gives us a gorgeous description of the apparatus of North's solitary confinement when writing for *Blackwood*; his daughter's unvarnished account of the same process agrees exactly as to time, rate of production, and so forth, but substitutes water for the old hock and "Scots pint" (magnum) of claret, a dirty little terra-cotta inkstand for the silver utensil of the *Noctes*, and a single large tallow candle for Christopher's "floods of light." He carried the whim so far as to construct for himself— his *Noctes* self—an imaginary hall-by-the-sea on the Firth of Forth, which in the same way seems to have had an actual resemblance, half of likeness, half of contrast, to the actual Elleray, and to enlarge his own comfortable town house in Gloucester Place to a sort of fairy palace in Moray Place. But that which has most puzzled and shocked readers are the specially

Gargantuan passages relating to eating and drinking. The comments made on this seem (he was anything but patient of criticism) to have annoyed Wilson very much; and in some of the later *Noctes* he drops hints that the whole is mere Barmecide business. Unfortunately the same criticism applies to this as to the upholstery—the exaggeration is "done too natural." The Shepherd's consumption of oysters not by dozens but by fifties, the allowance of "six common kettles-full of water" for the night's toddy ration of the three, North's above-mentioned bottle of old hock at dinner and magnum of claret after, the dinners and suppers and "whets" which appear so often;—all these stop short of the actually incredible, and are nothing more than extremely convivial men of the time, who were also large eaters, would have actually consumed. Lord Alvanley's three hearty suppers, the exploits of the old member of Parliament in Boz's sketch of Bellamy's (I forget his real name, but he was not a myth), and other things might be quoted to show that there is a fatal verisimilitude in the Ambrosian feasts which may, or may not, make them shocking (they don't shock me), but which certainly takes them out of the category of merely humorous exaggeration. The Shepherd's "jugs" numerous as they are (and by the way the Shepherd propounds two absolutely contradictory theories of toddy-making, one of which, according to the instructions of my preceptors in that art, who lived within sight of the hills that look down on Glenlivet, is a damnable heresy) are not in the least like the *seze muiz, deux bussars, et six tupins* of tripe that Gargamelle so rashly devoured. There are men now[1] living, and honoured members of society in Scotland, who admit the soft impeachment of having drunk in their

[1] 1886. Perhaps none *now* (1923).

youth twelve or fourteen "double" tumblers at a sitting. Now a double tumbler, be it known to the Southron, is a jorum of toddy to which there go two wineglasses (of course of the old-fashioned size, not our modern goblets) of whisky. "Indeed," said a humorous and indulgent lady correspondent of Wilson's, "indeed, I really think you eat too many oysters at the *Noctes*"; and any one who believes in distributive justice must admit that they did.

If, therefore, the reader is of the modern cutlet-and-cup-of-coffee school of feeding, he will no doubt find the *Noctes* most grossly and palpably gluttonous. If he be a very superior person he will smile at the upholstery. If he objects to horseplay he will be horrified at finding the characters on one occasion engaging in a regular "mill," on more than one corking each other's faces during slumber, sometimes playing at pyramids like the bounding brothers of acrobatic fame, at others indulging in leap-frog with the servants, permitting themselves practical jokes of all kinds, affecting to be drowned by an explosive haggis, and so forth. Every now and then he will come to a passage at which, without being superfine at all, he may find his gorge rise; though there is nothing quite so bad in the *Noctes* as the picture of the ravens eating a dead Quaker in the *Recreations*, a picture for which Wilson offers a very lame defence elsewhere. He must put all sorts of prejudice, literary, political, and other, in his pocket. He must be prepared not only for constant and very scurrilous flings at "Cockneys" (Wilson extends the term far beyond the Hunt and Hazlitt school, an extension which to this day[1] seems to give a strange delight to Edinburgh journalists), but for the wildest heterodoxies and inconsistencies of political, literary,

---

[1] 1886.

and miscellaneous judgment, for much bastard verse-
prose, for a good many quite uninteresting local and
ephemeral allusions, and, of course, for any quantity
of Scotch dialect. If all these allowances and provisos
are too many for him to make, it is probably useless
for him to attempt the *Noctes* at all. He will pretty
certainly, with the *Quarterly* reviewer, set their characters down as boozing buffoons, and decline the
honour of an invitation to Ambrose's or The Lodge, to
Southside or the tent in Ettrick Forest.

But any one who can accommodate himself to these
little matters, much more any one who can enter into
the spirit of days merrier, more leisurely, and if not
less straitlaced than our own, yet lacing their laces in
a different fashion, will find the *Noctes* very delightful
indeed. The mere high jinks, when the secret of being
in the vein with them has been mastered, are seldom
unamusing, and sometimes (notably in the long swim
out to sea of Tickler and the Shepherd) are quite
admirable fooling. No one who has an eye for the
literary-dramatic can help, after a few *Noctes* have
been read, admiring the skill with which the characters
are at once typified and individualised, the substance
which they acquire in the reader's mind, the personal
interest in them which is excited. And to all this,
peculiarly suited for an alternative in these solemn
days, has to be added the abundance of scattered and
incomplete but remarkable gems of expression and
thought that come at every few pages, sometimes at
every page, of the series.

Some of the burlesque narratives (such as the
Shepherd's Mazeppa-like ride on the Bonassus) are
inimitably good, though they are too often spoilt by
Wilson's great faults of prolixity and uncertainty of
touch. The criticisms, of which there are many, are

also extremely unequal, but not a few very fine passages
may be found among them. The politics, it must be
owned, are not good for much, even from the Tory
point of view. But the greatest attraction of the whole,
next to its sunshiny heartiness and humour, is to be
found in innumerable and indescribable bits, phrases,
sentences, short paragraphs, which have, more than
anything out of the dialogues of the very best novels,
the character and charm of actual conversation. To
read a *Noctes* has, for those who have the happy gift
of realising literature, not much less than the effect
of actually taking part in one, with no danger of head-
ache or indigestion after, and without the risk of being
playfully corked, or required to leap the table for a
wager, or forced to extemporise sixteen stanzas standing on the mantelpiece. There must be some peculiar
virtue in this, for, as is very well known, the usual
dialogue leaves the reader more outside of it than
almost any other kind of literature.

This peculiar charm is of necessity wanting to the
rest of Wilson's works, and in so far they are inferior
to the *Noctes*; but they have compensatory merits of
their own, while, considered merely as literature, there
are better things in them than anything that is to be
found in the colloquies of those men of great gorman-
dising abilities—Christopher North, James Hogg, and
Timothy Tickler. Of the four volumes of *Essays
Critical and Imaginative*, the fourth, on Homer and his
translators, with an unfinished companion piece on the
Greek drama, stands by itself, and has indeed, I believe,
been separately published. It is well worth reading
through at a sitting, which cannot be said of every
volume of criticism. What is more, it may, I think,
be put almost first in its own division of the art, though
whether that division of the art is a high or low one is

another question. I should not myself rank it very high. With Wilson, criticism, at least here, is little more than the eloquent expression of likes and dislikes. The long passages in which he deals with the wrath of Achilles and with the love of Calypso, though subject to the general stricture already more than once passed, are really beautiful specimens of literary enthusiasm; nor is there anything in English more calculated to initiate the reader, especially the young reader, in the love at least, if not the understanding, of Homer. The same enthusiastic and obviously quite genuine appreciation appears in the essay on the *Agamemnon*. But of criticism as criticism—of what has been called tracing of literary cause and effect, of any coherent and coordinated theory of the good and bad in verse and prose, and the reasons of their goodness or badness, it must be said of this, as of Wilson's other critical work, that it is to be found *nusquam nullibi nullimodis*. He can preach (though with too great volubility, and with occasional faults of taste) delightful sermons about what he likes at the moment—for it is by no means always the same; and he can make formidable onslaughts with various weapons on what he dislikes at the moment —which again is not always the same. But a man so certain to go off at score whenever his likes or dislikes are excited, and so absolutely unable to check himself whenever he feels tempted thus to go off, lacks the very first qualifications of the critic:—lacks them, indeed, almost as much as the mere word-grinder who looks to see whether a plural substantive has a singular verb, and is satisfied if it has not, and horrified if it has. His most famous sentence "The Animosities are mortal, but the Humanities live for ever" is certainly noble. But it would have been better if the Humanities had oftener choked the Animosities at their birth.

Wilson's criticism is to be found more or less everywhere in his collected writings. I have said that I think it a pity that, of his longest critical attempts, only one has been republished; and the reason is simple. For with an unequal writer (and Wilson is a writer unequalled in his inequality) his best work is as likely to be found in his worst book as his worst work in his best book; while the constant contemplation for a considerable period of one subject is more likely than anything else to dispel his habits of digression and padding. But the ubiquity of his criticism through the ten volumes was, in the circumstances of their editing, simply unavoidable. He had himself superintended a selection of all kinds, which he called *The Recreations of Christopher North*, and this had to be reprinted entire. It followed that, in the *Essays Critical and Imaginative*, an equally miscellaneous character should be observed. Almost everything given, and much not given, in the *Works* is worth consideration, but for critical purposes a choice is necessary. Let us take the consolidated essay on Wordsworth (most of which dates before 1822), the famous paper on Lord, then Mr, Tennyson's poems in 1832, and the generous palinode on Macaulay's *Lays* of 1842. No three papers could better show Wilson in his three literary stages, that of rather cautious tentative (for though he was not a very young man in 1818, the date of the earliest of the Wordsworth papers, he was a young writer), that of practised and unrestrained vigour (for 1832 represents about his literary zenith), and that of reflective decadence, for by 1842 he had ceased to write habitually, and was already bowed down by mental sorrows and physical ailments. In the first paper, or set of papers, it is evident that he is ambitiously groping after a more systematic style of criticism than he found in practice to be possible for him. Although he elsewhere scoffs at definitions, he tries to formulate very precisely the genius of Scott, of Byron, and of Wordsworth; he does his best to connect his individual judgments with these formulas; he shuns mere verbal criticism, and (to some extent) mere exaltation or depreciation of particular passages. But it is quite evident that he is ill at ease; and I do not think that any one now reading the essay can call it a successful one, or can attempt to rank it with those which, from different points of view, Hazlitt and De Quincey (Hazlitt nearly at the same time) wrote about Wordsworth. Indeed, Hazlitt is the most valuable of all examples for a critical comparison with Wilson; both being violent partisans and crotcheteers, both being animated with the truest love of poetry, but the one possessing and the other lacking the "tie-beam" of a consistent critical theory.

A dozen years later Wilson had cast his slough, and had become the autocratic, freespoken, self-constituted dictator, Christopher North. He was confronted with the very difficult problem of Mr Tennyson's poems. He knew they were poetry; that he could not help seeing and knowing. But they seemed to him to be the work of a "cockney" (it would be interesting to know whether there ever was any one less of a cockney than the author of *Mariana*), and he was irritated by some silly praise which had been given to them. So he set to work, and perpetrated the queerest jumble of sound and unsound criticism that exists in the archives of that art, so far as a humble but laborious student and practitioner thereof knoweth. He could not for the life of him help admiring *Adeline, Oriana, Mariana, The Ode to Memory*. Yet he had nothing but scorn for the scarcely less exquisite *Mermaid* and *Sea Fairies*—though the first few lines of the latter, excluded by this and other

pseudo-criticism from the knowledge of half a generation of English readers, equal almost anything that
the poet ever did. And only the lucky memory of a
remark of Hartley Coleridge's (who never went wrong
in criticism, whatever he did in life) saved him from
explicitly damning *The Dying Swan*, which stands at
the very head of a whole class of poetry. In all this
essay, to borrow one of his own favourite words, he
simply "plouters"—splashes and flounders about without any guidance of critical theory. Compare, to keep
up the comparative method, the paper with the still
more famous and far more deadly attack which Lockhart[1] made a little later in the *Quarterly*. There one finds
little, if any, generosity; an infinitely more cold-blooded
and deliberate determination to "cut up." But the
critic (and how quaint and pathetic it is to think that
the said critic was the author of *I ride from land to land*
and *When youthful hope is fled*) sees his theory of poetry
straight before him, and never takes his eye off it. The
individual censures may be just or unjust, but they fit
together like the propositions of a masterpiece of legal
judgment. The poet is condemned under the statute,—
so much the worse for the statute perhaps, but that
does not matter—and he can only plead No juris-
diction; whereas with Christopher it is quite different.
If he does not exactly blunder right (and he sometimes
does that), he constantly blunders wrong—goes wrong,
that is to say, without any excuse of theory or general
view. That is not criticism.

We shall not find matters much mended from the
strictly critical point of view, when we come, ten years
later, to the article on the *Lays*. Here Christopher, as
I hold with all respect to persons of distinction, is
absolutely right. He does not say one word too much

[1] See note at end of Essay on Lockhart.

of the fire and life of those wonderful verses, of that fight of all fights—as far as English verse goes, except Drayton's *Agincourt* and the last canto of *Marmion*; as far as English prose goes, except some passages of Malory and two or three pages of Kingsley's—*The Battle of the Lake Regillus.* The subject and the swing attracted him; he liked the fight, and he liked the ring as of Sir Walter at his very best. But he goes appallingly wrong all through on general critical points.

Yet, according to his own perverse fashion, he never goes wrong without going right. Throughout his critical work there are scattered the most intelligent ideas, the neatest phrases, the most appreciative judgments. How good is it to say that "the battle of Trafalgar, though in some sort it neither began nor ended anything, was a kind of consummation of national prowess." How good again in its very straightforwardness and simplicity is the dictum "it is not necessary that we should understand fine poetry in order to feel and enjoy it, any more than fine music." Hundreds and thousands of these things lie about the pages. And in the next page to each the critic probably goes and says something which shows that he had entirely forgotten them. An intelligent man may be angry with Christopher—I should doubt whether any one who is not occasionally both angry and disgusted with him can be an intelligent man. But it is impossible to dislike him or fail to admire him as a whole.

There is a third and very extensive division of Wilson's work which may not improbably be more popular, or might be if it were accessible separately, with the public of to-day, than either of those which have been surveyed. His "drunken *Noctes*," as Carlyle unkindly calls them, require a certain peculiar attitude of mind to appreciate them. As for his criticisms, it is frequently said, and it certainly would not become me to deny it, that nobody reads criticism but critics. But Wilson's renown as an athlete, a sportsman, and a lover of nature, who had a singular gift in expressing his love, has not yet died; and there is an ample audience now for men who can write about athletics, about sport, and about scenery. Nor is it questionable that on these subjects he is seen, on the whole, at his best. True, his faults pursue him even here, and are aggravated by a sort of fashion of the time which made him elaborately digress into politics, into literature, even (God rest his soul!) into a kind of quasi-professional and professorial sermonising on morals and theology, in the midst of his sporting articles. But the metal more attractive of the main subject would probably recommend these papers widely, if they were not scattered pell-mell about the *Essays Critical and Imaginative*, and the *Recreations of Christopher North*. Speaking generally they fall into three divisions—essays on sport in general, essays on the English Lakes, and essays on the Scottish Highlands. The best of the first class are the famous papers called *Christopher North in his Sporting Jacket*, and the scattered reviews and articles redacted in the *Recreations* under the general title of "Anglimania." In the second class all are good; and a volume composed of *Christopher at the Lakes*, *A Day at Windermere*, *Christopher on Colonsay* (a wild extravaganza which had a sort of basis of fact in a trotting-match won on a pony which Wilson afterwards sold for four pounds), and *A Saunter at Grasmere*, with one or two more, would be a thing of price. The best of the third class beyond all question is the collection, also redacted by the author for the *Recreations*, entitled *The Moors*. This last is perhaps the best of all the sporting and descriptive pieces, though not the least exemplary of its author's vagaries; for before he can get to the Moors, he gives us heaven knows how many pages of a criticism on Wordsworth, which, in that place at any rate, we do not in the least want; and in the very middle of his wonderful and sanguinary exploits on and near Ben Cruachan, he "interrupts the muffins" in order to deliver to a most farcical and impertinent assemblage a quite serious and still more impertinent sermon. But all these papers are more or less delightful. For the glowing description of, and the sneaking apology for, cat-worrying which the *Sporting Jacket* contains, nothing can be said. Wilson deliberately overlooks the fact that the whole fun of that nefarious amusement consists in the pitting of a plucky but weak animal against something much more strongly built and armed than itself. One may regret the P.R., and indulge in a not wholly sneaking affection for cock-fighting, dog-fighting, and anything in which there is a fair match, without having the slightest weakness for this kind of brutality. But, generally speaking, Wilson is a thoroughly fair sportsman, and how enthusiastic he is, no one who has read him can fail to know. Of the scenery of loch or lake, of hill or mountain, he was at once an ardent lover and a describer who has never been equalled. His accustomed exaggeration and false emphasis are nowhere so little perceptible as when he deals with Ben Cruachan or the Old Man of Coniston, with the Four Great Lakes of Britain, East and West (one of his finest passages), or with the glens of Etive and Borrowdale. The accursed influence of an un-chastened taste is indeed observable in the before-mentioned *Dead Quaker of Helvellyn*, a piece of un-relieved nastiness which he has in vain tried to excuse. But the whole of the series from which this is taken (*Christopher in his Aviary*) is in his least happy style, alternately grandiose and low, relieved indeed by touches of observation and feeling, as all his work is, but hardly redeemed by them. The depths of his possible fall may also be seen from a short piece which Professor Ferrier, obligingly describing it as "too lively to be omitted," has adjoined to *Christopher at the Lakes*. But, on the whole, all the articles mentioned in the list at the beginning of this paragraph, with the capital *Streams* as an addition, with the soliloquies on *The Seasons* and with part (*not* the narrative part) of *Highland Storms*, are delightful reading. The progress of the sportsman has never been better given than in *Christopher North in his Sporting Jacket*. In *The Moors* the actual sporting part is perhaps a little spoilt by the affectation of infallibility, qualified it is true by an aside or two, which so often mars the Christopherian utterances. But Wilson's description has never been bettered. The thunderstorm on the hill, the rough conviviality at the illicit distillery, the evening voyage on the loch, match, if they do not beat, anything of the kind in much more recent books far better known to the present generation. A special favourite of mine is the rather unceremonious review of Sir Humphry Davy's strangely over-praised *Salmonia*. The passage of utter scorn and indignation at the preposterous statement of the chief personage in the dialogues, that after an exceptionally hard day's walking and fishing "half a pint of claret per man is enough," is sublime. Nearly the earliest, and certainly the best, protest against some modern fashions in shooting is to be found in *The Moors*. In the same series, the visit to the hill cottage, preceding that to the still, has what it has since become the fashion to call the idyllic flavour, without too much of the rather mawkish pathos with which, in imitation of Mackenzie and the sensibility-writers of the last century, Wilson is apt to daub his pictures of rural and humble life. The passages on Oxford, to go to a slightly different but allied subject, in *Old North and Young North* (a paper not yet mentioned), may have full appeal to Oxford men, but I can hardly be mistaken in thinking that outsiders must see at least some of the beauty of them. But the list of specially desirable things in these articles is endless; hardly one of them can be taken up without discovering many such, not one of them without discovering some[1].

And, throughout the whole collection, there is the additional satisfaction that the author is writing only of what he thoroughly knows and understands. At the Lakes Wilson lived for years, and was familiar with every cranny of the hills, from the Pillar to Hawes Water, and from Newby Bridge to Saddleback. He began marching and fishing through the Highlands when he was a boy, enticed even his wife into perilous pedestrian enterprises with him, and, though the extent of his knowledge was perhaps not quite so large as he pretends, he certainly knew great tracts as well as he knew Edinburgh. Nor were his qualifications as a sportsman less authentic, despite the somewhat Munchausenish appearance which some of the feats narrated in the *Noctes* and the *Recreations* wear, and are indeed intended to wear. His enormous baskets of trout seem to have been, if not quite so regular as he sometimes makes them out, at any rate fully historical as occasional feats. As has been hinted, he really did win the trotting-match on the pony, Colonsay, against a thorough-bred, though it was only on the technical point of the thoroughbred breaking his pace. His walk from London to Oxford in a night seems to have been a fact, and

---

[1] If I accepted (a rash acceptance) the challenge to name the three very best things in Wilson I should, I think, choose the famous Fairy's Funeral in the *Recreations*, the Shepherd's account of his recovery from illness in the *Noctes*, and, in a lighter vein, the picture of girls bathing in *Streams*.

indeed there is nothing at all impossible in it, for the distance through Wycombe is not more than fifty-three miles; while the less certainly authenticated feat of walking from Liverpool to Elleray (eighty miles at least), without more than a short rest, also appears to be genuine. Like the heroes of a song that he loved, though he seems to have sung it in a corrupt text, he could wrestle and fight and jump out anywhere; and, until he was thoroughly broken by illness, he appears to have made the very most of the not inconsiderable spare time of a Scotch professor who had once got his long series of lectures committed to paper, and had nothing to do for the rest of his life but collect bundles of pound notes at the beginning of each session[1]. All this, joined to his literary gifts, gives a reality to his out-of-door papers which is hardly to be found else-where except in some passages of Kingsley, between whom and Wilson there are many and most curious resemblances, chequered by national and personal differences only less curious.

I do not think he was a good reviewer, even after making allowance for the prejudices and partisanships of the time, and for the monkey tricks of mannerism, which, at any rate in his earlier days, were incumbent on a reviewer in *Maga*. He is too prone to the besetting sins of reviewing—the right hand defections and left hand fallings off, which, being interpreted, consist first in expressing agreement or disagreement with the author's views, and secondly in digressing into personal statements of one's own views of things connected with them instead of expounding more or less clearly what

---

[1] This was just at Wilson's time, when they actually gave a man six months' leave between election and beginning work. *I* had a fortnight; and double or treble what Wilson had to do afterwards, besides constant change of subject. But 1 keep this passage though (or perhaps because) I used to, be chaffed about it by colleagues at Edinburgh (1923).

the book is, and addressing oneself to the great question, Is it a good or a bad piece of work according to the standard which the author himself strove to reach? I have said that I do not think he was on the whole a good critic (for a man may be a good critic and a bad reviewer, though the reverse will hardly stand), and I have given my reasons. That he was neither a great, nor even a very good poet or tale-teller, I have no doubt whatever. But this leaves untouched the attraction of his miscellaneous work, and its suitableness for the purpose of recreation. For that purpose I think it to be among the very best work in all literature. Its unfailing life and vigour, its vast variety, the healthy and inspiriting character of the subjects with which in the main it deals, are the characteristics which make its volumes easy-chair books of the best order. Its beauty no doubt is irregular, faulty, engaging rather than exquisite, attractive rather than artistically or scientifically perfect. I do not know that there is even any reason to join in the general lament over Wilson as being a gigantic failure, a monument of wasted energies and half-developed faculty. I do not at all think that there was anything in him much better than he actually did, or that he ever could have polished and sandpapered the faults out of his work. It would pretty certainly have lost freshness and vigour; it would quite certainly have been less in bulk, and bulk is a very important point in literature that is to serve as recreation. It is to me not much less certain that it never would have attained the first rank in symmetry and order. I am quite content with it as it is, and I only wish that still more of it were easily accessible[1].

---

[1] I find nothing to retract in this as criticism except in confessing that for a good many years 1 have certainly read Wilson less frequently than I did at one time (1923).

IX

DE QUINCEY[1]

In not a few respects the literary lot of Thomas De Quincey, both during his life and after it, has been exceedingly peculiar. In one respect it has been unique. I do not know that any other author of anything like his merit, during our time, has had a piece of work published for fully twenty years as his, only for it to be excluded as somebody else's at the end of that time. Certainly *The Traditions of the Rabbins* was very De Quinceyish; indeed, it was so De Quinceyish that the discovery, after such a length of time, that it was not De Quincey's at all, but "Salathiel" Croly's, must have given unpleasant qualms to more than one critic accustomed to be positive on internal evidence. But if De Quincey had thus attributed to him work that was not his, he has also had the utmost difficulty in getting attributed to him, in any accessible form, work that was his own. Three, or nominally four, editions—one in the decade of his death, superintended for the most part by himself; another in 1862, whose blue coat and white labels dwell in the fond memory; and another in 1878 (reprinted in 1880) a little altered and enlarged, with the *Rabbins* turned out and more soberly clad, but identical in the main—put before the British public for some thirty-five years a certain portion of his strange, long-delayed, but voluminous work. This work had occupied him for about the same period, that is to say for the last and shorter half of his extraordinary and yet uneventful life. Now, after much praying of readers, and grumbling of critics, we have a fifth and

[1] See Appendix A—De Quincey.

definitive edition from the English critic who has given most attention to De Quincey, Professor Masson[1].

Will readers of it form a different estimate from that which those of us who have known the older editions for a quarter of a century have formed, and will that estimate, if it is different, be higher or lower? To answer such questions is always difficult; but it is especially difficult here, for a certain reason which I had chiefly in mind when I said just now that De Quincey's literary lot has been very peculiar. I believe that I am not speaking for myself only; I am quite sure that I am speaking my own deliberate opinion when I say that on scarcely any English writer is it so hard to strike a critical balance—to get a clear definite opinion that you can put on the shelf and need merely take down now and then to be dusted and polished up by a fresh reading—as on De Quincey. This is partly due to the fact that his merits are of the class that appeals to, while his faults are of the class that is excused by, the average boy who has some interest in literature. To read the *Essay on Murder*, the *English Mail Coach*, *The Spanish Nun*, *The Cæsars*, and half a score other things at the age of about fifteen or sixteen is, or ought to be, to fall in love with them. And there is nothing more unpleasant for *les âmes bien nées*, as the famous distich has it, than to find fault in after life with that with which you have fallen in love at fifteen or sixteen. Yet most unfortunately, just as De Quincey's merits, or some of them, appeal specially to youth, and his defects specially escape the notice of youth, so age with stealing steps especially claws those merits into his clutch and leaves the defects exposed to derision. The most gracious state of authors is that they shall charm

---

[1] *The Collected Writings of Thomas de Quincey*; edited by David Masson. In fourteen volumes; Edinburgh, 1889–90.

at all ages those whom they do charm. There are others —Dante, Cervantes, Goethe are instances—as to whom you may even begin with a little aversion, and go on to love them more and more. De Quincey, I fear, belongs to a third class, with whom it is difficult to keep up the first love, or rather whose defects begin before long to urge themselves upon the critical lover (some would say there are no critical lovers, but that I deny) with an even less happy result than is recorded in one of Catullus's finest lines. This kind of discovery

Cogit amare *minus, nec* bene velle *magis.*

How and to what extent this is the case, it must be the business of this paper to attempt to show. But first it is desirable to give, as usual, a brief sketch of De Quincey's life. It need only be a brief one, for the external events of that life were few and meagre; nor can they be said to be, even after the researches of Mr Page and Professor Masson, very accurately or exhaustively known. Before those researches "all was mist and myth" about De Quincey. I remember as a boy, a year or two after his death, hearing a piece of scandal about his domestic relations, which seems to have had no foundation whatever, but which pretty evidently was an echo of the "libel" (published in a short-lived newspaper of the kind which after many years has again risen[1] to infest London) whereof he complains with perhaps more acrimony than dignity in a paper for the first time exhumed and reprinted in Professor Masson's edition. Many of the details of the *Confessions* and the *Autobiography* have a singular unbelievableness as one reads them; and though the tendency of recent biographers has been to accept them as on the whole genuine, I own that I am rather

---

[1] And has increasingly contaminated the Press (1923).

sceptical about many of them still. Was the ever-famous Malay a real Malay, or a thing of shreds and patches? Did De Quincey actually call upon the awful Dean Cyril Jackson and affably discuss with him the propriety of entering himself at Christ Church? Did he really journey pennilessly down to Eton on the chance of finding a casual peer of the realm of tender years who would back a bill for him? These are but a few out of a larger number of questions which in idle moods (for the answer to hardly one of them is of the least importance) suggest themselves; and which have been very partially answered hitherto even of late years, though they have been much discussed. The plain and tolerably certain facts which are important in connection with his work may be pretty rapidly summed up.

Thomas De Quincey, or Quincey, was born in Manchester—but apparently not, as he himself thought, at the country house of Greenhay which his parents afterwards inhabited—on 15th August, 1785. His father was a merchant, well-to-do but of weak health, who died when Thomas was seven years old. Of his childhood he has left very copious reminiscences, and there is no doubt that reminiscences of childhood do linger long after later memories have disappeared. But to what extent De Quincey gave "cocked hats and canes" to his childish thoughts and to his relations with his brothers and sisters, individual judgment must decide. I should say, for my part, that the extent was considerable. It seems, however, pretty clear that he was as a child, very much what he was all his life—emphatically "old-fashioned," retiring without being exactly shy, full of far-brought fancies and yet intensely concentrated upon himself. In 1796 his mother moved to Bath, and Thomas was educated first at the Grammar

School there and then at a privàte school in Wiltshire. It was at Bath, his headquarters being there, that he met various persons of distinction—Lord Westport, Lord and Lady Carbery, and others—who figure largely in the *Autobiography*, but are never heard of afterwards. It was with Lord Westport, a boy somewhat younger than himself, that he took a trip to Ireland, the only country beyond Great Britain that he visited. In 1800 he was sent by his guardians to the Manchester Grammar School in order to obtain, by three years' boarding there, one of the Somerset Exhibitions to Brasenose. As a separate income of £150 had been left by De Quincey's father to each of his sons, as this income, or part of it, must have been accumulating, and as the mother was very well off, this' roundabout way of securing for him a miserable forty or fifty pounds a year seems strange enough. But it has to be remembered that for all these details we have little security but De Quincey himself. However, that he did go to Manchester, and did, after rather more than two of his three years' probation, run away is indisputable. His mother was living at Chester, and the calf was not killed for this prodigal son; but he had liberty given him to wander about Wales on an allowance of a guinea a week. That there is some mystery, or mystification, about all this is nearly certain. If things really went as he represents them, his mother ought to have been ashamed of herself, and his guardians ought to have had, to say the least, an experience of the roughest side of Lord Eldon's tongue. The wanderings in Wales were followed by the famous sojourn in Soho, with its waitings at money-lenders' doors, and its perambulations of Oxford Street. Then, by another sudden revolution, we find De Quincey with two-thirds of his allowance handed over to him and permission to go to

Oxford as he wished, but abandoned to his own devices
by his mother and his guardians, as surely no mother
and no guardians ever abandoned an exceptionally
unworldly boy of eighteen before. They seem to have
put fifty guineas in his pocket and sent him up to
Oxford, without even recommending him a college,
and with an income which made it practically certain
that he would once more seek the Jews. When he had
spent so much of his fifty guineas that there was not
enough left to pay caution-money at most colleges, he
went to Worcester, where it happened to be low. He
seems to have stayed there, on and off, for nearly six
years. But he took no degree, his eternal caprices
making him shun *vivâ voce* (then a much more important
part of the examination than it is now) after sending
in unusually good written papers. Instead of taking
a degree, he began to take opium, and to make acquaintance with the "Lakers" in both their haunts of
Somerset and Westmorland. He entered himself at
the Middle Temple, he may have eaten some dinners,
and somehow or other he "came into his property,"
though there are dire surmises that it was by the
Hebrew door. At any rate in November, 1809, he gave
up both Oxford and London (which he had frequented
a good deal, chiefly, he says, for the sake of the opera
of which he was very fond), and established himself at
Grasmere. One of the most singular things about his
singular life—an oddity due, no doubt, in part to the
fact that he outlived his more literary associates instead
of being outlived by them—is that though we hear
much from De Quincey of other people we hear extremely little from other people about De Quincey.
Indeed what we do so hear dates almost entirely from
the last days of his life.

As for the autobiographic details in his *Confessions*

and elsewhere, anybody who chooses may put those Sibylline leaves together for himself. It would only appear certain that for ten years he led the life of a recluse student and a hard laudanum-drinker, varied by a little society now and then; that in 1816 he married Margaret Simpson, a dalesman's daughter, of whom we have hardly any personal notices save to the effect that she was very beautiful, and who seems to have been almost the most exemplary of wives to almost the most eccentric of husbands; that for most of the time he was in more or less ease and affluence (ease and affluence still, it would seem, of a treacherous Hebraic origin); and that about 1819 he found himself in great pecuniary difficulties. Then at length he turned to literature, started as editor of a little Tory paper at Kendal, went to London, and took rank, never to be cancelled, as a man of letters by the first part of *The Confessions of an Opium-Eater*, published in the *London Magazine* for 1821. He began as a magazine-writer, and he continued as such till the end of his life; his publications in book-form being, till he was induced to collect his articles, quite insignificant. Between 1821 and 1825 he seems to have been chiefly in London, though sometimes at Grasmere; between 1825 and 1830 chiefly at Grasmere, but much in Edinburgh, where Wilson (whose friendship he had secured, not at Oxford, though they were contemporaries, but at the Lakes) was now residing, and where he was introduced to Blackwood. In 1830 he moved his household to the Scotch capital, and lived there, and (after his wife's death in 1837) at Lasswade, or rather Polton, for the rest of his life. His affairs had come to their worst before he lost his wife, and it is now known that for some considerable time he lived, like Mr Chrystal Croftangry, in the sanctuary of Holyrood. But De

Quincey's way of "living" at any place was as
mysterious as most of his other ways; and, though he
seems to have been very fond of his family and not at
all put out by them, it was his constant habit to establish himself in separate lodgings. These he as constantly
shifted (sometimes as far as Glasgow) for no intelligible
reason that has ever been discovered or surmised, his
pecuniary troubles having long ceased. It was in the
latest and most permanent of these lodgings, 42 Lothian
Street, Edinburgh, not at Lasswade, that he died on
the 8th of December, 1859. He had latterly written
mainly, though not solely, for *Tait's Magazine* and
Hogg's Instructor. But his chief literary employment
for at least seven years before this, had been the
arrangement of the authorised edition of his works,
the last or fourteenth volume of which was in the press
at the time of his death.

So meagre are the known facts in a life of seventy-
four years, during nearly forty of which De Quincey,
though never popular, was still recognised as a great
name in English letters, while during the same period
he knew, and was known to, not a few distinguished
men. But little as is recorded of the facts of his life,
even less is recorded of his character, and for once it
is almost impossible to discover that character from
his works. The few persons who met him all agree as
to his impenetrability,—an impenetrability not in the
least due to posing, but apparently natural and fated.
De Quincey was at once egotistic and impersonal, at
once delighted to talk and resolutely shunning society.
To him, one is tempted to say, reading and writing
did come by nature, and nothing else was natural at all.
With books he is always at home. A De Quincey in a
world where there was neither reading nor writing of
books, would certainly either have committed suicide

or gone mad. Pope's theory of the master-passion, so often abused, justified itself here.

The quantity of work produced during this singular existence, from the time when De Quincey first began, unusually late, to write for publication, was very large. As collected by the author, it filled fourteen volumes; the collection was subsequently enlarged to sixteen, and though the new edition promises to restrict itself to the older and lesser number, the contents of each volume have been very considerably increased. But this printed and reprinted total, so far as can be judged from De Quincey's own assertions and from the observations of those who were acquainted with him during his later years, must have been but the smaller part of what he actually wrote. He was always writing, and always leaving deposits of his manuscripts in the various 'odgings where it was his habit to bestow himself. The greater part of De Quincey's writing was of a kind almost as easily written by so full a reader and so logical a thinker as an ordinary newspaper article by an ordinary man; and except when he was sleeping, wandering about, or reading, he was always writing. It is, of course, true that he spent a great deal of time, especially in his last years of all, in re-writing and re-fashioning previously executed work; and also that illness and opium made considerable inroads on his leisure. But I should imagine that if we had all that he actually wrote during these nearly forty years, forty or sixty printed volumes would more nearly express its amount than fourteen or sixteen.

Still what we have is no mean bulk of work for any man to have accomplished, especially when it is considered how extraordinarily good much of it is. To classify it is not particularly easy; and I doubt, myself, whether any classification is necessary. De Quincey himself tried, and made rather a muddle of it. Professor Masson tried again. But, in truth, except those wonderful purple patches of "numerous" prose, which are stuck all about the work, and perhaps in strictness not excepting them, everything that De Quincey wrote, whether it was dream or reminiscence, literary criticism or historical study, politics or political economy, had one characteristic so strongly impressed on it as to dwarf and obscure the differences of subject. It is not very easy to find a description at once accurate and fair, brief and adequate, of this peculiarity; it is best hinted at in a remark on De Quincey's conversation which I have seen quoted somewhere (whether by Professor Masson or not I hardly know), that it was, with many interesting and delightful qualities, a kind of "rigmarole." So far as I remember, the remark was not applied in any unfriendly spirit, nor is it adduced here in any such. But both in the printed works, in the remembrances of De Quincey's conversation which have been printed, in his letters, which are exactly like his articles, and in those astonishing imaginary conversations attributed to him in the *Noctes Ambrosianæ*, which are said, by good authorities, exactly to represent his way of talk, this quality of rigmarole appears. It is absolutely impossible for him to keep to his subject, or any subject. It is as impossible for him to pull himself up briefly in any digression from that subject. In his finest passages, as in his most trivial, he is at the mercy of the will-o'-the-wisp of divagation. In his later re-handlings of his work, he did to some extent limit his followings of this will-o'-the-wisp to notes, but by no means always; and both in his later and in his earlier work, as it was written for the first time, he indulged them freely in the text.

For pure rigmarole, for stories, as Mr Chadband has

it, "of a cock and of a bull, and of a lady and of a half-crown," few things, even in De Quincey, can exceed, and nothing out of De Quincey can approach, the passages about the woman he met on the "cop" at Chester, and about the Greek letter that he did not send to the Bishop of Bangor, in the preliminary part of the *Confessions*. The first is the more teasing, because with a quite elvish superfluity of naughtiness he has here indulged in a kind of double rigmarole about the woman and the "bore" in the river, and flits from one to the other, and from the other to the one (his main story standing still the while), for half a dozen pages, till the reader feels as Coleridge's auditors must have felt when he talked about "Ball and Bell, Bell and Ball." But the Greek letter episode, or rather, the episode about the Greek letter which never was written, is, if possible, more flagrantly rigmarolish. The-cop-and-bore-and-woman digression contains some remarkable description as a kind of solace to the Puck-led traveller; the other is bare of any such comfort. The Bishop's old housekeeper, who was De Quincey's landlady, told him, it seems, that the Bishop had cautioned her against taking in lodgers whom she did not know, and De Quincey was very angry. As he thought he could write Greek much better than the Bishop, he meditated expostulation in that language. He did not expostulate, but he proceeds instead to consider the possible effect on the Bishop if he had. There was a contemporary writer whom we can imagine struck by a similar whimsy: but Charles Lamb would have given us the Bishop and himself "quite natural and distinct" in a dozen lines, and then have dropped the subject, leaving our sides aching with laughter, and our appetites longing for more. De Quincey tells us at great length who the Bishop was, and how he was the Head of Brasenose, with some remarks on the relative status of Oxford Colleges. Then he debates the pros and cons on the question whether the Bishop would have answered the letter or not, with some remarks on the difference between strict scholarship and the power of composing in a dead language. He rises to real humour in the remark, that as "Methodists swarmed in Carnarvonshire," he "could in no case have found pleasure in causing mortification" to the Bishop, even if he had vanquished him. By this time we have had some three pages of it, and could well, especially with this lively touch to finish, accept them, though they be something tedious, supposing the incident to be closed. The treacherous author leads us to suppose that it is closed; telling us how he left Bangor, and went to Carnarvon, which change gradually drew his thoughts away from the Bishop. So far is this from being the case, that he goes back to that Reverend Father, and for two mortal pages more, speculates further what would happen if he had written to the Bishop, what the Bishop would have said, whether he would not have asked him (De Quincey) to the Palace, whether, in his capacity of Head of a House, he would not have welcomed him to that seat of learning, and finally smoothed his way to a fellowship. By which time, one is perfectly sick of the Bishop, and of these speculations on the might-have-been, which are indeed by no means unnatural, being exactly what every man indulges in now and then in his own case, which, in conversation, would not be unpleasant, but which, gradually and diffusedly set down in a book, and interrupting a narrative, are most certainly "rigmarole."

Rigmarole, however, can be a very agreeable thing in its way, and De Quincey has carried it to a point of perfection never reached by any other rigmaroler.

Despite his undoubted possession of a kind of humour, it is a very remarkable thing that he rigmaroles, so far as can be made out by the application of the most sensitive tests, quite seriously, and almost, if not quite, unconsciously. These digressions or deviations are studded with quips and jests, good, bad, and indifferent. But the writer never seems to suspect that his own general attitude is at least susceptible of being made fun of. It is said, and we can very well believe it, that he was excessively annoyed at Lamb's delightful parody of his *Letters to a Young Man whose Education has been Neglected*; and, on the whole, I should say that no great man of letters in the century, except Balzac and Victor Hugo, was so insensible to the ludicrous aspect of his own performances. This in the author of the *Essay on Murder* may seem surprising, but, in fact, there are few things of which there are so many subdivisions, or in which the subdivisions are marked off from each other by such apparently impermeable lines, as humour. If I may refine a little I should say that there was very frequently, if not generally, a humorous basis for these divagations of De Quincey's; but that he almost invariably lost sight of that basis, and proceeded to reason quite gravely away from it, in what is (not entirely with justice) called the scholastic manner. How much of this was due to the influence of Jean Paul and the other German humorists of the last century, with whom he became acquainted very early, I should not like to say. I confess that my own enjoyment of Richter, which has nevertheless been considerable, has always been lessened by the presence in him, to a still greater degree, of this same habit of quasi-serious divagation. To appreciate the mistake of it, it is only necessary to compare the manner of Swift. The *Tale of a Tub* is in appearance as daringly discursive as anything can be, but the author in the first place never loses his way, and in the second never fails to keep a watchful eye on himself, lest he should be getting too serious or too tedious. That is what Richter and De Quincey fail to do.

Yet though these drawbacks are grave, and though they are (to judge from my own experience) felt more seriously at each successive reading, most assuredly no man who loves English literature could spare De Quincey from it; most assuredly all who love English literature would sooner spare some much more faultless writers. Even that quality of his which has been already noted, his extraordinary attraction for youth, is a singular and priceless one. The Master of the Court of the Gentiles, or the Instructor of the Sons of the Prophets, he might be called in a fantastic nomenclature, which he would have himself appreciated, if it had been applied to any one but himself. What he somewhere calls his "extraordinary ignorance of daily life" does not revolt youth. His little pedantries, which to the day of his death were like those of a clever schoolboy, appeal directly to it. His best fun is quite intelligible; his worst not wholly uncongenial. His habit (a certain most respected professor[1] in a northern university may recognise the words) of "getting into logical coaches and letting himself be carried on without minding where he is going" is anything but repugnant to brisk minds of seventeen. They are quite able to comprehend the great if mannered beauty of his finest style—the style, to quote his own words once more, as of "an elaborate and pompous sunset." Such a schoolmaster to bring youths of promise, not merely

---

[1] Edward Caird, afterwards Master of Balliol. The words were used of and to the present writer. But it is unfortunately too late for Caird to recognise them now (1923).

to good literature but to the best, nowhere else exists. But he is much more than a mere schoolmaster, and in order that we may see what he is, it is desirable first of all to despatch two other objections made to him from different quarters, and on different lines of thought. The one objection (I should say that I do not fully espouse either of them) is that he is an untrustworthy critic of books; the other is that he is a very spiteful commentator on men.

This latter charge has found wide acceptance and has been practically corroborated and endorsed by persons as different as Southey and Carlyle. It would not in any case concern us much, for when a man is once dead it matters uncommonly little whether he was personally unamiable or not. But I think that De Quincey has in this respect been hardly treated. He led such a wholly unnatural life, he was at all times and in all places so thoroughly excluded from the natural contact and friction of society, that his utterances hardly partake of the ordinary character of men's speech. In the "vacant interlunar caves" where he hid himself, he could hardly feel the restraints that press on those who move within ear-shot and jostle of their fellows on this actual earth. This is not a triumphant defence, no doubt; but I think it is a defence. And further, it has yet to be proved that De Quincey set down anything in malice. He called his literary idol, Wordsworth, "inhumanly arrogant." (Does anybody— not being a Wordsworthian and therefore out of reach of reason—doubt that Wordsworth's arrogance was inhuman?) He, not unprovoked by scant gratitude on Coleridge's part for very solid services, and by a doubtless sincere but rather unctuous protest of his brother in opium-eating against the *Confessions*, told some home truths against that magnificent genius but most unsatisfactory man. A sort of foolish folk has recently arisen which tells us that because Coleridge wrote *The Ancient Mariner* and *Kubla Khan*, he was quite entitled to leave his wife and children to be looked after by anybody who chose, to take stipends from casual benefactors, and to scold, by himself or by his next friend Mr Wordsworth, other benefactors, like Thomas Poole, who were not prepared at a moment's notice to give him a hundred pounds for a trip to the Azores. The rest of us, though we may feel no call to denounce Coleridge for these proceedings, may surely hold that *The Ancient Mariner* and *Kubla Khan* are no defence to the particular charges. I do not see that De Quincey said anything worse of Coleridge than any man who knew the then little, but now well-known facts of Coleridge's life, was entitled to say if he chose. And so in other cases. That he was what is called a thoughtful person—that is to say that he ever said to himself, "Will what I am writing give pain, and ought I to give that pain?"—I do not allege. In fact, the very excuse which has been made for him above is inconsistent with it. He always wrote far too much as one in another planet for anything of the kind to occur to him, and he was perhaps for a very similar reason rather too fond of the "personal talk" which Wordsworth wisely disdained. But that he was in any proper sense spiteful, that is to say that he ever wrote either with a deliberate intention to wound or with a deliberate indifference whether he wounded or not, I do not believe.

The other charge, that he was a bad or rather a very untrustworthy critic of books, cannot be met quite so directly. He is indeed responsible for a singularly large number of singularly grave critical blunders—by which I mean of course not critical opinions disagreeing with my own, but critical opinions which the general consent of competent critics, on the whole, negatives. The minor classical writers are not much read now, but there must be a sufficient jury to whom I can appeal to know what is to be done with a professed critic of style—at least asserting himself to be no mean classical scholar—who declares that "Paganism had no more brilliant master of composition to show than"—Velleius Paterculus! Suppose this to be a mere fling or freak, what is to be thought of a man who evidently sets Cicero, as a writer, if not as a thinker, above Plato? It would be not only possible but easy to follow this up with a long list of critical enormities on De Quincey's part, enormities due not to accidental and casual crotchet or prejudice, as in Hazlitt's case, but apparently to some perverse idiosyncrasy. I doubt very much, though the doubt may seem horribly heretical to some people, whether De Quincey really cared much for poetry as poetry. He liked philosophical poets:— Milton, Wordsworth, Shakespeare (inasmuch as he perceived Shakespeare to be the greatest of philosophical poets), Pope even in a certain way. But read the interesting paper which late in life he devoted to Shelley. He treats Shelley as a man admirably, with freedom alike from the maudlin sentiment of our modern chatterers and from Puritanical preciseness. He is not too hard on him in any way, he thinks him a pleasing personality and a thinker distorted but interesting. Of Shelley's strictly poetical quality he says nothing, if he knew or felt anything. In fact, of lyrical poetry generally, that is to say of poetry in its most purely poetical condition, he speaks very little in all his extensive critical dissertations. His want of appreciation of it may supply explanation of his unpardonable treatment of Goethe. That he should have maltreated

Wilhelm Meister is quite excusable. There are fervent
admirers of Goethe at his best who acknowledge most
fully the presence in *Wilhelm* of the two worst characteristics of German life and literature, bad taste and
tediousness. But it is not excusable that much later,
and indeed at the very height of his literary powers and
practice, he should have written the article in the
Encyclopædia Britannica on the author of *Faust*, of
Egmont, and above all of the shorter poems. Here he.
deliberately assents to the opinion that *Werther* is
"superior to everything that came after it, and for
mere power, Goethe's paramount work," dismisses
Faust as something that "no two people have ever
agreed about," sentences *Egmont* as "violating the
historic truth of character," and mentions not a single
one of those lyrics, unmatched, or rather only matched
by Heine, in the language, by which Goethe first gave
German rank with the great poetic tongues. His
severity on Swift is connected with his special "will-
worship" of ornate style, of which more presently, and
in general it may be said that De Quincey's extremely
logical disposition of mind was rather a snare to him
in his criticism. He was constantly constructing general
principles and then arguing downwards from them; in
which case woe to any individual fact or person that
happened to get in the way. Where Wilson, the "only
intimate male friend I have had" (as he somewhere
says with a half-pathetic touch of self-illumination
more instructive than reams of imaginative autobiography), went wrong from not having enough of general
principle, where Hazlitt went wrong from letting prejudices unconnected with the literary side of the matter
blind his otherwise piercing literary sight, De Quincey
fell through an unswervingness of deduction more
French than English. Your ornate writer must be

better than your plain one, *ergo*, let us say, Cicero must be better than Swift.

One other curious weakness of his (which has been glanced at already) remains to be noticed. This is the altogether deplorable notion of jocularity which he only too often exhibits. Mr Masson, trying to propitiate the enemy, admits that "to address the historian Josephus as 'Joe,' through a whole article, and give him a black eye into the bargain, is positively profane." I am not sure as to the profanity, knowing nothing particularly sacred about Josephus. But if Mr Masson had called it excessively silly, I should have agreed heartily; and if any one else denounced it as a breach of good literary manners, I do not know that I should protest. The habit is the more curious in that all authorities agree as to the exceptional combination of scholarliness and courtliness which marked De Quincey's colloquial style and expression. Wilson's daughter, Mrs Gordon, says that he used to address her father's cook "as if she had been a duchess"; and that the cook, though much flattered, was somewhat aghast at his *punctilio*. That a man of this kind should think it both allowable and funny to talk of Josephus as "Joe," and of Magliabecchi as "Mag," may be only a new example of that odd law of human nature which constantly prompts people in various relations of life, and not least in literature, to assume most the particular qualities (not always virtues or graces) that they have not. Yet it is fair to remember that Wilson and the *Blackwood* set, together with not a few writers in the *London Magazine*—the two literary coteries in connection with whom De Quincey started as a writer—had deliberately imported this element of horse-play into literature, that it at least did not seem to interfere with their popularity, and that De Quincey himself, after 1830, lived too little in touch with actual life to be aware that the style was becoming as unfashionable as it had always, save on very exceptional subjects, been ungraceful. Even on Wilson, who was to the manner born of riotous spirits, it often sits awkwardly; in De Quincey's case it is, to borrow Sir Walter's admirable simile in another case, like "the forced impudence of a bashful man." Grim humour he can manage admirably, and he also—as in the passage about the fate which waited upon all who possessed anything which might be convenient to Wordsworth, if they died—can manage a certain kind of sly humour not much less admirably. But "Joe" and "Mag," and, to take another example, the stuff about Catalina's "crocodile papa" in *The Spanish Nun*, are neither grim nor sly, they are only puerile. His staunchest defender asks, "why De Quincey should not have the same license as Swift and Thackeray?" The answer is quick and crushing. Swift and Thackeray justify their license by their use of it; De Quincey does not. After which it is hardly necessary to add, though this is almost final in itself, that neither Swift nor Thackeray interlards perfectly and unaffectedly serious work with mere fooling of the "Joe" and "Mag" kind. Swift did not put *mollis abuti* in the *Four last years of Queen Anne*, nor Thackeray his *Punch* jokes in the death-scene of Colonel Newcome. I can quite conceive De Quincey doing both.

And now I have done enough in the fault-finding way, and nothing shall induce me to say another word of De Quincey in this article save in praise. For praise he himself gives the amplest occasion; he might almost remain unblamed altogether if his praisers had not been frequently unwise, and if his *exemplar* were not specially *vitiis imitabile*. Few English writers have touched so large a number of subjects with such competence both in information and in power of handling. Still fewer have exhibited such remarkable logical faculty. One main reason why one is sometimes tempted to quarrel with him is that his play of fence is so excellent that one longs to cross swords. For this and for other reasons no writer has a more stimulating effect, or is more likely to lead his readers on to explore and to think for themselves. In none is that incurable curiosity, that infinite variety of desire for knowledge and for argument which age cannot quench, more observable. Few if any have the indefinable quality of freshness in so large a measure. You never quite know, though you may have a shrewd suspicion, what De Quincey will say on any subject; his gift of sighting and approaching new facets of it is so immense. Whether he was in truth as accomplished a classical scholar as he claimed to be I do not know; he has left few positive documents to tell us. But I should think that he was, for he has all the characteristics of a scholar of the best and rarest kind—the scholar who is exact as to language without failing to comprehend literature, and competent in literature without being slipshod as to language. His historical insight, of which the famous *Cæsars* is the best example, was, though sometimes coloured by his fancy, and at other times distorted by a slight tendency to *supercherie* as in *The Tartars* and *The Spanish Nun*, wonderfully powerful and acute. He was not exactly as Southey was, "omnilegent"; but in his own departments, and they were numerous, he went farther below the surface and connected his readings together better than Southey did. Of the two classes of severer study to which he specially addicted himself, his political economy suffered perhaps a little, acute as his views in it often are, from the fact that in his time it was practically a new study, and that he had neither sufficient facts nor sufficient literature to go upon. In metaphysics, to which he gave himself up for years, and in which he seems really to have known whatever there was to know, I fear that the opium fiend cheated the world of something like masterpieces. Only three men during De Quincey's lifetime had anything like his powers in this department. Of these three men, Sir William Hamilton either could not or would not write English. Ferrier could and did write English; but he could not, as De Quincey could, throw upon philosophy the play of literary and miscellaneous illustration which of all the sciences it most requires, and which all its really supreme exponents have been able to give it. Mansel could do both these things; but he was somewhat indolent, and had many avocations. De Quincey could write perfect English, he had every resource of illustration and relief at command, he was in his way as "brazen-bowelled" at work as he was "golden-mouthed" at expression, and he had ample leisure. But the inability to undertake sustained labour, which he himself recognises as the one unquestionable curse of opium, deprived us of an English philosopher who would have stood as far above Kant in exoteric graces, as he would have stood above Bacon in esoteric value. It was not entirely De Quincey's fault. It seems to be generally recognised now that whatever occasional excesses he may have committed, opium was really required in his case, and gave us what we have as much as it took away what we have not. But if any one chose to write in the antique style a debate between Philosophy, Tar-water, and Laudanum, it would be almost enough to put in the mouth of Philosophy, "This gave me Berkeley and that deprived me of De Quincey."

De Quincey is, however, first of all a writer of ornate

English, which was never, with him, a mere cover to bare thought. Overpraise and mispraise him as anybody may, he cannot be overpraised for this. Mistake as he chose to do, and as others have chosen to do, the relative value of his gift, the absolute value of it is unmistakable. What other Englishman, from Sir Thomas Browne downwards, has written a sentence surpassing in melody that on Our Lady of Sighs: "And her eyes, if they were ever seen, would be neither sweet nor subtle; no man could read their story; they would be found filled with perishing dreams and with wrecks of forgotten delirium"? Compare that with the masterpieces of some later practitioners. There are no out-of-the-way words; there is no needless expense of adjectives; the sense is quite adequate to the sound; the sound is only what is required as accompaniment to the sense. And though I do not know that in a single instance of equal length—even in the still more famous, and as a whole justly more famous, *tour de force* on Our Lady of Darkness—De Quincey ever quite equalled the combined simplicity and majesty of this phrase, he has constantly come close to it. The *Suspiria* are full of such passages—there are even some who prefer *Savannah la Mar* to the *Ladies of Sorrow*. Beautiful as it is I do not, because the accursed superfluous adjective appears there. The famous passages of the *Confessions* are in every one's memory; and so I suppose is the *Vision of Sudden Death*. Many passages in *The Cæsars*, though somewhat less florid, are hardly less good; and the close of *Joan of Arc* is as famous as the most ambitious attempts of the *Confessions* and the *Mail Coach*. Moreover, in all the sixteen volumes, specimens of the same kind may be found here and there, alternating with very different matter; so much so, that it has no doubt often occurred to readers that the author's occasional divergence into questionable quips and cranks is a deliberate attempt to set off his rhetoric, as dramatists of the noblest school have often set off their tragedy, with comedy, if not with farce. That such a principle would imply confusion of the study and the stage is arguable enough, but it does not follow that it was not present. At any rate the contrast, deliberate or not, is very strong indeed in De Quincey—stronger than in any other prose author except his friend, and pupil rather than master, Wilson.

The great advantage that De Quincey has, not only over this friend of his but over all practitioners of the ornate style in the century, lies in his sureness of hand in the first place, and secondly in the comparative frugality of means which perhaps is an inseparable accompaniment of sureness of hand. To mention living persons would be invidious; but Wilson and Landor are within the most scrupulous critic's right of comparison. All three were contemporaries; all three were Oxford men—Landor about ten years senior to the other two—and all three in their different ways set themselves deliberately to reverse the practice of English prose for nearly a century and a half. They did great things, but De Quincey did, I think, the greatest and certainly the most classical in the proper sense, for all Landor's superior air of Hellenism. Voluble as De Quincey often is, he seems always to have felt that when you are in your altitudes it is well not to stay there too long. And his flights, while they are far more uniformly high than Wilson's, which alternately soar and drag, are much more merciful in regard of length than Landor's, as well as for the most part much more closely connected with the sense of his subjects. There is scarcely one of the *Imaginary Conversations* which would not be the better for very considerable thinning, while, with the exception perhaps of *The English Mail Coach*, De Quincey's surplusage, obvious enough in many cases, is scarcely ever found in his most elaborate and ornate passages. The total amount of such passages in the *Confessions* is by no means large, and the more ambitious parts of the *Suspiria* do not much exceed a dozen pages. De Quincey was certainly justified by his own practice in adopting and urging as he did the distinction, due, he says, to Wordsworth, between the common and erroneous idea of style as the *dress* of thought, and the true definition of it as the *incarnation* of thought. The most wizened of coxcombs may spend days and years in dressing up his meagre and ugly carcass; but few are the sons of men who have sufficient thought to provide the soul of any considerable series of avatars. De Quincey had; and therefore, though the manner (with certain exceptions heretofore taken) in him is always worth attention, it never need or should divert attention from the matter. And thus he was not driven to make a little thought do tyrannous duty as lay-figure for an infinite amount of dress, or to hang out frippery on a clothes-line with not so much as a lay-figure inside it. Even when he is most conspicuously "fighting a prize," there is always solid stuff in him.

Few indeed are the writers of whom so much can be said, and fewer still the miscellaneous writers, among whom De Quincey must be classed. On almost any subject that interested him—and the number of such subjects was astonishing, curious as are the gaps between the different groups of them—what he has to say is pretty sure, even if it be the wildest paradox in appearance, to be worth attending to. And in regard to most things that he has to say, the reader may be pretty sure also that he will not find them better said elsewhere. It has sometimes been complained by students, both of De Quincey the man and of De Quincey the writer, that there is something not exactly human in him. There is certainly much in him of the dæmonic, to use a word which was a very good word and really required in the language, and which ought not to be exiled because it has been foolishly abused. Sometimes, as has also been complained, the demon is a mere familiar with the tricksiness of Puck rather than the lightness of Ariel. But far oftener he is a more potent spirit than any Robin Goodfellow, and as powerful as Ariel and Ariel's master. Trust him wholly you may not; a characteristic often noted in intelligences that are neither exactly human, nor exactly diabolic, nor exactly divine. But he will do great things for you, and a little wit and courage on your part will prevent his doing anything serious against you. To him, with much greater justice than to Hogg, might Wilson have applied the nickname of Brownie, which he was so fond of bestowing upon the author of *Kilmeny*. He will do solid work, conjure up a concert of aerial music, play a shrewd trick now and then, and all this with a curious air of irresponsibility and of remoteness of nature. In ancient days when kings played experiments to ascertain the universal or original language, some monarch might have been tempted to take a very clever child, interest him so far as possible in nothing but books and opium, and see whether he would turn out anything like De Quincey. But it is in the highest degree improbable that he would. Therefore let us rejoice, though according to the precepts of wisdom and not too indiscriminately, in our De Quincey as we once, and probably once for all, received him.

APPENDIX A

DE QUINCEY

A SHORT time after the publication of my essay on De Quincey I learnt, to my great concern, that it had given offence to his daughter Florence, the widow of one of the heroes of the Indian Mutiny, Colonel Baird Smith. Mrs Baird Smith complained, in a letter to the newspapers, that I had accused her father of untruthfulness, and requested the public to suspend their judgment until the publication of certain new documents, in the form of letters, which had been discovered. I might have replied, if my intent had been hostile, that little fault could be justly found with a critic of the existing evidence if new evidence were required to confute him. But as the very last intention that I had in writing the paper was to impute anything that can be properly called untruthfulness to De Quincey, I thought it better to say so and to wait for the further documents. In a subsequent private correspondence with Mrs Baird Smith, I found that what had offended her (her complaints being at first quite general) was certain remarks on De Quincey's aristocratic acquaintances as appearing in the *Autobiography* and "not heard of afterwards," certain comments on the Malay incident and others like it, some on the mystery of her father's money affairs, and the passage on his general "impenetrability." The matter is an instance of the difficulty of dealing with recent reputations, when the commentator gives his name. Some really unkind things have been said of De Quincey; my intention was not to say anything unkind at all, but simply to give an account of the thing "as it strikes" if not "a contemporary" yet a well-willing junior. Take for instance the Malay incident. We know from De Quincey himself that, within a few years, the truth of this famous story was questioned, and that he was accused of having borrowed it from something of Hogg's. He disclaimed this, no doubt truly. He protested that it was a faithfully recorded incident: but though the events were then fresh, he did not produce a single witness to prove that any Malay had been near Grasmere at the time. And so elsewhere. As I have remarked about Borrow, there are some people who have a knack of recounting truth so that it looks as if it never had been true. I have been informed by Mr James Runciman that he himself once made considerable inquiries on the track of *Lavengro*, and found that that remarkable book is, to some extent at any rate, apparently historic. On the other hand I have been told by another Borrovian who knew Borrow (which I never did) that the *Life of Joseph Sell* never existed. In such cases a critic can only go on internal evidence, and I am sure that the vast majority of critics would decide against most of De Quincey's stories on that. I do not suppose that he ever, like Lamb, deliberately begat "lie-children": but opium-eating is not absolutely repugnant to delusion, and literary mystification was not so much the exception as the rule in his earlier time. As to his "impenetrability," I can only throw myself on the readers of such memoirs and reminiscences as have been published respecting him. The almost unanimous verdict of his acquaintances and critics has been that he was in a way mysterious, and though no doubt this mystery did not extend to his children, it seems to have extended to almost every one else. I gather from Mrs Baird Smith's own remarks that from first to last all who were concerned with him treated him as a person unfit to be trusted with money, and while his habit of solitary lodging is doubtless capable of a certain amount of explanation, it cannot be described as other than curious. I had never intended to throw doubt on his actual acquaintance with Lord Westport or Lady Carbery. These persons or their representatives were alive when the *Autobiography* was published, and would no doubt have protested if De Quincey had not spoken truly. But I must still hold that their total disappearance from his subsequent life is peculiar. Some other points, such as his mentioning Wilson as his "only intimate male friend" are textually cited from himself, and if I seem to have spoken harshly of his early treatment by his family I may surely shelter myself behind the touching incident, recorded in the biographies, of his crying on his deathbed, "My dear mother! then I was greatly mistaken." If this does not prove that he himself had entertained on the subject ideas which, whether false or true, were unfavourable, then it is purely meaningless.

In conclusion, I have only to repeat my regret that I should, by a perhaps thoughtless forgetfulness of the feelings of survivors, have hurt those feelings. But I think I am entitled to say that the view of De Quincey's character and cast of thought given in the text, while imputing nothing discreditable in intention, is founded on the whole published work and all the biographical evidence then accessible to me, and will not be materially altered[1] by anything since published or likely to be so in future. The world, though often not quite right, is never quite wrong about a man, and it would be almost impossible that it should be wrong in face of such autobiographic details as are furnished, not merely by the *Autobiography* itself, but by a mass of notes spread over seven years in composition and full of personal idiosyncrasy. I not only acquit De Quincey of all serious moral delinquency,—I declare distinctly that no imputation of it was ever intended. It is quite possible that some of his biographers and of those who knew him may have exaggerated his peculiarities, less possible I think that those peculiarities should not have existed. But the matter, except for my own regret at having offended De Quincey's daughter, will have been a happy one if it results in a systematic publication of his letters, which, from the specimens already printed, must be very characteristic and very interesting[2]. In almost all cases a consider-

---

[1] It has not been (1923).

[2] They were not quite as much so as might have been expected (1923).

able collection of letters is the most effective, and especially the most truth-telling, of all possible "lives." No letters indeed are likely to increase the literary repute of the author of the *Confessions* and of the *Cæsars*; but they may very well clear up and fill in the hitherto rather fragmentary and conjectural notion of his character, and they may, on the other hand, confirm that idea of both which, however false it may seem to his children, and others who were united to him by ties of affection, has commended itself to careful students of his published works.

Since the above Essay, and the Appendix to it, were written, not inconsiderable additions have been made to De Quincey's works besides the *Letters* referred to. It may I think be said without rashness that though a few minor points in his life have been cleared up, they have made no alterations in *criticism* of the very slightest importance, necessary. I fear, however, that these accretions have not resulted in much, if any, increased appreciation. My friend the late Mr Henley made a sort of "dead set" at De Quincey: and independently of this he seems to have fallen out of Edwardian and Georgian taste (1923).

X

ROBERT SOUTHEY

NEARLY seventy years ago Macaulay expressed a doubt whether Southey's poems would be read in half a century, but was certain that, if read, they would be admired. The doubt has been certainly justified; the certainty may seem more than a little doubtful. Southey's character, which was once subjected to the most unjust, though not perhaps the most unintelligible or inexcusable, obloquy, has long been cleared; and those who most dislike his matured views in political and ecclesiastical matters are the first to admit that few English men of letters have a more stainless record. His prose style, the merits of which were indeed never denied by any competent judges, has won more and more praise from such judges as time went on. But he is less read than ever as a whole, and his poems are the least read part of him. These poems, which the best critics of his own generation admired, if not without reserve in detail, without any misgiving on the whole; on which he himself counted, not in boastfulness or in pique, but with a serene and quiet confidence, to make him as much exalted by the next age as he thought himself unduly neglected by his own; which Landor admired to enthusiasm and many others to warmth, while they extorted a grudging tribute even from the prejudice of Byron,—now find hardly any readers, and still fewer to praise than to read. Even among the few who have read them, and who can discern their merits, esteem rather than enthusiasm is the common note, and esteem is about the most fatal sentiment that can be accorded to poetry.

It is of the prose rather than of the verse that Macaulay's prognostication has been thoroughly fulfilled. *The Life of Nelson* represents it a little less forlornly, but with hardly less injustice than *The Battle of Blenheim* and one or two other things represent the verse in the public memory. The stately quartos of *The History of Brazil* and *The Peninsular War*, the decent octavos of *The Colloquies on the Progress and Prospects of Society* and *The Book of the Church*, the handy little duodecimos of *Espriella* and *Omniana*, with all the rest, have to be sought in catalogues and got together, not indeed with immense research (for none of them is exactly rare) but with some trouble and delay. In any other country a decent, if not a splendid, complete edition would long ago have enshrined and kept on view work so admirable in style always, frequently so excellent in mere substance, so constantly enlivened with flashes of agreeable humour or hardly less agreeable prejudice, and above all informed by such an astonishing knowledge of books. Johnson may have been fitted to grapple with whole libraries; but Southey did grapple with them, his industry being as notoriously untiring as the great Lexicographer's was notoriously intermittent.

Even in the article of biography the same malign, and to some slight degree mysterious, fate has pursued him. His life was extremely uneventful; but, except for the great catastrophe of Sir Walter's speculative career, it was not much more uneventful than Scott's. He was a delightful, though a somewhat too copious letter-writer, he knew at all times of his life some of the most interesting people of the day, and scanty as were his means he was a very hospitable host and an untiring cicerone in a country flooded every year with tourists. But he was as unlucky in his biographers as

Scott and Byron were lucky. Cuthbert Southey appears to have been an excellent person of good taste and fair judgment, but possessed of no great literary skill in general, and of no biographical genius in particular; while he had the additional disadvantage of being the youngest child, born too late to know much of his father, or of his father's affairs during earlier years. Dr Warter, Southey's son-in-law, had more literary ambition than Cuthbert; but he was deficient in judgment and in the indispensable power of selecting from the letters of a man who seems often to have written much the same things to three or four correspondents on the same day. The result is that, though the *Life and Correspondence* is a charming book as a book, with portraits and frontispieces showing the dead and delightful art of line-engraving at its best, and though both it, the *Selected Letters* and the *Letters of Southey to Caroline Bowles* are full of interest, that interest is so frittered and duplicated, watered down and wasted in the eleven volumes, that only patient and skilled extractors can get at it. An abridgment, putting the life together in Southey's own words, has, I believe, been executed and by no incompetent hand; but there is always a curse on abridgments. And besides, the charm of a biography consists hardly more in the actual autobiographic matter, found in letters or otherwise, than in the connecting framework. It is because Boswell and Lockhart knew how to execute this framework in such a masterly fashion that their books possess an immortality which even the conversations of Johnson, even the letters of Scott, could not have fully achieved by themselves.

Southey, for whose early years there is practically no source of information but an autobiographic fragment written rather late in life, and dwelling on detail with interesting though rather disproportionate fulness, was born in Wine Street, Bristol, on the 12th of August 1774. His birthday gave him, according to an astrological friend, "a gloomy capability of walking through desolation," but does not seem to have carried with it any sporting tendencies. At least his only recorded exploit in that way is the highly eccentric, and one would think slightly hazardous, one of shooting wasps with a horse-pistol loaded with sand[1]. His father, also a Robert, was only a linen-draper, but the Southeys, though, as their omnilegent representative confesses, "so obscure that he never found the name in any book," were Somerset folk of old date and entitled to bear arms. They had moreover actual wealth in the possession of one of their members, the poet's uncle, John Cannon Southey, and expectations in the shape of estates entailed upon them in default of the male heirs of Lord Somerville. Southey, however, never benefited by either, for his uncle's fortune went out of the family altogether, and it turned out that Lord Somerville had somehow got the entail barred. His father too failed and died early, and all the family assistance that he ever had came from the side of his mother, Margaret Hill, who was pretty well connected. Her half-sister, Miss Tyler, extended a capricious and tyrannical protection to the boy in his extreme youth (turning him out of doors later on the score of Pantisocracy and Miss Fricker), while her brother, Mr Hill, a clergyman, was Southey's Providence till long after he reached manhood. After a childhood (unimportant though interesting to read about) in which he very early developed a passion for English literature, he was sent by his uncle to Westminster in the spring of 1788, and re-

---

[1] I have myself, sixty or seventy years ago, though unintentionally, slain a grasshopper with the wad projected from a cannon (1923).

mained there with not much intermission till it was time for him to go to Oxford.

This latter translation, however, was not effected without alarums and excursions. Although Southey, neither as boy nor yet as man, was the kind of person thoroughly to enjoy or thoroughly to profit by a public school, he was on the whole loyal to his own, and it produced a valuable and durable impression on him. The coarser and more hackneyed advantage of "making friends" he had to the uttermost; for it was there that he made the acquaintance of Charles Watkin Williams Wynn, who was through life his patron as well as his friend, and of Grosvenor Bedford, his constant correspondent and intellectual double. He also profited as much as need be in the matter of education, though, as has happened with other boys who have gone to school with more general information than solid instruction, he was promoted rather too rapidly to become a thorough scholar in the strict sense. Nor did some rough experiences in his early days do him much, if any, harm.

But the end of his stage was in a way unfortunate. Nothing could have less resembled the real man than his enemies' representation of him as a supple and servile instrument, keen to note and obstinate to seize the side on which his bread was buttered, and born to be a frequenter of "Mainchance Villa." As a matter of fact he was always an uncompromising and impracticable idealist, though with some safeguards to be noticed presently. In his last days at school he showed this quality just as he did twenty or forty years later, when he constantly struggled to write in *The Quarterly Review* as if he were sole proprietor, sole editor, and sole contributor thereof, just as he did when the heat of his Jacobinism was not at fullest, by "declining to drink Suwarrow," just as he did after he had thoroughly rallied to the Party of Order by refusing, in spite of the personal instances of the Duke of Wellington, to alter a judgment in his *Peninsular War*. It is needless to say that in his time, as earlier and later, any Westminster boy of ability rather above the average and of tolerable character and conduct, had his future made plain by the way of Christ Church or Trinity as the case might be. But Southey must needs start a periodical called *The Flagellant*, whereof the very title was in the circumstances seditious, and in an early number made a direct attack on corporal punishment. This arousing the authorities, he confessed and expressed contrition; but the head-master, Dr Vincent, was implacable, and not only insisted on his leaving the school, but directly or indirectly caused Dean Cyril Jackson to refuse to receive him even as a commoner at Christ Church.

He fell back, however, upon Balliol, and matriculated without demur in November 1792, going into residence in January. Perhaps, indeed, though his fortunes were now entering on a rather prolonged low tide, this particular ill luck was, even from the lowest point of view, not such very bad luck after all. At Christ Church even as a commoner, much more as a junior student, under such a Dean as Jackson, who bore the sword by no means in vain, a youngster of Southey's tone and temper, full of Jacobinism and all its attendant crazes, would have come probably, and rather sooner than later, to some signal mischance, even more decided and damaging to his prospects than the close of his Westminster career. At Balliol, though he was in no particularly good odour, they seem to have left him very much alone, not resenting even the shocking innovation of his wearing his hair uncropped and unpowdered in hall. His tutor, with perhaps more frankness than sense of duty, said to him, "Mr Southey, sir, you won't learn anything by my lectures; so if you have any studies of your own, you had better pursue them." This he did by getting up at five o'clock in the morning to breakfast (one shudders to hear) on "bread and cheese and red wine negus," walking all over the country, learning to swim and to row, and associating chiefly with men of his old school. He seems to have kept terms or not with a casualty somewhat surprising even in that age of lax discipline and few or no examinations; and after about a year and a half of this sort of thing, he ceased to reside at all. It is scarcely surprising that he should have felt very little affection for a place where he stayed so little and sat so loose; and long afterwards he notes that, though he was constantly dreaming of Westminster, he never dreamed of Oxford.

In fact he was busy with thoughts and schemes quite alien from the existing scheme, or indeed from any possible scheme, of the university. He had made the acquaintance of Coleridge; his boyish friendship with the Miss Frickers had ripened into an engagement with one of them, Edith; he had, though the atrocities of the Terror had much weakened his Gallomania, written *Joan of Arc*, and he had plunged ardently into the famous schemes of "Pantisocracy" and "Aspheterism." Of these much has been heard, though I never could make out, why, of these two characteristic specimens of Estesian language, Pantisocracy should have secured a place in the general memory while its companion has not. As Coleridge's many biographers have made known, Pantisocracy, a scheme for a socialist colony in Pennsylvania or Wales or anywhere, broke down; and it pleased Coleridge to consider that the blame was mainly Southey's. As a matter of fact it was impossible to start it without money, of which most of the Pantisocrats had none, and the others very little; and no doubt Southey who, visionary as he still was, had some common sense and a very keen sense of what was due to others, saw that to attempt it would be cruel and criminal. While Coleridge had been ecstatically formulating his enthusiasm in such sentences as "America! Southey! Miss Fricker! Pantisocracy!" his more practical friend was inquiring of Mr Midshipman Thomas Southey, his brother, "What do your common blue trousers cost?" Alas! when a man combines even an enthusiastic love for Aspheterism with a sense of the cost of common blue trousers, the end cannot be doubtful.

If, however, anybody imagined (and indeed the manufacturers of "Mr Feathernest" did try to set up such a notion) that Southey relinquished his generous schemes of honest toil abroad for a life of pensioned and voluptuous infamy at home, it was a very vain imagination. For a time, in October 1794, and later, his prospects were about as little encouraging as those of any young man in England. He had steadfastly resolved not to take Orders, the cardinal point of his benevolent uncle's scheme for him; his aunt turned him out of doors; his mother had nothing to give him; and his intended bride was penniless. His wants, however, were exceedingly modest, but fifty pounds a year. He delivered historical lectures at Bristol, lectures of the beautiful sweeping sort ("from the Origin of Society to the American War") which the intelligent undergraduate delights in; and they seem to have been not unsuccessful. John Scott, the future victim of that unlucky duel, undertook to find him journalism at a guinea and a half a week, though it is not clear that this ever came to anything. Cottle (Joseph of Bristol, the brother of Amos) gave him fifty guineas for *Joan of Arc*, and as many copies of the book to get rid of by subscription. Lastly, Mr Hill, his unwearied uncle, suggested that, as he would not take Orders, he should go to Lisbon (where Mr Hill was chaplain) for six months to "simmer down," and should then read law. Southey consented, but resolving to make desertion of his betrothed impossible, married Edith Fricker on 14th November, 1795, and parted from her at the church-door.

This marriage, and the Portuguese journey which immediately succeeded, may be said to have finally settled Southey's fortunes in life, young as he was at the time. He was never the man to shirk a responsibility, and though for some time to come he loyally attempted to read law, he soon made up his mind that it was never likely to give him a livelihood. On the other hand, his visit to the Peninsula, with the interest thus created in its history and languages, gave him that central subject and occupation which is almost indispensable to a working man of letters (such as he was marked out to be and soon became) if he is not to be a mere bookseller's hack. Directly, indeed, Southey's Spanish and Portuguese books and studies were about the least remunerative of all his mostly ill-paid work. The great *History of Portugal*, planned almost at once, never saw the light at all; and *The History of Brazil*, its more manageable offshoot and episode, was but an unprofitable work. But this visit to Lisbon, and another of somewhat longer duration which he took with his wife some years later, were of immense service. They thoroughly established his health, which had been anything but strong; they gave him, as has been said, a central subject to work upon in which he became an authority and which served as tie-beam and king-post both to his multifarious work; and they furnished him with one of those invaluable stores of varied and pleasurable memory than which nothing is of more consequence to a man whose life is to be passed in apparently monotonous study. He more than once planned a third visit, but war, scanty finances, unceasing occupations, and other things prevented it; and though in his later years he took a fair allowance of holidays, not unfrequently on the Continent, he never returned to Cintra and the Arrabida and those charmed territories of the "Roi de Garbe" to which he looked back as a sort of earthly Paradise, for all his consciousness that neither the things nor the people there were in all ways very good.

Nor were many years to pass before he was established in the district with which his name is connected only less indissolubly than that of Wordsworth. He had indeed no special fancy for the Lakes, nor for their climate after that of Portugal, and for some years at least had great difficulty in reconciling himself to them. But he hated London, where, when he at last gave up the Bar, there was nothing particular to keep him; death and other chances weakened his ties to Bristol, and he had none elsewhere, while his fast-growing library made some settled abode imperative. At last Coleridge, who had already settled himself at Keswick in a house too large for him, pressed the Southeys to join him there. Mrs Southey naturally was glad to have the company of her sister, and they went, at first for a short time, but soon took root. Meanwhile the chief practical question had been settled first by the acceptance from his friend Wynn, a man of means, of an annuity of £160, and, secondly, by much miscellaneous newspaper work in the form of poems and reviews.

Thalaba, which had been finished in Portugal (where *Kehama*, under the name of *Keradon*, was begun), brought him some fame, though his gains from this kind of work were always insignificant. But Southey, if he had expensive tastes, did not indulge them; his wife was an excellent manager—too excellent indeed as the sequel was thought to show, for her housewifely cares seemed to have helped to break down her health of mind and body at last. So he contrived in some incomprehensible manner not only to keep out of debt, but to help his own family liberally and strangers with no sparing hand.

The sojourn at Keswick began in 1801, and only ceased with Southey's life, though immediately after his arrival an appointment, which he soon gave up, as secretary to Mr Corry, the Irish Chancellor, interrupted it. Various attempts were made by himself and his friends to get him something better, but without success, and his own preferments, until quite late in his life Sir Robert Peel supplemented them with a fresh pension, were a Government annuity of £200 a year (much reduced by fees), which enabled him to relinquish Wynn's, and which was given him by the Whigs in 1808, and the Laureateship in 1814 with its pay of rather less than £100 a year. Such were the ill-gotten gains for which, according to the enemy, "Mr Feathernest" sold his conscience.

Although Southey was but seven-and-twenty when he settled at Keswick, and though he lived for more than forty years longer, it is as unnecessary as it would be impracticable to follow his life during this later period as minutely as we have done hitherto. The ply was now taken, the vocation distinctly indicated, and the means and place of exercising it more or less secured. Thenceforward he lived in laborious peace, disturbed only by the loss in 1816 of his beloved son Herbert, about ten years later by that of his youngest daughter Isabel, and later by the mental illness and death of his wife. He never recovered this last shock; and though he married again, his second wife being the poetess Caroline Bowles, it was as a nurse rather than as a wife that Edith's successor accepted him, and he died himself after some years of impaired intelligence on 21st March, 1843.

An almost extravagantly Roman nose (the other Robert, Herrick, is the only Englishman I can think of who excelled him in this respect) and an extreme thinness did not prevent Southey from being a very handsome man. His enemy Byron, who had no reason to be discontented with his own, declared that "to possess Southey's head and shoulders he would almost have written his Sapphics"; and, despite his immense labours and his exceedingly bad habit of reading as he walked, he was till almost the last strong and active. The excellence of his moral character has never been seriously contested by any one who knew; and the only blemish upon it appears to have been a slight touch of Pharisaism, not indeed of the most detestable variety which exalts itself above the publican, but of the still trying kind which is constantly inclined to point out to the publican what a publican he is, and what sad things publicans are, and how he had much better leave off being one. We know even better than was known fifty years ago what were Coleridge's weaknesses, yet it is impossible not to wish that Coleridge's brother-in-law had not written, and difficult not to wonder that Coleridge's nephew did not refrain from printing, certain elaborate letters of reproof, patronage, and good advice. So, too, the abuse and misrepresentation which Byron, and those who took their cue from Byron, lavished on Southey were inexcusable enough; but again one cannot help wishing that he had been a little less heartily convinced of the utter and extreme depravity and wickedness of these men. Still, there was no humbug in Southey; there was a great deal of virtue, and a virtuous man who is not something of a humbug is apt to be a little of a Pharisee unless he is a perfect saint, which Southey, to do him justice, was not. On the contrary, he was a man of middle earth, who was exceedingly fond of gooseberry tart and black currant rum, of strong ale and Rhenish, who loved to crack jokes, would give his enemy at least as good as he got from him, and was nearly as human as any one could desire.

Of his famous so-called tergiversation little need be said. Everybody, whatever his own politics, who has looked into the matter has long ago come to the conclusion that it was only tergiversation in appearance. Southey once said that political writing required a logical attitude of mind which he had not; and this is quite true, so true that it was a great pity he ever took to it. From sympathising in a vague youthful way with what he imagined to be the principles of the French Revolution, he changed to a hearty detestation of its practice. His liking for the Spaniards and his dislike of the French turned him from an opponent of the war to a defender of it, and it was this more than anything else that parted him from his old Whig friends. In short he was always guided by his sympathies; and as he was never in his hottest days of Aspheterism anything like a consistent and reasoned Radical, so in his most rancorous days of reaction he never was a consistent or reasoned Tory.

Of his life, however, and his character, and even of his opinion, interesting as all three are, it is impossible to say more here. We must pass over with the merest mention that quaint freak of Nemesis which made a mysterious Dissenting Minister produce from nobody knew where *Wat Tyler*, and publish it as the work of a Tory Laureate twenty-three years after it was written by an undergraduate Jacobin, the oddity of the thing being crowned by Lord Eldon's characteristic refusal to grant an injunction on the ground that a man could not claim property in a work hurtful to the public. Which refusal assured the free circulation of this hurtful work, instead of its suppression. And we can only allude to the not yet clearly intelligible negotiations, or misunderstandings, as to his succession to the editorship of *The Quarterly Review* when Gifford was failing. In these Southey seems to have somehow conceived that the place was his to take if he chose (which he never intended) or to allot to some one else as he liked; with the very natural result that a sort of bitterness, never completely removed and visible in the Review's notice of his life, arose between him and Lockhart after the latter's appointment. His selection by Lord Radnor (who did not know him) as member for Downton in the last days of rotten boroughs, and his election without his knowing it, was another odd incident. The last important event of his life in this kind was the offer of a baronetcy and the actual conferring of an additional pension of £300 by Peel, who, whatever faults he may have had, was the only Prime Minister since Harley who has ever taken much real interest in the welfare of men of letters.

But we must turn to the works; and a mighty armful, or rather several mighty armfuls they are to turn to. The poems, which are the chief stumbling-block, were collected by Southey himself in ten very pretty little volumes in 1837–8. After his death they were more popularly issued in one, his cousin, the Rev. H. Hill, son by a late marriage of the uncle who had been so good to him, editing a supernumerary volume of rather superfluous fragments, the chief of which was an American tale called *Oliver Newman*, on which Southey had been engaged for very many years. He had the good sense and pluck (indeed he was never deficient in the second of these qualities, and not often in the first), to print *Wat Tyler* just as the pirates had launched it after its twenty-three years on the stocks. It is very amusing and exactly what might be expected from a work written in three days by a Jacobin boy who had read a good many old plays. Canning, Ellis, and Frere together could have produced in fun nothing better than this serious outburst of Wat's:

> Think ye, my friend,
> That I, a humble blacksmith, here in Deptford,
> Would part with these six groats, earned with hard toil,
> All that I have, to massacre the Frenchmen,
> Murder as enemies men I never saw,
> Did not the State compel me?

One would like to have heard Mr Wopsle in this part. For the rest, the thing contains some good blank verse, and a couple of very pretty songs,—considerably better, I should think, than most other things of the kind published in the year 1794, which was about the thickest of the dark before the dawn of the *Lyrical Ballads*. *Joan of Arc*, Wat's elder sister by a year, though not published till a year after *Wat* was written, is now in a less virgin condition than her brother, Southey having made large changes in the successive (five) early editions, and others in the definitive one more than forty years after the first. The popularity (for it was really popular) of the poem, shows rather the dearth of good poetry at the time of its appearance than anything else. It displays very few of the merits of Southey's later long poems, and it does display the chief of all their defects, the defect which Coleridge, during the tiff over Pantisocracy, hit upon in a letter of which the original was advertised for sale a few years ago. This fault, least observable in *Thalaba* and *Kehama*, but painfully obvious in the others, consists in conveying to the reader a notion that the writer has said, "Go to, let us make a poem," and has accordingly, to borrow the language of Joe Gargery's forge-song,

> Beat it out, beat it out,
> With a clink for the stout,

but with very little inspiration for the poetical. *Joan of Arc* is a most respectable poem, admirable in sentiment and not uninteresting as a tale in verse. But the conception is pedestrian and the blank verse is to match:

> While thus in Orleans hope had banished sleep,
> The Maiden's host had prayed their evening prayer,
> And in the forest took their rest secure.

Very unexceptionable no doubt, but also extremely uninspiring. It is in its own way written very well; but one sees not why it should ever have been written at all.

Between this crude production and the very different *Thalaba* which followed it at some years' distance, Southey wrote very many, perhaps most, of his minor poems; and the characteristics of them may be best noticed together. In the earliest of all it must be confessed that the crotchet of thought and the mannerism of style which drew down on him the lash of the *Anti-Jacobin* are very plentifully exhibited. A most schoolboy Pindaric is *The Triumph of Woman*. The strange mixture of alternate childishness and pomposity which is almost the sole tie between the Lake Poets in their early work, pervades all the Poems on the Slave Trade,

the Botany Bay Eclogues, the Sonnets and the Mono-
dramas. Even in the Lyrical Poems written at Bristol,
or rather Westbury, in the years 1798–9, there would
be no very noticeable advance if it were not for the
delightful *Holly Tree*, from which Hazlitt has extracted
the well-deserved text of a compliment more graceful
than Hazlitt is usually credited with conceiving, and
which, with the later but not better *Stanzas written in
my Library*, is Southey's greatest achievement as an
occasional poet in the serious kind. His claims in the
comic and mixed departments are much more considerable. *Abel Shufflebottom* is fun, and being very early
testifies to a healthy consciousness of the ridiculous.
For his English Eclogues I have no great love; but it
is something to say in their favour that they were the
obvious originals of Tennyson's English Idylls as much
in manner as in title.

The Ballads, with the much discussed *Devil's Walk*
as an early outsider in one key, and the curious *All for
Love* as a late one in another, have much more to be
said for them than that in the same way they are the
equally obvious originators of the *Ingoldsby Legends*.
They are not easily criticised in a few words. In themselves they were not quite ancestorless, for "Monk"
Lewis, no great man of letters, but something of a man
of metre, had taught the author a good deal. They are
nearly as unequal as another division of Southey's own
verse, his Odes, of which it is perhaps sufficient to say
here that they were remarkably like Young's, especially
in the way in which they rattle up and down the whole
gamut from sublimity to absurdity. The Ballads frequently underlie the reproach of applying Voltairian
methods to anything in which the author did not
happen to believe, while nothing made him more indignant than any such application by others to things

in which he did believe—a reproach urged forcibly by Lamb in that undeserved but not unnatural attack in *The London Magazine*, which Southey met with a really noble magnanimity. But at their best they are very original for their time, and very good for all time. *The Old Woman of Berkeley*, one of the oldest and probably the most popular in its day, is perhaps the best. It has a fair pendant in *Bishop Hatto*, and the Bishop perhaps meets the modern taste even better than the Old Woman. The Fastrada story is too much vulgarised in *King Charlemain*, and it may be generally confessed of Southey that to the finest touches of romance he was rather insensitive, his nature lacking the "strange and high" feeling of passion. But he is thoroughly at home in *The King of the Crocodiles*. Everybody knows *The Inchcape Rock*, and *The Well of St Keyne*, and *The Battle of Blenheim*; indeed it is very possible that they are the only things of Southey that everybody does know. The Spanish Ballads are not nearly so good as Lockhart's: but Lockhart had the illegitimate advantage of grafting Scott's technique on Southey's special knowledge. Nevertheless, it may be said that all the ballads and metrical tales are to this day well worth reading, that both Scott and Byron owed them not a little, and that they indicate a vein in their author which might have been worked in different circumstances to even better advantage.

Still Southey's chief poetical claim is not here; and the best of the things as yet mentioned have been equalled by men with whom poetry was a mere occasional pastime. Nor do his Inscriptions, for which he has received high praise from some good critics, seem to me quite of the first class. They are, as a rule, too long, whereas an inscription, whether verse or prose, can hardly be too short. And what is worse, they too frequently have the elevation on stilts, the monumental effort in plaster, the slightly flatulent rhetoric, so incomparably parodied and ridiculed in the *Anti-Jacobin* by means of the immortal lines on Mrs Brownrigg. The *style noble* is the most dangerous of all styles. Of *The Vision of Judgment* it cannot be necessary to say anything in detail. It is not so bad as those who only know it from Byron's triumphant castigation may think, but otherwise I can only suppose that the Devil, tired of Southey's perpetual joking at him, was determined to have his revenge, and that he was permitted to do so by the Upper Powers in consequence of the bumptious Pharisaism of the preface. *The Pilgrimage to Waterloo* and *The Tale of Paraguay* are poetically no better though rather more mature than *Joan of Arc*; *Madoc* was admired by good men at its appearance, but frequent attempts, made with the best good will, to read it have not enabled me to place it much higher than these.

Roderick, the last of the long poems in blank verse, is also, I think, by far the best. The absence of pulse and throb in the verse, of freshness and inevitableness in the phrase and imagery is indeed not seldom felt here also; but there is something which redeems it. The author's thorough knowledge of the details and atmosphere of his subject has vivified the details and communicated the atmosphere; the unfamiliarity and the romantic interest of the story are admirably given, and the thing is about as good as a long poem in blank verse which is not of the absolute first class can be.

Of *Thalaba the Destroyer* and *The Curse of Kehama* we must speak differently. The one was completely written, the other sketched and well begun in that second sojourn at Lisbon which was Southey's golden time:

> When, friends with love and leisure,
> Youth not yet left behind,
> He worked or played at pleasure,
> Found God and Goddess kind;

when his faculties, tolerably matured by study, were still in their first freshness, and when he had not yet settled down, and was not yet at all certain that he should have to settle down, to the dogged collar-work of his middle and later age. I have no hesitation as to which I prefer. The rhymeless Pindarics of *Thalaba*, written while Southey was following Sayers in that anti-rhyming heresy which nobody but Milton has ever rendered orthodox by sheer stress of genius, are a great drawback to the piece; there are constant false notes like this of Maimuna,

> Her *fine* face raised to Heaven,

where the commonplace adjective mars the passionate effect; and though the eleventh and twelfth books, with the journey to Domdaniel and the successful attack on it, deserved to produce the effect which they actually did produce on their own generation, the story as a whole is a little devoid of interest.

All these weak points were strengthened and guarded in *The Curse of Kehama*, the greatest thing by far that Southey did, and a thing, as I think, really great, without any comparatives and allowances. Scott, always kind and well-affected to Southey as he was, appears to me to have been a little unjust to *Kehama*; an injustice which appears between the lines of his review of it, and in those of his reference to it in his biography. It is perfectly true, as he suggests, that Southey was specially prone to the general weakness of insisting on and clinging to his own weakest points. I often think, when I read him, of a distinguished man of letters whom I once heard reply to a very modest remonstrance (not made by me), "I should write it again to-morrow," setting his teeth as he did so. But this foible as it seems to me is less, not more, obvious in *The Curse of Kehama*. In the first place the poet has actually given up the craze for irregular blank verse, and the additional charm of rhyme makes all the difference between this poem and *Thalaba*. In the second place the central idea—the acquisition, through prescribed means, allowed by the gods, of a power greater than that of the gods themselves, by even the worst man who cares to go through the course—communicates a kind of antinomy of interest, a conflict of official and poetical justice which is unique, or if not unique, rare out of Greek tragedy. In the mediæval legends, delightful as they are, the interest is sometimes weakened by the illegitimate way in which the Virgin, or somebody else, will interfere to set things right. The defeat of Kehama by his own wilful act in demanding the Amreeta-cup is as unexpected and as artistically effective as the maxim,

> Less than Omniscience could not suffice
> To wield Omnipotence,

is philosophically sound.

Moreover the characters are interesting, at least to me. No *Rejected Addresses* shall avail to make me laugh at the blessed Glendoveer, who behaves throughout like a gentleman and a Trojan, as does also Ladurlad. It may be that Kailyal is almost too good a young person; but nowadays in particular, when we have an almost unvarying supply of the other kind in literature, she ought to be welcome if only for a change. Arvalan, though a very bad man, is a most excellent ghost; Lorrinite is a good witch. And then, to supplement these several attractions, there are for the wicked men who love "passages," who like "patches," quite delectable things. The author pretended ("not that it was really so," as Lamb says) to think the famous and beautiful,

> They sin who tell us love can die,

claptrap; if it be so, would he had sinned a little oftener in the same style! Nobody, except out of mere youthful paradox, can affect to undervalue the Curse itself. It is thoroughly good in scheme and in execution, in gross and in detail; there are no better six-and-twenty lines for their special purpose in all English poetry. And the first operation of the Curse is good, and the recovery of Kailyal, and the picture of the Swerga (though really Indra is but a cool and insignificant Divine Person) and that of Mount Meru. But the finest scenes of the poem are no doubt ushered in by the description of the famous Sea City which Landor re-described in the best known of all his stately phrases in verse, and from this to the end there is no break. The scenes in Padalon more especially want reading; they are in no need of praise when they have once been read, and a right melancholy thing it is to think how few probably have read them nowadays. *The Curse of Kehama* may not place Southey in the very highest class of poets, if we demand those special qualities in the poet which distinguish certain of the greatest names. But it puts him in the very first rank of the second.

I am aghast when I see how little room is left for the enormous and interesting subject of Southey's prose. As has been said, there is no collected edition of it; and there could be none which should be complete. There are, it is believed, no documents for identifying his earlier contributions to newspapers and magazines; but he wrote nearly a hundred articles in *The Quarterly Review*, many in many other Reviews, and the historical part (amounting to something like a volume on each occasion) of the Edinburgh *Annual Register* for three years. He translated or revised translations of *Amadis*, *Palmerin*, and the *Chronicle of the Cid*. He edited the *Morte d'Arthur*, Cowper's Poems, divers Specimens and Selections from English Poets and other things. His *Specimens of the Later English Poets* which, with some help from Grosvenor Bedford, he produced for Longmans in three very pretty volumes (1805), is particularly interesting because of its dealing with bards most of whom are utterly forgotten. And of solid independent books in prose he published, besides the three biographies of Nelson, Wesley, and Bunyan, nearly a dozen substantive works, some of them of very great size. None of these is so well known as the biographies, especially those of Nelson and Wesley. The latter only just misses the very first rank among the longer biographies—those which enter into full detail and give documents. The *Life of Nelson*, by common consent of all the competent, does attain the first rank among biographies of the shorter class. It will probably be considered by posterity one of the capital examples of that pedantic folly which is always repeating itself that persons, at best qualified to add footnotes of correction and amplification to it, have presumed in recent days to speak of it with disrespect. But the less known prose works must also receive attention.

At the date of *Letters from Spain and Portugal* (1797), Southey had not outgrown (indeed he was only twenty-three) that immature pomposity of style which has been already referred to, and which is apparent both in his verse and in his letters of all this time. The *Letters from England*, by Don Manuel Espriella, ten years later in date, are also at least ten years better in matter and form. The scheme, that of enabling Englishmen to see themselves as others see them, was indeed rather old-fashioned, and not of those things which are none the worse for being a little out of fashion; but it is very pleasantly carried out, and I doubt whether there is anywhere a more agreeable picture of the country and its ways in the first decade of the century. In three pocket volumes the road from Falmouth to London, the sights, ways, manners of the capital, the life (chiefly of the well-to-do middle classes), the chief country towns, the Lake district, and a great number of other matters, are described with a liveliness not seriously injured, and perhaps to some tastes even improved, by the admixture of a considerable amount of political and other reflection. It is surprising that it has not been reprinted. *Omniana*, which was to have been written by Southey and Coleridge together, but to which the latter made only a very small contribution, is less original, being a rather questionable cross between a commonplace-book (such as, after Southey's death, was actually issued in four huge volumes) and a "table-talk" or miscellany of short abstracts, summaries, comments, etc., of and on curious passages in books. Nevertheless these *Horæ Otiosiores*, as their second title goes, contain much curious and not a little interesting reading; and they, too, thoroughly well deserve reprinting. .

The *History of Brazil* followed, the chief, and, with *The Peninsular War*, the only pair actually erected of what Southey used fondly to call "my pyramids"— pyramids alas! not often visited now, though still in existence, and solidly enough built and based. The latter suffered perhaps more than any other of Southey's books from the necessity which their author's poverty imposed on him of constantly laying them aside for the bread-winning work of the hour as it offered itself.

This delay gave time for it to be caught up and passed by Napier's rival history which, though more brilliantly written, is at least as partial and prejudiced on the other side of opinion, and (some authorities will have it) not really more trustworthy in fact. However, *The Peninsular War* was one of the few works of Southey which brought him a solid, though inadequate, sum of money,—a thousand pounds to wit. Neither *The Book of the Church*, nor its appendix the *Vindiciæ Anglicanæ*, had any such satisfactory result, though both had a fair sale, and though both aroused considerable, if mainly angry, attention. The merits are indeed rather impaired by the peculiarity of their author's ecclesiastical attitude, which was that of a violent "Protestant" towards the Roman Church, and of an uncompromising Anglican towards Protestant Nonconformists. In fact Southey seems to have been singularly unlucky in his money transactions, for reasons partly indicated by Scott in a passage given by Lockhart. The large comparative profits which Cottle's apparently venturesome purchase of *Joan of Arc* brought to the publisher, together with his own unshaken conviction of the lasting quality of his work, seem to have made Southey fall in love with, and obstinately cling to, the system of half-profits, which, in the case of not very rapid sales, has a natural tendency to become one of no profits at all. For his Naval History, or *Lives of the Admirals*, he was paid down, and very fairly paid; but I do not know that he made anything out of *The Doctor*, his last, and one of his largest works, a quaint miscellany of reading, reflection, and humour, like a magnified *Omniana* with a thread of connection, which is, I believe, little read now, and which never was popular, but which a few tastes (my own included) regard as, for desultory reading, one of the most delightful books in English. Macaulay, who, politics apart, cannot be called an unfair critic of Southey, is unduly hard on his humour. But the temper of Macaulay's mind, whether owing to his Scotch blood or not, was, though keenly appreciative of wit, and open enough to at least some kinds of humour, always intolerant of nonsense, of pure cap-and-bells ·fooling, wherein Southey took a specially English delight.

Of this delight his poems bear frequent testimony and his letters are full of it—those especially describing the *Lingo Grande*, as he chose to call the curiosities of language which he attributed, justly or unjustly, to his sister-in-law, Mrs Coleridge. But *The Doctor* is its chief exercising ground and home. Not that this huge and charming book is by any means a mere compound of alternate horse-play and book-learning. The descriptions of the early home of Daniel Dove in the dales —where Northern scenery is deftly worked in with reminiscences of the author's youth in the West—are of singular beauty, and contain some of the very best specimens of Southey's admirable English. The famous "Story of the Three Bears," though the most finished, is very far from being the only separable episode in the endless, but by no means incoherent sequence of matter. And of the treasures of learning, never merely dry in itself, and constantly sweetened and moistened by fantastic humour, there is no stint.

The characteristics of this wide and neglected champaign of letters,—a whole province of prose, as it may be called,—especially when we add the huge body of published letters, present the widest diversity of subject, and cannot fairly be said to suffer from any monotony of style. To some tastes in the present day, indeed, Southey may seem flat. He scornfully repudiated, on more than one occasion, the slightest attempt at "fine writing," and ostensibly limited his efforts to the production of clear and limpid sentences in the best classical English. Not that he was by any means alarmed at an appearance of neologism now and then. His merely playful coinages in *The Doctor* and the Letters do not, of course, count; but precisian as he was, he was not of those precisians who will not have a word, however absolutely justified by analogy and principle, unless there is some definite authority for it. On the contrary he took the sounder course of actually rejecting words with good authority but bad intrinsic titles. His sentences are of medium length but inclining to the long rather than the short, and distinctly longer than the pattern, which the gradually increasing love of antithetic balance had made popular in the eighteenth century. His most ornate attempts will be found in the descriptive passages of *The Colloquies*, a book which, though Macaulay's strictures are partly justified, is of extreme interest and beauty at its best, and is chiefly marred by the curiously unhappy selection of the interlocutor,—an instance, with the plan of *The Vision of Judgment* and some other things, of a gap or weakness in Southey's otherwise excellent sense and taste. But in all his prose writings, no matter what they be, even in those unlucky political Essays, which he reprinted in two very pretty little volumes at the most unfortunate time and with the least fortunate result, he displays one of the very best prose styles of the century, perhaps the very best (unless Lockhart's, which is more technically faulty, be ranked with it) of the quiet and regular kind in English.

In the case of no writer, however, is it more necessary to look at him as a whole, to take his prose with his verse, his writings with his history and his character, than in the case of Southey. Neither mere bulk, nor mere variety of writings can, of course, be taken as a voucher for greatness; a man is no more a good writer because he was a good man than because he was a bad one, which latter qualification seems to be accepted by some; and even learning and industry will not exempt their possessor from inclusion among the *dulli canes*, as Southey himself has it. But when all these things are found together with the addition of a rare excellence in occasional passages of verse, with the composition of at least one long poem which goes near to, if it does not attain, absolute greatness, with an admirable prose style and a curious blending of good sense and good humour, then most assuredly the mass deserves at least equal rank with excellences higher in partial reach, but far smaller in bulk and range.

In the general judgment, perhaps, there is a certain reluctance to grant this. There is plausibility in asking, not if a man can do many things well, but if he has done one thing supremely; and unquestionably it is dangerous to multiply the tribe of literary Jacks-of-all-trades. There is no fear, however, of an extensive multiplication of Southeys; happy would our state be if there were any chance. For the man *knew* enormously; he could write admirably; it may be fairly contended that he only missed being a great poet by the constant collar-work which no great poet in the world has ever been able to endure; he had the truest sensibility with scarcely any touch of the maudlin; the noblest sense of duty with not more than a very slight touch of spiritual pride. If he thought a little too well of himself as a poet, he was completely free alike from the morose arrogance of his friend Wordsworth and from the exuberant arrogance of his friend Landor. Only those who have worked through the enormous mass of his verse, his prose, and his letters can fully appreciate his merits; nor is it easy to conceive any scheme of collection that would be possible, or of selection that would do him justice. But if no one of the Muses can claim him as her best beloved and most accomplished son, all ought to accord to him a preference never deserved by any other of their innumerable family. For such a lover and such a practitioner of almost every form of literature, no literature possesses save English, and English is very unlikely ever to possess again.

APPENDIX B

COLERIDGE AND SOUTHEY

I HAVE in the text expressed my opinion that Southey was, perhaps, a little too didactic in his dealings with Coleridge. But it must be remembered that the roundest and most uncompromising denunciation of Coleridge that we have comes from Wordsworth, not Southey; and I cannot help thinking that the late Mr Dykes Campbell, inestimable as are his dealings with the Lake set, and little as any one who knew him is likely to feel disposed to quarrel with him, was rather unfair to Southey, whom he accused of "meddlesomeness" in bringing on the marriage of Coleridge and Sara, and of whose letter to Mrs Hughes on the occasion of Coleridge's death he speaks severely. I should like to examine these two points a little. For the modern memory is rather short, and the modern judgment rather too apt to take things at second-hand: and I have seen this "meddlesomeness" recently taken as a thing proved and granted, by reviewers and others.

Let us then take it first. The facts are not in dispute. Coleridge, after engaging himself to Miss Fricker, took one of his fits of abscondence, left Cambridge, went to London, and abode there smoking and being smoked with Lamb at the *Salutation and Cat*, but giving no sign of life to his fiancée and his Bristol friends. Southey, visiting town either specially or for other purposes, sought him out, brought him back, and so it was that there was a *redintegratio amoris* and a marriage. Surely it is going not a little far to call this "meddlesomeness." Southey had been Miss Fricker's friend from childhood; he had himself introduced Coleridge to her; he was going to marry her sister; and it does not appear that she had any male relatives to act for her. Would any gentleman not have done what he did? Let it be remembered, too, that, after all, he could not simply tuck Coleridge under his arm and drag him to the altar; that no compulsion appears to have been required; that Coleridge was at least as much in love with his pensive Sara, both before and for some time after marriage, as it was in his nature to be; and that Southey, himself a very young man, had had no time as yet to become acquainted with the hopeless vacillation and instability of his future brother-in-law's character. He did the duty next him; well would it be for most men if they had nothing to reproach themselves with but that.

And now as to the letter to Mrs Hughes. "What he wrote," said Mr Campbell, "is better forgotten." What *did* he write? That Coleridge "Had long been dead to me, but his decease has naturally wakened up old recollections." That "Whosoever edits his letters will have a difficult and delicate task" (*cf.* Mr Ernest Coleridge's preface to these letters, and not all of them, sixty years later); that "all of his blood were in the highest degree proud of his reputation, but this was their only feeling concerning him"; that "Hartley has far greater powers than anyone who *now* bears the same name." This is absolutely all, and it will be observed that Southey does not as a matter of fact express any personal opinion whatever of an unfavourable kind, though, no doubt, he may be thought to guard himself rather carefully against expressing a favourable one except in point of "genius." There might have been a little more sentiment, perhaps; but Southey was not a sentimentalist, and the simple phrase "wakened up old recollections" from him means more than pages of regret and remorse would have meant from Coleridge's own pen. There is no doubt some evidence of the "natural death of love." Coleridge had wearied Southey out as he wearied out his family, Wordsworth, Wedgwood, everybody with whom he had to do—except people like the Morgans and the Gillmans, who were sufficiently below him in intellectual rank to think it an honour as well as a charity to dry-nurse him—as he once at least was close to wearying out the angelic goodness, the humorous tolerance, and the rock-fast friendship of Charles Lamb himself. Now Southey was not quite an angel, and tolerance was not his strong point: but nothing worse than this need, I am convinced, be said of his relations with the "archangel a little damaged," to whose forsaken family he was a father.

XI

WILLIAM COBBETT

To acquaint oneself properly with the works of Cobbett is no child's play. It requires some money, a great deal of time, still more patience, and a certain freedom from superfineness. For, as few of his books have recently been reprinted, and as they were all very popular when they appeared, it is frequently necessary to put up with copies exhibiting the marks of that popularity in a form with which Coleridge and Lamb professed to be delighted, but to which I own that I am churl enough to prefer the clean, fresh leaves of even the most modern reprint.

And the total is huge; for Cobbett's industry and facility of work were both appalling, and while his good work is constantly disfigured by rubbish, there is hardly a single parcel of his rubbish in which there is not good work. Of the seventy-four articles which compose his bibliography, some of the most portentous, such as the *State Trials* (afterwards known as Howell's) and the *Parliamentary Debates* (afterwards known as Hansard's), may be disregarded as simple compilation; and it is scarcely necessary for any one to read the thirty years of *The Register* through, seeing that almost everything in it that is most characteristic reappeared in other forms. But this leaves a formidable residue. The *Works of Peter Porcupine*, in which most of Cobbett's writings earlier than the nineteenth century and a few later are collected, fill twelve volumes of fair size. The only other collection, the *Political Works,* made up by his sons after his death from *The Register* and other sources, is in six volumes, none of which contains less than five hundred, while one contains more than eight hundred large pages, so closely printed that each represents two if not three of the usual library octavo. The *Rural Rides* fill two stout volumes in the last edition: besides which there are before me literally dozens of mostly rather grubby volumes of every size from Tull's *Husbandry*, in a portly octavo, to the *Legacy to Labourers*, about as big as a lady's card-case. If a man be virtuous enough, or rash enough, to stray further into anti-Cobbett pamphlets (of which I once bought an extremely grimy bundle for a sovereign) he may go on in that path almost for ever. And I see no rest for the sole of his foot till he has read through the whole of "the bloody old *Times*" or "that foolish drab Anna Brodie's rubbish," as Cobbett used with indifferent geniality to call that newspaper,—the last elegant description being solely due to the fact that he had become aware that a poor lady of the name was a shareholder.

Let it be added that this vast mass is devoted almost impartially to as vast a number of subjects, that it displays throughout the queerest and (till you are well acquainted with it) the most incredible mixture of sense and nonsense, folly and wit, ignorance and knowledge, good temper and bad blood, sheer egotism and sincere desire to benefit the country. Cobbett will write upon politics and upon economics, upon history ecclesiastical and civil, upon grammar, cookery, gardening, wood-craft, standing armies, population, ice-houses, and almost every other conceivable subject, with the same undoubting confidence that he is and must be right. In what plain men still call inconsistency there never was his equal. He was approaching middle life when he was still writing cheerful pamphlets and tracts with such titles as *The Bloody Buoy, The Cannibal's*

Progress, and so on, destined to hold up the French
Revolution to the horror of mankind; he had not passed
middle life when he discovered that the said Revolution
was only a natural and necessary consequence of the
same system of taxation which was grinding down
England. He denied stoutly that he was anything but
a friend to monarchical government, and asseverated
a thousand times over that he had not the slightest
wish to deprive landlords or any one else of their
property. Yet for the last twenty years of his life he
was constantly holding up the happy state of those
republicans, the profligacy, injustice, and tyranny of
whose government he had earlier denounced. He
frequently came near, if he did not openly avow, the
"hold-the-harvest" doctrine; and he deliberately proposed that the national creditor should be defrauded
of his interest, and therefore practically of his capital.
A very shrewd man naturally, and by no means an
ill-informed one in some ways, there was no assertion
too wildly contradictory of facts, no assumption too
flagrantly opposed to common sense, for him to make
when he had an argument to further or a craze to
support. "My opinion is," says he very gravely, "that
Lincolnshire alone contains more of those fine buildings
[churches] than the whole continent of Europe." The
churches of Lincolnshire are certainly fine; but imagine
all the churches of even the western continent of Europe,
from the abbey of Batalha to Cologne Cathedral, and
from Santa Rosalia to the Folgoët, crammed and
crouching under the shadow of Boston Stump! He
"dared say that Ely probably contained from fifty to
a hundred thousand people" at a time when it is rather
improbable that London contained the larger number
of the two. Only mention Jews, Scotchmen, the
National Debt, the standing army, pensions, poetry,

tea, potatoes, larch trees, and a great many other things, and Cobbett becomes a mere, though a very amusing, maniac. Let him come across in one of his peregrinations, or remember in the course of a book or article, some magistrate who gave a decision unfavourable to him twenty years before, some lawyer who took a side against him, some journalist who opposed his pamphlets, and a torrent of half humorous but wholly vindictive Billingsgate follows; while if the luckless one has lost his estate, or in any way come to misfortune meanwhile, Cobbett will jeer and whoop and triumph over him like an Indian squaw over a hostile brave at the stake. Mixed with all this you shall find such plain shrewd common sense, such an incomparable power of clear exposition of any subject that the writer himself understands, such homely but genuine humour, such untiring energy, and such a hearty desire for the comfort of everybody who is not a Jew or a jobber or a tax-eater, as few public writers have ever displayed. And (which is the most important thing for us) you shall also find sense and nonsense alike, rancorous and mischievous diatribes as well as sober discourses, politics as well as trade-puffery (for Cobbett puffed his own wares unblushingly), all set forth in such a style as not more than two other Englishmen, whose names are Defoe and Bunyan, can equal.

Like theirs it is a style wholly natural and unstudied. It is often said, and he himself confesses, that as a young man he gave his days and nights to the reading of Swift. But except in the absence of adornment, and the uncompromising plainness of speech, there is really very little resemblance between them, and what there is is chiefly due to Cobbett's following of the *Drapier's Letters*, where Swift, admirable as he is, is clearly using a falsetto. For one thing, the main characteristic of

Swift—the perpetual unforced unflagging irony which is the blood and the life of his style—is utterly absent from Cobbett. On the other hand, if Cobbett imitated little, he was imitated much. Although his accounts of the circulation of his works are doubtless exaggerated as he exaggerated everything connected with himself, it was certainly very large; and though they were no doubt less read by the literary than by the non-literary class, they have left traces everywhere. As a whole Cobbett is not imitable; the very reasons which gave him the style forbade another to borrow it. But certain tricks of his reappear in places both likely and unlikely; and since I have been thoroughly acquainted with him I think I can see the ancestry of some of the mannerisms of two writers whose filiation had hitherto puzzled me —Peacock and Borrow. In the latter case there is no doubt whatever; indeed the kinship between Borrow and Cobbett is very strong in many ways. Even in the former I do not think there is much doubt, though Peacock's thorough scholarship and Cobbett's boisterous unscholarliness make it one of thought rather than of form, and of a small part of thought only.

Therefore Cobbett is very well worthy studying, the study being part of that never-ending and delightful game of tracing literary genealogies, of filling in the literary maps, which is at once the business and the pastime of the critic. His political importance has seldom been questioned, and I think that on the whole it has been even underrated. His personality is extremely interesting and nearly always amusing, though the amusement may sometimes go a little close to disgust,—for no man ever illustrated both the faults and the merits of *l'Anglais*, if not of *l'homme sensuel moyen*, as did Cobbett. And last of all, though to me not least, there are few more simply delightful writers to read

without bothering yourself at all about literary filia-
tions or ancestries, about political revolutions or
conversations, about Cobbett the man, or England the
nation. It is indeed true (and this is the curse óf all
political writing, though less of his than of most) that
the lapse of time has made it impossible to leave all
trouble about politics aside, unless you happen to be
thoroughly well acquainted with politics. Even the
Rural Rides, even the *English Gardener*, nay, even the
very *Grammar* itself, cannot be read currently if you
do not know who and what "the Thing" and "the
Wen" and "the Fool-Liar" and "Anna Brodie" and
"my dignitary Dr Black" were; if you are not acquainted with all the circumstances which made the
very words "tea" or "taxes," "paper-money" or
"potatoes," throw Cobbett into a kind of epilepsy; if
you are not in the secret of his perpetual divagations
on locust-trees and swede turnips, on "Cobbett's corn"
and ridge cultivation. But my experience is that, when
you once do know these things, you bother yourself
very little about them afterwards so far as the mere
reading of Cobbett goes. The hottest Tory gospeller
could not think of getting angry with Cobbett, or
indeed getting into controversy with him at all; and
I should doubt whether even our modern Socialists,
though some of his ideas are very hke theirs, would
greet him very warmly as an ally. He *disreasons* too
much (to use a word which is very much wanted in
English and has the strictest titles to admission), and
his disreasoning, powerful as it was at the time, has lost
too much of its hold on present thought and present
circumstance.

He has left an agreeable and often quoted account
of his own early life in an autobiographic fragment
written to confound his enemies in America. He was

born on 9th March, 1762[1], at Farnham; and the chief of his interests during his life centred round the counties of Hampshire and Surrey, with Berkshire and Wiltshire thrown in as benefiting by neighbourhood. His father was a small farmer, not quite uneducated, but not much in means or rank above a labourer, and all the family were brought up to work hard. After some unimportant vicissitudes, William ran away to London and, attempting quill-driving in an attorney's office for a time, soon got tired of it and enlisted in a marching regiment which was sent to Nova Scotia. This was in the spring of 1784. As he was steady, intelligent, and not un-educated, he very soon rose from the ranks, and was sergeant-major for some years. During his service with the colours he made acquaintance with his future wife (a gunner's daughter of the literal and amiable kind), and with Lord Edward Fitzgerald. The regiment came home in 1792, and Cobbett got his discharge, married his beloved, and went to France. Unfortunately he had other reasons besides love and a desire to learn French for quitting British shores. He had discovered, or imagined, that some of his officers were guilty of malversation of regimental money, he abused his position as sergeant-major to take secret copies of regimental documents, and when he had got his dis-charge he lodged his accusation. A court-martial was granted. When it met, however, there was no accuser, for Cobbett had gone to France. Long afterwards, when the facts were cast up against him, he attempted a defence. The matter is one of considerable intricacies and of no great moment. Against Cobbett it may be said to be one of the facts which prove (what indeed hardly needs proving), that he was not a man of any

---

[1] Cobbett himself says 1766, and the dates in the fragment are all adjusted to this; but biography says 1762.

chivalrous delicacy of feeling, and did not see that in no circumstances can it be justifiable to bring accusations of disgraceful conduct against others and then run away. In his favour it may be said that, though not a very young man, he was not in the least a man of the world, and was no doubt sincerely surprised and horrified to find that his complaint was not to be judged off-hand and Cadi-fashion, but with all sorts of cumbrous and expensive forms.

However this may be, he went off with his wife and his savings to France; and enjoyed himself there for some months, tackling diligently to French the while, until the Revolution (it was, let it be remembered, in 1792) made the country too hot for him. He determined to go to Philadelphia, where, and elsewhere in the United States, he passed the next seven years. They were seven years of a very lively character; for it was the nature of Cobbett to find quarrels, and he found plenty of them here. Some accounts of his exploits in offence and defence may be found in the biographies, fuller ones in the books of the chronicles of Peter Porcupine, his *nom de guerre* in pamphleteering and journalism. Cobbett was at this time, despite his transactions with the Judge Advocate General, his flight and his selection of France and America for sojourn, a red-hot Tory and a true Briton, and he engaged in a violent controversy, or series of controversies, with the pro-Gallic and anti-English party in the States. The works of Peter, besides the above-quoted *Bloody Buoy* and *Cannibal's Progress*, contain in their five thousand pages or thereabouts, other cheerfully named documents, such as: *A Bone to Gnaw for the Democrats, A Kick for a Bite, The Diplomatic Blunderbuss, The American Rushlight*, and so on. This last had mainly to do with a non-political quarrel into which Cobbett got with a person of some professional fame, the "American Sydenham," otherwise Dr Benjamin Rush[1]. Rush got Cobbett cast in heavy damages for libel; and though these were paid by subscription, the affair seems to have disgusted our pamphleteer and he sailed for England on 1st June, 1800.

There can be little doubt, though Cobbett's own bragging and the bickering of his biographers have rather darkened than illuminated the matter, that he came home with pretty definite and very fair prospects of Government patronage. More than one of his Anti-Jacobin pamphlets had been reprinted for English consumption. He had already arranged for the London edition of "Porcupine's" *Works* which appeared subsequently; and he had attracted attention not merely from literary understrappers of Government but from men like Windham. Very soon after his return Windham asked him to dinner, to meet not merely Canning, Ellis, Frere, Malone and others, but Pitt himself. The publica-

---

[1] Soon after the original appearance of this essay, in which I referred to Cobbett's antagonist as "a certain quack doctor named Rush," I received from America, and especially from Philadelphia, lively remonstrances against this description of him. Mr Rosengarten of the Quaker city, assuming that I had "taken Rush on Cobbett's report," very kindly furnished me with some documents, especially a pamphlet-lecture by Dr Pepper, Provost of the University of Pennsylvania, highly eulogistic of one whom Mr Rosengarten himself describes as "the medical beau-ideal of this city, and of the medical profession in this country." I promised to make some explanation if I ever republished the essay, and I now do so. The fact is that I ought not to have called Rush "quack" *simpliciter*: for his education and degrees were quite regular. But I had not entirely taken Cobbett's word (he would be a rash man who should do so on any subject), and I must say that it still appears to me that Rush, even on his advocate's showing, belonged to what may be called the quack division of the faculty. He was essentially a faddist, and between a faddist and a quack there is not much more than a syllable. He opposed capital punishment. He said himself, "I have no more doubt of every crime having its cure in moral and physical influence than I have of the efficacy of Peruvian bark in intermittent fever." He was an anti-alcohol man, an anti-tobacco man, an anti-classical education man. All this shows the quack *ethos*: even though a man may have an array of diplomas that would have covered the backs of the army of Pentapolin of the Naked Arm in their natural sheepskin condition.

tion of the host's diary long afterwards clearly established the fact, which had been rather idly contested or doubted by some commentators.

How or why Cobbett fell away from Pitt's party is not exactly known, and is easier to understand than definitely to explain; even when he left it is not certain. He was offered, he says, a Government paper or even two; but he refused and published his own *Porcupine*, which lasted for some time till it lapsed (with intermediate stages) into the famous *Weekly Register*. In both, and in their intermediates for some three or four years at least, the general policy of the Government, and especially the war with France, was stoutly supported. But Cobbett was a free-lance born and bred, and he never during the whole of his life succeeded in working under any other command than his own, or with any one on equal terms. He got into trouble before very long owing to some letters, signed *Juverna*, on the Irish executive; and though his contributor (one Johnson, afterwards a judge) gave himself up, and Cobbett escaped the fines which had been imposed on him, his susceptible vanity had no doubt been touched. It was also beyond doubt a disgust to his self-educated mind to find himself regarded as an inferior by the regularly trained wits and scholars of the Government press; and I should be afraid that he was annoyed at Pitt's taking no notice of him. But, to do Cobbett justice, there were other and nobler reasons for his revolt. His ideal of politics and economics (of which more presently), though an impossible one, was sincere and not ungenerous; and he could not but perceive that a dozen years of war had made its contrast with the actual state of the British farmer and labourer more glaring than ever.

The influence which he soon wielded through the

Register, and the profit which he derived from it, at once puffed him up and legitimately encouraged the development of his views. He bought, or rather (a sad thing for such a denouncer of "paper"), obtained, subject to heavy mortgages, a considerable estate of several farms at and near Botley, in Hampshire. Here for some five years (1804 to 1809), he lived the life of a very substantial yeoman, almost a squire, entertaining freely, farming, coursing, encouraging boxing and single-stick, fishing with drag-nets, and editing the *Register* partly in person and partly by deputy. Of these deputies, the chief were his partner, and afterwards foe, the printer Wright, and Howell of the *State Trials*. This latter, being unluckily a gentleman and a university man, comes in for one of Cobbett's characteristic flings as "one of your college gentlemen," who "have and always will have the insolence to think themselves our betters; and our superior talents, industry and weight only excite their envy." Prosperity is rarely good for an Englishman of Cobbett's stamp, and he seems at this time to have decidedly lost his head. He had long been a pronounced Radical, thundering or guffawing in the *Register* at pensions, sinecures, the debt, paper-money, the game-laws (though he himself preserved), and so forth; and the authorities naturally enough only waited for an opportunity of explaining to him that immortal maxim which directs the expectations of those who play at any kind of bowls.

In July, 1809, he let them in by an article of the most violent character on the suppression of a mutiny among the Ely Militia. This had been put down, and the ringleaders flogged by some cavalry of the German Legion; and Cobbett took advantage of it to beat John Bull's drum furiously. It has been the custom to turn up the whites of the eyes at Lord Ellenborough who tried the case, and Sir Vicary Gibbs who prosecuted; but I do not think any sane man who remembers what the importance of discipline in the army was in 1809, can find fault with the jury who, and not Ellenborough or Gibbs, had to settle the matter, and who found Cobbett guilty. The sentence no doubt was severe,—as such sentences in such cases were then wont to be— two years in Newgate, a fine of a thousand pounds, and security in the same amount for seven years to come. Here, no doubt, Ellenborough's responsibility comes in, and he may be thought to have looked before and after as well as at the present. But the *Register* was not stopped, and Cobbett was allowed to continue therein without hindrance a polemic which was not likely to grow milder. For he never forgot or forgave an injury to his interests, or an insult to his vanity; and he was besides becoming, quite honestly and disinterestedly, more and more of a fanatic on divers points both of economics and of politics proper.

I cannot myself attach much importance to the undoubted fact that after the trial, which happened in June, 1810, but before judgment, Cobbett, aghast for a moment at the apparent ruin impending, made (as he certainly did make) some overtures of surrender and discontinuance of the *Register*. Such a course in a man with a large family and no means of supporting it but his pen, would have been, if not heroic, not disgraceful. But the negotiation somehow fell through. Unluckily for Cobbett, he on two subsequent occasions practically denied that he had ever made any offer at all; and the truth only came out when he and Wright quarrelled, nearly a dozen years later. This, the affair of the court-martial, and another to be mentioned shortly, are the only blots on his conduct as a man that I know, and in such an Ishmael as he was they are not very fatal.

He devoted the greater part of his time, during the easy, though rather costly, imprisonment of those days, to his *Paper against Gold*, in which, with next to no knowledge of the matter, he attacked probably the thorniest of all subjects, that of the currency; and the *Register* went on. He came out of Newgate in July, 1812, naturally in no very amiable temper. A mixture of private and public griefs almost immediately brought him into collision with the authorities of the Church. He had long been at loggerheads with those of the State; and it was now that he became more than ever the advocate (and the most popular advocate it had) of Parliamentary Reform. He was, however, pretty quiet for three or four years, but at the end of that time, in September, 1816, he acted on a suggestion of Lord Cochrane's, cheapened the *Register* from one shilling to two-pence, and opened the new series with one of his best pamphlet-addresses, "To the Journeymen and Labourers of England, Wales, Scotland and Ireland." For a time he was very much in the mouths of men; but Ministers were not idle, and the suspension of the Habeas Corpus and the famous *Six Acts* prepared for him a state of things still hotter than he had experienced before. Cobbett did not give it time to heat itself specially for him. He turned his eyes once more to America, and, very much to the general surprise, suddenly left Liverpool on 22nd March, 1817, arriving in May at New York, whence he proceeded to Long Island, and established himself on a farm there. Unluckily there were other reasons for his flight besides political ones. His affairs had become much muddled during his imprisonment, and had not mended since; while though his assets were considerable they were of a kind not easy to realise. There seems no doubt that Cobbett was generally thought to have run away from a gaol in more senses than one, and that the thought did him no good.

But he was an impossible person to put down; even his own mistakes, which were pretty considerable, could not do it. His flight, as it was called, gave handles to his enemies, and not least to certain former friends, including such very different persons as Orator Hunt and Sir Francis Burdett; it caused a certain belatedness, and, for a time, a certain intermittency, in his contributions to the *Register*; it confirmed him in his financial crazes, and it may possibly have supported him in a sort of private repudiation of his own debts, which he executed even before becoming legally a bankrupt. Finally it led him to the most foolish act of his life, the lugging of Tom Paine's bones back to a country which, though not prosperous, could at any rate provide itself with better manure than that. In this famous absurdity the purely silly side of Cobbett's character comes out. For some time after he returned he was at low water both in finances and in popularity; while such political sanity as he ever possessed may be said to have wholly vanished. Yet, oddly enough, or not oddly, the transplanting and the re-transplanting seem to have had a refreshing effect on his literary production. He never indeed again produced anything so vigorous as the best of his earlier political works, but in non-political and mixed styles he even improved; and though he is more extravagant than ever in substance occasionally, there is a certain mellowness of form which is very remarkable. He was not far short of sixty when he returned in 1819; but the space of his life, subsequent to his flight, yielded the *Year's Residence in America*, the *English Grammar*, the *Twelve*

Sermons, the *Cottage Economy*, the *English* (altered from a previous *American*) *Gardener*, the *History of the Reformation*, the *Woodlands*, *Cobbett's Corn*, the *Advice to Young Men*, and a dozen other works original or compiled, besides the *Rural Rides* and his other contributions to the *Register*.

He could not have lived at Botley any longer if he would, for the place was mortgaged up to the eyes. But to live in a town was abhorrent to him; and he had in America rather increased than satisfied his old fancy for rural occupations. So he set up house at Kensington, where he used a large garden (soon supplemented by more land at Barnes, and in his very last years by a place near Ash, in his native district) as a kind of seed farm, selling the produce at the same shop with his *Registers*. He also utilised his now frequent rural rides —partly to provide himself with political subjects and to deliver political addresses, partly as commercial travelling for the diffusion of locust-trees, swede turnip seed, and "Cobbett's corn"—a peculiar kind of maize, the virtues of which he vaunted loudly.

Also he began to think seriously of sitting in Parliament. At the general election after George the Third's death he contested Coventry, but without even coming near success. Soon afterwards he had an opportunity of increasing his general popularity—which, owing to his flight, his repudiation, and the foolery about Paine's bones, had sunk very low—by vigorously taking Queen Caroline's side. But he was not more fortunate in his next Parliamentary attempt at Preston, in 1826. Preston, even before the Reform Bill, was, though the Stanley influence was strong, a comparatively open borough, and had a large electorate; but it would not have Cobbett, nor was he ever successful till after the Bill passed. Before its passing the very Whig Government which had charge of it was obliged to pull him up. If he had been treated with undeserved severity before he was extremely fortunate now, though his rage against his unsuccessful Whig prosecutors was, naturally enough, much fiercer than it had been against his old Tory enemies. I do not think that any fair-minded person who reads the papers in the *Register*, and the cheaper and therefore more mischievous *Two-penny Trash*, devoted to the subject of "Swing," can fail to see that under a thin cloak of denunciation and dissuasion their real purport is "Don't put him under the pump," varied and set off by suggestions how extremely easy it would be to put him under the pump, how well he deserves it, and how improbable detection or punishment is. And nobody, further, who reads the accounts of the famous Bristol riots can fail to see how much Cobbett (who had been in Bristol just before in full cry against "Tax-Eaters" and "Tithe-Eaters") had to do with them. It was probably lucky for him that he was tried before instead of after the Bristol matter, and even as it was he was not acquitted; the jury disagreed. After the Bill, his election somewhere was a certainty, and he sat for Oldham till his death. Except for a little tomfoolery at first, and at intervals afterwards, he was inoffensive enough in the House. Nor did he survive his inclusion in that Collective Wisdom at which he had so often laughed many years, but died on 19th June, 1835, at the age of seventy-three. If medical opinion is right the Collective Wisdom had the last laugh; for its late hours and confinement seem to have had more to do with his death than any disease.

I have said that it is of great importance to get if possible a preliminary idea of Cobbett's general views on politics. This not only adds to the understanding of his work, but prevents perpetual surprise and possible fretting at his individual flings and crazes. To do him justice there was from first to last very little change in his own political ideal; though there was the greatest possible change in his views of systems, governments, and individuals in their relations to that ideal and to his own private interests or vanities. In this latter respect Cobbett was very human indeed. The son of a farmer-labourer, and himself passionately interested in agricultural pursuits, he may be said never, from the day he first took to politics to the day of his death, to have really and directly considered the welfare of any other class than the classes occupied with tilling or holding land. In one place he frantically applauds a real or supposed project of King Ferdinand of Spain for taxing every commercial person who sold, or bought to sell again, goods not of his own production or manufacture. If he to a certain extent tolerated manufactures, other than those carried on at home for immediate use, it was grudgingly, and indeed inconsistently with his general scheme. He frequently protests against the substitution of the shop for the fair or market; and so jealous is he of things passing otherwise than by actual delivery in exchange for actual coin or payment in kind, that he grumbles at one market (I think Devizes) because the corn is sold by sample and not pitched in bulk on the market-floor.

It is evident that if he possibly could have it, he would have a society purely agricultural, men making what things the earth does not directly produce as much as possible for themselves in their own houses during the intervals of field-labour. He quarrels with none of the three orders,—labourer, farmer, and landowner—as such; he does not want "the land for the people," or the landlord's rent for the farmer. Nor does he want any of the lower class to live in even mitigated idleness. Eight hours' days have no place in Cobbett's scheme; still less relief of children from labour for the sake of education. Everybody in the labouring class, women and children included, is to work and work pretty hard; while the landlord may have as much sport as ever he likes provided he allows a certain share to his tenant at times. But the labourer and his family are to have "full bellies" (it would be harsh but not entirely unjust to say that the full belly is the beginning and end of Cobbett's theory), plenty of good beer, warm clothes, staunch and comfortably furnished houses. And that they may have these things they must have good wages; though Cobbett does not at all object to the truck or even the "Tommy" system. He seems to have, like a half socialist as he is, no affection for saving, and he once, with rather disastrous consequences, took to paying his own farm-labourers entirely in kind. In the same way the farmer is to have full stack-yards, a snug farm-house, with orchards and gardens thoroughly plenished. But he must not drink wine or tea, and his daughters must work and not play the piano.

Squires there may be of all sorts, from the substantial yeoman to the lord (Cobbett has no objection to lords), and they may, I think, meet in some way or other to counsel the king (for Cobbett has no objection to kings). There is to be a militia for the defence of the country, and there might be an Established Church provided that the tithes were largely, if not wholly, devoted to the relief of the poor and the exercise of hospitality. Everybody, provided he works, is to marry the prettiest girl he can find (Cobbett had a most generous weakness for pretty girls) as early as possible, and have any number of children. But though there is to be plenty of game, there are to be no game-laws.

There is to be no standing army, though there may be a navy. There is to be no, or the very smallest, civil service. It stands to reason that there is to be no public debt; and the taxes are to be as low and as uniform as possible. Commerce, even on the direct scale, if that scale be large, is to be discouraged, and any kind of middleman absolutely exterminated. There is not to be any poetry (Cobbett does sometimes quote Pope, but always with a gibe), no general literature (for though Cobbett's own works are excellent, and indeed indispensable, that is chiefly because of the corruptions of the times), no fine arts—though Cobbett has a certain weakness for church architecture, mainly for a reason presently to be explained. Above all there is to be no such thing as what is called abroad a *rentier*. No one is to "live on his means," unless these means come directly from the owning or the tilling of land. The harmless fund-holder with his three or four hundred a year, the dockyard official, the half-pay officer, are as abhorrent to Cobbett as the pensioner for nothing and the sinecurist. This is the state of things which he loves, and it is because the actual state of things is so different, and for no other reason, that he is a Radical Reformer.

I need not say that no such connected picture as I have endeavoured to draw will be found in any part of Cobbett's works[1]. The strokes which compose it are taken from a thousand different places and filled in to a certain extent by guess-work. But I am sure it is faithful to what he would have drawn himself if he had been given to imaginative construction. It will be seen at once that it is a sort of parallel in drab homespun, a more practical double (if the adjective may be used

---

[1] The nearest approach is in the *Manchester Lectures* of 1831; but this is not so much a *projet* of an ideal State as a scheme for reforming the actual.

of two impracticable things,) of Mr William Morris's agreeable dreams. The artistic tobacco-pouches and the museums, the young men hanging about off Biffin's to give any one a free row on the river, and so forth, were not in Cobbett's way. But the canvas, and even the main composition of the picture, is the same. Of course the ideal State never existed anywhere, and never could continue to exist long if it were set up in full working order to-morrow. Labourer A would produce too many children, work too few hours, and stick too close to the ale-pot; farmer B would be ruined by a bad year or a murrain; squire C would outrun the non-existent constable and find a Jew to help him, even if Cobbett made an exception to his hatred of placemen for the sake of a Crown tooth-drawer. One of the tradesmen who were permitted on sufferance to supply the brass kettles and the grandfathers' clocks which Cobbett loves would produce better goods and take better care of the proceeds than another, with the result of a better business and hoarded wealth. In short, men would be men, and the world the world, in spite of Cobbett and Mr Morris alike.

I doubt whether Cobbett, who knew something of history, ever succeeded in deceiving himself, great as were his powers that way, into believing that this State ever had existed. He would have no doubt gone into a paroxysm of rage, and have called me as bad names as it was in his heart to apply to any Hampshire man, if I had suggested that such an approach to it as existed in his beloved fifteenth century was due to the Black Death, the French wars, and those of the Roses. But the fair vision ever fled before him day and night, and made him more and more furious with the actual state of England,—which was no doubt bad enough. The labourers with their eight or ten shillings a week and their Banyan diet, the farmers getting half-price for their ewes and their barley, the squires ousted by Jews and jobbers, filled his soul with a certainly not ignoble rage, only tempered by a sort of exultation to think in the last case that the fools had brought their ruin on their own heads by truckling to "the Thing." "The Thing" was the whole actual social and political state of England; and on everything and everybody that had brought "the Thing" about he poured impartial vitriol. The war which had run up the debt and increased the tax-eaters at the same time; the borough-mongers who had countenanced the war, the Jews and jobbers that negotiated and dealt in the loans; the parsons that ate the tithes; the lawyers that did Government work,—Cobbett thundered against them all.

But his wrath also descended upon far different, and one would have thought sufficiently guiltless, things and persons. The potato, the "soul-destroying root" so easy to grow (Cobbett did not live to see the potato famine, or I fear he would have been rather hideous in his joy), so innutritious, so exclusive of sound beef and bread, has worse language than even a stock-jobber or a sinecurist. Tea, the expeller of beer, the pamperer of foreign commerce, the waster of the time of farmers' wives, is nearly as bad as the potato. I could not within any possible or probable space accorded me follow out a tithe or a hundredth part of the strange ramifications and divagations of Cobbett's grand economic craze. The most comical branch perhaps is his patronage of the Roman Catholic Church, and the most comical twig of that branch his firm belief that the abundance and size of English churches testify to an infinitely larger population in England of old than at the present day. His rage at the impudent Scotchman who put the population at two millions when he is sure it was twenty, and the earnestness with which he proves that a certain Wiltshire vale, having so many churches capable of containing so many people must have once had so many score thousand inhabitants, are about equally amusing. That in the days which he praises so much, and in which these churches were built, the notion of building a church to "seat so many," or with regard to the population at all, would have been regarded as unintelligible if not blasphemous; that in the first place the church was an offering to God, not a provision for getting worship done; and that in the second, the worship of old, with its processions, its numerous altars in the same churches, and so on, made a disproportionate amount of room absolutely necessary, —these were things you could no more have taught Cobbett than you could have taught him to like *Marmion* or read the *Witch of Atlas*.

It is however time, and more than time, to follow him rapidly through the curious labyrinth of work in which, constantly though often very unconsciously keeping in sight this ideal, he wandered from Pittite Toryism to the extreme of half socialist and wholly radical Reform. His sons, very naturally but rather unwisely, have in the great selection of the *Political Works* drawn very sparingly on Peter Porcupine. But no estimate of Cobbett that neglects the results of this, his first, phase will ever be satisfactory. It is by no means the most amusing division of Cobbett's works; but it is not the least characteristic, and it is full of interest for the study both of English and of American politics. The very best account that I know of the original American Constitution, and of the party strife that followed the peace with England, is contained in the Summary that opens the *Works*. Then for some years we find Cobbett engaged in fighting the Jacobin party, the fight constantly turning into skirmishes on his private account, conducted with singular vigour if at a length disproportionate to the present interest of the subject. Here is the autobiography before noticed, and in all the volumes, especially the earlier ones, the following of Swift, often by no means unhappy, is very noticeable. It is a little unlucky that a great part of the whole consists of selections from *Porcupine's Gazette*, that is to say, of actual newspaper matter of the time,—"slag-heaps," to use Carlyle's excellent phrase, from which the metal of present application has been smelted out and used up long ago.

This inconvenience also and of necessity applies to the still larger collection, duplicating, as has been said, a little from Porcupine, but principally selected from the *Register*, which was published after Cobbett's death. But this is of far greater general importance, for it contains the pith and marrow of all his writings on the subject to which he gave most of his heart. Here, in the first volume, besides the selection from Porcupine, are the masterly *Letters to Addington on the Peace of Amiens*, in which that most foolish of the foolish things called armistices is treated as it deserved, and with a combination of vigour and statesmanship which Cobbett never showed after he lost the benefit of Windham's patronage and (probably) inspiration. Here too is a defence of bull-baiting after Windham's own heart. The volume ends with the *Letters to William Pitt*, in which Cobbett declared and defended his defection from Pitt's system generally. The whole method and conduct of the writings of this time are so different from the rambling denunciations of Cobbett's later days, and from the acute but rather desultory and extremely personal Porcupinades, that one is almost driven to accept the theory of "inspiration." The literary model too has shifted from Swift to Burke—Burke upon whom Cobbett was later to pour torrents of his foolishest abuse; and both in this first and in the second volume the reformer, wandering about in search of subjects not merely political but general—Crim. Con., Poor-laws, and so forth—appears. But in the second volume we have to notice a paper, still in the old style and full of good sense, on Boxing.

In the third Cobbett is in full Radical cry. Here is the article which sent him to Newgate; and long before it a series of virulent attacks on the Duke of York in the matter of Mrs Clarke, together with onslaughts on those Anti-Jacobins to whom Cobbett had once been proud to belong. It also includes a very curious *Plan for an Army*, which marks a sort of middle stage in Cobbett's views on that subject. The latter part of it, and the whole of the next (the fourth) consists mainly of long series on the Regency (the last and permanent Regency), on the Regent's disputes with his wife, and on the American War. All this part displays Cobbett's growing ill-temper, and also the growing wildness of his schemes—one of which is a sliding-scale adjusting all salaries, from the civil list to the soldier's pay, according to the price of corn. But there is still no loss of vigour, if some of sanity; and the opening paper of the fifth volume, the famous Address to the Labourers aforesaid, is, as I have said, perhaps the climax of Cobbett's political writing in point of force and form—which thing I say utterly disagreeing with almost all its substance. This same fifth volume contains another remarkable instance of Cobbett's extraordinary knack of writing, as well as of his rapidly decreasing judgment, in the *Letter to Jack Harrow, an English labourer, on the new Cheat of Savings Banks*.

At least half of the volume dates after Cobbett's flight, while some is posterior to his return. The characteristics which distinguish his later years, his wild crotchets and his fantastic running-a-muck at all public men of all parties, and not least at his own former friends, appear both in it and in the sixth and last, which carries the selection down to his death. Yet even in such things as the *Letter to Old George Rose* and that from *The Labourers of the ten little Hard Parishes* [this was Cobbett's name for the district between Winchester and Whitchurch, much of which had recently been acquired by the predecessors of Lord Northbrook] *to Alexander Baring, Loan-monger*, we can see, at a considerable distance of time, the strength and the weakness of this odd person in conspicuous mixture. He is as rude, as coarse, as personal as may be; he is grossly unjust to individuals and wildly flighty in principle and argument; it is almost impossible to imagine a more dangerous counsellor in such, or indeed in any times. Except that he is harder-headed and absolutely unchivalrous, his politics are very much those of Colonel Newcome. And yet the vigour of the style is still so great, the flame and heat of the man's conviction are so genuine, his desire according to the best he knows to benefit his clients, and his unselfishness in taking up those clients, are so unquestionable that it is impossible not to feel both sympathy and admiration. If I had been dictator about 1830 I think I should have hanged Cobbett; but I should have sent for him first and asked leave to shake hands with him before he went to the gallows.

These collections are invaluable to the political and historical student; and I hardly know any better models, not for the exclusive, but for the eclectic attention of the political writer, especially if his education be academic and his tastes rather anti-popular. But there is better pasture for the general student in the immense variety of the works, which, though they cannot be called wholly non-political—Cobbett would have introduced politics into arithmetic and astronomy, as he actually does into grammar—are non-political in main substance and purport. They belong almost entirely, as has been said, to the last seventeen or eighteen years of Cobbett's life; and putting the *Year's Residence* aside, the *English Grammar* is the earliest. It is couched in a series of letters to his son James, who had been brought up to the age of fourteen on the principle (by no means a bad one) of letting him pick up the Three R's as he pleased, and leaving him for the rest "To ride and hunt and shoot, to dig the beds in the garden, to trim the flowers, and to prune the trees." It is like all Cobbett's books, on whatsoever subject, a wonderful mixture of imperfect information, shrewd sense, and fantastic crotchet. On one page Cobbett calmly instructs his son that "prosody" means "pronunciation"; on another, he confuses "etymology" with "accidence." This may give the malicious college-bred man cause to be envious of his superior genius; but there is no doubt that the book contains about as clear an account of the practical and working nature and use of sound English speech and writing as can anywhere be found.

The grammar was published in 1818, and Cobbett's next book of note was *Religious Tracts*, afterwards called *Twelve Sermons*. He says that many persons had the good sense to preach them; and indeed, a few of his usual outbursts excepted, they are as sound specimens of moral exhortation as anybody need wish to hear or deliver. They are completed characteristically enough by a wild onslaught on the Jews, separately paged as if Cobbett was a little ashamed of it. Then came the *Cottage Economy*, instructing and exhorting the English labourer in the arts of brewing, baking, stock-keeping of all sorts, straw-bonnet making, and ice-house building. This is perhaps the most agreeable of all Cobbett's minor books, next to the *Rural Rides*. The descriptions are as vivid as *Robinson Crusoe*, and are further lit up by flashes of the genuine man. Thus, after a most peaceable and practical discourse on the making of rushlights, he writes: "You may do any sort of work by this light; and if reading be your taste you may read the foul libels, the lies, and abuse which are circulated gratis about *me* by the Society for Promoting Christian Knowledge." Here too is a charming piece of frankness: "Any beer is better than water; but it should have *some* strength and *some* weeks of age at any rate."

A rearrangement of the *Horse-hoeing Industry* of Jethro Tull, barrister, and the *French Grammar*, hardly count among his purely and originally literary work; but the *History of the Reformation* is one of its most characteristic if not one of its most admirable parts. Cobbett's feud with the clergy was now at its height; he had long before been at daggers drawn with his own parson at Botley. The gradual hardening of his economic crazes made him more and more hate "Tithe-Eaters," and his wrath with them was made hotter by the fact that they were as a body opponents of Reform. So with a mixture of astounding ignorance and of self-confidence equally amazing, he set to work to put the crudest Roman view of the Reformation and of earlier times into his own forcible English. The book is very amusing; but it is so grossly ignorant, and the virulence of its tirades against Henry VIII and the rest so palpable, that even in that heated time it would not do. It may be gathered from some remarks of Cobbett's own that he felt it a practical failure; though he never gave up his views, and constantly in his latest articles and speeches invited everybody to search it for the foundation of all truth about the Church of England.

The more important of his next batch of publications, the *Woodlands, The English Gardener, Cobbett's Corn*, restore a cooler atmosphere; though even here there are the usual spurts. Very amusing is the suppressed wrath of the potato article in the *English Gardener*, with its magnanimous admission that "there appears to be nothing unwholesome about it; and it does very well to qualify the effects of the meat or to assist in the swallowing of quantities of butter." Pleasing too is the remark, "If this turnip really did come from Scotland, there is something good that is Scotch." *Cobbett's Corn*, already noticed, is one of the most curious of all his books, and an instance of his singular vigour in taking up fancies. Although he sold the seed, it does not appear that he could in any case have made much profit out of it; and he gave it away so freely that it would, had it succeeded, soon have been obtainable from any seedsman in the kingdom. Yet he wrote a stout volume about it, and seems to have taken wonderful interest in its propagation, chiefly because he hoped it would drive out his enemy the potato. The English climate was naturally too much for it; but the most amusing thing, to me at least, about the whole matter is the remembrance that the "yellow meal" which it, like other maize, produced, became, a short time after Cobbett's own death, the utter loathing and abomination of English and Irish paupers and labourers, a sort of sign and symbol of capitalist tyranny. Soon afterwards came the last of Cobbett's really remarkable and excellent works, the *Advice to Young Men and Incidentally to Young Women*, one of the kindliest and most sensible books of its kind ever written. The other books of Cobbett's later years are of little account in any way; and in the three little *Legacies* (*to Labourers, to Peel*, and *to Parsons*) there is a double portion of now cut-and-dried crotchet in matter, and hardly any of the old power in form.

Yet to the last, or at any rate till his disastrous election, Cobbett was Cobbett. The *Rural Rides*, though his own collection of them stopped at 1830, went on to 1832. This, the only one of his books, so far as I know, that has been repeatedly and recently reprinted, shows him at his best and his worst; but almost always at his best in form. Indeed, the reader for mere pleasure need hardly read anything else, and will find therein to the full the delightful descriptions of rural England, the quaint, confident, racy, wrong-headed opinions, the command over the English language, and the ardent affection for the English soil and its children, that distinguish Cobbett at his very best.

I have unavoidably spent so much time on this account of Cobbett's own works—an account which without copious extract must be, I fear, still inadequate —that the anti-Cobbett polemic must go with hardly any notice at all. Towards the crises of the Reform Bill it became very active, and at times remarkable. Among two collections which I possess, one of bound tracts dating from this period, the other of loose pamphlets ranging over the greater part of Cobbett's life, the keenest by far is a certain publication called *Cobbett's Penny Trash*, which figures in both, though one or two others have no small point. The enemy naturally made the utmost of the statement of the condemned labourer Goodman, who lay in Horsham Gaol under sentence of death for arson, that he had been stirred up by Cobbett's addresses to commit the crime; but still better game was made controversially of his flagrant and life-long inconsistencies, of his enormous egotism, of his ter-giversation in the matter of the offer to discontinue the *Register*, and of his repudiation of his debt to Sir Francis Burdett. And the main sting of the *Penny Trash*, which must have been written by a very clever fellow indeed, is the imitation of Cobbett's own later style, its italics, its repetitions, its quaint mannerisms of fling and vaunt. The example of this had of course been set much earlier by the Smiths in *Rejected Addresses*, but it was even better done here.

Cobbett was indeed vulnerable enough. He, if any one, is the justification of the theory of Time, Country, and *Milieu*, and perhaps the fact that it only adjusts itself to such persons as he is the chief condemnation of that theory. Even with him it fails to account for the personal genius which after all is the only thing that makes him tolerable, and which, when he is once tolerated, makes him almost admirable. Only an English *Terræ Filius*, destitute of the education which the traditional *Terræ Filius* had, writing too in the stress of the great Revolutionary struggle and at hand-grips with the inevitable abuses which that struggle at once left unbettered, after the usual gradual fashion of English betterment, and aggravated by the pressure of economic changes—could have ventured to write with so little knowledge or range of logical power, and yet have written with such individual force and adaptation of style to the temper of his audience. At a later period and in different circumstances Cobbett could hardly have been so acrimonious, so wildly fantastic, so grossly and almost impudently ignorant, or if he had been he would have been simply laughed at or unread. At an earlier period, or in another country, he would have been bought off or cut off. Even at this very time the mere circumstantial fact of the connection of most educated and well-informed writers with the Government or at least with the regular Opposition, gave such a Free-lance as this an unequalled opportunity of making himself heard. His very inconsistency, his very ferocity, his very ignorance, gave him the key of the hearts of the multitude, who just then were the persons of most importance. And to these persons that characteristic of his which is either most laughable or most disgusting to the educated—his most unparalleled, his almost inconceivable egotism—was no drawback. When Cobbett with many italics in an advertisement to all his later books told them, "When I am asked what books a young man or young woman ought to read I always answer: 'Let him or her read *all the books that I have written,*'" proceeding to show in detail that this was no humorous gasconade but a serious recommendation, one "which it is my *duty* to give," the classes laughed consumedly. But the masses felt that Cobbett was at any rate a much cleverer and more learned person than themselves, had no objection on the score of taste, and were naturally conciliated by his partisanship on their own side. And, clever as he was, he was not too clever for them. He always hit them between wind and water. He knew that they cared nothing about consistency, nothing about chivalry, nothing about logic. He could make just enough and not too much parade of facts and figures to impress them. And above all he had that invaluable gift of belief in himself and in his own fallacies which no demagogue can do without. I do not know a more fatal delusion than the notion, entertained by many persons, that a mere charlatan, a conscious charlatan, can be effective as a statesman, especially on the popular side. Such a one may be an excellent understrapper; but he will never be a real leader.

In this respect, however, Cobbett is only a lesson, a memory, and an example, which are all rather dead things. In respect of his own native literary genius he is still a thing alive and delectable. I have endeavoured, so far as has been possible in treating a large subject in little room, to point out his characteristics in this respect also. But, as happens with all writers of his kidney, he is not easily to be characterised. Like certain wines he has the *goût du terroir*; and that gust is rarely or never definable in words. It is however I think critically safe to say that the intensity and peculiarity of Cobbett's literary savour is in the ratio of his limitation. He was content to ignore so vast a number of things, he so bravely pushed his ignorance into contempt of them and almost into denial of their real existence, that the other things are real for him and in his writings to a degree almost unexampled. I am not the first by many to suggest that we are too diffuse in our modern imagination, that we are cumbered about too many things. No one could bring this accusation against Cobbett; for immense as his variety is in particulars, these particulars group themselves under comparatively few general heads. I do not think I have been unjust in suggesting that this ideal was little more than the belly-full, that Messer Gaster was not only his first but his one and sufficient master of arts. He was not irreligious, he was not immoral; but his religion and his morality were of the simplest and most matter-of-fact kind. Philosophy, æsthetics, literature, the more abstract sciences, even refinements of sensual comfort and luxury he cared nothing for. Indeed he had a strong dislike to most of them. He must always have been fighting about something; but I think his polemics might have been harmlessly parochial at another time. It is marvellous how this resolute confinement of view sharpens the eyesight within the confines. He has somewhere a really beautiful and almost poetical passage of enthusiasm over a great herd of oxen as "so much splendid meat." He can see the swells of the downs, the flashing of the winterbournes as they spring from the turf where they have lain hid, the fantastic outline of the oak woods, the reddening sweep of the great autumn fields of corn, as few have seen them, and can express them all with rare force and beauty in words. But he sees all these things conjointly and primarily from the point of view of the mutton that the downs will breed and the rivers water, the faggots that the labourer will bring home at evening, the bread he will bake and the beer he will brew—strictly according to the precepts of *Cottage Economy*.

This may be to some minds a strange and almost incredible combination. It is not so to mine, and I am sure that by dint of it and by dint of holding himself to it he achieved his actual success of literary production. To believe in nothing very much, or in a vast number of things dispersedly, may be the secret of criticism; but to believe in something definite, were it only the belly-full, and to believe in it furiously and exclusively is, with almost all men, the secret of original art.

XII

MISS FERRIER

An old novel is to some people, I believe, a piece of literature worthy to be ranked with an old newspaper or an old almanack—not quite so dull as the last, a good deal duller than the first, but sharing with both the same distinguishing quality, that of essential incapacity to fulfil the reason of its existence. Students of the philosophy of language may be left to decide whether this is or is not a proof of the singular tyranny of names—an unconscious practical syllogism with the major premiss that a novel must be new. But no one, I think, is likely to contest the fact that such a view of old novels does prevail. If it prevails with any one who is accustomed to read for something else than the mere story, this must be set down to a conviction that in at least the majority of novels there is nothing more than the story, and very often exceedingly little of that. But the books which form the subject of the present essay have been exempted by high authorities and repeated reappearance from the reproach of more or less hardy annuals[1]. They have very high testimonials,

[1] This essay was originally written on the text of the six-volume edition of Miss Ferrier's novels published by Messrs Bentley in 1882. Twelve years later the publisher of this present book issued another edition the introduction of which contained a not inconsiderable selection of unpublished letters, furnished, I understand, by Miss Ferrier's nephew, who has since been good enough to inform me that he has a much larger store of them. They are of no small intrinsic interest, which may be a little obscured to modern eyes by the fact that, in the earlier ones at any rate, Miss Ferrier pretty obviously had before her the letter-writers of the novelists from Richardson downwards and so herself writes in a kind of falsetto; while the severity of touch which is apparent in the novels is even more marked here. But at the same time they exhibit the masculine strength of their author's understanding, her shrewd observation, and the excellent use she could make of it.

some of which must be known to many people in whose way the books themselves have never fallen. Scott praised them highly, not only, as he was wont to do with perhaps more generosity and good nature than strictly critical exactness, in private, but in his published works. Mackintosh read *Destiny* with an absorption sufficient to make him forget all about an impending dissolution of Parliament, for the news of which he was anxiously waiting. There is praise of Miss Ferrier in the *Noctes*—praise which certainly does not require forgiveness as in Tennyson's case.

But, above all, there is something curious and, at the present day especially, almost portentous in the fact that Miss Ferrier was content to write three novels, and three only. She had no imperative private reasons for ceasing to write; she had won a great deal of reputation by her books, and (a consideration which certainly would not have weakened the case with most people) she had made money in a most agreeably increasing proportion by her three ventures. *Marriage* brought her in £150; not a magnificent sum, certainly, but more than most novelists even of greater genius have made by their first novels. *The Inheritance* was sold for £1000, and *Destiny* for £1700. She might probably have depended on at least as much for a fourth novel. But she persistently refused to write any more, and the probable reason for this refusal (as to which I may have something to say) rather heightens than impairs the merit of the refusal. So she remains in literary history a singular and almost unique figure. Men and women of one book—a book in most cases inspired by some peculiar circumstance or combination of circumstances —are not uncommon. But that an author should live many days, should try the game three several times with result of praise and profit, and then retire from the field without any disgust such as checked Congreve or any sufficient disabling cause, this is certainly a most unusual thing.

Susan Edmonstone Ferrier was born at Edinburgh on the 7th of September, 1782. The memoirs which have been prefixed to the various editions of her works, and to which I am indebted for the facts of her biography, enter after the manner of the Scotch with some minuteness into her genealogy and family connections. Among these latter in various distances of ascent, descent, and collateral relation figure Archbishop Tait of Canterbury, Lord Braxfield (famous as the hero of many anecdotes of judicial and jocular brutality), and some other persons of note. But the principal fact of interest in this kind about Miss Ferrier is that she was aunt of "the last of the metaphysicians" as he has sometimes been called, the late Professor Ferrier of St Andrews. Her father was a Writer to the Signet, and among his clients was the fifth Duke of Argyll. He and his daughter were frequent visitors at Inveraray, and these visits are said, with pretty evident truth, to have had not a little influence in supplying Miss Ferrier with subjects of study and determining the character and personal arrangement of her books. Miss Clavering, her most frequent correspondent, was the Duke's niece: Lady Charlotte Campbell (afterwards Bury) was also an intimate of hers, and friends and members of the Argyll family are said to have sat for not a few personages of the novels. Whatever criticism these works may be exposed to, even Madame de Staël, in the mood in which (according to a priceless anecdote recounted by Mr Austen Leigh in his life of his aunt) she returned one of Miss Austen's novels with the disdainful comment, "vulgaire," could not have objected to the *ton* of Miss Ferrier's people. Her first heroine is an earl's granddaughter; her second, a countess in her own right; her third, the only surviving child of a great Highland chieftain; and in all her books, countesses and duchesses, baronets and Honourable Mr So-and-so's, "do be jostling each other." This, it is true, was very much the way of the novel of the period, and Miss Austen was almost the first to break through it— indeed, it may be shrewdly suspected that Corinne's fine feelings were secretly shared by a large number of readers, and that this had not a little to do with the comparatively limited success of *Pride and Prejudice* and its fellows. There is, perhaps, present in Miss Ferrier herself, the least little feeling of the same kind; her books contain some excellent sentiments on the vanity of rank and fashion, but somehow they leave on the reader's mind an impression that the author is secretly of Major Pendennis's mind as to the value of good acquaintances, and that it was more comfortable to her to walk down her literary St James's Street on the arm of an earl than on that of a simple commoner who would have been puzzled to tell the name and status of his grandfather. However this may be, her sketches were at least taken from the life, and she did not, like certain writers of our own day, talk familiarly of "the Honour-able Jem and the Honourable Jemima" on the strength of seeing the one at a respectful distance in a club smoking-room, and the other across some yards of gravel and the railings of Rotten Row.

It is not quite clear at what time *Marriage* was actually begun, but that it was begun in consequence of the Inveraray visits and of the company of "fashion-ables" and of originals there open to inspection, is pretty clear. It seems to have been planned with the before-mentioned Miss Clavering, who was not only confidante, but was allowed to hold in some small degree the more honourable and responsible position of collaborator. The book was certainly in great part written before 1810, and was read in manuscript to Lady Charlotte Campbell, who approved of it highly. But though the author saw a great deal of literary society—she and her father visited Scott at Ashestiel soon after the date just mentioned—the book did not appear till 1818, when it was published by Blackwood. It may be suspected that part of the reason for hesitation was the audacious extent to which (as is acknowledged in the correspondence with Miss Clavering) the characters were taken from living originals. However this may be, it appeared at last and was highly popular, drawing forth, immediately after its appearance, a public compliment from Sir Walter.

The original idea of *Marriage* is stated correctly enough in a letter to Miss Clavering. It is the introduction of a spoilt child of English fashionable life to a rough Highland home abounding with characters. Miss Ferrier's way of working out this conception was to a certain extent conventional—it is doubtful whether, with all her power, she ever got quite as clear of convention as did her admirable contemporary, Jane Austen—but it brings about many very comical and delightful situations. Lady Juliana Lindore is the daughter of a somewhat embarrassed English peer, the Earl of Courtland. Having no idea beyond her collection of pets, the society to which she has been accustomed, and a certain varnish of romance about handsome lovers and love in a cottage with a double coach-house, she receives with consternation her father's announcement that she is to marry an ugly duke. For a time she vacillates, chiefly owing to the splendour of the duke's presents, but at last the good looks of her handsome lover, Harry Douglas, prevail, and the pair elope to

Scotland and are married. Douglas has a commission in the Guards, and though he is only the second son of a petty landowner, he has fortunately attracted the attention of a rich bachelor, General Cameron. But the general is disgusted with his favourite's escapade, Lord Courtland disowns his daughter, and after a brief honeymoon there is nothing for it but to accept his father's invitation to the ancestral mansion in the Highlands. The pair set out with man and maid, pug, macaw, and squirrel, and Lady Juliana has pleasant visions of a romantic, but at the same time elegant, retreat where they will sojourn for a short time, receiving the attentions of the countryside and giving *fêtes champêtres* in return, till they once more enjoy the pleasures of London with a handsome endowment from her husband's father. The husband has some misgivings, but having left his home at a very early age, and looking back at it through the "filmy blue" of the past, is by no means prepared for the actual condition of Glenfern. The introduction of the pair to the reality of things takes place as follows:—

"The conversation was interrupted; for just at that moment they had gained the summit of a very high hill, and the post-boy, stopping to give his horses breath, turned round to the carriage, pointing at the same time, with a significant gesture, to a tall thin gray house, something resembling a tower, that stood in the vale beneath. A small sullen-looking lake was in front, on whose banks grew neither tree nor shrub. Behind rose a chain of rugged cloud-capped hills, on the declivities of which were some faint attempts at young plantations; and the only level ground consisted of a few dingy turnip fields, enclosed with stone walls, or dykes, as the post-boy called them. It was now November; the day was raw and cold; and a thick drizzling rain was beginning to fall. A dreary stillness reigned all around, broken only at intervals by the screams of the sea-fowl that hovered over the lake, on whose dark and troubled waters was dimly described a little boat, plied by one solitary being.

"'What a scene!' at length Lady Juliana exclaimed, shuddering as she spoke. 'Good God, what a scene! How I pity the unhappy wretches who are doomed to dwell in such a place! and yonder hideous grim house—it makes me sick to look at it. For Heaven's sake, bid him drive on.' Another significant look from the driver made the colour mount to Douglas's cheek, as he stammered out, 'Surely it can't be; yet somehow I don't know. Pray, my lad,' letting down one of the glasses, and addressing the post-boy, 'what is the name of that house?'

"'Hoose!' repeated the driver; 'ca' ye thon a hoose? Thon's gude Glenfern Castle.'"

Disenchantment follows disenchantment. Glenfern is a sufficiently commodious but quite uncivilised mansion, and its inhabitants consist of the father, a well-meaning chieftain, his three maiden sisters (Miss Jacky, the sensible woman of the parish, Miss Nicky, who is a notable house-wife, and Miss Grizzy, who is nothing in particular), and five daughters. The eldest son with his wife abides at a short distance. Very short experience of these circumstances suffices to reduce Lady Juliana to hysterics, which are treated by the aunts in the following fashion:

"'Oh, the amiable creature!' interrupted the unsuspecting spinsters, almost stifling her with their caresses as they spoke: 'Welcome, a thousand times welcome, to Glenfern Castle,' said Miss Jacky, who was esteemed by much the most sensible woman, as well as the greatest orator in the whole parish; 'nothing shall be wanting, dearest Lady Juliana, to compensate for a parent's rigour, and make you happy and comfortable. Consider this as your future home! My sisters and myself will be as mothers to you; and see these charming young creatures,' dragging forward two tall frightened girls, with sandy hair and great purple arms; 'thank Providence for having blest you with such sisters!' 'Don't speak too much, Jacky, to our dear niece at present,' said Miss Grizzy; 'I think one of Lady Maclaughlan's composing draughts would be the best thing for her.'

"'Composing draughts at this time of day!' cried Miss Nicky; 'I should think a little good broth a much wiser thing. There are some excellent family broth making below, and I'll desire Tibby to bring a few.'

"'Will you take a little soup, love?' asked Douglas. His lady assented; and Miss Nicky vanished, but quickly re-entered, followed by Tibby, carrying a huge bowl of coarse broth, swimming with leeks, greens, and grease. Lady Juliana attempted to taste it; but her delicate palate revolted at the homely fare; and she gave up the attempt, in spite of Miss Nicky's earnest entreaties to take a few more of these excellent family broth.

"'I should think,' said Henry, as he vainly attempted to stir it round, 'that a little wine would be more to the purpose than this stuff.'

"The aunts looked at each other; and, withdrawing to a corner, a whispering consultation took place, in which Lady Maclaughlan's opinion, 'birch, balm, currant, heating, cooling, running risks,' &c., &c., transpired. At length the question was carried; and some tolerable sherry and a piece of very substantial *shortbread* were produced."

What follows may be guessed without much difficulty, though the recital is well worth reading. Lady Juliana wearies her husband and his relatives with every possible demonstration of insolence and folly. The pipes make her faint; her favourite beasts and birds (which the old-fashioned politeness of the laird and a certain respect for her rank will not permit him to banish) become the nuisances of the house; and though she condescends to stay at Glenfern until she has enriched the family tree with a new generation— Major Douglas, the eldest son, has no children—she shows more and more her utter vacuity of mind, her want of real affection for her unlucky husband, and the impossibility of satisfying her by any concessions consistent with the means of the family. After a time, however, a new personage appears on the scene in the person of Lady Maclaughlan, one of the strongest and most original characters who had yet found a home in English fiction. Her defects are two only, that she is admitted to be very nearly a photograph from the life, and that, like too many of the characters of *Marriage*, she has but very little to do with the story. Lady Maclaughlan's humours are almost infinite and can hardly hope to represent themselves in any sufficient manner by dint of extract. She is a sort of cross between Lady Bountiful and Lady Kew, a mixture which will be admitted to be original, especially as one of the component parts had not yet been separately presented at all to the public. This is the fashion of her introduction:—

"Out of this equipage issued a figure, clothed in a light-coloured, large-flowered chintz raiment, carefully drawn through the pocket-holes, either for its own preservation, or the more disinterested purpose of displaying a dark short stuff petticoat, which with the same liberality, afforded ample scope for the survey of a pair of worsted stockings and black leather shoes, something resembling buckets. A faded red cloth jacket, which bore evident marks of having been severed from its native skirts, now acted in the capacity of a spencer. On the head rose a stupendous fabric, in the form of a cap, on the summit of which was placed a black beaver hat, tied *à la poissarde*. A small black satin muff in one hand, and a gold-headed walking-stick in the other, completed the dress and decoration of this personage."

Lady Maclaughlan has a husband (more like one of Smollett's characters than like any other product of English fiction) who is a hopeless cripple, and she is a tyrant to her friends, and especially to "the girls," as she calls the aunts at Glenfern; but she has plenty of brains. An excellent scene, though like many in the book rather of an extravagant kind, is that where the Glenfern party have come to dine with her on a wrong day. They make their way into the house with the utmost difficulty, surprise Sir Sampson Maclaughlan in undress, and only at last are ushered into the redoubtable presence:—

"After ascending several long dark stairs, and following divers windings and turnings, the party at length reached the door of the *sanctum sanctorum*, and having gently tapped, the voice of the priestess was heard in no very encouraging accents, demanding 'Who was there?'

"'It's only us,' replied her trembling friend.

"'Only us? humph! I wonder what fool is called *only us!* Open the door, Philistine, and see what *only us* wants.'

The door was opened and the party entered. The day was closing in, but by the faint twilight that mingled with the gleams from a smoky smouldering fire, Lady Maclaughlan was dimly discernible, as she stood upon the hearth, watching the contents of an enormous kettle that emitted both steam and odour. She regarded the invaders with her usual marble aspect, and without moving either joint or muscle as they drew near.

"'I declare—I don't think you know us, Lady Maclaughlan,'

said Miss Grizzy in a tone of affected vivacity, with which she strove to conceal her agitation.

"'Know you!' repeated her friend—'humph! Who you are, I know very well; but what brings you here, I do *not* know. Do you know yourselves?'

"'I declare—I can't conceive——' began Miss Grizzy; but her trepidation arrested her speech, and her sister therefore proceeded—

"'Your ladyship's declaration is no less astonishing than incomprehensible. We have waited upon you by your own express invitation on the day appointed by yourself; and we have been received in a manner, I must say, we did not expect, considering this is the first visit of our niece Lady Juliana Douglas.'

"'I'll tell you what, girls,' replied their friend, as she still stood with her back to the fire, and her hands behind her; 'I'll tell you what,—you are not yourselves—you are all lost—quite mad—that's all—humph!'

"'If that's the case, we cannot be fit company for your ladyship,' retorted Miss Jacky warmly; 'and therefore the best thing we can do is to return the way we came. Come, Lady Juliana—come, sister.'

"'I declare, Jacky, the impetuosity of your temper is—I really cannot stand it——' and the gentle Grizzy gave way to a flood of tears.

"'You used to be rational, intelligent creatures,' resumed her ladyship; 'but what has come over you, I don't know. You come tumbling in here at the middle of the night—and at the top of the house—nobody knows how—when I never was thinking of you; and because I don't tell a parcel of lies, and pretend I expected you, you are for flying off again—humph! Is this the behaviour of women in their senses? But since you are here, you may as well sit down and say what brought you. Get down, Gil Blas—go along, Tom Jones,' addressing two huge cats, who occupied a three-cornered leather chair by the fireside, and who relinquished it with much reluctance.

"'How do you do, pretty creature?' kissing Lady Juliana, as she seated her in this cat's cradle. 'Now, girls, sit down, and tell what brought you here to-day—humph!'

"'Can your ladyship ask such a question, after having formally invited us?' demanded the wrathful Jacky.

"'I'll tell you what, girls; you were just as much invited by me to dine here to-day as you were appointed to sup with the Grand Seignior—humph!'

"'What day of the week does your ladyship call this?'

"'I call it Tuesday; but I suppose the Glenfern calendar calls it Thursday: Thursday was the day I invited you to come.'

"'I'm sure—I'm thankful we're got to the bottom of it at last,' cried Miss Grizzy; 'I read it, because I'm sure you wrote it, Tuesday.'

"'How could you be such a fool, my love, as to read it any such thing? Even if it had been written Tuesday, you might have had the sense to know it meant Thursday. When did you know me invite anybody for a Tuesday?'

"'I declare it's very true; I certainly ought to have known better. I am quite confounded at my own stupidity; for as you observe, even though you had said Tuesday, I might have known that you must have meant Thursday.'

"'Well, well, no more about it. Since you are here you must stay here, and you must have something to eat, I suppose. Sir Sampson and I have dined two hours ago; but you shall have your dinner for all that. I must shut shop for this day, it seems, and leave my resuscitating tincture all in the deadthraw—Methusalem pills quite in their infancy. But there's no help for it. Since you are here you must stay here, and you must be fed and lodged; so get along, girls, get along. Here, Gil Blas—come, Tom Jones.' And, preceded by her cats, and followed by her guests, she led the way to the parlour."

The humours of Glenfern and its neighbourhood, however, come to an end before long. The offer of a farm to Harry Douglas by his good-natured old father and his wife's utter horror at the idea, the birth of twin girls for whom their mother entertains no feelings but profound disgust, and the general revolt of the whole family at Lady Juliana are happily succeeded by the relenting of General Cameron. He procures the restoration of the commission, which Douglas has forfeited by breaking his leave, and gives him a handsome allowance. One of the twins is left to the care of Mrs Douglas, the elder brother's wife, the other accompanies her parents to London. But Lady Juliana's senseless folly once more ruins her husband. Her discourtesy to General Cameron alienates him, her insane extravagance far outruns the allowance which even while marrying and disinheriting Harry he does not withhold. Douglas goes on foreign service, and practically nothing more is heard of him. Lady Juliana finds a home with her daughter Adelaide in the house of her brother, who has been deserted by his wife. A long gap occurs in the chronology, and the story is resumed when Adelaide and Mary (whom her mother has practically forgotten) are grown up. It is thought proper (much to Lady Juliana's disgust) that her daughter shall pay her a visit, and the second volume of the novel is occupied by the history of this. On the way to England there is a lively episode in which Mary Douglas is taken to see an ancient great-aunt in Edinburgh, whose account of the "improvements" of modern days is not a little amusing. Mrs MacShake, indeed, is one of those originals, evidently studies from the life, whom Miss Ferrier could draw with a somewhat malicious but an admirably graphic pen. Similar characters of a redeeming kind in the second part of the book are Dr Redgill, Lord Courtland's house physician, a parasite of a bygone but extremely amusing type, and Lady Emily, Lord Courtland's daughter, who is one of a class of young women of whom for some incomprehensible reason no novelist before Miss Austen dared to make a heroine[1]. Mary herself, who is the heroine, is a great trial to the modern reader.

"'I am now to meet my mother!' thought she; and, unconscious of everything else, she was assisted from the carriage, and conducted into the house. A door was thrown open; but shrinking from the glare of light and sound of voices that assailed her, she stood dazzled and dismayed, till she beheld a figure approaching that she guessed to be her mother. Her heart beat violently—a film was upon her eyes—she made an effort to reach her mother's arms, and sank lifeless on her bosom!

"Lady Juliana, for such it was, doubted not but that her daughter was really dead; for though she talked of fainting every hour of the day herself, still what is emphatically called a *dead-faint* was a spectacle no less strange than shocking to her. She was therefore sufficiently alarmed and overcome to behave in a very interesting manner; and some yearnings of pity even possessed her heart as she beheld her daughter's lifeless form extended before her—her beautiful, though inanimate features, half hid by the profusion of golden ringlets that fell around her. But these kindly

---

[1] Charlotte Grandison, afterwards "Lady G," the comic heroine of Richardson's novel, has sometimes been regarded as Lady Emily's original; and the Lady Honoria of *Cecilia* might have been instanced as a link between them. But Lady Emily is much less of a caricature than either.

feelings were of short duration; for no sooner was the nature of her daughter's insensibility ascertained, than all her former hostility returned, as she found every one's attention directed to Mary, and she herself entirely overlooked in the general interest she had excited; and her displeasure was still further increased as Mary, at length slowly unclosing her eyes, stretched out her hands, and faintly articulated, 'My mother!'"

In the same way "trembling violently" she is ready to fall upon her sister's neck, a proceeding to which her sister (a young woman leaving something to desire in point of morality, but sensible enough) strongly objects. This second volume includes, besides the capital figure of Dr Redgill (to whom I regret that justice cannot be done by extracts), not a few isolated studies of the ridiculous which can hardly be too highly spoken of. The drawback is that they have no more than the faintest connection with the story as such; indeed, it can hardly be said that there is any story in *Marriage*. It is a collection of exceedingly clever caricatures, some of which deserve a higher title, and the best of which will rank with the best originals in English fiction.

Six years passed between the appearance of *Marriage* and the appearance of *The Inheritance*. The practical success of the earlier book may best be judged by the fact that while *Marriage* brought Miss Ferrier in £150, Blackwood, who had published it, gave her more than six times as much for the new novel. For once difference of price and profit corresponded not unduly to difference of merit. The individual studies and characters of *The Inheritance* are as good as those of *Marriage*, while the novel, as a novel, is infinitely better. In her first work the author had been content to string together amusing caricatures or portraits without any but a rudimentary attempt at central interest. *The Inheritance*, if its plot is of no great intricacy (Miss Ferrier was never famous for plots), is at any rate decently *charpenté*, and the excellent studies of character, which make it delightful to read, are bound together with a very respectable cement of narrative. "The Inheritance" is the Earldom and estates of Rossville, which, by a chapter of accidents, devolve on Gertrude St Clair, the only daughter of a younger and misallied brother of the reigning earl, as inheritrix presumptive. She and her mother are invited to Rossville Castle, the inhabitants of which are the reigning earl and his sister, Lady Betty. Lady Betty is a nonentity, Lord Rossville a pompous fool, who delights in his own eloquence.

The Rossville society is completed by three nephews, with one of whom Gertrude is intended to fall in love, with another of whom she ought to fall in love, and (as a natural consequence) with the third of whom she does fall in love. The remaining characters of the book are more numerous than is the case in *Marriage*, and much better grouped. Miss Pratt, a talkative cousin of the Rossville family, is one of the few characters in Miss Ferrier's books who can afford comparison with those of Miss Austen. She is constantly citing the witticisms of a certain Anthony Whyte, who may be justly said to be an ancestor of Mrs Harris, inasmuch as he is always talked about and never seen. She is also fore-doomed to cross the soul of Lord Rossville, whose feelings of decency she outrages by proposing that a large company shall visit his dressing-room, whose elaborate sentences she constantly interrupts, and whom she finally kills, by making her appearance in a hearse, the only vehicle which she has been able to engage to convey her through a snowstorm. The other branch of Gertrude's connections, however, furnish their full share to the gallery of satirical portraits. One of them, the formidable "Uncle Adam," is said to have been drawn from the author's own father, while he has prophetic touches of no less a person than Carlyle. The Blacks, Mrs St Clair's closest relations, have improved somewhat in circumstances since she made a stolen match with her husband, and they are now on the outskirts of county society. The eldest daughter is engaged to a wealthy and fairly well-connected Nabob, Major Waddell, and on this unlucky pair Miss Ferrier concentrates the whole weight of her sarcasm, especially on Miss Bell Black, the bride elect, who is always talking about "my situation." The gem, however, of this part of the book is the following letter from Lilly Black, the second sister and bridesmaid, who, according to old fashion, accompanies Major and Mrs Waddell on their bridal tour. Jeffrey is said to have admired this particularly, which shows that the awful Aristarch of Craigcrook, when his prejudices were not concerned, and when new planets did not swim too impertinently into his ken, was quite ready to give them welcome.

"The following letters were put into Gertrude's hand one morning. The first she opened was sealed with an evergreen leaf; motto, *Je ne change qu'en mourant.*

"'I am inexpressibly pained to think what an opinion my dearest cousin must have formed of me, from having allowed so much time to elapse ere I commenced a correspondence from which, believe me, I expected to derive the most unfeigned and heartfelt delight. But you, my dear friend, whose fate it has been to roam, "and other realms to view," will, I am sure, make allowance for the apparent neglect and unkindness I have been guilty of, which, be assured, was very far from designed on my part. Indeed, scarce a day has elapsed since we parted that I have not planned taking up my pen to address you, and to attempt to convey to you some idea, however faint, of all I have seen and felt since bidding adieu to Caledonia. But, alas! so many of the vulgar cares of life obtrude themselves even here, in "wilds unknown to public view," as have left me little leisure for the interchange of thought.

"'Were it not for these annoyances, and the want of a congenial soul to pour forth my feelings to, I could almost imagine myself in Paradise. *Apropos*, is a certain regiment still at B., and have you got acquainted with any of the officers yet? You will perhaps be tempted to smile at that question; but I assure you there is nothing at all in it. The Major and Bell (or Mrs Major Waddell, as she wishes to be called in future, as she thinks Bell too familiar an appellation for a married woman) are, I think, an uncommon happy attached pair—the only drawback to their happiness is the Major's having been particularly bilious of late, which he ascribes to the heat of the weather, but expects to derive the greatest benefit from the waters of Harrowgate. For my part, I am sure many a "longing lingering look" I shall cast behind when we bid adieu to the sylvan shores of Winander. I have attempted some views of it, which may serve to carry to you some idea of its beauties. One on a watch-paper, I think my most successful effort. The Major has rallied me a good deal as to who that is intended for; but positively that is all a joke, I do assure you. But it is time that I should now attempt to give you some account of my travels, though, as I promise myself the delight of showing you my journal when we meet, I shall omit the detail of our journey, and at once waft you to what I call Lake Land. But where shall I find language to express my admiration!

"'One thing I must not omit to mention, in order that you may be able to conceive some idea of the delight we experienced, and for which we were indebted to the Major's politeness and gallantry. In order to surprise us, he proposed our taking a little quiet sail, as he termed it, on the lake. All was silence; when, upon a signal made, figure to yourself the astonishment and delight of Mrs Major and myself, when a grand flourish of French horns burst upon our ears, waking the echoes all round; the delightful harmony was repeated from every recess which echo haunted on the borders of the lake. At first, indeed, the surprise was almost too much for Mrs Major, and she became a little hysterical, but she was soon recovered by the Major's tenderness and assurances of safety. Indeed he is, without exception, the most exemplary and devoted husband I ever beheld; still I confess (but that is *entre nous*), that to me, the little taste he displays for the tuneful Nine would be a great drawback to my matrimonial felicity.

"'After having enjoyed this delightful concert, we bade a long adieu to the sylvan shores of Ulls Water, and proceeded to Keswick, or, as it is properly denominated, Derwent Water, which is about three miles long; its pure transparent bosom, studded with numberless wooded islands, and its sides beautifully variegated with elegant mansions, snow-white cottages, taper spires, pleasant fields, adorned by the hand of cultivation, and towering groves that seem as if impervious to the light of day. The celebrated Fall of Lodore I shall not attempt to depict; but figure, if you can, a stupendous cataract, rushing headlong over enormous rocks and crags, which vainly seem to oppose themselves in its progress.

"'With regret we tore ourselves from the cultivated beauties of Derwent, and taking a look, *en passant*, of the more secluded Grassmere and Rydall, we at length found ourselves on the shores of the magnificent Winander.

"'Picture to yourself, if it be possible, stupendous mountains rearing their cloud-capped heads in all the sublimity of horror, while an immense sheet of azure reflected the crimson and yellow rays of the setting sun as they floated o'er its motionless green bosom, on which was impressed the bright image of the surrounding woods and meadows, speckled with snowy cottages and elegant villas! I really felt as if inspired, so much was my enthusiasm kindled, and yet I fear my description will fail in conveying to you any idea of this never-to-be-forgotten scene. But I must now bid you adieu, which I do with the greatest reluctance. How thought flows upon me when I take up my pen! how inconceivable to me the distaste which some people express for letter-writing! *Scribbling*, as they contemptuously term it. How I pity such vulgar souls! You, my dear cousin, I am sure, are not one of them. I have scarcely left room for Mrs Major to add a PS. Adieu! Your affectionate

"'LILLY.'

"Mrs Waddell's postscript was as follows:—

"'MA CHERE COUSINE—Of course you cannot expect that I, a married woman, can possibly have much time to devote to my female friends, with an adoring husband, who never stirs from my side, and to whom my every thought is due. But this much. in justice to myself, I think it proper to say, that I am the happiest of my sex, and that I find my Waddell everything generous, kind and brave!

"'ISABELLA WADDELL.'"

There are not many better things than this of the kind, and it is matched by a long passage (too long, unhappily, to quote) as to a certain Miss Becky Duguid, an old maid, and a victim of commissions and such-like sacrifices to friendship. But one passage also dealing with the Black family must be given to show the keenness of Miss Ferrier's observation, and the neatness of her satirical expression:—

"Mrs Fairbairn was one of those ladies who, from the time she became a mother, ceased to be anything else. All the duties, pleasures, charities, and decencies of life were henceforth concentrated in that one grand characteristic; every object in life was henceforth viewed through that single medium. Her own mother was no longer her mother; she was the grandmother of her dear infants, her brothers and sisters were mere uncles and aunts, and even her husband ceased to be thought of as her husband from the time he became a father. He was no longer the being who had claims on her time, her thoughts, her talents, her affections; he was simply Mr Fairbairn, the noun masculine of Mrs Fairbairn, and the father of her children. Happily for Mr Fairbairn, he was not a person of very nice feelings or refined taste; and although at first he did feel a little unpleasant when he saw how much his children were preferred to himself, yet in time he became accustomed to it, then came to look upon Mrs Fairbairn as the most exemplary of mothers, and finally resolved himself into the father of a very fine family, of which Mrs Fairbairn was the mother. In all this there was more of selfish egotism and animal instinct than of rational affection or Christian principle; but both parents piqued themselves upon their fondness for their offspring, as if it were a feeling peculiar to themselves, and not one they shared in common with the lowest and weakest of their species. Like them, too, it was upon the bodies of their children that they lavished their chief care and tenderness, for, as to the immortal interests of their souls, or the cultivation of their minds, or the improvement of their tempers, these were but little attended to, at least in comparison of their health and personal appearance."

Such passages are fair, but not extraordinarily favourable examples of the faculty of satire (a little "hard" perhaps, as even her admirers acknowledged it to be, but admirably clear-sighted and felicitous in expression) with which Miss Ferrier illustrated all her novels, and especially this her masterpiece. The general story of *The Inheritance* is, however, quite sufficiently interesting and well-managed, even without the embroidery of character study. Lord Rossville, a well-meaning but short-sighted man, begins to suspect, rightly enough in general, but wrongly in particular, that his heiress is likely to be disobedient to his desire that she shall marry her cousin (and failing him, his next heir), Mr Delmour, a dull politician. She boldly tells him that she cannot marry Mr Delmour, and he threatens to disinherit her, but before his mind is fully made up he dies suddenly, and she succeeds. Her lover, the younger brother of Mr Delmour, has shown signs of interestedness which might be suspicious to a less guileless person than Gertrude, but the chapter of accidents enables him to regain his position, and he is more attentive than ever to the Countess of Rossville in her own right. Luckily an old promise to her mother prevents her from marrying at once. But at her lover's suggestion she goes up to London, is introduced by him to fashionable society, indulges in all sorts of expense and folly (Miss Ferrier is great on the expense and folly of London life, and the wickedness of absenteeism), and neglects the good works at Rossville, in which the third cousin, Lindsay, the virtuous hero of the story, has interested her before. At last she returns to her home, and a storm, which has long been brewing, breaks. A stranger, who has before been introduced as mysteriously threatening and annoying Mrs St Clair, makes himself more objectionable than ever, forcing his way into the castle, wantonly exhibiting his power over the mother, and through her over her indignant daughter, and by degrees making himself wholly intolerable. At last the mystery is disclosed. Gertrude is not Countess of Rossville at all, nor even daughter of Mrs St Clair. She is a supposititious child whom her ambitious mother (so called) has taken for the purpose of foisting her as heiress on the Rossville family. At first it seems as if she were to suffer the intolerable punishment of being handed over to the scoundrel Lewiston as his daughter, but his pretensions to her are so far disproved. *Cetera quis nescit?* The faithless Colonel Delmour flies off, the good Lindsay remains, and a course of accidents replaces Gertrude as mistress (though not in her own right) at Rossville Castle.

The Inheritance is a book which really deserves a great deal of praise. Almost the only exceptions to be taken to it are the rather violent alternations of ἀναγνώρισις and περιπέτεια, which lead to the conclusion, and the mismanagement of the figure of Lewiston. This ruffian is represented as a Yankee, but he is not in the least like either the American of history or the conventional Yankee of fiction and the stage.

He is clearly a character for whom the author had no type ready in her memory or experience, and whom she consequently invented partly out of her own head and partly from such rather inappropriate stock models of villains as she happened to be acquainted with. He is not probable in himself, nor are his actions probable, for a business-like scoundrel such as he is represented to be would have known perfectly well that forcing himself into Rossville Castle, and behaving as if it were his own property, was an almost certain method of killing the goose that laid the golden eggs. But these faults are not of the first importance, and the general merits of the book are very great. Gertrude herself is a consistent, lifelike, and agreeable character, neither too sentimental nor too humoursome, but perfectly human; all the other characters group well round her, and as for the merely satirical passages and personages they are wholly admirable.

The Inheritance was more popular even than *Marriage* had been; but the author still refused to be hurried into production. She had always been very coy about acknowledging her work—all her books were published anonymously—and she was accustomed to write (though that operation may seem a harmless one enough) with as much secrecy as Miss Austen herself observed. But Sir Walter Scott was taken into confidence as to the publication of *Destiny*, and through his good offices with Cadell she obtained a much larger sum for it than she had hitherto received. The book is an advance even upon *The Inheritance*, and much more upon *Marriage*, in unity and completeness of plot, and it contains two or three of Miss Ferrier's most elaborate and finished pictures of oddities. But, as it seems to me, there is a considerable falling off in *verve* and spontaneity. The story-interest of the book centres on the fortunes of

Glenroy, a Highland chieftain of large property, and his daughter Edith. In former days an appanage of considerable extent has been carved out of the Glenroy property, and this at the date of the story has fallen in to a distant relation of the family, who is childless, and who visits the country for the first time. Glenroy, petty tyrant though he is at home, condescends to court this kinsman for the sake of his inheritance. The old man, however, who is both ill-natured and parsimonious, and who is revolted by the luxurious waste of Glenroy's household, leaves the property, under rather singular conditions, to certain poor relations of Glenroy's, Ronald Malcolm, a boy about the same age as the chief's son, Norman and his nephew, Reginald, being the special heir. This boy goes to sea, and what may be called one branch of the plot concerns his disappearance and his unwillingness, by making himself known after a long absence, to oust his father from the property (as under the settlement he would be obliged to do). The other branch, which is reunited with this first branch rather adroitly, springs in this wise. Glenroy, somewhat late in life, and long after the birth of his children Norman and Edith, has re-married Lady Elizabeth Waldegrave, a reproduction of Lady Juliana in *Marriage*. She has one daughter, who, by the death of relations, becomes a peeress in her own right (Miss Ferrier, it will be observed, has a genuinely Scotch objection to limiting the descent of honours to heirs male), and Lady Elizabeth having quarrelled with her husband, is very glad to take her daughter Florinda away with her. Only after many years does she return, and the rivalry (unconscious on Edith's part) between Glenroy's daughter and the English peeress for the hand of Reginald gives rise to some good scenes. Norman Malcolm, the heir, has died already, and after a short period of dotage Glenroy himself follows, leaving his daughter totally unprovided for, in consequence of his belief in her approaching marriage to Reginald, on whom the estates devolve. Edith's subsequent fortunes (for, as may be readily imagined, the beautiful and wealthy Florinda carries the day); her stay with some Cockney connections of her mother's; the unlucky relations (again much copied from *Marriage*) of Reginald and Florinda, all lead up to the final reappearance of Ronald and the necessary marriage-bells.

The lighter dishes of this particular banquet consist of a *Hausfranzösin*, Madame Latour (who is perhaps somewhat indebted to Miss Edgeworth, though there are suspicions of a personal model and victim here as elsewhere); of the Cockney pair, Mr and Mrs Ribley, amusing but conventional; of the chief's two dependants and butts, Benbowie, a cocklaird of his own clan, and Mrs Macaulay, a good-hearted, poor relation, who plays the mother to Edith; and, above all, of Mr McDow, the minister of the parish. This last portrait is a satire of what Dryden called the "bloody" kind (the same word in the same sense is used to this day in the politest French, and I do not know why English should be more squeamish), on the foibles of the Presbyterian clergy. Jeffrey is said to have pronounced Mr McDow an entire and perfect chrysolite. With his "moderate" opinions, his constant hunger and thirst after decreets and augmentations (it may be explained to those who do not know Scotland that a minister of the Established Church, unlike his English compeer, is enabled, if he chooses, to be a perpetual thorn in the sides of the owners of real property in his parish by claims for increased stipend, repairs to the manse, etc.), his vulgarity, his stupid jokes, his unfailing presence as an uninvited guest at every feast, there is no doubt of the truth of the picture or of the strength of the satire. But Miss Ferrier occasionally lets her acid bite a little too deeply, and it may be thought that she has done this here. Mr McDow has the same fault as some of Flaubert's characters—he is too uniformly disgusting. A testimonial to this man, who is a model, be it remembered, of coarseness, ignorance, stupidity, and selfish neglect of his duties, is a good specimen of the sharp strokes which Miss Ferrier constantly dealt to the vices and follies of society—strokes sharper perhaps than any other lady novelist has cared or known how to aim:—

"MY DEAR SIR—It is with the most unfeigned satisfaction I take up my pen to bear my public testimony to worth such as yours, enriched and adorned as it is with abilities of the first order— polished and refined by all that learning can bestow. From the early period at which our friendship commenced few, I flatter myself, can boast of a more intimate acquaintance with you than myself; but such is the retiring modesty of your nature, that I fear, were I to express the high sense I entertain of your merit, I might wound that delicacy which is so prominent a feature in your character. I shall therefore merely affirm, that your talents I consider as of the very highest order; your learning and erudition are deep, various, and profound; while your scholastic researches have ever been conducted on the broad basis of Christian modera- tion and gentlemanly liberality. Your doctrines I look upon as of the most sound, practical description, calculated to superinduce the clearest and most comprehensive system of Christian morals, to which your own character and conduct afford an apt illustration. As a preacher, your language is nervous, copious, and highly rhetorical; your action in the pulpit free, easy, and graceful. As a companion, your colloquial powers are of no ordinary description, while the dignity of your manners, combined with the suavity of your address, render your company universally sought after in the very first society. In short, to sum up the whole, I know no man more likely than yourself to adorn the gospel, both by your precept and example. With the utmost esteem and respect,

"I am, dear Sir,
"Most faithfully and sincerely yours,
"RODERICK M'CRAW,
"*Professor of Belles Lettres.*"

Destiny was published in 1831, and was its author's last work. Nothing else from her pen has been published to my knowledge, except certain brief reminiscences of visits to Ashestiel and Abbotsford, and the letters above referred to. Her silence was not owing to want of invitation to write, for London publishers offered her handsome terms; but she could not please herself with any idea that occurred to her, and accordingly declined the offers. Indeed, there are not, I think, wanting signs in *Destiny* that a fourth book would have been a failure. She was no longer young; her stock of originals, taken *sur le vif*, was probably exhausted; her old sarcastic pleasure in cynical delineation was giving way to a somewhat pietistic view of things which is very noticeable in her last novel; and, to crown all, she was in failing health and suffered especially from impaired eyesight. Yet she survived the publication of *Destiny* for nearly a quarter of a century, and did not die till November, 1854, at the age of seventy-two.

Miss Ferrier's characteristics as a novelist are well marked and not likely to escape any reader. But nothing brings them out so clearly as the inevitable comparison with her great contemporary, Miss Austen. Of the many divisions which may be made between different classes of fiction writers, there is one which is perhaps as clearly visible, though it is perhaps not so frequently drawn, as any. There is one set of novelists (Le Sage, Fielding, Thackeray, Miss Austen, are among its most illustrious names) whose work always seems like a section of actual life, with only the necessary differentia of artistic treatment. There is another, with Balzac and Dickens for its most popular exponents, and Balzac alone for its greatest practitioner, whose work, if not false, is always more or less abnormal. In the one case the scenes on the stage are the home, the forum, the streets which all know or might have known if they had lived at the time and place of the story,

These writers have each in his or her own degree something of the universality and truth of Shakespeare. No special knowledge is needed to appreciate them; no one is likely in reading them to stop himself to ask— Is this possible or probable? In the other case the spectator is led through a series of museums, many if not most of the objects in which are extraordinary specimens, "sports," monstrosities; while some, perhaps, are like the quaint creations of Waterton's fancy and ingenuity—something more than monsters, mere deliberate things of shreds and patches more or less cleverly made to look as if they might have been at some time or other *viables*. Of these two schools, Miss Ferrier belongs to the last, though she is not by any means an extreme practitioner in it. A moment's thought will show that the system of relying for the most part on thumb-nail sketches which she avowedly practised leads to this result. Not only is the observer prompted to take the most strongly marked and eccentric specimens in his or her range of observation, but in copying them the invariable result of imitation, the deepening of the strokes, and the hardening of the lines, leads to further departure from the common form. These eccentricities, too, whether copied or imagined, fit but awkwardly into any regular plot. The novelist is as much tempted to let her story take care of itself while she is emphasising her "humours" as another kind of novelist is tempted to let it take care of itself while he is discoursing to his readers about his characters, or about things in general. Hence the sort of writing which was Miss Ferrier's particular *forte* leads to two inconveniences—the neglect of a congruous and sufficient central interest, and the paying of disproportionate attention to minor characters. The contrast, therefore, even of *The Inheritance* with, let

us say, *Pride and Prejudice*, is a curious one, and no
reader can miss the want in the later book of the wonderful perspective and proportion, the classical avoidance of exaggeration, which mark Miss Austen's
masterpiece. On the other hand, it is interesting enough
to let the imagination attempt to conceive what
Miss Ferrier would have made of Lady Catherine, of
Mr Collins, of the Meryton vulgarities. The satire would
be as sharp, but it would be rougher, the instrument
would be rather a saw than a razor, and the executioner
would linger over her task with a certain affectionate
forgetfulness that she had other things to do than to
vivisect.

Nor shall we find it uninteresting to extend the comparison to the third contemporary, who, by a singular
coincidence, completes with Miss Austen and Miss
Ferrier the trinity of English, Scotch, and Irish lady
novelists of the opening of the century. Miss Edgeworth
(on whose *Patronage* a rather direct critique exists in
one of Miss Ferrier's letters) had far more geniality, a
more fertile brain, and a wider and more catholic range
of interests and sympathies than her Scotch sister: but
it is fair to say that no one of her books is so good as
The Inheritance, and that several of them are much
worse than either *Marriage* or *Destiny*.

Notwithstanding these drawbacks, notwithstanding
her admitted inability to manage pathos (which in her
hands becomes mere *sensibilité* of an obviously unreal
kind), and lastly, notwithstanding her occasional
didactic passages which are simply a bore, Miss Ferrier
is an admirable novelist, especially for those who can
enjoy unsparing social satire and a masterly faculty of
caricature. She writes, as far as mere writing goes,
well, and not unfrequently exceedingly well. It is
obvious, not so much from her quotations, for they are

dubious evidence, as from the general tone of her work that she was thoroughly well read. There are comparatively few Scotticisms in her, and she has a knack of dry sarcasm which continues the best traditions of the eighteenth century in its freedom from mere quaintness and grotesque. The character of Glenroy at the beginning of *Destiny* is nearly as well written as Saint-Evremond himself could have done it, and the sentence which concludes it is a good example of its manner. "As it was impossible, however, that any one so great in himself could make a great marriage, his friends and followers, being reasonable people, merely expected that he would make the best marriage possible." This little sentence, with the admirable piece of *galimatias* in Mrs St Clair's interview with Lord Rossville, and the description in *Marriage* of Miss Becky Douglas's arms as "strapped back by means of a pink ribbon of no ordinary strength or doubtful hue," are examples taken at random of the verbal shafts which Miss Ferrier scatters all about her pages to the great delight of those who have alertness of mind enough to perceive, and good taste or ill-nature enough (for both explanations may be given) to enjoy them.

Her main claim, however, to be read is unquestionably in her gallery of originals, or (as it has been, with the dispassionateness of a critic who does not want to make his goose too much of a swan, called) her museum of abnormalities. They may or may not have places assigned to them rather too prominent for the general harmony of the picture. They may or may not be exaggerated. There may or may not be a certain likeness to the fiendish conduct of an ancestor of the author's friend, Lord Cassillis, in the manner in which she carefully oils them, and as carefully disposes them on the gridiron for roasting. But they are excellent

company. The three aunts, Lady Maclaughlan, Mrs
MacShake, Dr Redgill, and in a minor degree the Bath
Précieuses in *Marriage*, Lord Rossville, Miss Pratt,
Adam Ramsay, and above all "Mrs Major" in *The
Inheritance*, Molly Macaulay, Mr McDow, and the
Ribleys, in *Destiny*, are persons with whom the reader
is delighted to meet, sorry to part, and (if he have any
affection for good novels) certain to meet again. When
it is added that though she does not often indulge it,
Miss Ferrier possesses a remarkable talent for description, it will be seen that she has no mean claims. Indeed,
of the four requisites of the novelist, plot, character,
description, and dialogue, she is only weak in the first.
The lapse of nearly a century and a complete change
of manners have put her books to the hardest test
they are ever likely to have to endure, and they come
through it triumphantly.

XIII

ENGLISH WAR-SONGS—CAMPBELL

It has been admitted by a rather reluctant world,—at least since the days of Marmontel who gave three particularly exquisite reasons for the fact—that the English excel in poetry; and it is most scholastically true that he who excels in a subject shows his excellence best in treating the best parts thereof. Now of ancient times it has been laid down in various fashions that the two things best worth doing in this world are fighting and love-making; and though the curious little sectarian heresy which calls itself the Modern Spirit no doubt regards this doctrine as a barbarous and exploded crudity, it is not at all improbable that it may see many Modern Spirits out. Therefore poetry being, as we have all learnt, a criticism of life, and these two things being at least among the most notable and interesting things of life, it will follow that poetry will busy itself best with them. Further yet, I have been told that the natives of India, who have had some opportunity of observing us, declare that an Englishman is never happy unless he is doing either one or the other,—sport being included as partaking of both. Therefore, yet once more, we shall conclude that English poetry ought to sing well about them.

As a matter of fact it does. With the one branch we have nothing here to do, and indeed no human being could discuss it in the compass of a single essay. The War-song or War-poem, however, is by no means so unmanageable, and with it I may attempt to deal. And let it be stated at the outset that, if I do not begin at what some excellent persons think the beginning, it is not out of any intention to insult them. There is good fighting in Beowulf; but the average Englishman (I think not thereby forfeiting his national claim to good sense) absolutely declines to regard as English a language scarcely a word of which he can understand. For my own part, I cannot see why if I am to draw on this Jutish Saga (or whatever it is) I may not equally well reach my hand to the shelf behind me, take down my *Corpus Poeticum Boreale*, and draw on that; of which things there were no end. Therefore let these matters, and the Song of Brunanbürh, and all the rest of it, be uncontentiously declined, and let us start from what the plain man does recognise as English, that is to say from Chaucer.

I have elsewhere[1] ventured to question the wisdom of making pretty philosophical explanations of literary phenomena, and I do not purpose to spend much time in asking why in the earliest English poetry (as just defined) there is hardly anything that comes within our subject. Five very simple and indisputable facts,— that our earliest ancestors fought and sang of fighting, both in the most admirable fashion; that the great heroes of the Hundred Years' War did not apparently care to sing about fighting at all; that Elizabeth's wars gave us indirectly one of the few war-songs of the first class, Drayton's *Ballad of Agincourt*; that the English Tyrtæus during the desperate and glorious War of the Spanish Succession could get no further than Addison's *Campaign*; and that the Revolutionary struggle drew from a poet, not exactly of the first rank, three such masterpieces as *Hohenlinden, Ye Mariners of England,* and *The Battle of the Baltic*—five such facts as these, I think, should deter any one who has not a mere mania

---

[1] See *inf., Twenty Years of Political Satire.*

for reason-making from indulging in that process on this subject. The facts are the facts. There is much excellent literary description of fighting in Chaucer, but it is distinctly literary; there is nothing of the personal joy of battle in it. Eustache Deschamps was an infinitely inferior poet to Master Geoffrey, yet there is far more of the real thing in this particular way in *Car France est cimetière des Anglois*, than in any poetical compatriot and contemporary of the conquerors of Cressy. In the next century we have, so far as I know, nothing at all to match the admirable anonymous *War-song of Ferrand de Vaudemont*, which may be found in M. Gaston Paris' *Chansons Populaires*, and other anthologies. The Scotch literary poets are a little better, if not very much; but if we could attach any definite date to most of the Border and other ballads, we should be able to say when some of the most admirable fighting poetry in the world was written. Most of them, how-ever, are so thoroughly shot and veined with modern touches that no man can tell where to have them. For the actual spirit of mortal combat it is probably im-possible to surpass the two stanzas in *Helen of Kirk-connell*.

> As I went down the water side,
> None but my foe to be my guide,
> None but my foe to be my guide
>   On fair Kirkconnell Lea.
>
> I lighted down my sword to draw,
> I hachéd him in pieces sma',
> I hachéd him in pieces sma',
>   For her sake that died for me!

There is real *Berserk-gang* there: and yet the poem, and even the passage, distinctly shows the influence of the eighteenth century, to say no more. In its present cast and shape the whole of this ballad-question is a mere labyrinth. I do not know a more disheartening study than that of Professor Child's magnificent volumes, with their endless variants, which make a canonical text impossible. Therefore, despite the admirable fighting that there is in them, they will help us little.

Skelton Skeltonises in this as in other styles; but the *Ballad of the Doughty Duke of Albany and his Hundred Thousand Scots* is a mere piece of doggrel brag, utterly unworthy of the singer of *My Maiden Isabel* or even of the author of *Elinor Rumming*. The honour of composing the first modern English war-song has been recently, and I think rightly, given to Humphrey Giffard, whose *Posy of Gilloflowers*, published in 1580, just before the overture of the "melodious bursts that fill The spacious times of great Elizabeth," contains a quaint and rough but really spirited piece, *To Soldiers*, in this remarkable metre:

The time of war is come, prepare your corslet, spear and shield;
Methinks I hear the drum strike doleful marches to the field,
Tantara, tantara the trumpets sound, which makes men's hearts
    with joy abound:

The warning guns are heard afar and every thing announces war.
Serve God, stand stout: bold courage brings this gear about;
Fear not, forth run: faint heart fair lady never won.

This, it must be admitted, needs a good deal of licking into shape as regards form,—as regards spirit it has the root of the matter in it. Nor does the quaint prosaic alloy which so frequently affects the English as compared with the Scotch ballad prevent *The Brave Lord Willoughby* from being a most satisfactory document. The businesslike statement how, after that unluxurious meal of dead horses and puddle-water,

Then turning to the Spaniards
A thousand more they slew,

is no doubt destitute enough of the last indefinable touch which can transform words quite as simple and inornate into perfect poetry. But it misses it very narrowly, and almost provides a substitute by its directness and force.

I do not know, however, that the real joy of the thing is to be found anywhere before that wondrous *Battle of Agincourt to the brave Cambro-Britons and their Harp*, which Michael Drayton, an Englishman of Englishmen and a poet whose enormous versatility and copiousness have caused him to be rated rather too low than too high, produced in the early years of the seventeenth century. With the very first lines of it the fit reader must feel that there is no mistake possible about this fellow:

> Fair stood the wind for France
> When we our sails advance,
> Nor now to prove our chance
>   Longer would tarry:
> But putting to the main,
> At Caux, the mouth of Seine,
> With all his martial train
>   Landed King Harry.

There is no precedent for that dash and rush of metre; and if we look for followers it will bear the contrast as happily. The most graceful and scholarly poet of America, the greatest master of harmonies born in England during the nineteenth century, have imitated it. If *The Skeleton in Armour* is delightful, and *The Charge of the Light Brigade* (with its slight change of centre of gravity in the rhythm) consummate, what shall be said of this original of both? I know an enthusiast who declared that he would have rather written the single line "Lopped the French lilies" than any even in English poetry except a few of Shakespeare's. This was doubtless delirium, though not of the worst kind. But the intoxication of the whole piece is almost unmatched. The blood stirs all through as you read:

With Spanish yew so strong
Arrows a cloth-yard long
That like to serpents stung
  Piercing the weather:
None from his fellow starts,
But playing manly parts
And like true English hearts
  Stuck close together.

I always privately wish that he had written *Shot close together*, but why gild the lily? Still better is that gorgeous stanza of names:

Warwick in blood did wade,
Oxford the foe invade,
And cruel slaughter made
  Still as they ran up:
Suffolk his axe did ply,
Beaumont and Willoughby
Bare them right doughtily,
  Ferrers and Fanhope.

For some time it seemed as though the question with which the poem closes:

Oh! when shall English men
With such acts fill a pen?

was to be answered rather by the acts than by the pen. As few songs as triumphs wait on a civil war, and though Montrose might have done the thing he did not. The dishonest combats of the seventeenth century had to wait a couple of hundred years for their laureate and then he appeared on the wrong side. For even Mr Browning's *Cavalier Tunes* are not as good as *The Battle of Naseby*, which, Cavalier as I am, I wish I could think was "pinchbeck." No man perhaps ever lived who had more of the stuff of a Tyrtæus in him than Dryden; but his time gave him absolutely no subjects of an inspiriting nature, and did not encourage him to try any others. The *Annus Mirabilis* is fine enough in all conscience; but *Come if you dare*, and parts of *Alexander's Feast* show what might have been if the course of events had been more favourable. To tell the

honest truth, the cause was generally too bad in those
fights with the Dutch, and the fights themselves
(though we very properly call them victories) were too
near being defeats, to breathe much vigour into the
sacred bard; while for some fifty years of Glorious
John's manhood, from the battle of the Dunes to his
death, there was no land-fighting that could at once
cheer an Englishman and commend itself to a Jacobite.
In luckier circumstances Dryden was the very man to
have bettered Drayton and anticipated Campbell.

When he was dead there was no more question of
anything of the kind for a very long time. The Angel
passage in Mr Addison's poem is undoubtedly a very
fine one; I am exceedingly sorry for any one who doubts
or does not see that. But the essence of a war-song or
even a war-poem is that it should stir the blood; and
this stirs it just to the extent that is necessary to secure
the σοφῶς, in the sense of "Bravo," which Martial tells
us Roman reciters earned. It was really a pity. Cutts
is not such a pretty name as Ferrers or Fanhope; but
"the Salamander" did deeds of arms of which not the
greatest of bards need have disdained to be laureate.
Blenheim was most undoubtedly a famous victory:
the fighting, such as there was of it, at Ramillies was
of the best kind; and as for Malplaquet, it ranks for
sheer dingdong fighting, and on a far larger scale, with
Albuera or Inkerman. But sing these things our good
fathers could not. Yet they tried in all conscience. It
is a rough, but very sufficient test to take the copious
anthology of anthologies which Mr Bullen has recently
edited in half-a-dozen volumes for the beginning of the
seventeenth century and the last years of the sixteenth,
the collections variously called *Musarum Deliciæ* and
the *State Poems* for the middle of seventeenth, and the
odd sweeping together of poetry, sculduddery, music,

doggrel Verse of Society and what-not which Tom
D'Urfey made out of the songs of his time for the end
of the seventeenth and the beginning of the eighteenth.
In the first and second divisions we shall find hardly
any warlike verse; the third bristles with it.

The six volumes of the *Pills to Purge Melancholy* lie
beside me as I write, plumed with paper slips which I
have put in them to mark pieces of this sort. The
badness of them (a few lines of Dryden's, and one or
two not his, excepted) is simply astounding, even to
those who have pretty well fathomed already the poetic
depths of the late seventeenth and early eighteenth
centuries. They cover the whole period of William of
Orange's stout if not successful fights, and of the almost
unparalleled triumphs of Marlborough; yet there is
never a touch of inspiration. The following is on the
whole a really brilliant specimen:

> Health to the Queen! then straight begin
> To Marlborough the Great and to brave Eugene,
> With them let valiant Webb come in,
>   Who lately performed a wonder.
> Then to the ocean an offering make,
> And boldly carouse to brave Sir John Leak,
> Who with mortar and cannon Mahon did take
>   And made the Pope knock under.

Here is an effort on Oudenarde:

> Sing mighty Marlborough's story!
>   Men of the field,
>   He passes the shield,
> And to increase his glory,
> The French all fly or yield.
> Vendosme drew out to spite him
> Th' Household troops to fright him,
>   Princes o' the blood
>   Got off as best they cou'd
> And ne'er durst return to fight him.

Malplaquet inspires a yet nobler strain:

> Mounsieur! Mounsieur! Leave off Spain!
> To think to hold it is in vain,
> Thy warriors are too few.

> Thy Martials must be new,
> Worse losses will ensue,
> Then without more ado
> Be wise and call home petite Anjou!

At a still earlier period *The two Glorious Victories at Donawert and Hochstet* had stirred up somebody to write, to a tune by Mr Corbet, Pindaricks to this effect:

> Old Lewis, must thy frantic riot
>   Still all Europe vex?
> Methinks 'tis high time to be quiet
>   Now at sixty-six.

There is a little more spirit in a ditty beginning:

> From Dunkirk one night they stole out in a fright—

but it is political rather than battailous; and for a purely and wholly deplorable failure of combined loyal and Bacchanalian verse, I hardly know the equal of the following:

> Then welcome from Vigo,
> And cudgelling Don Diego,
> With——rapscallion
> And plundering the galleons.
> Each brisk valiant fellow
> Fought at Redondello,
>   And those who did meet
>   With the Newfoundland fleet.
> Then for late successes
> Which Europe confesses
> At land by our gallant Commanders,
> The Dutch in strong beer
> Should be drunk for one year
> With their Generals' health in Flanders!

I do not know how long the reader's patience will hold out against this appalling doggrel, which represents the efforts of the countrymen of Shakespeare and Shelley under the influence of victories which might have made a Campbell of "hoarse Fitzgerald." There is plenty more if any one likes it. I can tell him how the victory over the Turks proved that

> Christians thus with conquest crowned,
> Conquest with the glass goes round,

Weak coffee can't keep its ground
Against the force of claret.

How

The Duke then to the wood did come
In hopes Vendosme to meet,
When lo! the Prince of Carignan
Fell at his Grace's feet.

Oh, gentle Duke, forbear! forbear!
Into that wood to shoot,
If ever pity moved your Grace
But turn your eyes and look!

This is an extract taken from a delightful ballad in which the historical facts of Oudenarde are blended quaintly with the Babes in the Wood. Then we hear how

The conquering genius of our isle returns
Inspired by Ann the godlike hero burns.

We are told of Marlborough himself

Thus as his sprightly infancy was still inured to harms,
So was his noble figure still adorned with double charms.

While the selection may be appropriately finished by the exordium of an indignant bard who cries—

Ulm is gone,
But basely won,
And treacherous Bavaria there has buried his renown:
That stroling Prince
Who few years since
Was crammed with William's gold!

Macaulay, who read everything at some time or other, had probably not read these when he wrote on Addison, or he would have selected some of them to point still further the contrast of *The Campaign*. The poor man who wrote about the "capering beast" was a genius compared to most of the known or unknown authors of these marvellous exercitations, which would seem to have been composed after the effusion of liquor they generally recommend.

Few glories attended the British arms, on land and in Europe, from the setting of Corporal John's star to the rising of that of "the Duke"; but the true singer, if he had been anywhere about, might have found plenty of employment with the Navy. Unfortunately he was not, and his substitutes preferred to write *Admiral Hosier's Ghost*, or else melancholy lines like those of Langhorne, which no human being would now remember if Scott had not as a boy remembered them in the presence of Burns.

This last name brings us to a poet who ought to have sung of war even better than he did. As it is, there is as little mistake possible about *Scots Wha Hae*, as about *Agincourt*, or *Ye Mariners of England*; while for compressed and undiluted fire it has the advantage of both. It is characteristic, however, of the unlucky rant about freedom which Burns had got into his head, that the "chains and slavery" (which really were very little ones) play an even more prominent part than that pure and generous desire to thrash the person opposed to you, because he is opposed to you, because he is not "your side," which is the true motive of all the best war-songs. This (though in neither example is there equal poetical merit) is more perceptible in the light but capital "I am a Son of Mars" of the *Jolly Beggars*, and in those delightful verses of *Scotch Drink*, which so did shock the delicate nerves of Mr Matthew Arnold, and so do shock still the sensitive conscience of the modern person, who thinks war a dreadful thing, and carnage anything but God's daughter.

Our chief writer of war-songs, however (for Dibdin's capital songs are not quite such capital poetry), is beyond doubt or question Thomas Campbell; and a very hard nut is the said Thomas for "scientific" criticism to crack. He certainly belonged to a warlike family of a warlike nation; but he shared this advantage with some millions of other Scotchmen, and some thousands of other Campbells. His father, whose youngest child he was, and who was sixty-seven when Thomas was born on 27th July, 1777, was a Glasgow merchant, and he himself began life in a merchant's office. The "estho-psychological" (Heaven save us!) determining cause of his temperament is not precisely or eminently apparent. He was not, as Burns was, of a romantic or adventurous disposition, being all his life a quiet, literary gentleman. He was tolerably prosperous, despite his being an excessively bad arithmetician and husband of his money. He had, after early struggles as a tutor, a copying clerk and otherwise, a nice little pension (1805), a nicer little legacy (nay, several), some lucrative appointments and commissions. He lived chiefly at Sydenham and Boulogne (where, on 15th June, 1844, he died), though on his travels in Germany (in the dividing year of the centuries) he did hear, and even perhaps see, shots fired in anger. He also possessed at one period three hundred pounds in bank-notes rolled up in his slippers. He was not ungenerously devoted to port wine, was somewhat less generously *not* devoted to his poetical rivals, was well looked after by his wife (his cousin Matilda Sinclair) while she lived, and afterwards by a niece. He died on the verge of three score years and ten, if not an exceedingly happy or contented, yet on the whole a sufficiently fortunate man.

He was especially fortunate in this, that probably no man ever gained so early and kept so long such high literary rank on the strength of so small a literary performance. In the very year of his reaching man's estate, the *Pleasures of Hope* seated him at once on the Treasury Bench in the contemporary session of the Poets, and unlike most occupants of Treasury Benches, he was never turned off. Many far greater poets appeared during the nearly fifty years which passed between that time and his death; but they were greater in perfectly different fashions. That what may be called his official, and what may be called his real titles to his position were not the same, may be very freely granted. But he had real titles. The curious thing is that even the official titles were so very modest in volume. Setting his *Specimens* aside, all his literary work (which is not in itself very large) outside the covers of his Poems is as nearly as possible valueless. For some considerable time he was a journalist, and in later life he was for some ten years editor of the *New Monthly Magazine*, with a fair income, and very little to do. In 1806 he compiled *The Annals of Great Britain from the Accession of George II to the Peace of Amiens*, a work I have no doubt of the soundest Whig principles, but one which I confess I have never read. Much later he wrote or compiled divers *Lives of Petrarch*, of *Frederick the Great* (tenderly handled as from Whig to Whig in Macaulay's Essay), of *Mrs Siddons*. He was Perpetual Chairman of the Friends of Poland, and thrice Rector of the University of Glasgow. He thought at least that he originated the University of London.

The Poems themselves, the work of a long lifetime, do not fill three hundred small pages, and those of them which are really worth much, would not, I think, be very tightly packed in thirty. The *Pleasures of Hope* itself (published in April 1799, welcomed with extraordinary warmth, and having the good luck to precede by some years the new Renaissance of poetry in England) is beyond doubt the best of that which I should *not* include. It is one of the very best school exercises ever written; it has touches which only a schoolboy of genius could achieve. But higher than a school exercise it cannot be ranked. The other longer poems are far below it. *Gertrude of Wyoming* (1809) has several famous and a smaller number of excellent lines; but it is as much of an artificial conglomerate, and as little of an original organism as the *Pleasures of Hope*, and the choice of the Spenserian stanza is simply disastrous. "Iberian seemed his boot," the boot of the hero to the eyes of the heroine! To think that a man should, in a stanza consecrated to the very quintessence of poetical poetry—a stanza in which, far out of its own period and in mid-eighteenth century, Thomson had written the *Castle of Indolence*, in which, before Campbell's own death, Mr Tennyson was to write the *Lotos Eaters*,—deliver himself of the phrase, "Iberian seemed his boot"!

But by so much as *Gertrude of Wyoming* is worse than the *Pleasures of Hope* by as much is *Theodric* (1824) worse than *Gertrude of Wyoming*, and the *Pilgrim of Glencoe* (1842) worse again than *Theodric*. There are not more than five or six hundred lines, including as usual some good ones, in *Theodric*; but though I have just re-read it before writing this I have only the dimmest idea of what really happens. Theodric makes love to two young women, a most reprehensible though not uncommon practice, and they both die. One is named Constance and the other Julia: and the last lines of Constance's last letter to Theodric are rather pretty. She bids him not despair:

> I ask you by our love to promise this
> And kiss these words, where I have left a kiss;
> The latest from my living lips to yours.

But they are quite the best in the poem, which is too short to have any narrative interest, and too long to possess any other. Of the *Pilgrim of Glencoe* it is enough to say that the most enthusiastic Campbellites have seldom been able to say a word for it, that it is rather in Crabbe's style than in the author's own, and that Crabbe has not to my knowledge every written anything so bad as a whole.

Even when we come to the shorter poems (which were mostly written before *Gertrude of Wyoming*) almost endless exclusions and allowances have to be made. Campbell has left some exceedingly pretty love-songs, not I think very generally known, the best of which are "Withdraw not yet those Lips and Fingers," and "How Delicious is the Winning." But there is no great originality about them, and they are such things as almost any man with a good ear and an extensive knowledge of English poetry could write nearly as well. Almost everything (I think everything) of his that is really characteristic and really great is comprised in the dozen poems as his works are usually arranged (I quote the Aldine Edition) between *O'Connor's Child* and the *Soldier's Dream*, with the addition of the translated song of Hybrias the Cretan and, if anybody likes, *The Last Man*. Even here the non-warlike poems cannot approach the warlike ones in merit. The fighting passages of *O'Connor's Child* itself are much the best. *Glenara* (which by the way ends with a line of extraordinary imbecility) is not a very great thing except in the single touch,

Each mantle unfolding a dagger displayed.

The Exile of Erin is again merely pretty, and I should not myself care to preserve a line of *Lord Ullin's Daughter* except the really magnificent phrase

And in the scowl of Heaven each face
Grew dark as they were speaking.

As a whole the *Lines written on revisiting a Scene in Argyleshire*, with their admirable picture of the forsaken garden, seem to me the best thing Campbell did out of the fighting vein.

But in that vein how different a man was he! As a mere boy he had tried it, or something like it, feebly enough in *The Wounded Hussar*; and he showed what he could do in it, even when the subject did not directly touch his imagination, by his spirited paraphrase of the Hybrias fragment. His devotion to the style (which appears even in pieces ostensibly devoted to quite different subjects such as the *Ode to Winter*) is all the more remarkable that Campbell was a staunch member of the political party in England which hated the war. But it was a clear case of overmastering idiosyncrasy. It is an odd criticism of the late Mr Allingham's (to be matched, however, with several others in his remarks on Campbell) that the selection in the *Specimens* of Thomas Penrose's poem beginning

> Faintly brayed the battle's roar,
> Distant down the hollow wind,
> Panting terror fled before,
> Wounds and death were left behind,

shows "how tolerant a true poet like Campbell could be of the most frigid and stilted conventionality of diction." Most certainly he could be so tolerant; but his tolerance here had clearly nothing to do with the style. He was led away, as nearly everybody is, by his sympathy with the matter. Indeed before long Mr Allingham recollects himself, and says, "Battle subjects always took hold on him." They certainly did.

I do not care much for *The Soldier's Dream* as a whole. Most of it is trivial and there is an astonishing disregard of quantity throughout, any three syllables being apparently thought good enough to make an anapæst. Indeed Campbell was at no time very commendable for attention either as a metrist or as a rhymester. In the latter capacity he is often shocking, and in both he wants the aid of *furor poeticus* to enable him to surmount his difficulties. But the opening stanza of the *Dream* is grand:

Our bugles sang truce, for the night-cloud had lowered,
  And the sentinel stars set their watch in the sky;
And thousands had sunk on the ground overpowered,
  The weary to sleep and the wounded to die.

Pictorially and poetically both, that is about as good as it can be. *Lochiel's Warning* has no single passage as good: but it is far better as a whole, despite some of the same metrical shortcomings. The immortal "Field of the dead rushing red on the sight," the steed that "fled frantic and far" (and inspired thereby one of the finest passages of another Thomas), the hackneyed but admirable "All plaided and plumed in their tartan array," the "coming events" that a man may admire but hardly now quote—these and other things would save any copy of verses.

But still nothing can touch the immortal Three—*Hohenlinden*, *The Battle of the Baltic*, and *Ye Mariners of England*. What does it matter that no one of them is without a blemish, that *Ye Mariners* is almost a paraphrase of a good old ballad by good old Martin Parker, king of the ballad-mongers of England, that (as a certain kind of critic is never tired of telling us) there is not so much as a vestige of a wild and stormy steep at Elsinore, that to say "sepulchr*ee*," as we evidently must in *Hohenlinden*, is trying if not impossible? Campbell, who is in prose a little old-fashioned perhaps and slightly stilted, but on stilts with the blood in them if I may say so, who gave his reasons for thinking the launch of a line-of-battle ship "one of the sublime objects of artificial life," deserved to write the *Battle of the Baltic*. And he did more, Sempronius, he wrote it. There is not a stanza of it in which you may not pick out something to laugh or to cavil at if you choose. There is not one, at least in its final form, which does not stir the blood to fever-heat. *Ye Mariners of England* is much stronger in the negative sense of freedom from faults, only the last stanza being in any serious degree vulnerable; and the felicity of the rhythm is extraordinary. The famous second and third stanzas, "The spirits of your fathers" and "Britannia needs no bulwarks," are as nearly as possible faultless. Matter and manner could not be better wedded, nor could the whole fire and force of English patriotism be better managed so as to inform and vivify metrical language.

But I am not certain that if I were not an Englishman I should not put *Hohenlinden* highest of the three. It is less important "to *us*," it appeals less directly to our thought and sentiment, it might have been written by a man of any country,—always provided that his country had such a language to write in. Also it has a few of Campbell's besetting slips. "Scenery" is weak in the second stanza, and I could witness the deletion of the seventh altogether with some relief and satisfaction. "Sepulchre" is so exceedingly good in itself that the sense that we ought to call it "sepulchree" as aforesaid is additionally annoying (though by the way Glorious John would have called upon us to do the same thing without the slightest hesitation). But the poem is imitated from nothing and so stands above *Ye Mariners*; its blemishes are trifling in comparison with the terrible

> Then the might of England flushed
> To anticipate the scene

(where the last line except with much good will to help it is sheer and utter nonsense) and other things in *The Battle of the Baltic*. Moreover the concerted music of its rolling metre is unsurpassed. The triplets of each stanza catch up and carry on the sweep of the fourth line of the preceding in a quite miraculous manner; and that mixed poetic and pictorial touch which has been noted in Campbell appears nowhere so well. Although to me, as to everybody, it has been familiar ever since I was about seven years old, I never can get over my surprise at the effect of so hackneyed a word as "artillery." Indeed I knew a paradoxer once who maintained that this was due to the inspiration which made Campbell prefix "red"; "For," said he, "we are accustomed to see the Artillery in blue."

And it would be improper to leave this subject of Campbell—almost if not quite our greatest war-singer —without another observation. He was not only far below his best self in all other departments of poetry, but he had little taste for it in others. Though he lived till the nineteenth century was nearly half over, though he was junior to all the great men who founded nineteenth century poetry, he was himself only a belated son of the eighteenth century. He was an apprentice of the Popian tradition to the last, and never took out his freedom save in the single department of the war-song.

More than a hundred years, more fertile in good poetry and bad verse than any similar period in the history even of England, have passed since in the course of a few months Campbell sketched, if he did not finish, all his three masterpieces. The poetry and the verse both have done their share of battle-writing. Of the great poets who were Campbell's contemporaries and superiors none quite equalled him in this way; though Scott ran him hard, and Byron, never perhaps writing a war-*song* of the first merit, abounded in war-poetry of a very high excellence. Scott could do it better than he could do almost anything else in verse; and if volume and degrees of merit are taken together the prize must be his. Nothing can beat the last canto of *Marmion* as narrative of the kind; few things can equal the regular lyrics of which *Bonnie Dundee* if not the best is the best known, and the scores of battle-snatches of which Elspeth Cheyne's version of the battle of Harlaw may rank first. The Lakers were by temperament rather than by principle unfitted for the style: though if Coleridge, in the days of *The Ancient Mariner*, had tried it we should have had some great thing. Shelley, though a very pugnacious person, thought fighting wicked; and Keats, though he demolished the butcher, did not sing of war. Moore is not at his best in such things. In fact they have a knack of being written by poets otherwise quite minor, such as Wolfe of the not undeservedly famous *Burial of Sir John Moore*, a battle-piece surely rather than a mere dirge.

The Epigoni of the great school of 1800–1830 have been on the whole more fruitful than that school itself, though nothing that they have done can quite touch Campbell in fire, and though they have never surpassed Drayton in a sort of buoyant and unforced originality which excludes all idea of the mere literary copy of verses. One of the earliest and certainly one of the best of them in this kind (for Peacock's immortal *War Song of Dinas Vawr* is too openly satirical) was Macaulay. I wish I had space here to destroy once for all (it could easily be done to the satisfaction of any competent tribunal) the silly prejudice against Macaulay's verse which, as a result of an exaggerated following of the late Mr Arnold by criticasters, is still, among criticasters, common. In Mr Arnold himself I suspect the prejudice to have been partly mere crotchet (for great critic as he was in his day he was full of crotchets), partly perhaps due to some mere personal dislike of the kind which Macaulay very often excited in clever and touchy young men, but partly also and perhaps principally to the facts that Mr Arnold belonged to a generation which affected to look on war as a thing barbarous and outworn, and that he himself had no liking for and was absolutely unskilled in war-verse. *Sohrab and Rustum* is in parts and especially in its famous close a very fine poem indeed; but of the actual fighting part I can not say much.

Still if Mr Arnold really disliked the *Lays of Ancient Rome* he was quite right to say so; it is not easy to be equally complimentary to those who affect to dislike them because they think it the right thing to do. Tried by the standard of impartial criticism Macaulay is certainly not a great poet, nor except in this one line a poet at all. Even in this line his greatness is of the second not of the first order, for the simple reason that it is clearly derivative. "No Sir Walter, no *Lays*" is not a critical opinion; it is a demonstrable fact. Granting so much, I do not see how sane criticism can refuse high, very high, rank to the said *Lays*, and the smaller pieces of the same kind such as *Ivry* and *Naseby*, and those much less known but admirable verses which tell darkly what happened

When the crew with eyes of flame brought the ship without a name
    Alongside the Last Buccaneer.

For the test of this kind of verse is much simpler and more unerring than that of any other. If in the case of a considerable number of persons of different ages, educations, ranks, and so forth, it induces a desire to walk up and down the room, to shout, to send their fists into somebody else's face, then it is good and there is no more to be said. That it does not cause these sensations in others is no more proof of its badness than it is a proof that a match is bad because it does not light when you rub it on cotton wool.

The still common heresy on this subject has made it necessary to dwell a little thereon. The great mass of Victorian war-poetry it is only possible to pass as it were in review by way rather of showing how much there is and how good than of criticising it in detail. Tennyson was excellent at it. Some otherwise fervent admirers of his are, I believe, dubious about *The Charge of the Light Brigade*; I have myself no doubt whatever, though it is unequal. Still more unequal are *The Revenge* and *Lucknow*. But the quasi-refrain of the latter

> And ever upon the topmost roof our banner of England blew

is surpassed for the special merit of the kind by no line in the language, though it is run hard by the passage in the former, beginning

> And the sun went down and the stars came out far over the
> summer sea.

There are flashes and sparks of the same fire all over Lord Tennyson's poems, as in the splendid

> Clashed with his fiery few and won

of the *Ode on the Death of the Duke of Wellington*, or the still finer distich

> And drunk delight of battle with my peers
> Far on the ringing plains of windy Troy

and the first stanza of *Sir Galahad* and a score of others. Of Mr Browning's famous Cavalier Tunes already mentioned *Give a Rouse* is the only one I care much for; the two others are artificial with anything but Cavalier artificiality. *Hervè Riel* if not quite a war-song (albeit the art of judicious running away is art and part of war) has more of the root of the matter in it, *Through the Metidja* more still (for all its mannerism, it is the only successful attempt I know to give the very sound and rhythm of cymbals in English verse), and perhaps *Prospice*, though only metaphorically a fighting-piece, most of all. For, let it be once more repeated, it is the power of exciting the combative spirit in the reader that makes a war-song.

We shall find this power present abundantly in many poets during these last days. In hardly any department perhaps is Mr Swinburne's too great facility in allowing himself to be mastered by instead of mastering words more to be regretted, for no one has ever excelled him in command both of the rhythms and the language necessary for the style. Even as it is the *Song in Time of Order* hits the perfectly right note in respect of form and spirit. There is plenty of excellent stuff of the sort in Mr William Morris' *Defence of Guinevere*— plenty more in his later work. Charles Kingsley ought to have left us something perfect in the manner, and though he never exactly did, *The Last Buccaneer*, that excellent ballad where

> They wrestled up, they wrestled down,
> They wrestled still and sore,

the opening of

> Evil sped the battle-play
> On the Pope Calixtus' day,

and the last lines of the *Ode to the North-East Wind* have all the right touch, the touch which has guided us through this review. That touch is to be found again in Sir Francis Doyle's *Return of the Guards*, his *Private of the Buffs*, and most of all in his *Red Thread of Honour*, one of the most lofty, insolent and passionate things concerning this matter that our time has produced.

But here we are reaching dangerous ground, the ground occupied, and sometimes very well occupied, by younger living writers. It is better to decline this and close the survey. It has shown us some excellent, and even super-excellent things, some of surpassing and gigantic badness, a very great deal that is good and very good. I do not think any other language can show anything at all approaching it. Despite the excellence of old French in this kind, and despite the abundant military triumphs of the modern nation, the modern language of France has given next to nothing of merit in it. The *Marseillaise* itself, really remarkable for the way in which it marries itself to a magnificent tune is, when divorced from that tune, chiefly rubbish. The Germans,—with one imperishable thing, Körner's *Schwertlied* (sometimes sneered at by the same class of persons who sneer at Macaulay) in the pure style, and a few others, such as Heine's *Die Grenadiere* in the precincts of it—have little that is very remarkable.

In these and other European languages, so far as I know, you often get war-pictures rendered in verse not ill, but seldom the war-spirit rendered thoroughly in song or snatch. Certain unpleasant ones will tell us that as the fighting power dies down, so the power of singing increases, that "poets succeed better in fiction than in fact," as Mr Waller, both speaker and hearer being persons of humour, observed to his Majesty Charles II on a celebrated occasion. Luckily, however, that *Ballad to the Brave Cambro-Britons and their Harp*, and *The Battle of the Baltic* will settle this suggestion. It will hardly be contended that the countrymen and contemporaries of Drayton, that the contemporaries and countrymen of Campbell, had lost the trick of fighting. Look too at Le Brun *Pindare* and his poem on the *Vengeur*, a very few years earlier than *The Battle of the Baltic* itself. Le Brun belonged to very much the same school of poetry as the author of *The Pleasures of Hope*, and I do not know that on the whole he was a very much worse poet. The fictitious story of the

Vengeur, on which he wrote, and which he not at all improbably believed (as most Frenchmen do to this day) was even fresher than Copenhagen to Campbell, and far more exciting. Yet scarcely even those woful contemporaries of Corporal John, from whom I have unfilially drawn the veil, made a more hopeless mess of it than Le Brun. The spirit of all poetry blows where it listeth, but the spirit of none more than of the poetry of war. Let us hold up our hands and be thankful that it has seen fit to blow to us in England such things as *Agincourt*, as *Scots Wha Hae*, as *Ye Mariners of England*, and a hundred others not so far inferior to them.

APPENDIX C

SONGS OF THE CRIMEAN WAR

A RATHER curious and interesting paper, which would not badly illustrate the difficulty, more than once pointed at in the text, of making out any strict connection between opportunity and performance in the matter of War Songs, might be written on those of the Crimean War. It is, of course, true that *The Charge of the Light Brigade*, one of the capital things of our literature in this kind, owes its inspiration to the subject; and that indirectly it is responsible for a good deal of not the least powerful part of *Maud*. But when we have allowed for these, and for the strictly bellicose parts of Sydney Dobell's *England in time of War*, we have pretty well exhausted the very notable things to which the one great war in which England engaged for eighty years, gave birth. Archbishop Trench's *Alma* is estimable but hardly great; the other War Poems which Dobell's coadjutor Alexander Smith, the resipiscent Chartist Ernest Jones, and others produced, deserve no stronger epithet.

The truth is that, here as elsewhere, the reverse of Borrow's dictum about beer applies to poetry. "The goodness of ale," quoth he, "depends less upon who brews it than upon what it is brewed of." I am not quite certain even of this: but it is certain that the goodness of poetry depends much less on the matter of the song than on the gifts of the singer. And in this case Tennyson was the only great English singer whom the war found ready. The subject does not seem to have inspired Browning; it was not very likely to inspire Mr Arnold; Kingsley, who might have sung nobly on it, had already turned from poetry to prose. In fact the war exactly coincided with the interval in English verse, between the undisputed establishment of the power of Tennyson and Browning, and the rise of the second Victorian—the first purely Victorian—school with Mr William Morris. Only the "Spasmodics" occupied the field, and the Spasmodics, as has been said, did what they could.

But if the enquirer goes still further and says, "Yes; but why did not the Crimean war develop its Campbell, in addition to Tennyson, who was a universal not a specialist singer?" then no answer can be given except that, as a matter of fact, it did not, and there's an end on't. Even its unsatisfactory character in many ways will give us no help; for if there was blundering there was no disgrace, and it is only disgrace that seals the singer's lips. The hour had come, but the men had not; and that is the conclusion of the whole matter[1].

[1] The abundant war-songs of 1914–18 are too new to be judged on the same lines with those of this paper or even of its Appendix (1923).

XIV

MADAME D'ARBLAY

THERE are so many things that are interesting in the life and works of Fanny Burney, that it is difficult for any one to know "where to begin." Perhaps some smart person may rejoin that it is not necessary to begin at all, inasmuch as one of the acknowledged masters of what the French call "bio-bibliographical" writing made her the subject of a famous essay nearly a century ago. But, without presumption, this judgment may be disabled. In the first place it is the peculiarity—some may say the weakness—of critical writing that, though it may contain final things, it never can be as a whole final. Each generation takes its own view, never to be anticipated, and with great difficulty, in the absence of actual documents, to be recovered, as to the interesting books and persons of the past. Each deserves that this view should be put and kept on record: none can claim that the record shall be closed.

And, again, though Macaulay seldom wrote a more interesting essay than that on Madame D'Arblay, and though it would be exceedingly rash for any one to enter into competition with him in some points, there are others, in which he is exposed not merely to his well-known besetting sins, but to some special and peculiar objections. It was absurd and almost ignoble of him to call Croker a "bad writer." It was absurd, for Croker was not a bad writer, though he was an ill-conditioned person who had wreaked a very discreditable revenge on an old lady of a great past, an unblemished character, and a very amiable disposition, for her exceedingly pardonable refusal to put her knowledge of Johnson at his disposal. It was ignoble because, as instructed people then knew, and as everybody knows now, Croker's fault was the fault not of being a bad writer, but of being a good speaker, and having tripped up T. B. Macaulay in the Reform Bill debates more than once. Again, Macaulay's anxiety to vindicate the leaders of the Whig party for their persecution of Hastings is unduly prominent, all the more so because Hastings certainly was not supported in any particularly decided way by the leaders of the Tory party. And for a third complaint Macaulay, though he did not originate the exaggeration, exaggerates Miss Burney's sufferings as a *dame d'Atours*: while he is rather perfunctory and incomplete in his survey of her literary work. To some extent indeed he could not help this, for the old issue of the *Diary* was not carried to an end when he wrote, and the very delightful *Early Diary* was not published till some thirty years after his death. As usual, when the critic is a great one, these supplements of information have not in the least superannuated his work. As usual also they have justified an attempt, with however inferior powers, to supplement that work itself.

Besides, Macaulay, writing with good will, and "fighting a prize" against a rather ungenerous assailant, has not wholly grappled with the literary peculiarities of the problem, though he has admitted with fair confession, but also with a little avoidance, the astounding declension of Madame D'Arblay's literary talent. Her whole work has never yet, I think, been surveyed[1]. The readers and the critics of the later novels and the

---

[1] This was certainly true in 1895. Whether it has ceased to be true now I cannot say: but I apologise to any one who might be offended (1923).

Memoirs of Dr Burney were not acquainted with the charms of the *Diary*. The devotees of the *Diary* have very naturally said little or nothing—in some cases I believe they have known little or nothing—of anything but *Evelina* and *Cecilia*. In fact, while the *Memoirs* are not a very common book, *Camilla* and *The Wanderer* are now (in any decent condition) very uncommon ones. They were originally printed in large numbers, but they were never reprinted. The copies were worn steadily to death in circulating libraries; and the result is, that with the help of the recent mania among book-collectors for first editions of novels, good copies of both, especially of *The Wanderer*, fetch ridiculous prices. Indeed you may pay a fair number of shillings for copies, which a finical person will find it necessary to read in gloves, of books which possess in the case of *Camilla* little more than a remnant, and in the case of *The Wanderer* not so much as a remnant, of genius or even of talent.

It so happens that, as a result of the order of publication, though not of the dates of writing, Miss Burney's work falls into three natural and excellent sections for criticism. There are first the novels; then the *Memoirs of Dr Burney*; and lastly, the *Diary* and *Letters* early and late, though here the early comes after the late by the accident of posthumous publication. The novels pursue a steady sinking down from excellent to atrocious (for I cannot agree with some that *Cecilia* exceeds *Evelina* in anything but bulk); the *Memoirs* drop to a lower depth still; and then the *Diaries* rise to perhaps a higher height than that at which the novels began. It is unfortunate, doubtless, that the best work should be in fact all contemporaneous and all early. But it is fair to say that even in the latest written passages of the *Diary* and *Letters*, happy touches meet us which mày be looked for absolutely in vain in the much earlier *Wanderer* and *Memoirs of Dr Burney*.

Madame D'Arblay is so inimitable a historian of her own life, it has been so well dealt with by Macaulay, and it is in its general outline so commonly known that there is no great need to dwell at any very great length on it here, though certain points may require notice. She was born at Lynn on the 13th of June, 1752—a fact for the discovery of which Croker took unnecessary trouble, and for the revelation of which he received, as was meet, unnecessary abuse. There is not the slightest evidence that Fanny ever endeavoured to conceal her age: though the admitted childishness of her appearance made people think her younger than she was. And so far from her having ever attempted to represent *Evelina* as the work of a "girl of seventeen," we have her own distinct statement, which none but a fool could misunderstand, and none but a churl affect to misunderstand, that her heroine is the "girl of seventeen" and that she, the novelist, is "past" that interesting age. Her father was the Historian of Music, latterly Organist to Chelsea Hospital, and the friend of the best men of his time. One of her brothers was an officer of Cook's, and later as "Admiral" Burney the friend of Southey, Coleridge, and especially Lamb; another was a scholar justly renowned for Greek in the day of Porson. Her sisters were all clever, and one of them was herself a novelist. There are references in the *Diary* proper, and full ones in the early *Diary*, to Fanny's backwardness, shyness, and so forth as a girl and young woman. But she was always scribbling; she was in a singularly stimulating society, and she published *Evelina* in a clandestine sort of way (1778), not indeed at "seventeen," but at not quite twenty-six. Then she became a lioness, and remained so;

Cecilia (1782) bringing her more fame, and (which *Evelina* had not done), some money[1]. Later still came the famous incident of her becoming assistant Keeper of the Robes to Queen Charlotte (1786) in which employment she abode five years, pined, and grew positively ill.

A great deal of nonsense has been, in my humble judgment, written about this episode. Macaulay, no lover of kings, especially Tory ones, very handsomely acquits George the Third; but he is remorselessly severe on Queen Charlotte. Others have involved the royal family generally in condemnation; and almost everybody, from Macaulay himself downwards, has lamented the loss of immortal works during the period, and put down the subsequent drying up of Miss Burney's genius to its evil effect. Let us (in the greatest words, never to be hackneyed however often quoted, of her greatest friend) "clear our minds of cant." The offer of the appointment was, no doubt, a mistake of good nature, and its acceptance was one of bad judgment. Indeed, it seems to me that Dr Burney, to please whom Fanny accepted it against her wish, has never had his due measure of blame. Despite his amiability he seems always to have been rather a silly man, as indeed is not obscurely hinted in the oxymel of Mrs Thrale's verses on him, and as is established by the fact of his not only writing a poem on astronomy and pestering Herschel about it, but habitually keeping a doggrel diary after a fashion common in his day, and pardonable enough to schoolboys and undergraduates, but not so pardonable in elderly professional men. On this occasion, too, he was, I fear, not merely silly, but selfish.

---

[1] Macaulay had heard this money put at £2000, which is large; a letter printed later by Mrs Ellis from Charlotte Burney reduces it to £250, which seems unbelievably small.

It was the dream of his life—a dream already once or twice disappointed—to be "Master of the King's Band"; and he evidently thought that if his daughter were close about the royal person, he would secure this coveted post. It is satisfactory that he did not.

As to the Queen—for the King, as we have seen, is acquitted by a hostile judge—there are not so many excuses required for her as seems to be generally thought, and there are many more available than are required. It is equally history and human nature that royal personages, whether their royalty be political or metaphorical, should be apt to think that the honour of serving them is far more than sufficient recompense for the pains of it. But this need not be counted. Queen Charlotte had been accustomed to the slavish submission paid to German Transparencies and Serenities much humbler in rank than an English Queen. She knew perfectly well that hundreds of ladies in Germany and France, and dozens in England, would have gone on their knees for the place. She had the want of understanding of physical weakness, which is far too common in physically strong people, be they queens or not. Part of Miss Burney's sufferings was due to their Majesties' natural attachment to Mrs Schwellenberg, who, old cat as she was[1], was intensely faithful; and part to her own failure to assert herself and the equality which it would seem she titularly held. The restrictions of visitors and so forth, which are so bitterly complained of in the *Diary*, were almost unavoidable in a household which tried above all things to avoid the licence of the two previous reigns and of the Prince of Wales's establishment. The parsimony was not shown to Miss Burney only.

[1] Much may be forgiven to "Peter Pindar," for the way in which, chiefly by anticipation and certainly in ignorance, he avenged Fanny of "Cerbera" in some of the bitterest and most amusing of his satires.

But the important question for posterity is whether this residence at Court really did as it is pretended, "dry her vein" of novel writing, and this will be best treated later; it is enough to say for the present that facts and probabilities are equally against it.

When she was released (1791)[1], the interesting part of her life to others was practically over, though the most interesting part of it to herself was yet to begin. In the society of her friends, the Lockes of Norbury Park, she met an elderly and respectable *émigré*, the Chevalier D'Arblay, who had no money, and whose attractions generally were not very clear except to the eyes of love. They married (1793)—one suspects M. D'Arblay to have been a rather poor though probably no unamiable kind of creature—on nothing but the little pension which the Queen had given Frances when she left Court; and the Chevalier took to gardening and "invested the apartments with imperceptible cupboards," as his wife says in the unbelievable English of her later times. A baby—Alexander, who afterwards went to Cambridge, was heard of by Macaulay, his six years junior, as a rather remarkable mathematician, took orders in the Church of England, and died three years before his mother in 1837—was born in 1794. Then Madame D'Arblay wrote *Camilla*, which was published in the first place by subscription with great success, and brought her in some three thousand pounds, but kept no hold on the public. When Napoleon's power was established, M. D'Arblay returned to France and

---

[1] The recently published *Memoirs* of Mrs Pappendick, who some time after Fanny's day occupied the inferior position of " Wardrobe Woman," assert that it was a case of dismissal rather than of resignation, and that the Queen was displeased at Miss Burney's being always writing when her bell rang. Mrs Ellis has had no difficulty in pointing out that this is irreconcilable, not only with Fanny's own account, but with certain facts. It is, however, likely enough to have been a back-stairs tradition founded upon, or fostered by, some ill-tempered remark of the Schwellenberg's.

obtained a civil post; but towards the end of the Tyranny his wife and child took the opportunity to escape to England. He had better luck under the Restoration than under the Empire, but did not stay long in France, and returning to England, died at Bath in 1818. Meanwhile his wife had brought out the terrible failure of *The Wanderer* (which, however, was widely sold before people found out how bad it was), and in the same year (1814) lost her father. Not much is recorded of her later years by others, except a visit from Sir Walter Scott. She died aged eighty-eight on the 6th of January, 1840, having brought out the unlucky *Memoirs* of her father in 1832, her eightieth year.

Evelina delectable; *Cecilia* admirable; *Camilla* estimable; *The Wanderer* impossible; *The Memoirs of Dr Burney* inconceivable; the *Diary* and *Letters*, whether original or "early," unequal, but at their best seldom equalled;—this might serve in the snip-snap and flashy way for a short criticism of Madame D'Arblay's work. But that work is not, either in its merits or its defects, to be polished off so unceremoniously.

The special merits of *Evelina* and their source may be found indicated with remarkable felicity though with no intended application to Miss Burney in a very unlikely place, the opening of *Ernest Maltravers*, or rather in the preface of 1840, which the author prefixed thereto. Speaking of *Pelham*, Lord Lytton (or, as it is more natural to call him in connection with these early works, Bulwer) says that "it has the faults and perhaps the merits natural to a very early age, when the novelty of life itself quickens the apprehension, when we see distinctly and represent vividly what lies on the surface of the world, and when, half sympathising with the follies we satirise, there is a gusto in our paintings which atones for their exaggeration. As we grow older we observe less, we reflect more: and like Frankenstein we dissect in order to create." We shall find, I think, that this passage—one of many that show in the author a critical faculty with which he is too seldom credited, and which he certainly did not bestow on his own work so often as he might—supplies a tolerably complete key to Madame D'Arblay's weakness as well as to her strength: and indeed (certain things being added) explains the amazing inequality of her work. But for the present we are only concerned with the positive side of it, and the application is certainly very complete. For all the ungraciousness of the Crokerian chronology, *Evelina* was written virtually at a very early age: for Fanny Burney was admittedly a very backward child, with a haphazard and irregular education which made her less accomplished in the ordinary sense at six and twenty than more regularly trained misses at sixteen. She began, moreover, to scribble very early in actual years; and though most of these early attempts perished in the flames, we know that *Evelina* was connected with one of them, and it would be contrary to all literary experience if part of it was not written as early as they were. At any rate, nothing can depict more exactly and appropriately than these words of Bulwer's the special merits of the book—the quick observation, the distinct sight, the vivid presentation of surface things, and finally the "gusto"—obsolete but excellent word, which perhaps has dropped out of use because the thing to which it applies has dropped out of experience. "Gusto" was the reigning attribute—*engouement* they called it in France—characteristic of the eighteenth century: it steadily declined in the nineteenth.

What admirable subjects of experience Fanny had,

the diaries sixty and a hundred years later have amply told the world: and Macaulay has summed them up in one of his famous and favourite show passages. It is still not easily intelligible why Dr Burney, with all his amiability and talent, all the fancy of the time from the king downwards for music, and all the advantage that his association with the charmed circle of Johnson and Burke and Reynolds gave him, should with his extremely modest position (he was neither more nor less than a music master), his scanty fortune, and his poky house in St Martin's Street, have become such a pet of society. But he certainly was a pet of it, and his daughter had the *entrée* to the very best as well as the bluest of London sets, even before she made herself a new key to them by her work. In that work, too, we may note that half sympathy of which Bulwer also speaks. Miss Burney is a satirist to some extent or she could not be so amusing as she is: but it is very small and very good-natured satire. If we compare her with her famous sisters or rather nieces in the next generation we shall find nothing in her of the inexorable justice which has been called cruelty in Miss Austen, of the severity, which sometimes comes near to savagery, of Miss Ferrier. She is even more lenient to her puppets than Miss Edgeworth herself, though she may seem to this generation too tolerant of some things in that rougher society both as she represents them in fiction, and as she records them in her actual experience[1].

There is avowedly very little art in the book, and its characters, like its composition, remind us of the so-called humour-comedy of the time between Jonson and Wycherley, the principles of which had frequently been adopted by novel writers, even such great ones as

---

[1] Cf. particularly the atrocious conduct of the Packingtons at West-wood to poor "Lilies and Roses"—Miss W.—in the *Early Diary*.

Smollett. Sporadic eccentricities, accumulated more or less anyhow, form a catalogue which does as a matter of fact carry the reader from beginning to end of the story, but which exhibits hardly the slightest trace of regular plan. The "anagnorisis" of Evelina at the end is one of the very weakest of such things (which are rather apt to be weak), and the only excuse for Mr Villars and Mrs Selwyn in not having long before softened that "reed painted like iron," Sir John Belmont, is to be found in the fact that Mr Villars throughout his letters shows himself chiefly a fool, and that Mrs Selwyn is represented as chiefly a shrew. Evelina herself pants with propriety, and blushes becomingly: and Lord Orville is not more of a stick than most of his kind. But the outrageous practical jokes of Captain Mirvan on the hapless old harridan Duval and her more hapless because more respectable French friend are overdone, and have no sort of connection with the story, while Sir Clement Willoughby's wildness is shockingly tame. Yet all these faults are far more than atoned for by the youthful zest and freshness of the general picture, by the liveliness with which the incidents, desultory as they are, pick up and succeed each other, and above all, by the incomparable sketches of the Branghtons and Mr Smith. In Poland Street, where the Burneys had lived before moving to Queen's Square, and then to Sir Isaac Newton's house just south of Leicester Square, they seem to have associated with a rather lower class of neighbours than later, and Frances used her models royally. It cannot be said that she is not at home with the upper classes: she not only knew but could draw gentlemen and ladies. Her keen as well as kind Daddy Crisp was perfectly right in ejaculating in reference to some epistolary "conversation-piece" of hers: "If specimens of this kind had been preserved of the different *Tons* that have succeeded each other for twenty centuries last past, how interesting they would have been." But Fanny was more than a mere *Ton*-painter, her best characters are more than gentlemen and ladies: they are immortals, as perhaps no others of hers are, with the doubtful exception of Sir Sedley Clarendel, the chief spot of brightness in the respectable blank of *Camilla*.

With all my sense of its defects, I never read *Evelina* (and I have read it two or three times at least during the last decade or so, as well as often earlier) without delight. Of *Cecilia* I can only borrow the famous libel on marriage, and say that to me at least "it is good, but it is not delightful." One feels immediately the presence of a much more elaborate effort, of a much maturer art, than can be found in *Evelina*. Burneians have always differed as to the tradition that Johnson gave direct assistance. It is a matter purely of tradition and of internal evidence, and Johnson himself appears to have said (which does not settle the matter) that he had never seen it till it was printed. But it is fair to remember that Macaulay, who was not only a good critic but had access to stores of oral information long since closed, was in favour of it; and I own that I agree with Macaulay. However, even if we leave this open, it is impossible not to note the difference certain to exist, and existing, between a book written absolutely without skilled censors and published anyhow, and one deliberately composed under the eyes of two skilled scholars such as Dr Burney and Daddy Crisp: with a floating atmosphere, leaving Johnson out, of literary friends from Burkes and Windhams down to Murphys and Malones. It is not, I think, known who suggested the extension of scale to the enormous limits, or nearly so, which Richardson had induced readers to tolerate if not to expect. Perhaps it was the booksellers—which seems all the more likely as Miss Burney always clung to the five volumes afterwards. For myself I own that, after the second volume or thereabouts, I find *Cecilia* rather difficult to read. The introduction of the girl to town has much of the liveliness of *Evelina*: it was a theme evidently congenial: and though many of the details are exaggerated, especially the cockneyisms of Mr Briggs (the Branghtons, alas! are always far away), though the machinations and melodrama of the Harrels might be toned down with great advantage both to probability and pleasure, the whole is well grouped and well machined. Cecilia, moreover, has the advantage of her elder sister in character and sense. But after the point named the interest seems to me to die away and to be revived chiefly by Lady Honoria who, though she owes a good deal to Anna Howe and Charlotte Grandison, has the advantage over them of being a lady in fact as well as in name. All the Delviles are naught; Mr Monckton and Mr Albany, bad and good lay figures; while Miss Larolles, popular as she was with her own generation, does not possess very vital signs now. In other words, Miss Burney wrote *Evelina* because she had a mind to do so: she wrote *Cecilia* because she made up her mind to do so.

The signs of the collar are to me so evident in this book that I am wholly unable to accept the view of those who think that, had she been left unmolested by kings and queens, we should have had more *Evelinas* or even more *Cecilias* from her. In the first place there are in the *Diary* certain distinct avowals, which I see no reason for assigning to mere bashfulness or mock humility, that she felt herself written out. There is at least one almost explicit hint from the experienced and affectionate Crisp that he thought she might be. And most important of all, there are the books themselves— those which come before and those which follow. Let us pay a little attention to these latter before coming to the general question.

I can see no reason, apart from a freezing of the genial current, why *Camilla* should not have been at least as good a book as *Cecilia*. To listen to some of those who pity Miss Burney, one would imagine that five years of rather harassing and uncongenial employ- ment in the very noon of strength will ruin health and sterilise intellect for the rest of life. As a matter of fact, Miss Burney had had another five years of entire rest, the first two spent in her usual society and in pleasant travel, the last in retired but extremely happy married life with hospitable and accomplished neighbours. Her former range of experience had been enriched by her Court stage, which, confined as it was in some ways, could not fail to give her new types. It is said that she was hampered by the desire of writing nothing that could offend the Queen. Now this is surely rather childish. It would seem as if some admirers of Fanny Burney had got Charlotte of Mecklenburg on the brain. And they do not seem to consider that they are paying a very bad compliment to their own idol when they suggest that she was not only a hopelessly submissive courtier, but was destitute of versatility in her own art —that she could not write a good novel under certain not very difficult conditions of pleasing, which, I must add, I do not myself think were in the least incumbent on her. That *Camilla* is not a great novel I am afraid cannot be denied. It is one of its glories that Miss Austen was among the original subscribers, and the extreme Burneians have tried to extract a testimonial from this great pupil. This will not do. *Camilla* is indeed joined with *Cecilia* and *Belinda* in *Northanger Abbey* to receive one of those generous exaltings of contemporary work in its own craft in which young genius, as opposed to young cubbishness, often indulges. But it is deplorably noticeable that though the more elaborate depreciation of the book which follows is put in the mouth of John Thorpe, whose opinions the author certainly did not mean to endorse, no distinct vindication of it is attempted, and the illiberal sneer at "the woman who married an emigrant" is the only criticism which is distinctly held up to ridicule. The fact is that, as I must repeat, *Camilla* is *not* a great novel. The character of the absent and pedantic Dr Orkborne pleased good wits at the time —he is mentioned in *The Antiquary*, and it is almost the only allusion of Scott's that, to my shame, I must acknowledge not to have understood till a very recent period. Camilla herself is really a very nice girl, though one wishes for a more human revolt in her now and then. Sir Sedley Clarendel, the most complete of fops, has been praised before, and may be praised again: Mrs Arlbery is almost certainly Mrs Thrale, adapted with judgment and good taste, and there are other separate sketches which remind us that we are reading a book by the author of *Evelina*. But Sir Hugh Tyrold, who alters his will at every moment, not out of caprice, but out of sheer silliness, who maintains, teases, and fears the pedant Dr Orkborne, and who generally behaves like a senile baby, justifies John Thorpe's criticism to such an extent, that I have sometimes been really afraid that the *griffe de la lionne* appears in Miss Austen's own reference to the matter. The wicked governess, Miss Margland, is the most uninteresting of unamiable duennas; no undergraduate, who was not an utter fool as well as an infernal rascal, ever con-

sented as Lionel Tyrold does to blackmail his invalid
uncle by anonymous letters; Mr Tyrold, Camilla's
father, a learned, intelligent, and virtuous divine,
ought to be whipped for the way in which he treats
his family, and allows them to be treated. The hero,
Edgar Mandlebert, who vacillates between Camilla and
her beautiful fool and vixen of a cousin Indiana (the
name is interesting when we think of George Sand),
and who is held up as a pattern at once of chivalry
and brains, might have a set of halberts rigged up next
to Mr Tyrold's with great advantage.

The fact is that the whole thing, except a few separate
traits, is in the vague. The author has indeed still got
a plot, as she had in *Cecilia*, which is more than she had
in *Evelina*. She has got some good studies for the
filling in: but she does not in the least know what to do
with them, and she has no grasp of life as a whole.
She is constantly "off the rails"; indeed it is exceedingly rare that she is on them.

In *The Wanderer* it is not too much to say that she
never gets on them at all. The opening scene of this
unluckiest of books, a book which was expected, hailed,
welcomed by everybody, from veterans to novices, and
which sank as soon as it appeared, has a faint touch of
the personal experience which was always necessary
to Fanny, and which she sometimes utilised so well,
in the flight of the heroine by boat from France.
Madame D'Arblay had just had something very like
that experience. But the rest is all stark nought. The
fatal long-lost or misknown daughter business invited
her once more, as in *Evelina*; and she could no more,
as in *Evelina*, redeem it with humours and with the
fresh insight of an unjaded eye. The progress of "the
Wanderer," *alias* "the penetrated Juliet" from her
sufferings in the boat, and from the vulgar persecutions

of Mrs Ireton till the time when, united with Mr Harleigh, she is "embraced and owned by her honoured benefactress, the Marchioness," is a kind of nightmare of dulness. The hardened reviewer, "famoused for fight" with thousands of novels, but just saves his credit as he struggles through this fearful book, where nobody is alive, and where the adventures of the gibbering ghosts who figure in it are gibbered in a language such as hardly our own day—a nurse of monsters in style—has seen. The victims of Charlottophobia say that Miss Burney's sojourn at Court among half-Germans, and her subsequent sojourn in France, account for the frightful lingo which defaces *The Wanderer* and *The Memoirs of Dr Burney*. They forget again that only a weak plant could be stifled by such atmospheres. Macaulay set it down to Johnsonese unintelligently exaggerated, and there is something in this. But whatever the cause, the effect is not disputable, and it may be said, without remorse and without caricature, that nothing but the matter of *The Wanderer* could deserve such a style, and that the style of *The Wanderer* is, on the whole, almost too bad for the matter.

With the *Memoirs* things are, if possible, worse still in point of form, and the matter, though very much better, is almost hopelessly disfigured. Unfortunately the documents on which it is founded were mainly destroyed. Mrs Ellis, Madame D'Arblay's most faithful and most generous defender, laments the fatal misuse of these materials. They were, we know, abundant, superabundant; and Dr Burney had had opportunities such as few men have had. The actual book is a tedious rhapsody, exceedingly hard to read with any intelligent comprehension of dates and surroundings, barren in matter while full of the very worst art. Macaulay, doing his *devoir* gallantly, tried to maintain that, though there was deplorably bad writing, there was no "dotage." I cannot be sure of this. It is not merely that the style, as Macaulay himself fully admits, and shows by extract, is horrible and heartrending, not merely that not a few passages and themes which we have delightfully treated in the *Diary* are here re-presented "not in dog's likeness," as Mr Carlyle used to say. It would be cruel to multiply the specimens which Macaulay has already given of the hopeless *galimatias* which distinguishes the book. But one instance of something worse may be given. Madame D'Arblay quotes an anecdote of Bonaparte, who complained that her husband had written him "a devil of a letter," and added pleasantly, "However, I ought only to regard in it the husband of Cecilia." One only wishes that all the anecdotes of the Corsican presented him in so pleasant a light as this. But will it be believed that Madame D'Arblay herself, the "little charactermonger" of Johnson, the Fannikin of Crisp, the not too azure blue who had held her own at Streatham and in London, adds, "Of the author of *Cecilia* of course he meant"? She was eighty at the time, no doubt, she had lost father, husband, friends; but what a gap is here between the creator of the Branghtons and the commentator of a kindly and fairly *spirituel* confusion which is as common as any figure of speech! To quote much from that unhappy book would be unworthy of "decent gentility and education" (as Mark Pattison has it), for in more than language it *is* the "dotage," the clear dotage of a woman of delightful talent, and in some ways of true genius. It cannot be defended; to criticise it seriously were idle; and to laugh at it inhuman and base.

And so we come to the *Diary*, no part of which was issued during its author's lifetime, though it formed the

basis of much of the *Memoirs of Dr Burney*, and therefore exhibits, in a way even more curious than melancholy, the fashion in which it is possible for a painter
to paint his own good work into bad. This *Diary*, even
yet, is understood not to be published completely, and
probably never will be; but enough is extant to make
it one of the bulkiest things of the kind. Nor is this
surprising when it is remembered that the letter and
diary-writing habits of eighteenth century young ladies
are by no means caricatured in the works of Richardson, which, in their turn, helped to recommend and
prolong the practice. Until her marriage, and to some
extent after it, Fanny appears to have been incessantly
scribbling—for her father often, for herself almost as
often; while almost the whole of her Court life is
recorded in a sort of letter-journal to "Susan and
Fredy," *i.e.* her sister Susanna, the wife of the Colonel
Phillips who was afterwards Charles Lamb's friend,
and Frederica Locke of Norbury. In later years she
cut these diaries about very considerably;—she had
always, as in the famous instance of the early holocaust
of her manuscripts, at the direct or indirect instance
of her stepmother, that comparative readiness to part
with the fruits of her labours which usually, though not
invariably, accompanies extremely easy and rapid production. But she left much, and much of that much
would seem to be still extant.

Delightful as the *Diary* is, its extreme voluminousness, and the singular inequality which here as elsewhere shows itself in the author's work, have brought
upon it some rather harsh judgments, such as that
it is "tiresome." I do not myself find it tiresome
anywhere—even in the interminable conversations
with "Mr Turbulent" and "Mr Fairly," even in the
bewildering multitude of small details in the *Early*

Diary which Mrs Ellis, with a patience and skill which no editor could surpass, has devoted herself to explaining, adjusting and unravelling; hardly even, though I confess that the "hardly" sometimes needs to be accentuated, in the sketches of the later years when little happened, when Madame D'Arblay either was excluded from inspiriting society or left no account of that which she did see, and when the curse of jargon, though never so evident in the *Diary* as in the published books, had laid its grasp upon her. It will not, indeed, do to expect too much or the wrong sort of things; we must not look for perpetual epigram or for frequent good stories; we must carry about with us continually the remembrance that we are in the century of Richardson and of Horace Walpole, and that Miss Burney, with all her gifts, had not those of either, while she had the voluminousness of both. We must remember yet again Diderot's quaint excuse for his beloved English novelist that, after all, the actual conversations in *Grandison*, etc., would, if you took part in them, take longer than the record of them does in reading.

And in large parts of the book there is no need for any remembrance, any allowance at all. The brilliancy and charm of the Streatham parts of the *Diary*, of the best of the Court scenes, of the Hastings trial, have been acknowledged by all good judges ever since they first appeared. Macaulay in one of his most masterly exercises of joint literary divination and interpretation, constructed, out of the fragmentary and pompous notices in the *Memoirs*, a glowing picture of the *salon*, such a little one and so well attended, in St Martin's Street; but the actual documents of the *Early Diary* bring out the details of this with unexpected and seldom failing piquancy. The want of these indications made him perhaps a little wrong on "Daddy" Crisp and the Chesington circle; but the fuller descriptions of that odd person, and his odd household, are all the more welcome. Some hold that books of this sort ought never to be read straight through; I have read both the diaries in that fashion more than once, and with great pleasure. But for dipping they certainly have few superiors; nor have they very many equals even in that century of autobiography.

To what, then, are we to attribute the admitted inequalities of the *Diary* and the steady declension of power in the Novels? All sorts of causes, some already noted, have been assigned, besides that absurd one of Miss Burney's powers having been killed by five years' waiting at odd times to hand the queen's clothes to the wardrobe women, and fighting with Schwellenbergs at Windsor, very considerably tempered by flirtations with equerries, etc. The influence and the withdrawal of the influence of Johnson; the bad English spoken by that devoted household of George the Third; the worse or none at all heard for so many years in France; ill-health, narrow means, and divers other things have been alleged. There is perhaps no region in which the excellent French phrase about those who "seek noon at fourteen o'clock" is so constantly illustrated as in that of criticism. For, let us consider what Fanny Burney's special talents are; what they were considered to be by those who know her best; and what she thought of them herself. Perhaps the last may be ruled out as treacherous, but I do not think so. Vanity is common enough, and there are plenty of us who think that with choice and chance we could do great things. But persistent self-delusion about literary powers is, I believe, except in the case of poets, exceedingly rare, and Fanny was not a poet. Moreover, self-delusion, which takes the form of self-depreciation, is so rare both in poets and others, as to be very nearly unknown. And we know that Fanny at no time thought highly of her own talents, that she had pretty distinctly proposed to herself not to attempt anything after *Cecilia*, and that everything she did do afterwards, with a view to publication, was planned more or less under the pressure of necessity on the one hand and large offers on the other. The necessity of writing—the imperative impulse of which we sometimes hear—may be very rare. But the impulse not to write when it does not come from constitutional laziness (and Miss Burney was the most industrious of women) is very seldom a trick, very generally a kindly warning of nature.

Of what her friends thought we have fortunately one document which is worth a thousand. The researches of Mrs Ellis have shown that Macaulay's estimate of the chagrin of Daddy Crisp at the comparative failure of a play which might, with quite equal truth, have been said to have comparatively succeeded, was mistaken, though quite reasonably mistaken. It is impossible to argue (and Macaulay had far too much sense even to hint the argument) that Crisp, years after the incident, in a different line altogether, and in reference to a person for whom he had admittedly the fondest affection, was in the very least degree likely to be jealous of Fanny. Yet not in reference to *Evelina*, of which the sudden and so to speak accidental success might have encouraged a Job's comforter to try to "rub the gilt off," but in reference to *Cecilia*, which had been carefully engineered, had taken and kept the top of the tide, and really deserved very high praise, we find from this experienced, and if anything partial monitor, a strangely serious and, in the light of subsequent events, more strangely prophetic warning. It is not to be summarised in any single passage, but anybody who considers the published letters to and from Crisp during the progress of the book will see, I think, that he was profoundly sceptical of Fanny keeping up her vein and not too well satisfied even with this famous and admired production of it. He tells her, indeed, that there had been nothing so good since Fielding and Smollett, and he was right. Smollett had died seven years before the publication of *Evelina*, and for a good thirty years there was nothing published, there was nothing even written (except certain early works of the young lady who subscribed to *Camilla* and defended it at once), which could even touch *Evelina* and *Cecilia* in merit. But the author of certain remarks about Voltaire and Shakespeare which may be found in the *Diary* was not likely to go wrong on the negative side any more than on the positive; and he must have noted the seeds of decay in his "Fannikin," as keenly as he noted the flowers of flourishing.

The fact, as it seems to me, is, that Fanny Burney is in English literature our capital example of a kind of writer commoner in the old conditions of English life abroad than at home, and commoner in all countries among women than among men. In this class a talent of observation and presentation, real and charming to no small degree, is forced at a certain time, and by favourable circumstances, into not premature but perfect bloom. Its best members always remain happy and favourable subjects in point of receptivity; but they have, as a rule, no absolute root or spring of creative genius; and they do not assist the native want by any thorough study of good models. Many critics of Fanny Burney have expressed an amiable but not wholly intelligent surprise, at the very small amount

that she seems to have read—brought up among un-
guarded books as she was—and at the somewhat
limited intelligence which her critical remarks show.
The fact is that she was the very reverse of bookish,
and the innocent raptures over certain love letters (the
work of that clever bookmaker, William Combe) in
which she and her Mr Fairly indulged at Cheltenham,
the comparison which in an *Early Diary* she makes
between the *Vicar of Wakefield*, and some stuff of
which I should have to go to the book even to remember
the name, show what power of literary discrimination
she had. Nor was her really creative instinct strong
—*Evelina* is a chaos, though a delightful one, as far
as plot or construction goes; if *Cecilia* is better we know
that, putting Johnson out of question and admitting
his denial of having seen the book before it was in print
to the fullest, it was subjected to severe criticism and
radical alteration at Crisp's hand, and was talked about
between other members of the Burneian circle.

Then, it may be asked, what had she? She had much.
She had an eye for character—external character, no
doubt, chiefly, but still an eye for character—such as
nobody else born within many years of her had. And
she had, moreover, from almost her earliest youth till
almost past her fortieth year, the most extraordinarily
fertile field, the most extraordinarily stimulating atmosphere, of character study. The eighteenth century
is admittedly the special century of the word "Society";
and Fanny Burney was in the very hotbed of the
English eighteenth century. The habits of her family
were scribblative; its society was immense, various, incomparable. She might, if she had been more pert
and less modest, have inscribed on her *Diary* the
slightly altered line—

"We've had Johnson and Burke; all the wits have been here."

To her clear eyes, and her ready if not very critical pen, there presented itself from the early days in Poland Street, through those in Queen Square, and most of all in the *domus exilis Newtonia*, through Streatham and Mrs Montagu's peacock saloon, and all the rest to the stately if sometimes dismal halls of Windsor and St James's, and the dismal and not at all stately apartments of Kew, the phantasmagoria of all sorts of society. She registered it in her novels and in her diary alike, but best in the latter, with unflagging vigour, if with unequal success, while, as that passage from *Ernest Maltravers* which I have quoted puts it, "the novelty of life quickened the apprehension." At about middle age the stars grew less propitious. The actual society of London seems to have become decidedly less interesting and stimulating. The great wits of "the Club," who, partly by accident and partly by the fact of Burke's connection with politics, had made a junction between statesmanship and literature, died. The younger Pitt, though not himself a boor, was utterly indifferent to letters. The Whigs assumed the ferocious and limited partisanship of a small and hopeless opposition, a farther gap being made by the split between them and the Prince of Wales. Mrs Thrale, that "Welsh fairy," had made herself impossible by her second marriage; Fanny herself put herself out of Court by her first and only one. M. D'Arblay appears to have been an eminently respectable person, but, I should think, rather a dull one; and he carried his wife off to France. During the Empire she mixed with an interesting if a rather priggish and doctrinaire society, but we have no record of it from her hands and hardly any of her participation in it from others. She came back, an old woman, to domestic sorrows, to "new faces, other minds"; and it is scarcely wonderful that she came back with only the ashes of her old gifts.

I have always thought that if "eloquent, just, and mighty Death," the most merciful as the mightiest of all potentates, had not removed Charlotte Brontë, we should have had something of a parallel in her to Madame D'Arblay's later writings, though Miss Brontë's harder fortunes and more passionate temper would not have consoled us by anything like the *Diary*. There, too, was the excitement—of a sufficiently different sub-species, but parallel—of personal experience, with little aid from books, and with no great fund of independent artistic spirit. There, too, were the vivid, the original outpourings of this experience in novel-form. And there, too, had the experience been prolonged, must have been the break-down, the failure of the original impressions, with no new ones to make them good, the *Camillas* and the *Wanderers*—not perhaps the *Memoirs of Dr Burney*, because only an extraordinary conjunction of inauspicious stars could ever produce anything like that appalling production.

But this, it may be, is gratuitous; and it would be more gratuitous still to follow it out in the cases of other novelists of the same sex, as could, I believe (with the single exception of Miss Austen, the exception to all rules), be done. It is more germane to a reasonable matter to admit, and not to attempt to excuse the fact that Miss Burney—that at least Madame D'Arblay—was not one of those fortunate persons who, from the first to the last, with only human vicissitudes, persevere in being capable, who even persist in being great.

But if she was not one of these, she was one of the still not numerous band who, owing to no matter what cause, do delightful things. To her who gave us the Branghtons, Mr Smith, the first volume if not the two first volumes of *Cecilia*, Sir Sedley Clarendel even, let there be praise not in the lowest by any means. To her who gave us the quaint mixed presentation of Dr Burney's visitors, the picture of a Johnson always amiable and sometimes apologetic, the sketches of the sojourn of a young "lioness" in the most various menageries, always with credit to herself and with the result of something like immortality to the other beasts —let there be praise perhaps higher still. Historians may add that Miss Burney has given us almost our only English picture of an English Court, drawn completely from the inside, without any ill-nature such as that which. invalidates the truth, if it heightens the zest, of books like Hervey's, with distinct literary talent, and with total freedom from "purpose." As a diarist Miss Burney is with Pepys and Evelyn, as a letter-writer with Walpole and Chesterfield. And unlike all these, except Horace, she is a novelist as well, while I must confess that though I like the kind of *The Castle of Otranto* better than the kind of *Evelina*, I must put *Evelina* a good deal higher in its kind than *The Castle of Otranto*.

XV

TWENTY YEARS OF POLITICAL SATIRE

THOUGH it may seem to some a rather cowardly thing for a critic to say, I am myself much inclined to doubt whether any very satisfactory result comes of attempts to decide why this or that literary product came at that or this time. The "product-of-the-circumstances" theory was a very pretty and ingenious toy, which, like many toys in literature, in philosophy, and in other departments of toy-making, amused the town for a time, but has now had its day. Too surely does the critic who is not blinded by his affection for it discover that, if you pick your circumstances very carefully, you can indeed account for any product, but that you are exposed to two awkward inquiries—"How about the other circumstances which you have neglected?" and "Were not these circumstances on which you lay stress present at other times when the product was *not* produced?"

Of course we can see in general why certain times— the time when Greece became, from an insignificant collection of petty states the most formidable power in the Mediterranean, the time of the completest and most unchallenged Roman domination, the time when the "Dark" blossomed into the "Middle" Ages, the time of the Reformation and the discovery of America, the time of the French Revolution—should all have been fertile in literature. As a man is most inclined to perpetrate literature when he is excited, so is a world. But when you come down to minor matters I doubt very much whether any such explanation is possible. I could make twenty very pretty ones for the singular development of political and semi-political satire during the last twenty years of the eighteenth century in England; but I should be the first to admit that one was no better than another, and that any twenty-first was likely to be as good, or at least as sufficient, as the whole of them. The popularity and novelty of the swinging easy measures of Anstey's *Bath Guide*; the fact of the coincidence of the palmy days of the English public school and University system, as regards its peculiar style of scholarship, with the period when public school and University men had most direct, immediate, and easy entrance into politics; the keenness of political disputes, which till the Revolution itself broke out turned upon no vital question but were all the keener; the general curiosity and partial annoyance caused by the supremacy of Pitt at so early an age; the absence of any passionate or absorbing school of literature to divert literary talent from mere sport—these and a dozen other things may be detected by any tolerably acute observer, and justified by any tolerably diligent student. It is sufficient for me to indicate them in passing.

The fact, however, of the existence of a peculiar kind of political and semi-political verse at this time —which has been rather imitated than continued since, and which is quite different from the political satire of a hundred years earlier, at the head of which towers *Absalom and Achitophel*, from the still earlier form of Butler, and from the later work in which Churchill mixed Dryden with vitriol and dirty water—is indisputable; and it is equally indisputable that it produced some of the most amusing stuff to be found anywhere in English literature. Its crowning achievement, the inimitable though constantly imitated "Poetry of the *Anti-Jacobin*," has been frequently re-edited, the latest, or one of the latest, issues having appeared under the care of the late Mr Henry Morley. Mr Morley's indefatigable industry in selecting and editing much of the best work of English authors in cheap, easily accessible, and sometimes by no means uncomely forms, could never be too gratefully acknowledged by any person of taste. And this great merit, joined to that of having, as his pupils unanimously testified, inspired an unusual number of persons with his own love for our literature, may dispense any generous critic from examining too narrowly his critical powers and his methods of editing.

In the same volume Mr Morley included (chiefly it would appear for the reason that George Ellis was a contributor to both books) a very few specimens of the *Rolliad*, a much earlier and less finished production on the other side of politics, but, allowing for the absence of two such wits as Canning and Frere, not so much less amusing. As his concern was with the work of the trio exclusively, he also gave the *Microcosm* and other non-political matter. My aim being different, the subjects of this paper will be the *Rolliad*, with its dependent *Political Eclogues*, *Probationary Odes*, and *Political Miscellanies* at one end, and the *Poetry of the Anti-Jacobin* at the other, with, between them, the exceedingly diverting work of Peter Pindar.

The *Rolliad* (as its facetious authors themselves record, with greater literal accuracy than attaches to all their statements) "owed its existence to the memorable speech of the member of (*sic*) Devonshire on the first discussion of the Westminster scrutiny" which followed the famous Westminster election of 1784—the contest between Fox and Sir Cecil Wray. The *Political Eclogues*, and the *Probationary Odes for the Laureateship*, ostensibly occasioned by Whitehead's death, followed in 1785; while the *Political Miscellanies*

were originally appended to the *Rolliad* itself, or rather
to the criticisms of and specimens from that imaginary
epic. They were all the work of a knot of literary Whigs
—for Ellis, who was afterwards a staunch Tory, then
had Whiggish leanings—mostly members of Brooks's,
mostly personal friends of Fox, and all animated by
the keenest dislike of the boy Minister, Pitt. Various
"keys" have, as in other cases of the same kind, indicated, no doubt more or less correctly, their names,
though not all the pieces are attributable with certainty.
Dr Lawrence, the friend of Burke, seems to have been
the guiding spirit, and he was assisted by Lord John
and Lord George Townshend; by two clever Irishmen,
Tickell and Fitzpatrick; sometimes by Richard Burke;
by a still cleverer compatriot of theirs, Tierney; once
or twice by Sheridan; by General Burgoyne, who, as
is well known, was not quite so inefficient with the pen
as with the sword; and, besides others known or unknown, by Ellis, then a little over thirty, author only
of some contributions to the once famous *Bath-Easton
Vase*, and of a few other light verses in the eighteenth
century manner, but already a very wide, careful, and
accomplished student of literature. It has been thought
with some reason that the rondeaux which figure among
the *Rolliad* verses, for the first and last time for many
years in English literature, are due to him[1]. The variety
indeed of the form of the *Rolliad* is one of its principal
charms. The subjects are tolerably numerous—the
Westminster election, the wickedness of Hastings and
Impey, the follies and clownishness of the title-hero
Mr Rolle (a Devonshire squire of great wealth, popularity, and power, who was obnoxious to the Whigs

---

[1] A copy, however, of the 1799 edition, with apparently contemporary
pencil notes, which my friend Mr Austin Dobson lent me, attributes
them to Lawrence.

as a pillar of Pittism in the west), Sir Cecil Wray, Sir Joseph Mawbey, Dr Prettyman, and "those about" Pitt generally, with, for a constant resource and change whenever other subjects grew scarce or stale, Pitt himself, his policy, his character, and above all his supposed dislike of women. On this latter theme the wits were never tired of descanting, despite the discouraging fact that the British public obstinately refused to see the joke. Nor has political satire ever gone quite so far in this direction since. Mealymouthed persons have thought that the *Anti-Jacobin* writers gave themselves some licence, but they never came anywhere near the *Rolliad*. Indeed, short as was the interval between the two books, it may be doubted whether public sentiment would have endured it if they had.

It would, however, be quite a mistake to imagine that the appeal of the *Rolliad* lies in mere scurrility. On the contrary, it is uncommonly good fun, and, Tory as I am, I have not the least hesitation in admitting that now, and for some time to come, the Whig dogs, with Lawrence and his pack on one side, and Wolcot, he by himself, on the other, had very much the best of it. Pitt's notorious indifference, despite his scholarship, to English letters and English men of letters may have had something to do with this, but so it was. Nothing on the other side could touch the *Rolliad* and "Peter" till the French Revolution made half these Whig songsters themselves Tories, and considerably softened even the "savage Wolcot" himself. The *Rolliad* suffers, of course, from certain inevitable drawbacks of almost all political literature: the principal questions are not excessively interesting, the minor ones utterly dead and forgotten, there are constant allusions which hardly anybody, and some that probably no one, understands.

The work, as all work done by a great number of hands must be, is very unequal. But the sparkle of it, the restless energy, the constant change of form and front, the vitalities in short, are very attractive: especially, no doubt, because they are at least often combined with good literary form.

The thing was, of course, not original: it had more or less immediate ancestors in the miscellanies of Swift, Pope, Arbuthnot, and Gay, and its lineage might easily be traced even farther back. But I think that any one who reads the *Rolliad* will perceive in it that note of noteworthiness which consists in being much more like what has come after it than what came before it. Its epigrams are somewhat out of date—the epigram proper, more's the pity, has been very little cultivated of late[1]. Its Virgilian parodies appeal less than they appealed to a generation in which almost every educated man knew his Virgil by heart. Its skits of verse preserve the Popian style in a way which reminds us that that style was still omnipotent. And yet it has those vital marks which make the better class of literary work in all ages seem modern to the tolerably well-read reader. We should, alas!—for engraving has gone out with epigrams—find a difficulty in getting anything so well engraved nowadays as its frontispiece, with a genealogical tree starting out of the bowels of Duke Rollo and bearing roundels recording how divers Rolles were unfortunately "sus. per coll," or its title-page vignette, neatly exhibiting the arms of the family— three French rolls *or* between two rolls of parchment proper—and a demi-Master of the Rolls (Kenyon) for crest. But the text might (let us hope it would have been written equally well) have been, for most of its

---

[1] Quite recently my friend Mr F. P. Barnard has broken the fallow (1923).

turns and traits, written yesterday. "Mr Rous spoke for two hours to recommend expedition.... Sir Cecil's tastes, both for poetry and small beer, are well known; as is the present unfinished state of his newly-fronted house in Pall Mall."

These little flashes show the sprightliness of the authors, but soon they rise to greater things and grapple with the "Virtuous Boy" himself:

> Pert without fire, without experience sage,
> Young with more art than Shelburne gleaned from age,
> Too proud from pilfered greatness to descend,
> Too humble not to call Dundas his friend,
> In solemn dignity and sullen state,
> This new Octavius rises to debate.

The parody of Pope or, at least, of Akenside is good, but the true merit of the thing is that it gives us, as all political satire should give us, the real points in the object which were unpopular with his foes. The lines on Dundas are better still, and it is amusing to remember that both pieces are thought to be by Ellis:

> For true to public Virtue's patriot plan,
> He loves the Minister and not the Man;
> Alike the advocate of North and Wit,
> The friend of Shelburne, and the guide of Pitt.
> His ready tongue with sophistries at will,
> Can say, unsay, and be consistent still;
> This day can answer and the next retract,
> In speech extol and stigmatise in act;
> Turn and re-turn, whole hours at Hastings bawl,
> Defend, praise, thank, affront him, and recall;
> By opposition he his King shall court;
> And damn the People's cause by his support.

But it is not in this solemn kind of work that the book shows its charms. These lie in such things as the famous passage which, from having been frequently quoted, is probably known to many who do not know another line of it:

> Ah! think what danger on debauch attends:
> Let Pitt, once drunk, preach temperance to his friends;

> How as he wandered darkling o'er the plain,
> His reason drowned in Jenkinson's champagne,
> A rustic's hand, but righteous fate withstood,
> Had shed a Premier's for a robber's blood.

As these lines are generally quoted, a pleasant prose postscript to them is omitted in praise of "the wonderful skill of our poet who could thus bring together an orange girl [for the illustration has crowned a passage on temperance] and the present pure and immaculate Minister, a connection which it is more than probable few of our readers would have in any way suspected." And so poor Pitt gets equally laughed at for his proneness to one foible and his abstinence from another, a device never to be forgotten by those who lampoon statesmen. This is at once a neat and a quotable gird: of the others on the same subject most are not quotable, though there is an exception in the following very agreeable epigram (on the attempted coalition between the Duke of Portland and Mr Pitt, which failed because the parties could not agree as to what was "fair and equal"):

> On fair and equal terms to plan
>   A union is thy care;
> But trust me, Powis, in this case
> The *equal* should not please his Grace,
>   And Pitt dislikes the *fair*.

Nor is English the only language in which the hapless Rolle, his chief, and their friends are epigrammatised. Latin, French, Italian, even Greek (very fair Greek, though "without the accents"), figure, and in a parcel of "foreign epigrams" it is by no means uninteresting to read by chance on the same page a mention of the "University of Gottingen" and the name "Casimir." For the wits of the *Anti-Jacobin* undoubtedly knew their *Rolliad* well, and one of them, as we have said, had the best cause to know it.

The *Political Eclogues* which follow the *Rolliad* proper

are amusing enough though a little obvious, the best of them being the first, where Lawrence turns "Formosum pastor" into a gross but very funny assault on George Rose. But the *Probationary Odes* must rank higher, and if they were a little more compressed would rank higher still. They are but half political, and sometimes almost purely literary, till the *infandus dolor* (let me be permitted to speak in character) smarts again, and a whole sheaf of epigrams is fired at Mr Pitt's modesty, Sir Cecil Wray's statesmanship, and Dr Prettyman's apostolic virtues. Poor Tom Warton, a most excellent person and a very nice verse-writer in his day, is a constant butt, probably as the most likely actual candidate, and the Pittites come in for indiscriminate punishment with mere blue-stockings and busybodies. Here is imitated the stately style of the man who was not born to be Johnson's biographer, though he thought he was, dropping at the end into the artless verse:

> Here lies Sir John Hawkins,
> Without his shoes and stockings.

Here poor Hannah More, after some most improper insinuations, is made to say, "Heavens! what would this amiable baronet [Sir Joseph Mawbey] have been with the education of a curate!" Here Mrs George Anne Bellamy draws a delightful picture of herself "in a clean hackney coach, drawn by grey horses, with a remarkably civil coachman, fainting in my Cecil's arms." Here Warren Hastings's more laboured style is hardly caricatured in this description of the advocate who did his very best to lose him his cause, Major Scott:—"I can venture to recommend him as an impenetrable arguer; no man's propositions flowing in a more deleterious stream; no man's expressions so little hanging on the thread of opinion." And then come the odes themselves—Wray, Mulgrave, Mawbey, Macpherson, Wraxall, and a score more compete. A very bad and impossible imitation of Dundas's Scotch—the worst thing in the whole book, and showing how necessary it was that Burns and Sir Walter should show Englishmen what Scotch was really like—is redeemed a little later by a capital Hibernian pendant due to Fitzpatrick, and supposed to be Lord Mountmorres, a name of tragic associations yesterday, but then that of a favourite butt. This pindaric must have delighted Thackeray, and is very like his own Irish verse. Even better is the ode assigned to Thurlow, where the redoubtable Chancellor's favourite verb accompanies the piece all through with the most delectable crashes, the epode, if I may so call it, containing rather more d—ns than there are lines. And last of all we have the *Political Miscellanies*, which in a manner complete these odes, and in which most of the epigrams proper and minor pieces above referred to will be found. There is no doubt too much of the thing on the whole, but that is the fate of books that appear in parts and instalments.

Clever as the *Rolliad* is, interesting and stimulating as it proved to its own and the succeeding generations (it may give it an additional zest to some readers to know that in his famous essays on Hastings, Pitt, and others, Macaulay was evidently thinking of it far more often than any definite references show), the little finger of that prince of English lampooners who called himself Peter Pindar was thicker than the loins of any one of its company of wits. I have at different times of my life read Peter thrice right through (a very considerable task, for the standard edition of him, though it is said not to be complete, contains more than two thousand five hundred pages), and each time I have been more convinced that if he had only been a little more of a scholar, and a great deal more of a gentleman, he would have been a very great man indeed. As it is, his mere cleverness is something prodigious. But in the first place, he had very little, or a very intermittent, sense of style, and the ungirt flow of his Muse's gown is often far too slatternly. In the second place, he was a dirty Peter (dirty with a French rather than an English dirtiness, sniggering and Voltairian), a scurrilous Peter, a malevolent Peter, a Peter to whom at least in his flourishing days *non erant lachrymæ rerum*, a Peter who could beslaver George the Fribble at the moment that he was assuming airs of Republican independence towards George the Farmer, a Peter thoroughly coarse in grain and fibre, a Bœotian buzzard masquerading as a Theban eagle. To such bad language does he give irresistible temptation every now and then. And in another minute his shrewdness, his unexpected and delightful quips, the good-humour which in him was consistent with ill-nature, above all, as I have said, his prodigious cleverness, make one almost like, and very much more than almost admire him.

John Wolcot was born at Dodbrooke, a suburb of Kingsbridge in Devonshire, which is or was the head if not sole quarters of the manufacture of "white ale" —a rather terrible liquor which is supposed to represent the real Saxon brewage. Perhaps it was due to this that the future Peter was fond of ale all his life, and of cakes likewise. While he was still young, he went to live at Fowey, the quaintest if not the prettiest town in Cornwall, with an uncle who was a doctor, and was educated for his uncle's profession at Fowey itself, at Bodmin, in France, and in London. When he was nearly thirty, one of his Cornish neighbours, Sir William Trelawney, was made Governor of Jamaica, took

Wolcot with him, and made him "Physician-General" to the island. Then a thing happened which could hardly have happened at any other time than the eighteenth century. Trelawney thought he could give Wolcot better patronage in the Church, sent him to England to get ordained, and actually presented him to a living on his return. A more unclerical cleric than Wolcot perhaps never existed in our country. His morals were not only decidedly but avowedly and ostentatiously loose; and if he had any religion at all, it would seem to have been a sort of Gallic willingness to admit the existence of an easy-going *Etre Suprême*. He had, however, apparently no great opportunities of corrupting or scandalising the faithful in Jamaica; for one of the few things personally recorded of him is that no congregation usually appeared at his church, whereupon, after decently waiting ten minutes, he and the clerk would adjourn to the neighbouring sea-shore, and shoot ring-tailed pigeons. When he returned to England, as he did before long at Trelawney's death, he seems to have given up all views as to clerical profession or preferment, and resumed the practice of medicine in Cornwall. Here he discovered the painter Hoppy or Opie (a benefit which British art could have done without), and wrote poetical jests on his neighbours. His love of art, which was sincere and on the whole judicious, seems to have been the immediate cause of his beginning, in 1782, the series of odes to the Royal Academicians, which made a considerable stir, was continued annually for a time, and drew him once more to London. Here he remained for some quarter of a century, writing steadily for the booksellers despite the calamity of blindness which latterly fell on him. As a very old man he returned to Cornwall, and died there in 1819.

A great deal of Wolcot's work, all of which was published under the name of "Peter Pindar, Esq.," is not political at all. His biography has been very scantily written, but I should think it at least probable that the actual determination of his lampooning powers against Farmer George was due in great part to Farmer George's patronage of West. With West, Peter, who as has been said was really a good, though a harsh, partisan, and whimsical, art critic, could not away. The King's taste in music, and his parsimony towards musicians, were fresh faults in Wolcot's eyes. He had inherited the good old British aversion to "virtuosity," not in the sense of fiddles, but of collecting and what are now called scientific pursuits. The British Museum, the Royal Society, Sir Joseph Banks, Count Rumford, Sir William Hamilton (as archæologist, not as husband), and other similar things and persons, were all obnoxious to Peter; and as most of them were not unwelcome at Windsor and Buckingham House, the vials of Peter's wrath were all the more freely emptied on the Royal occupant of those palaces. If he wanted more stimulus, it was supplied by the fact that some well-known west-country persons, whom for this or that reason he disliked, were King's men. He too laughed at Rolle, and at Lord Mount-Edgcumbe. He uses the most terrific language concerning Mr Justice Buller. About the middle of his literary career, Gifford, a Devonshire man like himself, aroused in him the kind of frantic hatred which that strange personage seems to have had the gift of arousing, and which Wolcot vented in verse and in prose scarcely less furious than the almost Bedlamite scream of Hazlitt's much later *Letter*. For all these personal reasons and others, rather than, as it seems to me, from any definite political predilections or antipathies, Peter fixed on the King, occasionally distributing a share of his attentions to the King's favourite Minister:—

(Yes: I detested Pitt and all his measures,
And wrote *Will*ippics on administration,

as he says somewhere), to that Minister's associates, Jenkinson, Rose, Dundas, and to certain noblemen and Court favourites. Of these were the Lord Salisbury who enriched Peter's *Margate Hoy* with the lines—

Happy, happy, happy fly!
Were I you, and were you I!
But you will always be a fly
And I remain Lord Salisbury—

(and who, as another authority tells us, used actually to stuff all the carriage pockets of the post-chaises he travelled in with original manuscript verses), Lord Cardigan, the Duke of Leeds, and others. Finally a large, if not the largest, portion was given to Queen Charlotte and the officials, especially the German officials, of the household.

There is no doubt, though there are happy strokes all about his work, that posterity has been (as it generally though not always is) right in fixing on Peter's personal lampoons on the King and, in the good old sense, his "family" as the things to remember Peter by. The *Odes to the Academicians* are very good, *Sir Joseph Banks and the Emperor of Morocco* excellent, many other things of the same kind capital. *Bozzy and Piozzi* I am inclined to think the very best thing of its particular kind ever written: the singular folly of the various claimants to the "showmanship" of Johnson could hardly be better ridiculed than in these answering strains of James and the Lady. In serious eighteenth century verse ("Know, lovely virgin, thy deluding art, Hath lodged a thousand scorpions in my breast," and so forth) of which Wolcot, strange to say, has left copious specimens, he may be a little better or a little worse than Hayley, though he could sometimes turn a very happy half-serious epigram, as here:

> Ah! tell me not that I grow old,
> That love but ill becomes my tongue;
> Chloe, by me thou ne'er wert told,
> Sweet damsel, that *thou* wert too young!

In the same way, when he gets very serious even in his satire he is not usually good, perhaps because he then imitates Churchill, without possessing Churchill's indubitable gift of Drydenian verse. His denunciation of Lord Lonsdale, for the not very terrible crime of pointing out to the inhabitants of Whitehaven that, pending a final decision as to his legal liability for the sinking of ground above his coal-mines, it would be necessary for him, at great loss to himself as well as to them, to suspend the working, is one of the funniest examples of explosion of good useful wrath through the touch-hole that I know. Wolcot's best literary mood is that of a cat—not a cat in a rage, but a cat in a state of merriment, purring and mumbling, and rolling about. In which state, as all judicious lovers of the animal know, you may look out for a shrewd scratch or bite shortly as part of the game. When he gets really "savage" (the epithet Macaulay assigns to him) he is seldom amusing. His best form is such as this, which I take almost at random from his longest and most famous poem, the piece with the ugly name:

> Thus, when Burgoyne, opposing all the Fates,
> Defied, at Saratoga, General Gates,
> Sudden the hero dropped his threatening fist,
> And wisely deemed it folly to resist.

I could write a long dissertation to show why I can never read or repeat to myself "defied, at Saratoga, General Gates," without laughing, but it is better to laugh again and not write it.

Of this mood the almost world-famous visit to Whitbread's brewery house (the somewhat delusive title of which is "Instructions to a Celebrated Laureate"), and (in the Devonshire dialect which no one has ever written so well as Wolcot) the Royal visit to Exeter, are the best known and certainly among the best examples. But it is impossible to turn over many pages of Peter (even in his late and rather chapfallen *Tristia*, where it is hard to be very certain whether his jokes about making friends with the powers that be are jokes on the right or the wrong side of the mouth) without finding instances of it. I do not know whether he has ever been "selected." It might be impossible to perform that always dubious and dangerous process on a person who has as much of the satyr as of the satire. But on the face of him few writers call for it more. Here, as indeed was noted above, Wolcot avenges the *carum caput* of Fanny Burney on her enemy Schwellenberg in so dreadful a manner that even the soul of Daddy Crisp, with all his affection for Fannikin and all his hatred of the rest of the human race, might beg for mercy. Elsewhere he is, though more playfully, almost equally unkind to the great Mr Burke, for no particular reason that I can discover, inasmuch as they were at the time on the same side generally, except that Wolcot, who was a John Bull to the core, hated Scotchmen and Irishmen. This is horribly irreverent—

> When Mister Burke, so famous for fine speeches,
>   From trope to trope a downright rabbit skipping,
> Meant, schoolboy-like, to take down Hastings' breeches,
>   And give the noble governor a whipping.

And on the next page there is a much longer but equally uncomplimentary simile for the Edmundian eloquence. It would shock the admirable decency of the present day to know the epithet which, at the very opening of an ode, he gives to those useful functionaries, the Lords of the Bedchamber. But he was never quite so happy as in dealing with Great George our King himself; and if that monarch, who really knew something about literature, was half as good-natured as tradition makes him out, he must have been as much amused by Peter as it pleased Peter's waggery sometimes to assert that he was. In such a mood Peter, offering an amnesty to King and Queen, but maintaining the feud with the detested Schwellenberg, thus addresses his book:

> Sweet babe! to Weymouth shouldst thou find thy way,
>   The King, with curiosity so wild
> May on a sudden send for thee and say:
>   "See, Charly! Peter's child. Fine child, fine child!
> Ring, ring, for Schwellenberg, ring, Charly, ring:
>   Show it to Schwellenberg, show it, show it, show it.
> She'll say, 'Got dem de saucy stoopid thing;
>   I hate more worse as hell what come from poet!'"

Perhaps the happiest, by the way, of these curious Royal repetitions which Peter was never tired of playing upon is in prose, and told in a note, to the effect that when the King was visiting Mount-Edgcumbe, he strayed a little from the rest of the party to see a monument which had been put up to a departed pet pig named Cupid. Her Majesty Queen Charlotte called to him to know what he was looking at, and the King with perfect gravity replied, "Family grave, Charly! family grave, family grave." And the two next best things attributed to the Royal pair are expressions of repentance and amendment for the (on the whole purely imaginary) crimes with which Master Peter thought good to charge them. Rebuking the horrid eagerness of the monster Pitt to oppress the public, His Majesty frankly declares:

> "Yes! yes! I know, I know, the hounds are howling.
> God, Pitt! I don't, I don't much like their growling.

> Hey, hey? Growl, growl? What, what? Things don't go right?
> Why, quickly, quickly, Pitt, the dogs may *bite*?
> That would be bad, bad, bad, a sad mishap,
> Hey, Pitt, hey, hey? I should not like a *snap*."

And his consort magnanimously chimes in:

> "I geef my chewells to de Peepel's sighs,
> All tings from Mistress Hastings as I gote;
> I geef de fine pig diamond of Arcote,
> Iss, dat vich Rumbold geef, I geef again,
> Rader dan see de Peepels suffer pain.
> De Emperor presents, Lord! I vil not tush,
> Although de duty coss so *very* mush."

For as Her Majesty unanswerably asks:

> "Vat signifies de millions in our purses,
> If moneys do profoke de Peepel's curses?"

In one (and not the worst) of Wolcot's squibs, pretending to be silenced by the severer legislation which followed the excesses of the French, he laments sadly:

> No more must we laugh at an ass,
> No more run on topers a rig,
> Since Pitt gets as drunk as Dundas,
> And Dundas gets as drunk as a pig.
>
> . . . . .
>
> Now farewell to fair Buckingham House,
> To Richmond and Windsor and Kew,
> Farewell to the tale of the L——e,
> Mother Redcap! and monarchs, adieu!

A worse thing came upon him and the other Opposition lampooners than the checks of the law, which so far as I know, were never seriously applied to any of them. Peter remained valiantly singing, and years afterwards accomplished very respectable *Epistles to Mrs Clarke*, and jeremiads on his own exclusion from the Carlton House *fêtes*. But the satiric Muse was tired of her escapade for some years in Whig company, or else was frightened back by the French Revolution to the older quarters where she had laughed of old with Aristophanes and Lucian, with Butler and Swift. On 20th November, 1797, appeared the first number of the *Anti-Jacobin,* and three years later the *Poetry of the Anti-Jacobin* was collected and published.

So much more is generally known about this book than about my earlier subjects, neither of which has, to my knowledge, been reprinted for many years, that it is the less necessary to say much about its author- ship and intention here. That its name neatly and accurately expressed its purpose, that its editor was Gifford, and its most brilliant contributors Canning, Ellis, and Frere, though one or two others did good work, are matters of universal knowledge. Frere, who was the youngest, had also the cleanest political record of the three, for he was a Tory from the first, while Canning, as is well known, hovered a little before settling, and Ellis was a convert. Pitt cared nothing at all for literary praise or blame, and is said to have addressed to Ellis the neatest quotation of that century of classical quotations next to Harley's famous con- solation to Prior. Both were present when some person, thoughtless, ignorant, or malicious, asked Ellis about the *Rolliad,* whereupon Pitt promptly set any possible awkwardness straight by the line:

Immo age et a prima dic, hospes, origine nobis.

I have not observed that many of the persons who are justly proud of calling the poet "Vergil" quote him as aptly as that. But whatever the antecedents of any of the three might be, they all thoroughly meant business in these attacks on the Jacobins English and French, and the enemies of Pitt. The great opening poem on Mrs Brownrigg is most probably assigned to all the three, the still greater "Knifegrinder" to Canning and Frere. In the third of these charming parodies (which, oddly enough, Southey never seems to have had magnanimity enough quite to forgive—the weakest thing I know about him), the delightful dactylics about

the "nice clever books by Tom Paine the philanthro-
pist" Ellis may have shared. It must have been a little
awkward for him when Canning in an early number
gibed at those who

> sit
> Midst Brooks's elders on the bench of wit,
> Where Hare, Chief Justice, frames the stern decree,
> While with their learned brother sages three,
> Fitzpatrick, Townshend, Sheridan, agree.

For his own name had been in the commission with
these very same learned brethren a bare dozen years
before, and the *Rolliad* was the result of it. But these
little accidents will happen, and he had been personally and in a rather unmannerly fashion ("by Ellis'
sapient prominence of nose") attacked in the piece that
Canning was ridiculing. At any rate there was no
mistake about him now. He seems to have written
by himself the capital parody of "Acme and Septimius"
—"Fox with Tooke to grace his side," with its refrain:

> He spoke, and to the left and right,
> Norfolk hiccupped with delight.

And he took part in nearly all the most famous things
of the collection, "The Loves of the Triangles," "The
Progress of Man," "The Rovers," "New Morality,"
and the rest.

It is important to observe that all these pieces are
in a more or less direct sense political, and much more so
than is sometimes thought nowadays. Professor Morley,
perhaps to soothe his own or other persons' feelings,
talks of the *Anti-Jacobin* as chiefly an attack on "false
sentiment" generally. "The Loves of the Triangles"
has often been regarded as a mere literary "skit" on
Darwin and his likes; and "The Rovers" has a false air
of being pretty free from politics. Look a little deeper,
and different conclusions will, I think, be reached. It
was no doubt a godsend to the Anti-Jacobins that so

much external folly of various kinds happened to be associated with the maintenance of the new opinions in politics and (horrid word, then not invented!) sociology. But Canning's inexhaustible wit, Frere's audacious humour and whimsical erudition (some of his prose notes are unsurpassable), Ellis's eighteenth century polish and Voltairian elegance, always drove straight at the principles of innovation generally, of fantastic sympathies and antipathies, of topsy-turvy theories, which underlay the frippery of the outside. The great Mr Higgins, the eidolon-author of the two didactic poems and the drama (ah, when will researches in St Mary Axe give us the *Catastrophe of Mr and Mrs Gingham and the episode of Hipponia*, the *Conspiracy against the Ordinate*, and the scene in "The Rovers" where "several children: fathers and mothers unknown," are "produced on all sides"?), constantly enunciates in those very confidential letters which he wrote to his treacherous editors, the exact sentiments which we know so well to-day. When he talks about privilege and prejudice, about the vicious refinement of civilised society in regard to marriage, the cumbrous establishments which the folly, pride, and self-interest of the worst part of our species have heaped up, the certainty of man's perfectibility were he freed from kingcraft and priestcraft and other incidents of the present social system—all these things are perfectly unmistakable. We have them with us as fresh as ever. Substitute *The Doll's House* for *Stella*, read "Fabian Society" for poor Mr Higgins's clubs (but the works of the Fabian Society are not so amusing as Mr Higgins's), and 1798 becomes any present year of grace you please[1]. The very names of "Sedition's evening host" are startling; and we can fill in the blanks of that great hymn with

---

[1] And almost any since (1923).

names "after the chances and changes of the times," according to the author's direction, without the slightest difficulty. There can be no manner of reasonable doubt that if it had not been for the maudlin Socialism (they did not call it Socialism then, but it was the same thing) of Southey's sapphics and dactylics, the windy Republicanism of his poem on Marten, his metrical freaks would have been left alone by the mockers. Payne Knight and Darwin had follies enough; but if the one had not been avowedly, and the other in a sort of half-hearted way Jacobinical, they too might have disported themselves in safety. Even "The Rovers" is full of politics. Does the reader think that "Crown and Anchor" in that beautiful jumble of Beefington's ("England...our country...Magna Charta...it is liberated...a new era...House of Commons...*Crown and Anchor*...opposition") is mere miscellaneous farce? Not in the least. It was at the authentic "Crown and Anchor" tavern that, on Fox's birthday, the Duke of Norfolk gave "Our Sovereigns' health—the Majesty of the People." The dignity, chivalry, and courage of the immortal waiter enforce the great doctrine that "the conscience of a poor man ought to be more valuable to him than that of a prince in proportion as it is generally more pure." The satirists may, according to the excellent advice of their own troubadour, "by a song conceal their purposes." But those purposes are constantly what they are in one place avowed to be—to ridicule and baffle the appetite for change, to enforce the old proverb that "seldom comes a better," to confound ideas of equality, and the like. The *Anti-Jacobin* is thus not only more constantly but much more thoroughly political than the gibes of Brooks's, because patronage and power were in the hands of a thin man who did not like women instead of in those of a fat man who did, or the personal lampoons of Wolcot on the foibles and favourites of a king.

The fact of this unity and directness of purpose must, I think, be counted in for some of the merit of the book, as well as the fact that Ellis had incomparably stronger colleagues now than before, and that the crimes of the political and the follies of the social Jacobins gave a much better subject. At any rate the merit is certainly much greater. Of "The Rovers," that Ibsenism before Ibsen, it is impossible to tire. I am told that it was once tried on the stage and failed. This does not surprise me, for even *The Critic* is said not to be popular now, and "The Rovers" requires much more literary, political, and miscellaneous knowledge to appreciate it than *The Critic* does. But I believe that all boys of any brains, however little they may know of its ante-cedents, delight in "The Rovers": and I am sure that all middle-aged and aged persons of any sense delight in it. Nobody can exceed me in respect for Southey: but if I had to choose between his poems in the vein which the *Anti-Jacobin* parodied and the parodies of the *Anti-Jacobin*, I should certainly take the parodies. The "Address to the Gunboats" (some "Keys" attribute it to Lord Morpeth; but he never could have written it, and if the translation of "Pictis Puppibus" is not Frere's or, less probably, Canning's, I am no two-legged creature) is not, I believe, so great a favourite with some as it is with me. But surely the last couplet—

> Beware the *Badger's* bloody pennant,
> And that d——d invalid lieutenant!—

has an extraordinary charm. All the world is agreed as to the "Elegy or Dirge" on Jean Bon Saint-André, and I suppose there is not much more difference on the two didactic poems. Time may make one gouty and grey-haired, may bring disappointment at things that

are not and disgust at things that are, but scarcely
shall it deprive us of the faculty, nay, the irresistible
need of laughter as the well-known words recur:

> The feathered race with pinions skim the air,
> Not so the mackerel, and still less the bear;

as

> Each shepherd clasped with undisguised delight
> His yielding fair one—in the captain's sight;

as that incomparable note of Frere's to "blue-eyed
wanton" "*Hyperbola*: not figuratively speaking as in
rhetoric, but mathematically, and therefore blue-eyed";
or that other on "Pons Asinorum," where Mr Higgins,
with the combined fairness of a man of science and an
enlightened politician, after observing that "having
frequently watched companies of asses during their
passage of a bridge he never discovered in them any
symptoms of geometrical instinct," admits that "with
Spanish asses, which are much larger (*vide* Townsend's
Journey through Spain) the case may possibly be
different." And the whole is appropriately crowned
with "The New Morality," wherein the connection
between the modes of thought satirised is given.

Of course, it is impossible that political sympathy
should not make one's enjoyment of such things rather
keener. But as I have made no secret of the amusement
with which I read the *Rolliad* and Peter Pindar, having
in neither case any such sympathy with the writers,
I do not think the difference here is likely to carry
me very far to leeward of the truth in thinking that
the superior excellence of the *Anti-Jacobin* lies not
more in its greater literary polish than in the superior
sanity and largeness of its spirit. Though the personal
satire is sometimes pretty sharp, it is never as in the
other cases merely personal; and I think I can imagine
(I am rather inclined to think that I know one or two)

persons who, though by no means sympathising with Toryism, appreciate to the full the unsparing and un-erring fashion in which the *Anti-Jacobin* lashes what may be called the Fool on the other side of politics;— the Fool who believes in political nostrums and political revolutions, the Fool who gushes over the inevitable and ineradicable inequalities of the world, the Fool who drops a tear over criminals, the Fool who fails to see that, though certain social rules may pinch individuals now and then, the permission of general licence would simply make the world unworkable.

It is, I think, to this heightening and enlargement of the political aim that we must at any rate in part attribute the fact that the *Poetry of the Anti-Jacobin* remains unsurpassed as a collection of political verse-satire. We have had excellent practitioners of that art since the century began. Moore, Praed, and Mansel produced, and there is at least one living[1] writer[2] who produces work which Canning himself need not have refused to sign. But all such writers have been ex-posed to the inconvenience that the main "dependence," in the old phrase, of the political quarrel has not altered much, has altered very little, since 1800. As I have said, the inimitable prefaces of Mr Higgins reproduce them-selves every day in our midst, and "Divine Nonsensia" has found little or nothing new, call she it by whatever new names, to talk about since she furnished subjects to "The Rovers" and "The Knifegrinder." But as yet, whatever may be coming, neither the excitement of popular imagination, nor the liberty of popular follies, nor the exaggeration of popular crimes, has equalled the state of things of 1793–1800. There has been no such death-grapple as there was then, no such storm for the Pilot to weather, no such topsy-turvifying of public

[1] Again alas! not now (1923).   [2] The late Mr Traill.

sentiment as could bring men like Goethe and Coleridge and Southey (let it be remembered that each of them saw the error of his ways) to write the rubbish that kindled the "Singing Flames" of the *Anti-Jacobin's* correction. They were kindly flames[1] after all, and a God did save the culprits—more happy than those referred to in Heine's famous warning. If the occasion comes again—which Heaven forbid!—why, let the same God send us "such hounds, such hawks, and such a leman" —such Anti-Jacobins and such a Pilot[2]!

[1] An American critic once gravely commented on the ignorance of the present writer in not knowing that Heine wrote "sengenden," "singeing." Possibly this was part of the "great American joke." If not, it can only be said, in the first place, that Heine did not; and in the second, that if he did, "why, the less Heine he."

[2] Amen! (1923).

XVI

SOME GREAT BIOGRAPHIES

It is one of the best worn of commonplaces that there is no book so generally interesting as a well done biography, and none which is so rarely well done or so difficult to do well. But there is often a good deal of truth in commonplaces, and there is a very great deal of it in this. Putting aside books read owing to some fashion or fancy of the time, and those which lend themselves to reading simply because they require absolutely no knowledge or intelligence in those who read them, and those in which positive genius insists upon attention being paid to it, no books have been so steadily popular with the best class of readers as the great biographies. On the other hand an un-deviating consensus of critics (whose natural depravity could hardly have avoided slipping into truth now and then if their opinion was feigned) agrees that nothing is so bad as the average biography. It may not be unamusing or unprofitable to take some admittedly successful examples, in the chief different kinds, and endeavour to see what makes them good; it will certainly not be difficult to discern and indicate in passing what makes the others bad.

All biography is obviously and naturally divided into two kinds. There is the biography pure and simple, in which the whole of the materials is passed through the alembic of the biographer, and in which few if any of these materials appear except in an altered and digested condition. This, though apparently the oldest, is artistically the most perfect kind. Its shortest examples are always its best, and some of the best and shortest are among the best things in literature. The *Agricola* of Tacitus at one end of the list and Southey's *Nelson* almost at the other may save us the trouble of a long enumeration of the masterpieces; while nobody needs to be told that the list ranges from masterpieces like these down to those that *ego vel Cluvienus* may write. There has always been a considerable demand for this sort of thing; but it is not quite the kind of biography which has been specially popular for the last century, and which has produced the famous books to which I have already alluded. This is the kind of "applied" or "mixed" biography, including letters from and to the hero, anecdotes about him, and the like, connected and wrought into a whole by narrative and comment of the author, or, as he sometimes calls himself, the editor. To this belong more or less wholly the great biographies which I shall take for texts, Boswell's *Johnson*, Moore's *Byron*, Lockhart's *Scott*, Carlyle's *Sterling* (much smaller than the others, for reasons, but distinctly on the same lines with them), and, of books more recent, Sir George Trevelyan's *Macaulay*. And to this class also, for reasons very easy to understand, belong almost all the biographies recently produced of men recently living. The reasons I say are easy to find. There is the great popularity of the great examples: there is the demand arising from this popularity; but most of all there is the fatal facility of the proceeding in appearance, and in appearance only.

There can of course be no doubt that to the inexperienced it looks easy enough. In the first kind of biography the writer must to some extent master a considerable quantity of matter and subject it to some kind of intellectual or quasi-intellectual process of his own. At the very worst, the absolutely least, he must frame a sufficient number of sentences in his own head and (unless he dictates) write them with his own fingers—a number sufficient to fill the space between the covers of the book. And, unless he is a quite abnormally stupid or conceited man, he will be more or less conscious that he is doing this well or ill, sufficiently or insufficiently. He cannot to any great extent merely extract or quote. He must create, or at any rate build, or do something that may at least cheat himself into the idea that he is building or creating.

The second path is in comparison quite a primrose one. In most cases the biographer by hypothesis finds himself in possession of a certain, often a considerable, stock of material in the way of diaries, letters and what not. Even if he has struck out the notion of the book for himself and is not ready furnished with his materials by executorship, appointment of friends, and the like, his own unskilled labour or that of a few jackals at public and other libraries will generally stock him amply with all the stuff he wants. Very often this stuff is, in part at least, really interesting. What more simple than to calendar it; to omit whatever is more than is wanted to fill the one, two or three volumes ordered or accepted by the publisher; to string the rest together with a " John-a-Nokes was born on the —th of——. Of his earliest years we find" and so on; to insert here and there a reference, a reminiscence, a reflection, or a connecting narrative; and, if the operator be very conscientious, to wind up with an appreciation or summary, "We have thus followed a remarkable (or a painful, as the case may be) career to its close. Had this," and so forth? What, I repeat, more simple?

"It is not more stiff than that," says the engaging idiom of the Gaul. At any rate there is certainly a large and apparently an increasing number of persons, many of them educated, presumably not unintelligent, certainly not unacquainted with books, things, and men, who consider that there is no greater "stiffness" in it. Any competent critic, even any tolerably intelligent reader who dutifully studies or skims his new volumes from Mudie's, could name books of this kind within the last few years, nay, within the last few months, some of which had no justification whatever for their existence; others which a really skilful hand would have reduced to a small volume or even to an ordinary quarterly essay; others which, though capable of having been made into books of the right sort by the right treatment, had only been made into books of the wrong sort by the wrong treatment. Anybody on the other hand who remembers many thoroughly satisfactory books of the kind for some years past must either be a much more fortunate or a much less fastidious reader and critic than I can pretend to be[1]. Let us therefore turn over once more those famous biographies of the kind that are good, and see if the secrets of their goodness are capable of being disengaged.

It will be evident, and may possibly have been already objected by some thorough-going Boswellian, that the first, and as he would say the greatest, has some marked differences from the others. This may be partly due to the fact that Boswell had practically no model when he wrote his extraordinary book, while the others all wrote with that book more or less consciously before them. It may be due also to the other fact that for by far the greater part of his hero's life

[1] It so happens that since this paper first appeared a rather unusually large number of biographies—sometimes of the first interest in subject—have been published. But I fear hardly one of them is likely to challenge admission into the select class on the score of execution. (1895: but is it better in 1923?)

he did not know him at all; while for the rest he had exceptionally full stores of personal communication to draw upon. A considerable variation of treatment was therefore almost of necessity imposed on him. To generalise about Boswell is a very perilous task. Almost everything possible has been said: and most, or at least many, of these things clash and hurtle like the elements in chaos. I shall give no opinion here whether Boswell was the specially inspired zany of Macaulay, or the man of some foibles but of good brain and heart on the whole, and of an intelligent rather than blind devotion to his master, whom Carlyle preferred and who has been of late years more and more the favourite. I do not myself pretend to rank in the most ardent section of Boswellians. Full of delightful matter as the book is, it seems to me a book rather for perpetual dips—dips which should leave no part of it unexplored, but interrupted and comparatively short—than for the long steady swim which the very greatest literary streams invite, sustain, and make delightful. It would indeed scarcely be possible for even the most rapid reader to read Boswell or Lockhart or Moore through at a sitting, unless it were as long as the gambling sederunt in *The Young Duke*. But I have read Lockhart often, and I hope to read him often again, on successive evenings from beginning to end. I have read Moore at least once if not twice through in the same way, besides countless dippings into both. I have never succeeded, and I have more than once failed, in reading Boswell through on the same plan.

This however may be my fault, not Boswell's: and I am sure that there is not a page of him that I have not read, and that often, with delight. For he had, and he revealed to the others, the secret of this kind of biography. And he had it, if not so much as Lockhart (who seems to me the prince of all biographers, past, present, and to come) much more than any of those others, though they had it too. This secret consists in fixing the attention of the reader, even if it be unconsciously, at once on the character of the subject; and, so far as possible, never giving a touch afterwards which does not in some way fill out and fill up that character. The satire poured on Bozzy's minuteness by Wolcot and others is often (in Peter Pindar himself at least) admirably good fun, and not always quite unjust from certain points of view[1]. And yet if we pause and with hand on heart ask ourselves, "Is the most trivial of these trivialities really superfluous?" it will be very difficult to answer in the affirmative. There is hardly one incident, there is hardly one saying of Johnson's, there is even hardly one of those astounding platitudes or sillinesses of Bozzy's own which support the "zany" theory, that does not in some subtle and cunning fashion elaborate and furnish forth that extraordinary personality which some will have to be the most faithful portraiture of a human being that

[1] As *Bozzy and Piozzi* has been twice praised, here and in the Essay on *Twenty years of Political Satire*, it may be well to give a brief specimen of its method, for it is not, I suspect, in all hands. Perhaps the best passage of all is the version of Boswell's wonderful account of his conduct to the Duchess of Argyle in her own house, but it is rather long. The following may be better:

> With glee the Doctor did my girl behold,
> Her name Veronica, just four months old,
> This name Veronica, a name though quaint,
> Belonged originally to a saint;
> But to my old great-grandam it was given,
> As fine a woman as e'er went to Heaven;
> And what must add to her importance much,
> The Lady's genealogy was Dutch.
> The man who did espouse this Dame divine,
> Was Alexander, Earl of Kincardine;
> Who poured along my body, like a sluice,
> The noble, noble, noble blood of Bruce:
> And who that owned this blood could well refuse
> To make the world acquainted with the *news*? &c., &c., &c.

we possess in books, and others the most astonishing example of an *eidolon* heightened and transcendentalised by art. I have no doubt that much of Boswell's attraction for the extreme Boswellians consists in what his earliest thorough-going defender would have called his "marine-stores" of detail about all sorts of things and persons besides Johnson. No one except Horace Walpole has given us such a collection of *ana in excelsis*, of miscellanies miscellanied into quintessence, as Boswell; and Horace lacks the central tie-beams that Bozzy provides. For yet once more it must be said that in Boswell the whole has a tendency and an aim—a tendency which reaches its end, an aim which is hit by the archer. It is in this that the supremacy of Boswell's art consists. Apparently desultory, he is never really so; apparently sucking in everything and disgorging everything by turns with the indiscriminating action of a whirlpool, he is really subjecting the whole to a cunning chemical process.

How different the process, or at least how different the success is in the case of the bad and even of the less good biographies the memory, full of fright, of many a double-volumed night shall easily tell us. In the selection and editing of documents and in the construction of linking narrative we shall find better models among the biographers referred to than Boswell. But we shall nowhere find a better—I am not quite sure that we shall anywhere find one so good— in this central requirement of always keeping the character of the subject before the reader, and building up the notion of it with here a little and there a little of successive detail and touch. It may be that Bozzy had so steeped himself in his hero that he at last thought and saw all things in Johnson; and that everything extraneous to that subject naturally dropped off and became unimportant to him. But this would be only a scientific, not a critical, explanation of the fact: and the fact itself remains. Now the very last thing that we find in the average modern biographer is this omnipresence of the subject in its quiddity. The biographer may be earnestly, even tediously, desirous to put a certain side or what he thinks a certain side, of his subject before us. But "the whole," as Empedocles (not Mr Arnold's but the man himself) said, "few boast to find." We turn over pages of surplusage, pages of repetition, pages of triviality; but the central idea and personality of the man, the idea that disengages itself, once for all and unmistakably, from the pages of Boswell, we are either altogether baffled in seeking, or have to piece and patch out laboriously for ourselves. There may be amusing stories about the subject, or about other people: there may be meritorious bursts of original writing from the author or editor; but the central idea, the central tie-beam, is too often wanting. There is no composition, and therefore there is no art. In Boswell there is this composition, though it is of a very peculiar and perhaps a not easily imitable kind.

The next book in chronological order, Moore's *Byron*, has very different lessons to teach. It must of course be judged in the first place with a most unusual amount of allowance. The mere circumstances of the antecedent destruction of the *Memoirs* imposed upon Moore such a necessity of dancing in fetters that probably, if poverty, and perhaps a little vanity combined, had not dictated to will, he never would have consented to undertake the exercise. He wrote too soon after Byron's death not to have been, even if this most harassing condition had been absent, encumbered by innumerable considerations of this person's feelings, of what that person had written, of what the moral British public still thought, of what the enthusiastic British public still felt. Frequent as are Byron's own laudations of Moore's attitude towards "the great," and creditable as on the whole that attitude must be pronounced to have been, Moore suffered under various personal disabilities in grappling with his task. He was an Irishman writing of English society; a somewhat irregularly educated Irishman dealing with English public school and university education; a Whig writing of a period of almost unbroken Tory rule; a reformed Thomas Little writing of a very unreformed Don Juan. But he was a man of thorough literary faculty, and literary faculty (which is a branch of wisdom) is, like wisdom, justified of her children in all ways and at all seasons. He had, in those letters and other documents of Byron's which had escaped the flames, illustrative matter of unsurpassed interest: for there is a practical agreement between the admirers and the depreciators of Byron's poetry, that his prose letters are of the very best in their kind. Moore had, moreover, a central subject which, if not of the least enigmatic, was intensely individual, and concerning which the intensest curiosity was entertained by his readers. With a man of the great literary faculty already mentioned this conflict of drawbacks and advantages was certain to produce something notable.

The book is indeed full of faults, all of which (with some things which are not faults at all) may be found censured in his most florid style by Wilson in the *Noctes Ambrosianæ*. It was a mistake, at least as obvious as the reason for it, to be excessively reticent as to the poet's English freaks and unnecessarily loquacious as to his Italian dissipations. It was a worse mistake to drop the pen of the biographer now and then, and thump the cushion of the preacher, an exercise which suited the genial Thomas uncommonly ill. It was a still more unwise extension of that mistake to indulge in abstract discussions about education, marriage, and what not, for which Moore (who was one of the worst hands in the world at abstract dissertation) was very badly equipped, and which, if they had been handled by a combination of Solomon and Berkeley, would still have been out of place in the particular book. It would be quite easy to pick other and minor faults all through.

But who that reads the book with heart's as well as mind's eye cares to do any such thing? Here too we have the main and principal thing, which was in this case to let the subject speak for himself. One of the more legitimate faults which may be found with Moore is that he has not "edited" quite enough, that he has frequently allowed Byron (who like most letter-writers from foreign parts necessarily had to repeat himself to his various correspondents) to appear in the book as tautologous to a rather unjust extent. But even in this there is justification for the biographer. He knew, being a man of letters and a great man of letters, that what was wanted was precisely this—to let Byron speak for himself. There had been endless speaking *about* him.

God's great gift of speech abused
Made the memory confused

of almost everybody on the subject. Moore had been prevented from giving full liberty of speech to his client even in this instance; so, like a judicious advocate he gave the fullest liberty that he could in the matter left to him. At any rate he too earns the meed due to the thorough painting of the portrait, the finished construction of the character. We have had all manner of "real Lord Byrons" and of false Lord Byrons since; we have had things that Moore might have told us had he chosen and been free to speak, and things that he was too sensible to tell however free his tongue had been. But it may be safely said that nothing that can ever come out will be incompatible with the Lord Byron made known to us by Moore. He is done, like Pantagruel, *dans son naturel*; and the natural or unnatural additions will be found to answer thereto.

Far different again is this procedure from that of the ordinary biographer. He copies Moore in giving us much unnecessary matter; he copies him in giving us far more unnecessary comment. The only things he does not copy him in are the excuses for these two faults, and the merit which, were they far greater, would redeem them.

The next example seems to me, as I have already said, to be the capital example of the kind. It is true that Lockhart had everything in his favour. He had ample material; he had complete knowledge of it; he had a real affection for his subject; he had nothing to conceal; he had, if not the same sort of personal curiosity, half-genuine, half-morbid, which Moore had to cater for in the case of Byron, a general interest in his hero which has seldom been equalled and never exceeded. But in literature, as in other games, it is not sufficient to have cards; you must know how to play them. Lockhart played his admirable cards to even greater admiration. His play has indeed been subjected to tests that may be called hardly fair. The later publication, first of Scott's complete *Diary*, and then of a large additional collection of his *Letters*, was such a test; and it is not necessary to dwell much on the triumphant fashion in which Lockhart emerged from it. Except a very little which for divers reasons he could not have published, and a very little more which on the whole it was better taste for him not to publish, there may be said to have been absolutely nothing of interest or importance in the complete *Diary* which he had not given in his extracts. We had more in bulk, but we had nothing new in kind. We learnt nothing, and there was no fear of our learning anything, derogatory to Sir Walter and hitherto concealed; but we learnt also nothing favourable to him that had, either by maladroitness or bad faith, been held back. Some of the new matter was painful; almost all of it was superfluous.

Of the *Letters*, no doubt, this could not be said. The additions they made to our knowledge were always interesting, sometimes intensely so. But whatever their degree of importance, it was always easy to see why Lockhart had not given them, and seldom possible to refuse approval to his holding of them back. What is proper enough to be known sixty years after a man's death is often improper to be known on the morrow of it. Yet perhaps few men in Lockhart's position, well knowing the unjust aspersions which had been cast on his action in the Scott-Christie duel, would have had the combined good taste and self-denial not to publish the acquittal, by an authority from which there could be no appeal, the Duke of Wellington, which these unpublished letters contain.

But only they of little faith or little intelligence can have been much surprised or greatly relieved by this passage of Lockhart's through the ordeal. To any really good literary judge the thing was certain beforehand. This *Life* had the "certain vital marks." I am aware of course that, putting entirely aside the usual vague and intangible prejudice against Lockhart, some good and well-disposed judges have expressed themselves as not wholly satisfied with parts of his treatment —have considered him unfair to Constable and the

Ballantynes and so forth. But the elaborate justification of Constable which was published some years ago
left on my mind no feeling that Lockhart had treated
him unfairly; and those who disapprove of the treatment of the Ballantynes usually incriminate not the
Life itself, but divers side controversies and appendices
with which we have here nothing to do. What we have
to do with is the presentation of the life and conversation of a great man on a great scale; and that this has
never been done better I am sure, that it ever will be
done better I find great difficulty in believing. The
special point of the work is the unmatched combination
of excellence in the selection and editing with excellence
in the connecting narrative. Boswell's matter is delightful, and excellently arranged for his purpose. But
whenever he becomes at all original he becomes (were
it not for the pleasingness of his coxcombry and its
advantages as a set-off) a bore. Moore's dissertations
are sometimes superfluous, and not always intrinsically
very sound. In the examples to be noticed later
Carlyle's monologue, as was his wont, has sometimes
a habit of submerging Sterling; and the biographer is
altogether so much greater a man than his subject,
that there is an occasional sense of incongruity. Sir
George Trevelyan, whose relation to his hero may be
said to have been very similar to that of Lockhart to
Scott, and who, like Lockhart, was fortunate in possessing abundant material, sometimes seems to have
found himself a little cramped by the relationship, and
nowhere seems to me to have attained the full and
equable command both of his pen and his subject which
is so remarkable in his predecessor.

It is in this full and equable command both of his
materials and his own arrangement of them that Lockhart's unique excellence consists. He had to deal with

an almost faultless subject—for there is absolutely no stain on Scott's memory except his clandestine tradings with the Ballantynes, where it is evident that some strange delusion held him from the first as to the distinctly unprofessional, nay as to the questionably honest, character of these relations. There was therefore a not inconsiderable danger that he should present (as so many biographers have presented to us) a faultless monster, or should busy himself in tedious endeavours to whitewash small faults into positive virtues. The best evidence that he has not done this is the almost incredible but actual fact that there have been people, both at the time and since, who have thought him unfair to Scott. The truth of course is that he has contrived with consummate art to let the character of his hero show itself as good but not in the least goody, as heroic but not in the least theatrical. Yet another distinguishing grace of this great book—"the best book in the world" as a person who was not ignorant of the other best books in the world once called it to me—is the singular skill with which the author, while never obtruding, never obtrusively effaces himself. He is often actually on the scene: he is constantly speaking in his own person; and yet we never think of him as the man with the pointing-stick at the panorama, as the beadle at the function, as the ringmaster of the show. He seems to stand rather in the relation of the epic poet to his characters, narrating, omnipresent, but never in the way.

No other biographer, I repeat, seems to me to have reached quite this pitch of art. It is true that Bozzy plays monkey to his master's bear in a very diverting and effective manner; but still the relation may always be stigmatised by foes, and must sometimes be admitted even by friends, as that of bear and monkey, a contrast diverting and effective, but almost too violent for the best art. There is nothing of this in the *Life of Scott*. Whether Scott is speaking for himself in the autobiography, the diary, and the letters; or whether Lockhart is speaking of and for him, the presentation is continuous, uniform, uninterrupted. Two phrases, often foolishly used but in their original meaning not only harmless but excellent, may be used in that original meaning of this book. It is "as interesting as a novel," and it is "as good as a play." That is (to translate these artless words into more elaborate phraseology), it has the uniform grasp, the sustained and absorbing attraction, of the best works of narrative and dramatic art. It is easy to say that this is due to the subject, that "all depends on the subject," and that here the subject is matchless. I think this can, as it happens, be rather crushingly rebutted by instance. I do not think that the appreciation of Moore above quoted is grudging. But let any one who knows the two books well ask himself soberly what Moore would have made of Scott, and what Lockhart would have made of Byron. As for the ordinary biographer it is perhaps too heartrending to think what he could have made, if he had given his mind to it, of either. Let any one who knows remember what Lord John Russell made of Moore himself, a subject not of course of the same interest as Scott or Byron, but of interest much above the common; let him remember much more recent instances of even more promising matter, treated by hardly less approved artists, and what came of them. Then, if he does not bless Lockhart and award the crown to him, I have nothing more to say but to repeat that I for my part know no book of the kind equal to this.

Here then we have something like the type and

standard example of the elaborate biography of the composite kind, the kind which not stinting itself of any one possible sizing allowable to the biographer, admitting great portions of original matter, and permitting the subject to a great extent to illustrate himself, keeps a perpetual regulating hand on these materials, adjusts the connecting links of narrative and comment to one consistent plan of exposition, and so presents the subject "in the round," on all sides, in all lights, doing this not merely by ingenious management in the original part, but by severe and masterly selection in that which is not original. It has been rumoured from time to time that in addition to the *Diary* and even to the additional *Letters*, further instalments of the Abbotsford papers are to be given to the public. They can hardly be otherwise than welcome in themselves, though it seems idle to wish for the pinched-off clay, the marble chips, the bronze filings when you have the sculptor's finished statue. But after the crucial example of the *Diary* itself, I think it may be taken for granted that the results will be uniform whatever is published. We shall have no lower, but also no really fuller idea of Scott; and we shall have a higher idea of what Lockhart gave and did, by beholding what he deliberately refrained from doing and giving.

The next in order of our books is in a certain way the greatest, as in a certain other way the smallest, of all. But I do not think that the superlative belongs to it as a biography. Of its merits as a book there can be no question, and there never has been any with competent judges. It has sometimes indeed been thought the very best of Carlyle's books, or second only to *The French Revolution*. Its modest length kept the author from the voluminous digressions which beset him so easily; the frequent changes of scene, and the constant necessity for making more or less brief reference to distinguished or interesting persons, excited and fed his unrivalled power of description and characterisation to an extraordinary degree. The sense of battle (for the book begins, if it does not go on, as a polemic against Hare's view of Sterling) gave zest and spirit to the performance. And there can be little doubt that personal memories and affections helped likewise.

The result is astonishingly happy. It is brief enough to be read at a moderate stretch; and for my part, often as I have read it, I have seldom been able to begin it again or even to consult it for a casual reference, without following it right through. Although full enough of the author's characteristic manner, it does not show his mannerism at anything hke its furthest. The preaching is necessarily subdued: it is administered dramatically and in short doses. The whole is an inculcation of Carlylism no doubt; but it is effected by object-lessons, and with swift and variegated change of scene and character. The famous chapter on Coleridge (admittedly the masterpiece of the book if not of the author) is only the best of infinite good things. The Welsh sketches; the remarks on Cambridge and Sterling's friends there; the ingenious economy of the Torrijos episode, where the hapless expedition gets its full share of celebration and Sterling's own not exactly heroic part in it is skimmed without any dishonesty but with consummate art; the scores of portrait vignettes scattered about, and the admirable composition of all these things, make up such a book as few that the world's libraries contain.

Such a book; but such a biography? Here I am not so sure. You can of course "see" Sterling plainly enough in it: but you hardly see what others must have seen. To his friends and relations he was no doubt dear; perhaps not the less dear, as women often and men sometimes are, for his weaknesses physical and mental. I should be sorry to hurt any one's feelings in speaking of his personality: and it must be distinctly understood that it is of Carlyle's Sterling, not of Sterling himself, that I speak. That he was, apparently, the first of all such as cannot "make up their minds to be damned" (in his biographer's words of another person of somewhat sturdier substance) and yet want better bread than is made of wheat by virtue of which they may be saved—the father of all the deplorable family that includes the Arthur Cloughs of real life and the Robert Elsmeres of fiction—the conductor and coryphæus of the caitiff choir who sing undogmatic anthems to a Nehushtan of negation—should not perhaps count too much against him. And no wise man will bear too hardly on the fact of his having turned his back on a certain troublesome and probably dangerous business, to which he had put his hand, in order to dry the tears of a "blooming young lady with black eyes." But it is too evident that Sterling, his physical health no doubt aggravating his metaphysical complaints, was a man not strong, amiable and not ungifted, but with no great originality in him, and without a very great capacity for taking trouble in order to make up for the lack of originality. Very fortunate indeed was it for him that he was called upon to play no other part than that of an affluent scholarly invalid, and that he died before youth had quite departed, and therefore before his weakness had ceased to be pathetic and begun to be painful to his friends.

This is a brutal reduction to plain prose of Carlyle's portrait of him. But the mere fact that it will seem brutal shows on the one hand how skilful the painter is, and on the other that the merits of his picture are the merits not of biography—that is to say the presentation of a man as he is—but of romance, or the presentation of something as it is not. All through the book Carlyle plays Socrates to this poor friend of his (with very little fight in him at any time and with none left now) and protects him from the onset of the enemy. That he sometimes effects the rescue by concentrating our attention on himself, is part of the recognised procedure in such cases. But it is by no means always thus that he champions Sterling. I have not the slightest doubt that the variety and brilliancy of the scene-painting, the divergences into side portraits, and all the other purple patches referred to above, had a more or less conscious purpose of avoiding the concentration of too much attention on the reader's part on the nominal hero. The result no doubt is in a way triumphantly successful. The book has practically founded an immortal Sterling Club; there will always be voices to sing *Tu Marcellus eras* in honour of Sterling; and I protest that I am rather ashamed of myself for having said what I believe to be the truth about him just now. Nor can it be said that the biographer may not smooth a little and apologise a good deal; especially where, as in Sterling's case, the faults are only weaknesses and wants. But still if the standard of biography which has been set up earlier is at all a true one, Sterling never could have furnished a subject for one of the very best of biographies as such. There was simply not enough substance in him for one. And we shall accordingly find that what Carlyle with wonderful art has done is to reverse the tricks of the conjurers, and lead us to believe that we are reading a life of Sterling while Sterling is really "vanished,"

and we are actually reading an extraordinarily interesting history of the places that he lived in, the
men he knew, the actions which he shared or did not
share, and the personality of his redoubtable and
admirable friend and biographer, all thrown up on a
background of the shortcomings of the Church and
State of England in the nineteenth century.

No two books could in this respect stand in much
greater contrast to each other than the *Sterling* and
Sir George Trevelyan's *Life and Letters of Macaulay*.
The requirements of this last were entirely different:
they were met with a just consciousness of their
difference, and the result is a success of a perfectly
different kind. Macaulay is still a difficult subject to
handle. He had grave faults as a writer and some foibles
as a man, accompanying great merits as a man and
greater gifts as a writer. By an almost unexampled
coincidence he has been depreciated by some in a
manner which makes others forgive him where he
ought not to be forgiven; and he has been admired
by some in a way which makes others unduly shy of
admiring him. But this applies to his writing chiefly.
Speaking under correction, I should say that for some
fifteen years after his death, the ideas of him among
those who had not known him personally were pretty
uniform, and not much more unfavourable among
those who rather disliked his writings than among
those who admired them. That is to say, he was
thought of as an undoubtedly clever, a very generous,
and an entirely honourable man, who had retained the
faults of a clever and precocious boy—"cocksureness,"
inordinate loquacity, intolerance of fair give-and-take
in conversation to a hardly tolerable degree—a man
whose "rough, pistolling ways" extended from literature into life, who was not too scrupulous about carrying

personal and political antipathies into his writings, and who was not only "cocksure" but also cock-a-hoop to a degree barely if at all excusable.

And I think it is also not too much to say that Sir George Trevelyan's biography changed this almost at once, changed it even for some who were rather prejudiced against Macaulay, and made it almost impossible for any future generation which takes the trouble to acquaint itself with him at all to entertain that notion of him which Lord Melbourne's *mot*, the Windsor Castle incident, and a few other things had helped his writings to establish in the minds of the generation before. For it is, I venture to think, one of Sir George's amiable mistakes (of which there are a few in the book) to think that Macaulay's writings "give us no more idea of the author than Shakspeare's do." I should say myself that they give a very decided though, as it happens, a very false or at any rate a very incomplete idea of him. There is scarcely a page of the *Essays* or the *History* in which we do not seem to see a man of unquestionable knowledge and of equally unquestionable power, with no small range of sympathy and taste, but with a huge pair of blinkers on for everything and everybody with whom or with which he is not in sympathy, positive to or beyond the verge of arrogance, ready to pronounce and perhaps even to think everyone who does not agree with him a fool or a knave or an egregious combination of both, never quite dishonest, but often quite unjust, with little real geniality even in his appreciation of humour, and with little real sympathy even in his appreciation of sentiment.

I do not know whether the family tradition was too strong in Sir George for him even to be aware of this notion of his uncle, which certainly existed at the time he wrote in persons neither infantine nor ill-blooded nor ill-informed. But he could have taken no happier way to substitute something better and juster for it than the way he actually took. He is sincerely, even desperately, loyal to "the bluid of McAulay." With Mr Napier I am unable to see that Johnson, who was very frequently in the wrong, was wrong at all when he smote the Reverend Kenneth and the Reverend John for speaking unadvisedly with their lips. But Sir George, the faithful, is sure that he was wrong; and of his fidelity there are many other odd examples in the book. The very preface, however, to the second edition shows that, despite this amiable weakness, he had the root of the biographical matter in him. "It was my business," says he, "to show my uncle as he was, and not as I or any one else would have had him." "Oh brave we!" as Johnson himself might have said. Not of course that the principle extends to publishing *tacenda* of any kind. There are things which are not disgraceful to a man to have done or written, but of which the publication is obviously unfair to him, which any biographer may suppress, and which in some notable later examples of biography have not been suppressed—to the discredit of the subject in the minds of fools, of the biographer in the minds of the wise.

But to quote, or rather to paraphrase Sir George again, if a faithful picture of the subject cannot be drawn without injuring his memory, let the drawing alone; if the drawing be undertaken, let it be faithful. Consider what would have happened if Sir George had set himself to cut away all the early and later priggishness, all the evidences of extreme partisanship in the Croker and other matters, if he had given us a Macaulay all family affection, all sweet reasonableness, all pathetic humanity, a trimmed, shorn, and varnished Macaulay. We should have revolted, we should have said that this was absurd: and we should have liked Macaulay even less than before, and had a strong suspicion that Sir George was a garbler and a humbug. Whereas, by giving the rough with the smooth, and letting the man exhibit himself as he actually was, yet with no treacherous or unfair revelation, the revolution of opinion in the minds of some, the establishment once for all of a good opinion in those of others, was done and done thoroughly, so that it will never need to be done again and may defy not merely the critic but also the indiscreet busybody.

If anybody says that by much comparison of instances I have made clear two *secrets de Polichinelle*, first that the "life" of a man should give us the man and his life and not a collection of dead and inhuman things, secondly that a good "life" of a man will be found to have been well done itself, and done probably in a rather different way from any other, I bow to the remark. It is more and more becoming clear to me that the only secrets much worth finding out are *secrets de Polichinelle*, things already known to all the world. To convince yourself of the obvious, neither to fail to see it for mere blindness like the $_f oo_{ls}$, nor to fail to see it because of elaborate and persistent turning away from it like the clever ones, is certainly in these days, and perhaps has been in all, a very important and by no means an extremely simple task. Yet it may be pleaded that if the secret of writing biographies is known to all the world, no small number of persons in that world (to wit, the writers of biographies) seem to be for the most part absolutely guiltless of the knowledge. And yet "Lives" are being more and more written. In the notes to his translation of Heine's *Deutschland* Mr Leland informs us that "in one of the best-known minor libraries in Europe" he "found two lives of a

distinguished English poet and not a line of his works."
It is entirely conceivable; it would not surprise me very
much if he had said that he knew an author who had
written one of the lives without having read a line
of the works. Such things have happened, and are
happening. But still, things being so, it might be
supposed that the books for which there is such a
demand would be supplied good. That would be a
gross and grievous mistake. Demand may create
supply; it certainly does not necessarily create good
supply.

The examples I have taken are pretty well spread
over the century (or rather less) in which they all
appeared; and though the latest of them made its
appearance so to speak yesterday, it is less satisfactory
to remember that the subject of that life was born
nearly at its beginning, and died very shortly after
this nineteenth century had come to the end of its
first half. It is quite possible that the materials for
biography are not so promising as they used to be.
Some persons pretend that the cry about the decay
of letter-writing is nonsense. The cautious arguer will
confine himself to replying that at any rate there are
great temptations not to write letters. Telegrams, post-
cards, correspondence-cards, letter-cards—all of these
things the truly good and wise detest and execrate;
it is not quite so certain that they abstain from them.
I believe that the habit of keeping a diary has really
gone out to a great extent. Too often moreover
nowadays the unauthorised person steps in with his
privateering before the authorised person is ready for
sea; and then the authorised person too often indulges
in undignified chasings and cannonadings of his predecessor. Above all there seems to have been lost,
in this and other things, the all-important sense of

proportion in books, and we get "Lives" that would have been excellent in one volume watered out into two, "Lives" that would have been pleasant places in two, becoming pathless deserts in four. These things have had a bad effect on the class of persons who are likely to find biographers. One hears of their destroying materials with a "Please God, nobody shall deal with *me* as —— dealt with ——." Or else, as was the case with Cardinal Newman, they enjoin a method of dealing with their materials, which, though it permits any one of tolerable intelligence to construct a biography for himself with comparatively little difficulty, does not give him the biography actually made. For it cannot be too often repeated that a real biography ought to be something more than the presentation of mere materials, however excellently calendared, something more than Memoirs, Letters, Diary and so forth. The whole ought to be passed through the mind of a competent and intelligent artist, and to be presented to us, not indeed in such a way that we are bound to take his word for the details, but in such a way that we see a finished picture, a real composition, not merely a bundle of details and *data*.

END OF VOLUME ONE

PRINTED IN GREAT BRITAIN
BY W. LEWIS, UNIVERSITY PRESS
CAMBRIDGE

WS - #0087 - 120623 - C0 - 229/152/24 - PB - 9781330346396 - Gloss Lamination